COMPOSITION AND APPLIED GRAMMAR

THE WRITING PROCESS

12

Miles C. Olson

Carol B. Kuykendall

Cherie A. Lyons

Nancy Tia Brown

Allyn and Bacon, Inc.

Boston   Rockleigh, N.J.   Atlanta   Dallas   San Jose

London   Sydney   Toronto

The Writing Process—Books 7 through 12

Authors and Consultants

Miles C. Olson, Senior Author—Professor of English Education, University of Colorado at Boulder; Director, Colorado Writing Project.

Allen Berger, Consultant—Professor of Language Communications, University of Pittsburgh; Director, Pittsburgh Reading and Writing Consultants; Editor, *English Education.*

Nancy Tia Brown, Coauthor, Book 12—Project Director in Career Education and Gifted Education, Jefferson County Public Schools, Colorado; former high-school foreign languages teacher.

Warren E. Combs, Coauthor, Book 8—Writing Consultant, Clarke and DeKalb County Schools, Georgia.

Philip DiStefano, Coauthor, Book 11—Professor of English Education and Reading, University of Colorado at Boulder; Co-Director, Colorado Writing Project; Consultant, National Assessment of Educational Progress.

Michael G. Gessner—Research Associate, Center for the Study of Reading and Writing, University of Colorado at Boulder. Contributing Author, Book 11.

Gale Dugas Hulme, Coauthor, Books 7 and 10—Language Arts Consultant for Gwinnett County Public Schools, Lawrenceville, Georgia; former high-school English teacher and department chair.

Sandra Jones—Language Arts Supervisor for the Dougherty County Schools, Albany, Georgia. Contributing Author, Book 7.

Daniel R. Kirby, Coauthor, Books 7 and 10—Professor of English Education, University of Georgia at Athens.

Kathleen Kirby—Instructor, University of Georgia, Athens, Georgia. Contributing Author, Book 10.

Carol B. Kuykendall, Coauthor, Books 9 and 12—Executive Director, English Language Arts, Houston (Texas) Independent School District.

Cherie A. Lyons, Coauthor, Book 12—Project Director in Career Education, Jefferson County Public Schools, Colorado; former high-school English teacher.

Iris M. Tiedt, Coauthor, Book 10—Professor, San Jose State University (California); Director, South Bay Writing Project.

Acknowledgments for material quoted from other sources will be found on page 342 which is an extension of this page.

Senior Editor: Patricia A. Browne
Senior Designer: Beverly Fell
Preparation Services Coordinator: Martha E. Ballentine
Production and Art Services by Tonia Noell-Roberts

Library of Congress Catalog Card No. 81-68466

Printed in the United States of America
ISBN 0-205-07550-9

2   3   4   5   6   7   8   9   89   88   87   86   85   84   83   82

CONTENTS

Realizing Self

There is no description as difficult as describing oneself.

—Montaigne

Chapter **1**

Finding a Focus

Writing is a way of realizing. Think for a moment about the word *realize*. Usually, it means "to become aware of" or "to understand." Taken literally, though, it means "to make real."

Writing can help you do both. It can help you understand your own thoughts and experiences. It can also help you make those thoughts and experiences real to someone else.

This book is about writing to realize. Each chapter will suggest ways of discovering, exploring, and expanding your own stockpile of raw material for writing. Each chapter will also offer techniques for shaping that material into interesting pieces to be read by others.

Just reading these chapters won't do much for your writing. You'll need to practice. As novelist MacKinlay Kantor said, "There is a mystery about stringing words together which cannot well be solved until one has strung a lot of words together." The activities in this book require you to do exactly that—to string a lot of words together. In the process, you will realize a great deal about yourself, about the world around you, and about the power of writing.

Your first subject will be yourself—the one subject that offers an unlimited supply of material and upon which you are the ultimate expert. At first glance, that subject seems easy. In a way, it is really hard. When you write about most subjects, you can step back and see those subjects from different angles, but you can't step back from yourself. You know the face in the mirror, but you can't see that face as it reflects joy, disappointment, surprise, boredom. You know what you think and feel, but it's hard to sort out those thoughts and feelings when they are yours. Being so close to your subject—indeed *being* your subject—doesn't allow you to move back and see it in perspective.

There are some very practical reasons to begin this course by writing about yourself. For one thing, you will soon be applying for college admission or for a job. You may even be applying for both. College

3

admissions offices as well as prospective employers often request applicants to submit an autobiographical sketch. How well you write about yourself may help determine whether you are admitted by the college of your choice or hired by a prospective employer.

There is a second good reason to begin this course by writing about such a familiar subject. Because you need not strain for material to write about, writing about yourself frees you to concentrate on the composing process. Since this is your last high school writing course, it is particularly important that you make that process your own—in other words, that you become an independent writer.

As you work through this initial unit, keep in mind that writing about self is just a starting point. In subsequent units, you will move outward. You will write about other people, about observations and ideas, about literature, and even about the future. In every sense of the word, you will seek to *realize* these things through writing. In this chapter, you will begin by writing to realize self.

Zooming In

A good writer, like a good photographer, zooms in on a subject. Suppose that a photographer wants to capture the pain of defeat exemplified by a losing quarterback as he leaves the football field after a close game. That photographer would not simply aim the camera in the general direction of the quarterback and click the shutter. Such a shot would include everything within range: an expanse of football field, a cluster of players and coaches, and any spectators who happened to be milling around. The quarterback would be only one image among many. To capture the quarterback's moment of defeat, a good photographer would zoom in on that one dejected figure. The resulting close-up might focus on the quarterback's face, on his downcast eyes and grimly clenched lips. Everything else would fade into the background.

Cameras are unselective. They do not automatically focus on the most significant image within their viewfinders. It is the photographer who consciously selects a subject and zooms in on it. A writer must do the same thing.

It is not enough to decide that you will turn the camera around and zoom in on yourself. That subject is too ambitious. There is too much to be captured in one picture.

Although you are still young, you've seen more and done more than you'll ever be able to put on paper. With so much to write about, you may be tempted to cover too much ground in a single piece. If you do, the result will be much like that photograph in which the quarterback disappears into the post-game crowd. You can't write about everything at once. Even when you write about yourself, you must choose a focal point and push everything else into the background.

Most writers don't *start* with a good focal point. They have to look for one. They have to sort through their experiences, observations, and ideas for something worth writing about. This preliminary collecting and sifting of possibilities, often called *pre-writing,* is an essential step in the writing process.

In previous English classes, you may have tried free writing, jotlisting, and brainstorming. You may have recorded observations, thoughts, and feelings in a journal or writer's notebook. All of these activities help you collect raw material for writing and explore promising possibilities.

During this course, you will continue to practice a variety of pre-writing strategies. In doing so, you will sometimes discover new ideas as well as uncover old ones. As you add to your reservoir of ideas and become more adept at tapping it, you will gain ease and confidence as a writer.

As you start your collection of raw material for writing, don't hold out for the grand or the dramatic. Think small. Remember writer Robert Persig's story of a student who wanted to write a theme about the United States. When she couldn't think of a single word to say, her teacher suggested that she write about her home town instead. When the girl still couldn't get started, the teacher suggested that she narrow her attention to the front of the opera house on Main Street, beginning with the upper left-hand brick. The challenge worked, and the student wrote an interesting, original paper.

Keeping a notebook will help you grow as a writer. Henry David Thoreau, one of the great journal-keepers of all time, once commented on the way ideas seem to multiply when they are collected: "Thoughts accidentally thrown together become a frame in which more may be developed and exhibited." The more ideas you collect, the more likely they are to develop into something extra.

Start a Writer's Notebook to be kept throughout the course. Label the first section **Idea Bank**. Use this section to collect your pre-writings, beginning with the ones that follow:

Getting It Started

1. Something concrete often sparks ideas. When writing about yourself, concrete objects can be especially helpful because they

provide an external reference point. So, go through a scrapbook, photograph album, autograph book, or souvenir box you kept when you were younger. Look for items that especially reflect you or have some special meaning. List those items and make notes on what they show about you or about why they are important.

2. Now try another way of looking at yourself. Figures like the following are sometimes called *webs* because they spin out from a central point. Copy the web on a separate page in your Writer's Notebook, leaving plenty of room for your own additions. Write your name in the center.

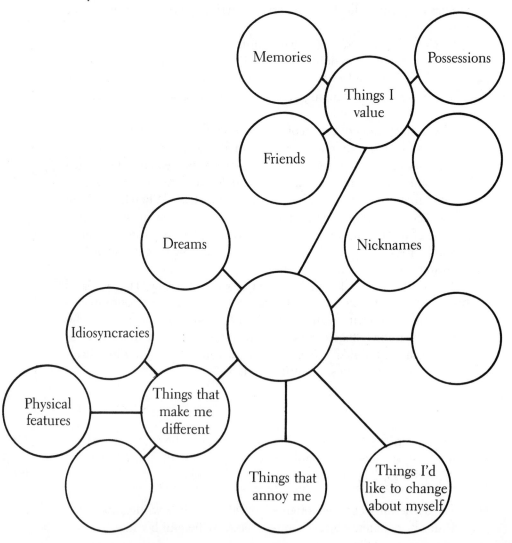

Notice that some cells of the web have been left blank. Those blanks are just to remind you that you can add your own—not just where there are blanks, but anywhere you like.

Keep in mind that *you* are the center of the web. The point is to move out in all directions and see where various categories lead. For example, here is just one part of a web developed by another student.

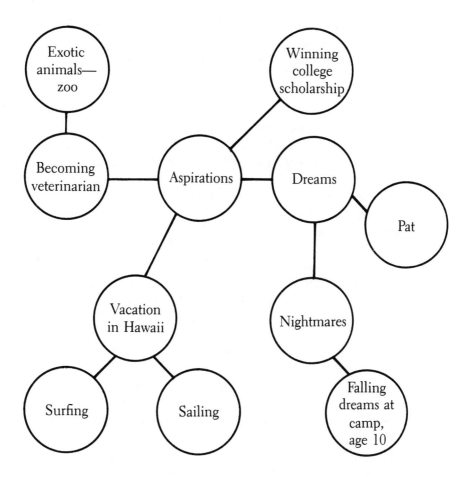

Pat branched off into two kinds of dreams, aspirations, and nightmares. The latter didn't seem to lead anywhere besides the childhood memory of one vivid nightmare at camp. The branch labeled *aspirations* was more productive. It reminded Pat of her ambition to become a veterinarian, perhaps treating exotic animals in a zoo. Another aspiration, a trip to Hawaii, reminded the writer of her interests in surfing and sailing. Notice how the web traces each chain of association.

Now you are ready to complete the web in your Writer's Notebook. Work rapidly, letting one association lead to another. Get down as much as you can.

~~~~~~~~~~~~~~~~~~~~~~~~~~~~~~~~~~~~~

The point of pre-writing exercises like the ones you have just completed is to survey some of the possibilities for writing about a subject—in this case, you. There is no commitment to a single focus. At this stage of the process, the writer is like the photographer who pans almost at random, looking through the viewfinder of a camera for promising subjects.

Now that you have surveyed some possibilities for writing about yourself, choose one of those possibilities and explore it in detail. Free writing provides one good way to do so.

If you have practiced free writing in previous courses, you know that it is a way of getting ideas down fast. You write freely, without paying much attention to form. In most free writing, you don't worry about staying on one subject or making logical connections. You just write whatever comes to mind for a prescribed time, usually about ten minutes. The only rule is "Don't stop."

During the next activity, you will do a slightly more controlled kind of free writing. You will still write nonstop, and you will still write fast. This time, however, you will write within the boundaries of a single subject. In other words, your free writing will be focused.

~~~~~~~~~~~~~~~~~~~~~~~~~~~~~~~~~~~~~

Getting It Down

Look back over the notes you made going through a scrapbook or some other collection of memorabilia. Also look back over the topics spun out on your web. Find one item or cluster of items that suggests something important about you or that offers some insight into what makes you who you are.

Use the topic selected as the focus for a free writing about yourself. For ten minutes, write as fast as you can. Don't worry about how your sentences look or sound—or even whether your words make sentences. Don't worry about the order in which ideas land on the page. Just keep thinking about yourself in terms of the particular topic you selected, and keep your pen or pencil moving.

~~~~~~~~~~~~~~~~~~~~~~~~~~~~~~~~~~~~~

Put your focused free writing away for later use. Keep it in mind as you work through some related activities. Now that your thoughts have been captured in rough form, they need time to germinate.

Meanwhile, you will sample some writing others have done about themselves. In this case, the writing is by professionals. As an apprentice writer, see how much you can learn from these masters of the craft.

SPOTLIGHT

E. B. White's essay "About Myself" was written in 1945. In this brief excerpt from that essay, notice how the author personalizes himself by focusing on one thing that concerns him deeply.

> I am a man of medium height. I keep my records in a Weis Folder Re-order Number 8003. The unpaid balance of my estimated tax for the year 1945 is item 3 less the sum of items 4 and 5. My eyes are gray. My selective service order number is 10789. The serial number is T1654. I am in Class IV-A and have been variously in Class 3-A, Class 1-A (H), and Class 4-H. My social security number is 067-01-9841. I am married to U.S. Woman 067-01-9807. Her eyes are gray. This is not a joint declaration, nor is it made by an agent; therefore it need be signed only by me—and, as I said, I am a man of medium height. . . .
>
> I owe a letter to Corporal 32413654, Hq and Hq Sq, VII AAF S.C., APO 953 c/o PM San Francisco, Calif., thanking him for the necktie he sent me at Christmas. In 1918 I was a private in the Army. My number was 4,345,016. I was a boy of medium height. I had light hair. I had no absences from duty under G.O. 31, 1912, or G.O. 45, 1914. The number of that war was Number One.

Consider these questions and compare your responses with those of your classmates:

1. E. B. White never states his concern directly, but the distinct pattern of details leaves no doubt about the focal point of the essay. What personal concern do these paragraphs zoom in on?
2. At first glance, the author doesn't seem to deliver what the title promises. He doesn't seem to tell much about himself. What clues do you find to the author's age, family life, past? What physical details about himself does he include? Which does he repeat? Why do you think he does so?

3. Actually, the seemingly impersonal details about numbers add up to a strong impression of the author. What kind of man would be troubled by all those anonymous numbers? How can you tell that he *is* troubled? (Notice especially the last sentence of each paragraph.)
4. E. B. White could have stated his concern directly and explained to the reader what that concern showed about him as a person. Instead, the author presents details that dramatize that concern and thus offer a flash of insight into the person who felt it. Why is this approach more powerful than a more general and more direct explanation?

Sharpening the Image

In "About Myself," E. B. White doesn't try to tell everything about himself. He doesn't tell about his career as a journalist or his adventures in driving across the continent in a Model A Ford. Those are the subjects of other pieces. "About Myself" focuses on one point: White's concern about the depersonalizing effect of classifying and numbering human beings and everything around them.

Without such a focal point, a piece of writing blurs. But a well-defined focus is not enough. Good writers like E. B. White choose just the right details to make the word picture rich and vivid as well as clear. White does not stop with the bare outlines. He fills in with specifics ranging from gray eyes to social security numbers to the Christmas necktie from Corporal 32413654.

When writing about yourself, you will want to be just as explicit and to elaborate just as fully. You can add lots of pertinent details without cluttering a word picture or losing focus. In fact, well-chosen details *sharpen* focus. Two more passages by professional writers illustrate this point.

Notice that the next piece was prompted by a family scrapbook, one of the sources you tapped earlier. This paragraph appears in John Updike's autobiographical essay "Boyhood in the Forties."

> Leafing through a scrapbook my mother long ago made of my childhood drawings, I was greeted by one I had titled "Mr. Sun Talking to Old Man Winter in His Office." Old Man Winter, a cloud with stick legs, and his host, a radiant ball with similar legs, sit at ease, both smiling, on two chairs that are the only furniture of the solar office. That the source of all light should have, somewhere, an office, suited my conception of an artist, who was someone who

lived in a small town like Shillington, and, who, equipped with pencils and paper, practiced his solitary trade as methodically as the dentist practiced his. And indeed, that is how it is at present with me.

This single childhood drawing presents a strong image of Updike, both as child artist and adult novelist. Here, the focus is upon self as artist.

Every detail has been chosen accordingly. Think for a moment about the selectivity at work here. Think about the details that are *not* included. The writer doesn't tell how he happened to be going through the album, how the album looked, whether the drawing was done with pencil or crayon, where he had been, and how he had felt years earlier when he had done the drawing. Such details may have occurred to him as he looked at the drawing, and some may have piqued his interest, but a good writer knows what to leave out as well as what to put in. Here, Updike includes only those details that show how he views himself as an artist.

Notice how much the writer manages to say with so few deftly chosen details. Notice also how he uses comparison to intensify those details and to give them extra meaning. First, the author compares the stick figure representing the sun to the artist. What does this comparison suggest about artists? In what way is the artist a source of light? Later, Updike highlights the image of the sun-like artist's sitting in an office by comparing his methodical approach to that of a dentist. How does this unexpected comparison add to his view of the artist?

Ralph W. Ellison also uses comparison to intensify well-chosen details in one of his autobiographical sketches. The passage you will read, which appears near the end of the sketch, describes a favorite possession that reflects the author. On the web you completed earlier, you may have identified some of your own favorite possessions. Here, Ellison begins by recounting how he found this boyhood treasure and goes on to tell what it meant to him:

> . . . I recall finding, about this time, while seeking adventure in back alleys—which possess for boys a superiority over playgrounds like that which kitchen utensils possess over toys designed for infants —a large photographic lens. I remember nothing of its optical quali- ties, of its speed or color correction, but it gleamed with crystal mystery and it was beautiful.
>
> Mounted handsomely in a tube of shiny brass, it spoke to me of distant worlds of possibility. I played with it, looking through it with squinted eyes, holding it in shafts of sunlight, and tried to use it for a magic lantern. But most of this was as unrewarding as my attempts

to make the music come from a phonograph record by holding the
needle in my fingers.

I could burn holes through newspapers with it, or I could
pretend that it was a telescope, the barrel of a cannon, or the third
eye of a monster—*I* being the monster—but I could do nothing at all
about its proper function of making images; nothing to make it yield
its secret. But I could not discard it.

In the opening sentence, find the comparison Ellison uses to illustrate the
appeal of back alleys to boys. Why is this comparison so apt? In the last
sentence of the second paragraph, find the comparison that shows the

futility of the writer's attempts to put the lens to practical use. Why does this comparison work so well?

The first comparison helps lead the reader into the piece. It helps set the stage and show something about the boy at the time he found the lens. The second is much more important because it intensifies the dominant image in the essay, the handsome lens that was treasured for its mystery rather than its utility. Notice how other phrases keep this image in the foreground. The lens "gleamed with crystal mystery." It spoke to its young owner of "distant worlds of possibility." It refused to "yield its secret." Here again, careful selectivity is at work.

Take a moment to glance back over the short pieces by White, Updike, and Ellison. All three share a common subject, the author himself. But here the similarity ends. The first shows an individualist concerned about the dehumanizing side effects of progress in the twentieth century. The second offers a glimpse of the artistic vision that has influenced a novelist since boyhood. The third recalls the love of beauty and mystery invested in a favorite possession by another fledgling writer.

The three pieces are as different in form as they are in focus. White's piece reads like a monologue. Updike's is primarily description. Ellison's moves along like a narrative. Each writer has chosen the approach that works best for him and adapted it freely. For other autobiographical sketches—and all three have written many—these same writers have chosen other forms and adapted them just as freely.

In writing about yourself, you have all of these options and more. The point of reading professional models is not to imitate them. It is to open up new options and stimulate your own ideas.

If the models did indeed stimulate ideas for writing about yourself, you may have already jotted some of them down. If not, you may want to do so as you reread the free writing you did earlier.

Don't be disappointed if your free writing seems pretty pale beside the sketches of White, Updike, and Ellison. They are professional writers. Besides, their pieces weren't written in ten minutes! Your free writing was just a way of getting preliminary thoughts down on paper, perhaps not even in complete sentences. A free writing isn't even a first draft.

Up to this point, you've been concerned with what to say, not how to say it. To some extent, you still are. As you begin to plan the first draft of a focused paper about yourself, you will want to add details to the ones you captured earlier. You may want to think of ideas, phrases, and even sentences that might be repeated to highlight a dominant image. You may want to try different comparisons to intensify key details.

In later chapters of this book, you will practice all of these writing techniques. However, choosing details around a central focus and inventing comparisons are not just writing techniques. They are *thinking* techniques. By focusing on details and experimenting with comparisons, you discover more things to say as well as better ways of saying them. (Remember that upper left-hand brick on the front of the opera house?) That is exactly what you are supposed to do as you move from pre-writing to drafting.

───

Getting It Down

Using your free writing and any other notes you may have made during the course of this chapter, write a short piece about yourself. Focus that piece around one object, experience, interest, or characteristic that reveals something about you as a person. Use lots of explicit detail and try for some good comparisons to intensify key points.

───

Checking It Out

When you have finished, read your paper over, perhaps aloud. Be sure that all sentences are complete and that two or more don't run together. Mark any sentences that you suspect might be either sentence parts (often called fragments) or sentences that run together (often called run-ons). ● If you have such questionable sentences, consult pages H-11–12 in the Writer's Handbook. Then reconsider the possible trouble-spots you marked and make any necessary corrections. Ask your teacher to check any sentences you still aren't sure about.

Although what you have written is only a first draft, it is undoubtedly worth sharing with someone else. Almost every time you write in this course, you will be asked to try out what you have written on someone, usually your classmates and teacher but sometimes another audience. After all, writing is to be read!

Read your paper aloud to a small group of classmates. Ask each of them to jot down the most important thing that comes through about you—in other words, the focal point of the paper. Did all readers see what you intended? Also, ask what each reader liked *best* about the paper. (You might also share your paper at home with at least one family member and get responses to the same questions.)

Consider the responses of your readers. Make marginal notes about how your paper might be improved if you were to revise it—as you may do later.

Moving Toward Independence

In this chapter you have concentrated on pre-writing and drafting, on finding interesting things to say and saying them with ease. In other words, you have begun to work toward fluency in writing. The next chapter will continue this emphasis, but it will move further into the writing process.

Before you leave this chapter, think back through the process so far. Think about the techniques you used to tap both inner and outer resources for something worthwhile to say about yourself in writing. Think about how you used the material that surfaced during pre-writing activities in drafting a paper about yourself.

Think also about the fact that this is the last writing course you will take in high school. By the end of this year, you need to understand the writing process so well that you can work your way through it without step-by-step instructions. For this reason, many chapters in this book will conclude with an assignment that challenges you to apply independently the techniques you have just practiced. This is the first such chapter.

Develop the habit of reviewing the techniques you have practiced and writing them down in your Writer's Notebook. Start a section— perhaps in the back—titled **Notes on the Writing Process**. Head the first page "Pre-writing Strategies." Then, start a list with the two strategies practiced in this chapter, free writing and webbing. Opposite each, you may wish to write a brief explanation for future reference. Head the next page "Guidelines for Drafting." Enter *focus* as the first item on that list. Again, you may wish to jot down what the term means to you now that you have worked through the chapter and written a first draft focusing upon one aspect of self. By maintaining this log of writing techniques throughout the year, you will reinforce your understanding of the writing process and thus move toward independence as a writer.

Having reviewed the pre-writing and drafting strategies practiced in this first chapter, you are ready to see how well you can apply them on your own. Here is your assignment:

<hr />

**Getting
It
Down**

During the years you have been in school, you have done a lot of writing. Though you may not think of yourself as such, you are already a writer. Like any other writer, you have your own accumulated feelings about the task of putting words on paper. You have your own strengths and weaknesses. You have your own writing habits.

Take a close look at yourself as writer. Write a short piece characterizing the writer you are right now.

<hr />

Although the two papers you have written during this chapter have not been revised and polished, your teacher will probably want you to turn them in. Both will help your teacher get to know you as a person and as a writer.

Before handing those papers in, read them one more time. Also take another look at the **Idea Bank** section in your Writer's Notebook. Have you done some hard thinking about who you are? Have you discovered—or rediscovered—anything interesting? In other words, have you begun to realize yourself more fully?

**Checking
It
Out**

Chapter 2

Capturing the Moment

Have you ever tackled a writing topic like "My Elementary School Days" or "What I Did Last Summer"? Such big topics almost guarantee failure. Because there is so much territory to cover, you condense days or even years into single sentences. Such writing doesn't move you toward greater self-awareness. Since you usually end up saying too little about too much, such writing doesn't do much for your reader either.

In this chapter, you'll work toward capturing moments rather than months or years. Of course, not all moments are worth capturing. But you have experienced plenty that are. The first task is to find them.

So far, all of your pre-writing warm-ups have been done solo. This time you will work with some classmates. Reminiscing aloud will jog your memory. Listening to the recollections of others will also help. Just think of all the conversations in which you have said, "That reminds me of the time. . . ."

Getting It Started

Turn to a clean page in the **Idea Bank** of your Writer's Notebook. Head the page "Moments to Remember." Use it to note personal experiences you recall during this activity.

After your teacher has divided the class into groups of four or five students, someone in each group will need to volunteer as leader. This person's job will be to keep the conversation on track and to keep it moving. Each group member will share recollections suggested by these questions. (Don't worry if you draw a blank on some items. As you go through the list, just recall as many experiences as you can.)

1. Do you remember the first time you
    saw a baby brother or sister?
    went to school?

were left all alone?

realized that you were different in some way?

found out that someone you loved or admired wasn't perfect?

met your best friend?

stayed away from home overnight?

thought you were in love?

were caught in a falsehood?

travelled on an airplane, a bus, or a train?

got behind the wheel of a car?

What other "firsts" do you remember?

2. Can you remember a time when you felt extremely

embarrassed?   triumphant?

lonely?   serene?

frightened?   surprised?

3. Can you remember a happening that was the opposite of what you were expecting—for example, a time when you

expected to fail but succeeded?

expected to be rewarded but were punished?

expected to laugh but cried?

expected to dislike someone but liked him or her a great deal?

4. What memory is your

earliest?   happiest?

saddest?   most cherished?

most ridiculous?

Recreating the Past

Some of the memories you just listed are probably very important to you. You would like to recall some of these experiences more clearly and more fully. Unfortunately, you cannot go back and recapture all of the sensations that made a particular moment memorable. You must be content with seemingly fragmentary flashes of recollection. For example, on your first day of school, you may recall the white-on-green manuscript letters displayed above the chalkboard, the smell of graham crackers served with morning milk, the sound of a jump rope slapping the sidewalk at recess, the taste of paste as you licked your fingers after art, the stiffness of new jeans. Alone, each detail doesn't mean much. Together, these impressions can go a long way toward re-creating what you experienced on that first day of school. After all, you experienced that day through your five senses.

Review the experiences you jotted down during the pre-writing activity. Decide which three are most vivid in your mind and seem the most worthwhile to explore in writing. Using the questions that follow, think back through each experience.

Getting
It
Started

Where did the experience occur? Who else was there? What do you recall seeing? Does any color stand out as a part of the scene you remember? What do you remember hearing? feeling? tasting? smelling?

Make five headings on a sheet of paper: **Sight, Sound, Touch, Taste, Smell**. Under each, list sensory impressions associated with one of the memories you have chosen. When you have listed as many sensory details as you can remember, do the same for each of the other two memories.

Put aside the list you just made. As you made the list, did you notice how the memory of one sensation helped trigger another? Almost before you knew it, you may have filled in enough background to make each memory stand out clearly. Exploring background is another way of getting ideas, of finding material to include in what you write. It is a way of helping you get in closer touch with your own subject.

Later, you will use your list of background details as you write a memory sketch about one of the three experiences you just explored. Including such sensory details in your paper will help your reader see, hear, feel, taste, and smell what you did at the time. In this way, your reader will be able to enter into your memory vicariously.

SPOTLIGHT

Thomas Wolfe's "Circus at Dawn" provides a good example. Although you may never have seen a circus train unload—a commonplace occurrence in small-town America fifty years ago—Wolfe's account will make you feel that you have. In this piece, the author recaptures the moments of wonder he felt as a boy each time he and his brother watched the circus come to town.

Talking in low excited voices we would walk rapidly back toward
town under the rustle of September leaves, in cool streets just grayed

now with that still, that unearthly and magical first light of day which seems suddenly to rediscover the great earth out of darkness. . . . At the sculptural still square where at one corner, just emerging into light, my father's shabby little marble shop stood with a ghostly strangeness and familiarity, my brother and I would "catch" the first streetcar of the day bound for the "depot" where the circus was—or sometimes we would meet someone we knew, who would give us a lift in his automobile.

Then, having reached the dingy, grimy, and rickety depot section, we would get out, and walk rapidly across the tracks of the station yard, where we could see great flares and streamings from the engines, and hear the crash and the bump of shifting freight cars, the swift sporadic thunders of a shifting engine, the tolling of bells, the sounds of great trains on the rails.

And, to all these familiar sounds, filled with their exultant prophecies of flight, the voyage, morning, and the shining cities—to all the sharp and thrilling odors of the trains—the smell of cinders, acrid smoke, of musty, rusty freight cars, the clean pine-board of crated produce, and the smells of fresh stored food—oranges, coffee, tangerines and bacon, ham, and flour and beef—there would be added now, with an unforgettable magic and familiarity, all the strange sounds and smells of the coming circus.

The gay yellow sumptuous-looking cars in which the star performers lived and slept, still dark and silent, heavily and powerfully still, would be drawn up in long strings upon the tracks. And all around them the sounds of the unloading circus would go on furiously in the darkness. The receding gulf of lilac and departing night would be filled with the savage roar of the lions, the murderously sudden snarling of great jungle cats, the trumpeting of the elephants, the stamp of the horses, and with the musty, pungent, unfamiliar odor of the jungle animals: the tawny camel smells, and the smells of panthers, zebras, tigers, elephants, and bears.

Then, along the tracks, beside the circus trains, there would be the sharp cries and oaths of the circus men, the magical swinging dance of lanterns in the darkness, the sudden heavy rumble of the loaded vans and wagons as they were pulled along the flats and gondolas, and down the runways to the ground. And everywhere, in the thrilling mystery of darkness and awakening light, there would be the tremendous conflict of a confused, hurried, and yet orderly movement.

. . . On the circus ground, the tents were going up already with the magic speed of dreams. All over the place (which was near the

tracks and the only space of flat land in the town that was big
enough to hold a circus) there would be this fierce, savagely hurried,
and yet orderly confusion. Great flares of gaseous circus light would
blaze down on the seared and battered faces of the circus toughs as,
with the rhythmic precision of a single animal—a human riveting
machine—they swung their sledges at the stakes, driving a stake into
the earth with the incredible instancy of accelerated figures in a
motion picture. And everywhere, as light came, and the sun appeared, there would be a scene of magic, order, and of violence.
The drivers would curse and talk their special language to their
teams; there would be the loud, gasping, and uneven labor of a
gasoline engine, the shouts and curses of the bosses, the wooden
riveting of driven stakes, and the rattle of heavy chains . . .

Meanwhile, the circus food tent—a huge canvas top without
concealing sides—had already been put up, and now we could see

the performers seated at long trestled tables underneath the tent, as they ate breakfast . . . They ate big fried steaks, pork chops, rashers of bacon, a half-dozen eggs, great slabs of fried ham and great stacks of wheat cakes which a cook kept flipping in the air with the skill of a juggler, and which a husky-looking waitress kept rushing to their tables on loaded trays held high and balanced marvelously on the fingers of a brawny hand. And above all the maddening odors of the wholesome and succulent food, there brooded forever the sultry and delicious fragrance—that somehow seemed to add zest and sharpness to all the powerful and thrilling life of morning—of strong boiling coffee, which we could see sending off clouds of steam from an enormous polished urn, and which the circus performers gulped down, cup after cup.

. . . And reluctantly, with full light come and the sun up, we would leave the circus grounds and start for home.

Before working further on your own memory sketch, consider these questions about the one you have just read:

1. What details in Wolfe's description appeal most strongly to the sense of sight? of smell? of hearing? of touch? Make a list of details in each category that you consider the most vivid. Underline words that you find particularly effective in conveying sensory impressions.
2. "Circus at Dawn" is crammed with detail, but details are not randomly selected. All details focus on the circus—not just the circus in general but the circus as it is remembered years later by someone who watched it being unloaded and set up in a small town at dawn. The way the narrator feels about what he is recounting provides even greater focus. Find as many words and phrases as you can that show the young boy's sense of wonder.
3. Besides being focused around one carefully limited topic and one feeling, this sketch is carefully arranged. Notice how the account begins with the walk across town toward the circus ground and ends with the boys' starting back home. The observations between unfold in the sequence in which they occur. Notice how often Wolfe uses transitional words like *then* to remind the reader of this chronological movement. List as many such transitional words and phrases as you can find.
4. "Circus at Dawn" contains recurrent references to the breaking of day. Locate the images of darkness and light. How do these images sharpen focus and reinforce chronological arrangement of details?

Return to the list of sensory impressions you made earlier. Have you thought of other sensations associated with the experiences you were recalling? If so, add them to your list.

~~~~~~

Choose from the three memories you explored earlier the one you consider most promising as the subject of a memory sketch. Refer to your list of sensory impressions as you write an account of the experience upon which the list is based. Be sure to narrate the events in the order in which they occurred. Bring each event alive with rich, sensory detail. Use the most descriptive words you can find to re-create the experience as vividly as possible.

**Getting
It
Down**

~~~~~~

Put aside the draft you have just completed, and think back for a moment to the Wolfe sketch. As an adult recounting an event from his childhood, this author did not write choppy, immature sentences. "Circus at Dawn" did not begin like this: "We would talk in low excited voices. We would walk rapidly. We would walk back toward town. September leaves would rustle overhead. The cool streets would turn gray. The first light of day seemed magical. It seemed unearthly. It seemed to rediscover the great earth out of darkness." No, indeed, the author included all of these details in one sentence: "Talking in low excited voices we would walk rapidly back toward town under the rustle of September leaves, in cool streets just grayed now with that still, that unearthly magical first light of day which seems suddenly to rediscover the great earth out of darkness." Although this sentence is long and tightly packed with detail, notice how smooth and easy-to-follow it is.

Although you probably will not write sentences as long and complicated as Thomas Wolfe's, it is a good idea to practice combining ideas into rich sentences. Such practice will help you write richer, more varied sentences of your own.

Writer's Workbench

Introduction to Sentence-Combining

Sentence-combining problems will appear regularly in the Writer's Workbenches in this book. They will help you explore and practice the options speakers and writers use in putting English sentences together. If such problems are new to you, don't worry. The problems are based on intuitive understanding of language. Serious work with sentence-combining problems will help you bring intuitive understanding to a conscious level and thus gain greater control of language.

A. In this Workbench, you will first work through some *cued* problems. The cues (signals) provided in the problems help you practice sentence patterns that you might not otherwise use. There are only a few cues to learn. Even if you haven't seen these cues before, you will probably be able to figure them out by seeing how they work in the following example.

> A gull came soaring over the waves.
> The gull was <u>silent.</u>
> The gull paused.   (,)
> The gull hovered.   (, and)
> The gull plummeted into the water for a fish dinner.
> (, finally -ing)

> A silent gull came soaring over the waves, paused, and hovered, finally plummeting into the water for a fish dinner.

As you can see, the cues are like glue used to fit pieces of the combined sentence together. The underlining cue means that only the underlined word or phrase appears in the combined sentence. Notice that repeated words, like "The gull" in the preceding example, show the place of the underlined part in the previous sentence. In this case, *silent* belongs in front of *gull*. All other cues in this sample problem are enclosed in parentheses. When whole words and punctuation marks appear in parentheses, they are moved to the front of the sentences they follow. Repeated words are usually crossed out before the sentence is combined with the previous one. Word parts, like *-ing* in this example, are usually connected to a verb of the sentence they follow. Again, repeated words are deleted before the sentence is combined with the previous one.

The one basic cue that does not appear in this example is the SOMETHING cue. This word, always written in capital letters, serves as a place-holder in the sentence in which it appears. It tells where the next sentence should be slotted in.

Work through the following problems on your own. Follow the cues and be certain that you use all of the information in the problem sentences in your combined sentences. Write your combined sentences in paragraph form and you will have part of a memory sketch written by another student in response to the assignment you have been working on.

1. The car stopped.   (As soon as)
    I tumbled out.   (,)
    I ran across the sand.   (and)
    The sand was blistering.
    I ran toward the water.
    The water stretched as far as I could see.   (that)

2. I neared the water.   (-ing)
    I looked down to see SOMETHING.   (,)
    A glaze was covering the sand.
    The glaze was wet.
    The glaze was soothing my feet.   (and)
    My feet were burning.

3. I was sitting.   (Soon)
    I was sitting on the sand.
    The sand was wave-drenched.
    I was scooping out holes.   (,)
    I was watching them fill with sea water.   (and)

4. I knew it.   (Almost before)
   I had ventured into the water.   (,)
   The water was <u>shallow.</u>
   The waves surged over my knees.   (, where)
   The waves splashed droplets into my face.   (and)
   The droplets were <u>salty.</u>

5. I heard a voice.   (When)
   The voice was <u>in the distance.</u>
   I ducked under the water.   (,)
   The roar of the gulf would drown out SOMETHING.   (so that)
   The words were "Come back, Becky."
   The words were <u>dreaded.</u>

Check your combined sentences with the model sentences supplied by your teacher. Be sure to ask questions about any cues that puzzle you. You will be using these cues again.

In reviewing your combined sentences, notice how the student writer used details that appeal to several of the senses. Notice also the use of transition to link sentences together and to signal chronological arrangement.

B. In this second part of the Workbench, you will try some *uncued* problems. Such problems consist of several short sentences which you may combine in any way you wish. Of course, you should try for the smoothest, most concise sentences possible.

In the next exercise, some words have been underlined. This time, underlining is not intended as a cue; it simply identifies a word or phrase that doesn't have much sensory appeal. As you combine the sentences, substitute more vivid words or phrases for those that have been underlined. Write your combined sentences in paragraph form, and you will have an improved version of another student's account of his first race. Begin your paragraph with the sentence combined for you as an example.

Example:

The coach <u>said</u> "Go."
I <u>came</u> from the starting line.
I <u>joined</u> the jumble of <u>bright</u> track suits and <u>moving</u> legs.

When the coach yelled "Go," I jumped from the starting line and joined the jumble of multi-colored track suits and churning legs.

1. I left the straightaway.
   I tried to forget the noise of the crowd.
   I tried to hear only the sound of shoes hitting the track.

2. Sweat already ran down my face.
   It hurt my eyes.
   It left a bad taste in my mouth.

3. Soon, I realized SOMETHING.
   Three of us had pulled away from the crowd.
   We were almost even.
   We took the course.
   We squinted against the bright sun.
   We took in great breaths of air.

4. I let out all stops.
   I felt myself <u>move</u> into the lead.
   A cramp <u>suddenly</u> <u>affected</u> my left leg.
   It sent me <u>falling</u> to the track.

5. I rolled off the track.
   I spit out the <u>unpleasant-tasting</u> cinders.
   I wiped my eyes.
   Tears now mingled with sweat.
   I hid my face in the <u>refreshing</u> grass.

Compare your version with those of several classmates. Which sentences are smoothest, clearest, and most economical? Which word substitutions create the sharpest word pictures?

Now that you have practiced combining sentences and sharpening word choices, return to the draft you completed earlier. Do you see any sentences that need to be combined or any word choices that need to be reconsidered? You might like to make these improvements before trying your sketch out on some of your classmates.

~~~~~~

**Checking
It
Out**

Read your memory sketch aloud to a small group. When you finish, ask whether there is any part of the narration that is not clear. Is there anything your readers would like to know more about? Is there anything that seems irrelevant and should be omitted? Also ask your classmates to tell you which sensory details they like best and which could be sharper. Finally, ask whether they could follow the sequence of events. Is there any passage that needs transition? Jot down responses for later reference.

~~~~~~

**Getting
It
Right**

Review the notes you made on your memory sketch. Consider these comments and suggestions as you revise your paper. Also take into account your own answers to these questions:

1. Is this paper focused around one memory—a memory that covers moments, not days or weeks or months?
2. Does the account of what happened contain lots of sensory

details to re-create the sights, sounds, smells, tastes, and feelings that you remember most vividly?

3.   Are events recounted in chronological order? Do transitions make one sentence lead smoothly into another?

4.   Are sentences rich and varied rather than thin and choppy?

5.   Is the paper free of distracting errors in mechanics and usage?

Revise your paper carefully. Make a final draft, perhaps to be added to a class scrapbook titled *Memorable Moments*.

Writing with Your Own Voice

If you listened to a tape recording of a class discussion or a conversation with friends, you would undoubtedly recognize your own voice. People close to you probably know who's calling even before you identify yourself on the telephone. One thing that makes your voice recognizable is the way it sounds—its pitch, quality, rate, intonation, and any regional accent. But the way it sounds is not the only thing that sets your voice apart. Your voice is actually a reflection of your personality.

Suppose for a moment that you didn't hear a tape recording of that class discussion or conversation with friends. Suppose that you read a word-for-word transcript instead. Even if you didn't remember exactly who said what, wouldn't you recognize some of the speakers, especially those you know well? Wouldn't you recognize their voices?

One of your major goals during this course will be to write with your own voice. Sometimes that voice will be conversational: you will write much as you talk. Often, however, your writing will be more formal. But writing formally does not mean sounding like someone else. Always, the voice on the page should be distinctively yours.

SPOTLIGHT

Here is a memory sketch in which poet Nikki Giovanni recalls her first day of school as a five-year-old. The author has just recounted how she had walked confidently toward the school with her mother, promising to call the teacher "Mrs. Hicks" rather than the family name of "Aunt Willa." Notice how strongly the voice of the narrator comes through.

I was bouncing up the stairs prepared to knock them dead when Mommy opened the door and I looked at all those little faces. I broke down. I didn't know these people . . . I started crying . . . Mommy, in the usual vanity that mothers possess, thought I didn't want to leave her but that wasn't it at all . . . Mommy—four-eleven, 90 pounds after Christmas dinner—walked out of that kindergarten room a little taller, a bit prouder . . . her baby girl really cared. The kids, in their usual indifferent way, stated, "Kim is a crybaby." I wanted to shout at them all—"You *dumbbumbs*"—but I restrained myself by burying my head in Aunt Willa's lap and softly pleading, "What shall I do?" Aunt Willa hit upon the saving idea: Go get Gary.

In She strode—like Cleopatra on her barge down the Nile, like Nefertiti on her way to sit for the statue, like Harriet Tubman before her train or Mary Bethune with Elenora; my big sister came to handle the situation. You could feel the room respond to her pres-

ence. It could have been San Francisco at the earthquake, Chicago as Mrs. O'Leary walked to her cow, Rome as Nero struck up his fiddle, Harlem when Malcolm mounted the podium; Gary came to handle the situation. Looking neither right nor left she glided from the door, her eyes searching for the little figure buried in Aunt Willa's skirt. "Kim"—her voice containing all the power of Cicero at the seashore, Elijah at the annual meeting—"Kim, don't cry." And it was over. Tears falling literally pulled themselves back into my eyes. In a gulp, with a wipe of the hand, it was over. "I'll walk you home for lunch. Come on, now, and play with the other kids. There's Donny, Robert's brother, and Pearl. They want to play with you." The pain, the absolute pain of wanting to be eight years old and in the fifth grade and sophisticated and in control. I could have burst! "I'm sorry." "Don't worry about it. Mommy just wouldn't want you to cry." She turned her full gaze on me. "I've got to go back to class now." She paused. Of course I understood. Oh, yes. I understood. "See you at lunch," she whispered. And as majestically as she had come—red turtleneck sweater, white short socks, and yes, sneakers (I still had to wear high-top shoes)—she vanished through the door.

Working with a small group of classmates, jot down answers to the questions that follow:

A. Begin by having one member of the group read the Giovanni sketch aloud as the author herself might read it.
   1. What two or three adjectives best describe the voice of the narrator in this particular piece?
   2. What two or three passages best illustrate these distinctive qualities? How?

B. Review the Wolfe sketch on pages 21–24, having one group member read at least part of it aloud. Jot down answers to the same two questions.

C. After the class reconvenes, compare the responses recorded by your group with those of other groups. Discuss any inconsistencies.

Few readers would confuse the voice of Nikki Giovanni with that of Thomas Wolfe. Even though Giovanni wrote other pieces reflecting the sense of wonder that permeates "Circus at Dawn" and Wolfe sometimes wrote whimsically as Giovanni did in the excerpt from "For a Four-Year-Old," their voices are never interchangeable. Each is distinctive.

Think back to the memory sketch you wrote earlier. Do you think you let your own voice come through? Does the narrator sound like *you*?

Moving Toward Independence

In this chapter, you have looked into the past for a glimpse of an earlier you. In seeking to capture a significant moment from the past, you have continued to concentrate on the process of discovering and shaping material from your own experience—in other words, on pre-writing and drafting. You have also begun to try out your writing on others and to use their responses as well as your own critical eye to guide revision.

At this point, you might like to glance back through the chapter and find items worth adding to the **Notes on the Writing Process** in your Writer's Notebook. For example, you might add *brainstorming* to your list of pre-writing strategies. Under "Guidelines for Drafting," you might add *sensory detail*. What else should you add? Beside each entry, write as much explanation as you think you'll need for later reference.

Now you are ready to apply what you have learned so far—not just in this chapter but in the preceding one as well. This assignment, like the one that concluded Chapter 1, will offer no step-by-step instructions. The point is to see how well you can do on your own.

Getting It Down

Nikki Giovanni's memory sketch is not just an account of the poet's first encounter with school; it is about her special relationship with big sister Gary. Think of some special person in your life. Recount an experience that shows what the person is like, how you feel about that person, and why.

Checking It Out

If time permits, share your paper with several classmates. Ask their impressions of the person as he or she emerges from the paper. Ask also what feeling about the person the paper conveyed. If you intended to create a different impression, make whatever changes are needed in order to do so.

If possible, make a copy of your revised paper to share with the special person you wrote about. Did capturing the relationship on paper help you become more aware of what the relationship means? Writing to realize special *others* is another way of writing to realize *self*.

Chapter **3**

Creating a Self-Portrait

The pieces you have written so far are like verbal snapshots or clips from home movies. Each focuses on a single subject, and each conveys a single impression. Collectively, these short autobiographical pieces project a strong image. The composite picture, however, is more like a collage than a self-portrait. In this chapter, you will compose an extended self-portrait that stands alone to give a clear idea of who you are and what you are becoming.

Before composing this self-portrait, you will continue to collect material and to write short sketches. Besides extending what you have already learned about discovering and developing ideas, you will concentrate on shaping those ideas into a polished piece. By the time you complete this chapter, you will have worked through the entire writing process: pre-writing, drafting, revising, and editing.

Exploring Comparisons and Contrasts

If you were describing raspberries to someone who had never seen or tasted them, you might say something like this: "Raspberries are shaped like blackberries, but they are more the color of strawberries. They don't taste quite as sweet as either." A person familiar with blackberries and strawberries would probably be able to recognize raspberries from this short description.

One of the best ways to describe the unfamiliar is by comparison to the familiar. Applying the known to the unknown can also spark imagination. Many great inventors have used comparison as a creative tool. The Wright brothers, for example, modeled the structure of the airplane on the anatomy of the bird. At one point in the NASA program, astronauts needed a way to get into and out of space suits faster than zippers and snaps would allow. An orange skin provided the inspiration for the invention of a self-gripping fastener that can be peeled open and pressed closed.

Such leaps of imagination are also productive for writers. In fact, the act of discovering new things to say is often called *invention*. In getting started on your next piece of writing, you will use comparison as a tool for invention.

Considering what a person is *like* and what he or she is *unlike* can help you take a fresh look at that person. Think of a close friend. What kind of music is that person most like—symphonic, country western, rock, operatic, disco, chamber, jazz? What qualities does your friend have in common with that kind of music? What kind of music is your friend *least* like? In what ways? By thinking of your friend in terms of music, you may see him or her in a new light.

~~~~~~

**Getting
It
Started**

In this exercise you will consider what *you* are like and unlike. Enter your responses in the **Idea Bank** of your Writer's Notebook.

A. Complete each of the following fifteen sentences with the items in each category that you consider most like yourself.
Example: If I were a city, I would be ___.

If you consider yourself romantic and perhaps artistic, you might write *Paris, France*. If you have a hardy, pioneering spirit, you might write *Barrow, Alaska*. There is sure to be some city that reflects the kind of person you think you are.

1. If I were an animal, I'd be a (an) ___.
2. If I were a vehicle, I'd be a (an) ___.
3. If I were a vegetable, I'd be a (an) ___.
4. If I were a machine, I'd be a (an) ___.
5. If I were a dance, I'd be a (an) ___.
6. If I were a toy, I'd be a (an) ___.
7. If I were a part of speech, I'd be a (an) ___.
8. If I were a plant, I'd be a (an) ___.
9. If I were a piece of furniture, I'd be a (an) ___.
10. If I were a season of the year, I'd be ___.
11. If I were a color, I'd be ___.
12. If I were a planet, I'd be ___.
13. If I were a sport, I'd be ___.
14. If I were a mark of punctuation, I'd be a (an) ___.
15. If I were a piece of clothing, I'd be a (an) ___.

B. Now go back and complete each of the preceding sentences with the thing in each category that you consider most *unlike* yourself.

　　　Example: If I were a city, I would NOT be ___.

C. Find someone in your class who completed at least one of the sentences in this exercise the same way you did. Talk about the reasons each of you thought a particular item seemed especially like or unlike yourselves. Make a jot list of those similarities and differences.

Also discuss your responses with a close friend or family member. Have that person guess the qualities that made you compare or contrast yourself with a particular animal, vehicle, vegetable, etc. Explain any comparisons and contrasts that may not be apparent. After discussing various responses with your friend or family member, make a jot list of specific similarities or differences in each category.

Checking
It
Out

Put your Writer's Notebook aside. Later, you may decide to develop some of the comparisons and contrasts you have explored and make them a part of your self-portrait. First, though, you will explore another approach to comparison and contrast.

SPOTLIGHT

Read the following excerpt from Joyce Maynard's "Old Before My Time," a chapter from her autobiography *Looking Back: A Chronicle of Growing Up Old in the Sixties.*

> To my friend Hanna, at five, I am a grown-up. I do not feel like one—at nineteen, I'm at the midway point between the kindergartner and her mother, and I belong to neither generation—but I can vote, and drink in New York, and marry without parental consent in Mississippi, and get a life sentence, not reform school, if I shoot someone premeditatedly . . . I have left childhood, and though I longed to leave it, when being young meant finishing your milk and missing "Twilight Zone" on TV because it came on too late, now that it's gone I'm uneasy. Not fear of death yet (I'm still young enough to feel immortal) or worry over wrinkles and gray hair, but a sense that the fun is over before it began, that I'm old before my time—why isn't someone holding *my* hand still, protecting *me* from the dangers of the city, guiding *me* home? . . .
>
> Hanna doesn't look where we're going, never bothers to make sure she can find her way home again, because she knows I will take care of those things, and though I feel I am too young to be so old in anybody's eyes, it's just a feeling, not a fact. When it rains, she gets the plastic rain hat, and when the ball of ice cream on her cone falls off, I give her mine. But if Hanna uses my ice cream and my hat, my knowledge of the subways and my hand, well, I use Hanna too: she's my excuse to ride the ferris wheel, to shop for dolls. And when the circus comes to town—Ringling Brothers, no less—and I take her, everything evens up. Walking to Madison Square Garden, stepping over sidewalk lines and dodging muggers, she is my escort more than I am hers.
>
> I think of one time in particular.
>
> There we sat, in our too-well-cushioned seats, Hanna in her navy blue knee socks, and flower barrettes, I beside her, holding the overpriced miniature flashlight she had shamed me into buying

(because everyone else on our row had one), earnestly obeying the
ringmaster's instructions to wave it when the lights went out—
frantically, a beacon in the night—because Hanna's hands were too
full of other circus-going apparatus: a celluloid doll whose arm
already hung loose, the Cracker Jack she wanted for the prize inside,
the Jujubes that she swallowed dutifully like pills. We all seemed a
little sad. Hanna and me and all the other flashlight wavers who
surrounded us, like people I'd see in a movie and feel sorry for—the
grown-ups, the ticket-buyers, because the admission fee hadn't really
brought us into youngness again, even the little kids, because most
of them had barely had it to begin with. We grew up old, Hanna
even more than I. We are cynics who see the trap door in the magic
show, the pillow stuffing in Salvation Army Santa Clauses, the
camera tricks on TV commercials ("That isn't really a genie's hand
coming out of the washing machine," Hanna tells me, "it's just an
actor with gloves on.") So at the circus, there was a certain lack of
wonder in the crowd, a calm, shrugging atmosphere of "So what else
is new?" . . .

  What all this has to do with growing up old—Hanna and me,
five and nineteen, watching the circus—is that Hanna has already
begun her aging and I, once having aged, am trying to return.

Either independently or with a small group of classmates, consider these questions:

1. Although Hanna seems to be the central figure in the essay, she is really a reference point for the author. By comparing and contrasting herself with five-year-old Hanna, Joyce Maynard tells a great deal about herself. Look back through the essay and find all the ways that the author at nineteen is *like* Hanna at five. Find all the ways she is *unlike* Hanna.

2. Notice that similarities and differences between Hanna and the author are not just stated in general terms. Each is brought alive with specific illustrative detail. Which details seem most vivid and most significant?

3. What do all the comparisons and contrasts add up to? In other words, what is the author's purpose? What insight into Joyce Maynard at age nineteen is the focal point of the essay?

One way to take stock of yourself is to probe your feelings about growing up. How do you feel about the child you were and about the adult you are becoming? You may find these questions easier to explore if you compare and contrast yourself to a particular child, especially if you have a Hanna in your life. In the next pre-writing activity, you will try some other ways to recall the kind of child you were and relate that child to your present self.

Getting It Started

Read through the approaches outlined in Options A and B. Choose the one that seems most promising for you.

Option A.   Exploring Attitudes About the Sexes

1. Across the top of a page in the **Idea Bank** section of your Writer's Notebook, write "When I was younger, I thought boys (girls) were . . ." Before completing this sentence, think back to the childhood games you played with members of the opposite sex. Think of how you perceived members of the opposite sex in elementary school. Then think of yourself as you were early in junior high. Picture yourself at your first party, perhaps a school dance. How did you feel about the others who were there? about the boys? about the girls? Complete the sentence about what you thought of the opposite sex. At the top of the next page, write

"Now I think . . ." Consider your present view and complete the sentence.

2.   Extend your exploration by interviewing people you were close to as a child.

   a.   Ask your mother or father what early advice they gave you about the opposite sex. Ask whether your parents recall any particular incident that showed how you felt about boys (or girls) at an early age.

   b.   Talk to a close childhood friend. Recall how you each felt about the opposite sex. Try to remember particular incidents or conversations. Did you have a stereotyped image of what men or women were like?

3.   Use the material you have just gathered as the impetus for a ten-minute free writing. Begin with the sentence you completed earlier about what you thought of boys or girls when you were younger. Include specific incidents from your own experience. Write as fast and as freely as you can, not stopping to worry about organization or form. Just get down as much as you can in ten minutes.

   Read over what you have just written. Spend a few minutes considering ways in which your views have changed. Think of recent conversations and experiences that show new attitudes about the opposite sex. Then do a ten-minute free writing on your current perceptions. Begin with the sentence you completed earlier about what you now think. Again, write rapidly and freely without concern for form.

Option B.   Exploring Ambitions

1.   Across the top of a page in the **Idea Bank** section of your Writer's Notebook, write "When I was younger, I wanted . . ." Think back over your childhood ambitions. Which were strongest or most persistent? Can you remember conversations with friends about what you wanted to be and do when you grew up? After reflecting on these questions, finish the sentence about what you wanted when you were younger. At the top of the next page, write "Now I want . . ." Think about what you hope to be ten years from now. Imagine that you are talking to a friend right after high school graduation. Your friend asks you what you want to do with your life. What do you tell him or her? Consider your present ambitions and complete the sentence.

2. Extend your exploration by interviewing people who are close to you.

   a. Talk to a parent or other close relative. Ask, "When I was young, what did you really think I'd turn out to be? What did I talk about wanting to be?"

   b. Ask an old friend, "What do you think I'll be doing ten years from now? Why do you think so?" If possible, ask a new friend the same questions.

3. Use the material you have just gathered as the impetus for two ten-minute free writings. Begin the first free writing with the sentence you completed earlier about what you wanted when you were younger. Writing as fast as you can, get down everything you can think of about your early childhood ambitions. Write freely, not stopping to worry about organization or form. Pause a few minutes to shift your thoughts to your present ambitions. Then begin your second free writing with the sentence you completed earlier about what you now want. Again, write freely and fast. Get down as much as you can in ten minutes.

In this first part of the chapter, you have practiced using comparison and contrast to generate ideas. Later, you may use some of the ideas you have collected in composing your self-portrait. Certainly you will find comparison and contrast useful in generating ideas on other topics you will write about throughout this course and even after you leave school.

SPOTLIGHT

Exploring Viewpoints

Still another way of generating ideas about a topic is to look at it from different points of view. See whether you can identify the point of view in the following poem. In other words, see whether you can determine who is speaking.

I am silver and exact. I have no preconceptions.
Whatever I see I swallow immediately
Just as it is, unmisted by love or dislike.
I am not cruel, only truthful—

The eye of a little god, four-cornered.
Most of the time I meditate on the opposite wall.
It is pink, with speckles. I have looked at it so long
I think it is a part of my heart. But it flickers.
Faces and darkness separate us over and over.

Now I am a lake. A woman bends over me.
Searching my reaches for what she really is.
Then she turns to those liars, the candles or the moon.
I see her back, and reflect it faithfully.
She rewards me with tears and an agitation of hands.
I am important to her. She comes and goes.
Each morning it is her face that replaces the darkness.
In me she has drowned a young girl, and in me an old woman
Rises toward her day after day, like a terrible fish.

Sylvia Plath

If this poem were not titled "Mirror," how would you know that the speaker is indeed a mirror? What details most clearly establish this point of view? Why is the mirror a good point of view for describing the unnamed woman's feelings toward growing old?

Getting It Started

Look in a mirror. Make a list of the physical features the mirror "sees." Describe each feature as sharply as possible.

Now imagine that the mirror not only "sees" you but also "knows" how you feel about the way you look. In other words, consider not just the image reflected in your mirror, but the image you *wish* were reflected. Make a list of the physical features you would *like* to see in the mirror.

The mirror provides a public view of self. The you in the mirror is the one observed by strangers on the street. The way you feel about the image in the mirror reflects a more private view. By comparing and contrasting the two, you may discover some interesting things about yourself.

The viewpoints of different people can also help you know yourself better. Think for a moment about how you appear to different people—your parents, your best friend, your teachers, your dentist, etc. What does each know about you? How do you act when you are with each person?

Getting It Started

A. Write three paragraphs, each describing you through the eyes of a particular person. You may wish to choose your three points of view from the following list. Be sure to choose points of view that will convey different perceptions of you.

a parent
your best friend
a younger sister or brother
an older sister or brother
an employer
your doctor
the principal of your school

a person your own age whom
   you dislike
a teacher you like
a teacher you dislike
a stranger on the street
a very old person

In writing each paragraph, speak through the voice of the person describing you. Speak of yourself in the third person—that is, by name or as *he* or *she*.

B. Now write a paragraph of response to each of the three descriptions. Use your own voice to describe yourself as you are with that particular person. In responding to the way your mother might have described you, for example, you might begin, "To my mother, I'm still a little boy. I guess I often act like one . . ." Be honest. Concentrate on details that would cause you to be seen in a certain way from that person's point of view. Try to sound like yourself. In other words, write in your own voice.

Again, put aside the material you have just collected. You may wish to use glimpses of yourself from different points of view in your self-portrait. Certainly you will continue to use point of view as a technique for examining all kinds of topics from a variety of angles.

Filling in Background

Photographers often use background to enhance their subjects. Celebrities, for example, are often photographed against a characteristic backdrop. Think of the pictures you have seen in magazines. A Nobel Prize winning novelist sits before a typewriter in a book-lined study. An Olympic skater stands at the railing of an ice rink. A TV newsperson appears against a wall of video monitors. In each case, setting helps the photographer underscore the celebrity's claim to fame.

Background can be equally helpful to a writer. Suppose that you were describing two friends, one very methodical and meticulous, the other freewheeling and oblivious to detail. You might describe each in his or her room after school on Friday afternoon. You could describe the way the first positions school books in their place on a tidy desk, hangs up a jacket in an uncluttered closet, and walks across the spotless floor to answer the telephone, which sits beside an alarm clock on the otherwise empty surface of a night table. You could describe the way the second tosses books and jacket onto a rumpled, unmade bed before dashing across a floor strewn with magazines and clothing to look for the telephone, which is hidden somewhere beneath several days' newspapers. In each case, the person's room would reflect a key personal trait.

Getting
It
Started

Consider the places that best reflect *you*. Where do you feel most at home? Against what characteristic setting might you be photographed?

In the **Idea Bank** of your Writer's Notebook, jot down answers to these questions:

1. If you have a room of your own, how does it look? If you share a room, how does your area of the room look?
2. If you could create the room of your dreams, how would it look?
3. When you want to be alone, where do you go?
4. When you were younger, did you have a favorite hideaway? Where was it and what was it like?
5. What is your favorite place where you like to go with friends, especially on weekends? What makes this place a favorite?
6. Do you and your family have a special vacation haven? If so, what particular spot in this area is your favorite?
7. If you have lived in more than one house or apartment, what place in the old neighborhood—or in the old house—do you especially miss? Why?
8. If you have a hobby or pastime, where do you go to practice it? What is this place like?

Put aside the notes you have just made. Later, you will describe at least one of these places in more detail and reflect further on how that place shows something about you. First, however, read the following excerpt from Ernesto Galarza's *Barrio Boy*. In this passage, Galarza tells about the family's move into a new neighborhood in Sacramento, California. The family—comprised of Ernesto, his mother, and his two uncles Gustavo and José—have been aided in the move by their former landlady, Mrs. Dodson, after they borrowed money to buy a bungalow across town.

SPOTLIGHT

As you read the excerpt, notice how the new neighborhood differs from the old. Notice also how much you learn about the author by seeing how he relates to each environment.

Our new bungalow had five rooms, and porches front and back. In the way of furniture, what friends did not lend or Mrs. Dodson gave us we bought in the secondhand shops. The only new item was an elegant gas range, with high oven and long, slender legs finished in enamel. Like the house, we would be paying for it in installments.

It was a sunny, airy spot, with a family orchard to one side and a vacant lot on the other. Back of us there was a pasture. With chicken wire we fenced the back yard, turned over the soil, and planted our first vegetable garden and fruit trees. José and I built a palatial rabbit hutch of laths and two-by-fours he gathered day by day on the waterfront. A single row of geraniums and carnations separated the vegetable garden from the house. From the vacant lots and pastures around us my mother gathered herbs and weeds which she dried and boiled the way she had in the pueblo. A thick green fluid she distilled from the mallow that grew wild around us was bottled and used as a hair lotion. On every side our windows looked out on

family orchards, platinum stretches of wild oats and quiet lanes, shady and unpaved.

We could not have moved to a neighborhood less like the *barrio*. All the families around us were Americans. The grumpy retired farmer next door viewed us with alarm and never gave us the time of day, but the Harrisons across the street were cordial. Mr. Harrison loaned us his tools, and Roy, just my age but twice my weight, teamed up with me at once for an exchange of visits to his mother's kitchen and ours. I astounded him with my Mexican rice, and Mrs. Harrison baked my first waffles . . .

Every member of the family, in his own way, missed the *barrio*. José and Gustavo could no longer join the talk of the poolrooms and the street corners by walking two blocks down the street. The sign language and simple words my mother had devised to communicate with the Americans at 418 L didn't work with the housewives on 7th Avenue. The families we had known were now too far away to exchange visits. We knew no one in Oak Park who spoke Spanish. Our street was always quiet and often lonely with little to watch from our front porch other than boys riding bicycles or Mrs. Harrison hanging out her wash. Pork Chops and the Salvation Army never played there.

I, too, knew that things were different. There was no corner where I could sell the *Union* and my income from running errands and doing chores around the rooming house stopped. There were no alleys I could comb for beer bottles or docks where I could gather saleable or edible things. The closest to Big Singh* I could find was a runty soothsayer in Joyland who sat on a rug with a feather in his turban and told your fortune.

Use the following questions as a guide for reviewing the author's use of background to reveal character:

1. Describe the Galarzas' old neighborhood. What does Ernesto miss from the old neighborhood?
2. Describe the new house and the new neighborhood. What clues can you find to Ernesto's feelings about the new family home? What is he proud of? (Notice revealing word choices as well as direct statement —for example, the "elegant" stove.) What features of the new neighborhood seem a little disappointing?

*a Hindu friend from the old neighborhood who ran a boarding house for other people from his country

3. What do Galarza's descriptions of these two childhood environments tell about him as a person? What words and phrases would you use to describe him at the stage of his life at which the family made the move?

Sometimes, the same surroundings appear one way to a child and another way to that same person a few years later. Consider the familiar example of your kindergarten or first-grade classroom as it looked to you when you entered it for the first time. Then think of that same classroom as it would appear to you today.

In a poem honoring his father, Gordon Parks presents such a dual view of the place in which he grew up.

Funeral

After many snows I was home again.
Time had whittled down to mere hills
The great mountains of my childhood.
Raging rivers I once swam trickled now
                like gentle streams.
And the wide road curving on to China or
        Kansas City or perhaps Calcutta,
Had withered to a crooked path of dust
Ending abruptly at the burying ground.
Only the giant who was my father
              remained the same.
A hundred strong men strained beneath his coffin
When they bore him to his grave.

Notice how the mountains, river, and roads seem to have been scaled down by time.

Option A. Describe two different places that you previously identified as being important to you. You might, for example, describe a place where you go to be alone and another place where you like to go with your friends. OR You might describe the place where you lived as a child and the place where you live now.

Getting It Down

Option <u>B.</u>   Choose one of the places you identified earlier as being special to you in some way during your childhood. Describe that place as it appeared to you when you first knew it. Then describe the place as it would appear to you now.

~~~~~~

Checking It Out

Read over the two descriptions you just wrote. Before putting them aside for later use, think about how each place fills in your personal background. How does that place reflect something important about you?

~~~~~~

Moving Toward Independence

During these first three chapters, you have collected a substantial stockpile of autobiographical material. You have even completed some brief but polished pieces about yourself. In the process, you have practiced many techniques for discovering material worth writing about. In other words, you have practiced invention. Though you have concentrated on pre-writing and to an extent on drafting, you have also worked a little bit on revising and editing.

During the last part of this unit, you will work completely through the composing process to produce a fully developed self-portrait. This self-portrait will offer more than a brief glimpse into the experiences and traits that distinguish you from others. It will stand alone to give a selective but clear picture of who you are at this point in your life.

Before beginning this major project, take a few minutes to review this chapter for invention strategies that should be added to the pre-writing section of **Notes on the Writing Process** in your Writer's Notebook. After making entries under "Pre-writing Strategies," wait until you finish the next few pages to make additional entries under "Guidelines for Drafting." You will be reminded to do so just before you start writing your self-portrait.

In writing this self-portrait, your first major task will be selecting a focus. Of all the approaches you could take to telling about yourself, which would be most significant and most interesting? Once you have decided upon a focus, you must select from the many details of your life those that will develop the insight you have chosen to convey.

Getting
It
Started

Make a list of important facts about your life. Include events, interests, hobbies, relationships, travels, likes and dislikes, and anything else you think makes you an individual. When you have finished the list, think of at least three different you's—for instance, the academic you, the rebellious you, the athletic you, the family you. Select details from the list that would fit into each self-portrait.

You may or may not want to use one of these you's as the focus for your self-portrait. The point is just to see how different self-images can be created from the same list of autobiographical details.

Getting
It
Started

Before you go much further, you must decide upon a focus for your self-portrait. Review the entries in the **Idea Bank** of your Writer's Notebook and the short papers you have written during these first three chapters. What patterns strike you? What insights seem especially clear? What view of yourself do you find most interesting and most revealing? Note two or three approaches to the writing of a self-portrait that seem especially promising.

In writing this self-portrait, another of your most important tasks will be organization. You have already practiced organizing small collections of details about yourself. In recounting memories, you probably organized details chronologically. In other words, you arranged your account of what happened in time order. In other pieces of writing, you may have organized details topically—that is, you used some overriding point to hold the piece together and supported that general point with specific illustrative details. Your last piece of writing about a significant place was organized topically; since you described first one place and then another, you probably organized by contrast as well.

Organization should never be arbitrary. It should always grow out of what you have to say. The material itself should suggest a structure. For example, suppose you decided to write your self-portrait as a series of autobiographical episodes that dramatize how you feel about growing up. The most natural and effective organization would almost certainly be chronological. On the other hand, suppose you decided to approach your self-portrait as a reflection on some dominant personal trait. That trait might be positive (like tenacity), negative (like clumsiness), or both (like loyalty, which may be well-placed or misguided). Although you would undoubtedly recount experiences to illustrate the trait and those experiences would be recounted chronologically, the overall organization of the self-portrait would be topical. Each illustrative incident would develop some aspect of the trait around which the self-portrait is focused.

Suppose that you decided to personalize yourself in terms of comparison and contrast. For example, you might base your entire self-portrait upon ways you are like and unlike a family member representing another generation. On the other hand, you might focus on times when you have (and have not) managed to meet certain expectations—perhaps your own or those of your parents or teachers. Like Ernesto Galarza, you might choose to compare and contrast your life in one home and neighborhood (or one school) to your later life in another.

Comparison and contrast lend themselves to topical arrangement. Within this kind of organization, the writer has a number of options. Similarities may be clustered in some paragraphs and differences in others, or the two kinds of details may be interspersed. (If you choose to use comparison and contrast as the basis of your self-portrait, you might like to review "Old Before My Time" and the excerpt from *Barrio Boy* to see how the authors handled organization.)

Before plunging into your first draft, review the section you have just read. To help you understand and remember key points, summarize those points under the heading *organization* in your "Guidelines for Drafting." Keep in mind what you have learned as you begin to shape the material you have collected into the first draft of a self-portrait.

Getting It Started

Make a final decision on the focal point for your self-portrait. Just for your own reference, state in one clear sentence the main idea you plan to develop. Then go back through the **Idea Bank** of your Writer's Notebook and all the other writings you have done so far. Mark everything that might contribute to the idea around which you plan to focus your self-portrait.

So far, you have only *identified* potential material. At this point, that material probably seems to you hopelessly jumbled. It probably is jumbled, but not hopelessly. Read back through notes and passages you have marked and look for items that seem to belong together. Does some kind of natural grouping emerge? Can the overall idea you are developing be divided into parts? If so, how many? What part does each piece of material fit into? Mark details that seem to go together. (You may use any method of marking that works for you—perhaps color-coding, numbers or letters, or sub-topics.)

After you have at least tentatively decided how to group various chunks of raw material, check to see that you have enough for each major part of your self-portrait. Fill in gaps. Add any interesting new details that occur to you. Also decide which cluster of material should come first, which should come next, and so on.

Next, sketch out an overall plan for your self-portrait. You need not make a formal outline unless you particularly like that method of getting your plan down on paper. A jot list will do nicely. Just note in order the details, episodes, points of comparison, or other pieces of material you plan to include in your paper. When you finish the list, you might bracket related items to remind you where one major section of the self-portrait will leave off and the next will begin.

~~~~~~~~~~~~~~~~~~~~~~~~~~~~~~~~~~~~~

Using your jot list to keep you on track, make a first draft of your self-portrait. Keep in mind that this piece of writing should stand alone to give a clear idea of who you are. In order for it to do so, your self-portrait must be rich in detail. Also, it must let your own voice come through.

**Getting
It
Down**

~~~~~~~~~~~~~~~~~~~~~~~~~~~~~~~~~~~~~

Share your paper with a small group of classmates. After a first reading, ask each to jot down a sentence summarizing what he or she considers the main idea or theme of the self-portrait. Without comparing notes, read the paper a second time. This time, ask each person in your group to jot down the word or phrase from the paper that best encapsulates the main idea and then a word or phrase *not in the paper* that captures the main idea. Compare notes, discussing any discrepancies between what you intended and how your readers interpreted your self-portrait. Ask what word choices, details, and passages the group found particularly apt or interesting. Ask also about the flow of the paper. Does anything seem out of place? Throughout the

**Checking
It
Out**

discussion, make notes to consider later as you revise your paper.

Don't try to start revising yet. You are still too close to your paper. Revision really means "seeing again." You can take a clearer second look if you put the paper away and let time put a little distance between you and what you have written.

Sometimes, it helps to see what other students have written. You have already read first drafts written by some of your classmates. In the process of responding to those drafts, you undoubtedly sharpened your ear for good writing. You could tell which self-portraits sounded just like the writer. You could tell what worked and what didn't.

Writer's Workbench

Sentence-Combining: Cued Problems

This sentence-combining exercise provides a sample of some *revised* self-portraits written by students. Both Part A and Part B consist of *cued* problems. You will follow the cues (signals) to make each group of sentences into a single sentence. One new cue is JOIN, which simply signals you to put two sentences together to form one. (If you need to review other cues, look back at the introductory Writer's Workbench on pages 25–30.)

A. Combine the following sentences as indicated by the cues. (Asterisks show where a paragraph begins.) Write the combined sentences in paragraph form, and you will have the *opening* of a self-portrait.

  * I was one of the children.
    Children were <u>2.8.</u>
    <u>Couples</u> <u>were</u> <u>supposed</u> <u>to</u> <u>have</u> 2.8 children <u>the</u> <u>year</u> I <u>was</u> <u>born.</u>
    (JOIN)

    Our block was statistically perfect.
    Two-thirds of the families had two children.   (:)
    The other third had three.   (and)

I grew up.
I watched TV the fifteen hours.   (-ing)
Hours were expected.
Hours were per week.

I ate food.
Food was nourishing.
I went to the doctor.   (and)
I went regularly.
I could live my years.   (so that)
Years were predicted.
Years were seventy-plus.

I played baseball.
I played in the summer.
I played football.   (,)
I played in the fall.
I played basketball.   (, and)
I played in the winter.

Doesn't it seem SOMETHING?
I would qualify as the boy.   (that)
The boy is average.
The boy is all-American.

That's the way it seems.
That's not the way it is.   (, but)

* I veered away from the conventional.
  I was three years old.   (before)

B. The next series of sentence-combining problems is based on a different student's self-portrait. If you follow the cues correctly and write the combined sentences in paragraph form, you will have the *ending* of that self-portrait.

* I'll be leaving for college.   (Since)
  I'll be leaving soon.
  I should SOMETHING.   (,)
  I send these relics to the city dump.
  I clear the closet.   (and)

There's no point in keeping the handprint.
The handprint is <u>ceramic.</u>
I made in first grade.   (that)
It's broken.   (, especially since)

Surely I could part with these report cards.
Cards are <u>old.</u>
Cards are <u>dog-eared.</u>   (,)
They do represent almost twelve years' work.   (even if)

These ballet shoes can certainly go.
Shoes are <u>beginner's.</u>
Hiking boots can go.   (and)
Boots are <u>outgrown.</u>

This stack of composition books takes space.
Books contain poems.   (-ing)
Poems are amateurish.
Books contain never-to-be-completed novels.   (and)
Space is valuable.

There's no doubt about it.
All this junk should go.   (:)

Maybe I'll leave it here.   (On the other hand ,)
No one will forget who I really am.   (—just so)

Compare your combined sentences with those of several classmates or with the models provided by your teacher. Get help with any sentences you may have missed. Keep asking questions until any confusion is resolved.

The introduction and conclusion in the preceding Writer's Workbench are finished products. Each is part of a carefully revised paper. A closer look at these student writing samples should help you get ready to revise your own paper.

Look first at the introduction. Notice how the paper grabs the reader's attention from the very beginning. The first draft didn't do so. The paper originally began, "I grew up in an ordinary family, in an ordinary house, on an average block. I seem like the average all-American boy." Not bad. Focusing the whole paper on how the writer seems average but really isn't is a good idea. The repetition in the first sentence makes it fairly interesting but not nearly as arresting as the first sentence of the revised version. Notice the effect of added detail. One of the main questions to keep in mind during revision is "What needs to be *added?*"

The introduction to this self-portrait is complete at the end of the first paragraph. The last statement in that paragraph ("That's the way it seems, but not the way it is.") really establishes the focal point of the self-portrait. Subsequent paragraphs can now illustrate that statement.

Notice how the next paragraph begins: "I veered away from the conventional before I was three years old." This sentence, which leads into the first illustrative anecdote, hasn't been changed much since the first draft. Originally it began, "I *turned* away from the conventional . . ." In revising his paper, the writer substituted the more vivid verb *veered* for *turned*. Sometimes substitutions are more extensive. In any case, another big question to keep in mind during revision is "What should be *substituted* for something else?"

Now look at the sample conclusion you reconstructed during Part B of the sentence-combining exercise. The self-portrait leading up to this conclusion focuses on the major interests that have shaped the writer's life. The self-portrait, which is written as an extended monologue, begins with the writer's thoughts as she sorts through her belongings before starting to pack for college. Items in her closet remind her of what she enjoys most—school, the outdoors, dancing, and writing. A section of the self-portrait goes into detail about each one.

Notice how the concluding paragraph subtly echoes the interests developed in the body of the self-portrait. The handprint and the report cards recall school; the hiking boots, the outdoors; the ballet shoes, dancing; the composition books, writing. The last sentence draws everything together and underscores the writer's feelings that these interests represent her identity as a person.

Remember that this concluding paragraph is a product of revision. The first draft was longer but less effective. It included several sentences about old scrapbooks and photograph albums. Besides being a little too obvious, these sentences had nothing to do with the four major interests featured in the self-portrait. Since they just cluttered the paragraph, these sentences were deleted. Another key question to keep in mind during revision is "What should be *omitted*?"

In the first draft of this concluding paragraph, the last sentence was placed right after the first. The paragraph began like this:

> Since I'll be leaving for college soon, I should send these relics to the city dump and clear the closet. On the other hand, maybe I'll leave everything here—just so no one will forget who I really am. I know I really shouldn't . . .

Notice how much impact the paragraph loses when it is arranged that way. The final draft surprises the reader a little with the decision not to throw everything away after all. By reserving this sentence until last, the writer has built to a climax. Still another big question to keep in mind during revision is "What should be *rearranged*?"

In revising your own self-portrait, you will want to keep in mind the four big questions that guide all writers during the revision process:

> What should be added?
> What should be omitted?
> What should be substituted?
> What should be rearranged?

You will also want to keep in mind the criteria your teacher will use in evaluating your self-portrait. These criteria are listed on the rating scale, called a Checkpoint, that appears on page 63.

Such a Checkpoint will conclude each unit. It will provide a means for assessing your application of techniques practiced in that unit. The descriptors on the right-hand side of each Checkpoint will help you set goals for a particular paper. Read the descriptors at the high end of the scale on page 63. Use them as goals for the final draft of your self-portrait.

First, however, turn to the **Notes on the Writing Process** section in your Writer's Notebook. Start a new subsection titled "Guidelines for Revision." Review the preceding pages and jot down the most important revision strategies. Keep these strategies in mind as you revise your self-portrait.

Reread the first draft of your self-portrait. During this first rereading, don't try to make changes. Don't even concern yourself with the suggestions of your classmates, the four big revision questions, or the criteria in the Checkpoint. The first time through, try to read the paper as if you had never read it before. Keep in mind only two questions: "Does the self-portrait say what I want it to say?" and "Does it sound like *me?*"

After you have read the whole paper and dealt with these two fundamental questions, go back through each part in detail. Consider the suggestions made earlier by your classmates, the revision strategies explained in this chapter, and the criteria in the Checkpoint. Note changes you think would improve the paper. Before beginning your final draft, read through the whole piece to see the overall effect of changes you have penciled in.

As you make a final draft, be careful about form. This is the stage at which you must edit. Since the paper will go public, it should contain no lapses in usage, mechanics, or spelling. ● If you aren't sure about a word or a sentence, consult the Writer's Handbook or ask your teacher for help. Be especially careful about sentence structure, avoiding both fragments and run-ons. Before you hand in your paper, you may want to have a friend or a parent proofread.

Getting It Right

After your paper has been evaluated and returned, your teacher may wish to add it to a Class Portrait scrapbook or display it on a special bulletin board, perhaps beside a recent snapshot or school picture of you. Before contributing your paper to the collection, you may want to make a copy for your parents, your grandparents, or a special friend. You may even want a copy of your own, since this may be your first major piece of writing this term and your most ambitious attempt at writing to realize self.

CHECKPOINT 1

	1	2	3	4	5

Focus   ×5=

I could never pin down your main idea. Paper goes off in all directions. Choose *one* and try again.

You have a clear focal point, but a few details don't seem related. Check for stragglers. Also tighten connections.

Focus is sharp and clear. Approach is original and paper strongly unified.

Voice   ×5=

Paper doesn't sound like *you.* Try writing the way you talk.

Your voice is coming through. Rewrite a few stilted passages and the paper will ring true.

Your voice comes through loud and clear. I'd recognize it even if your paper were unsigned!

Organization   ×4=

Self-portrait needs a clearer beginning, middle, and end. In the middle, try to keep related ideas in the same paragraph.

Essentially strong. Paper moves naturally and logically. Work on introduction and conclusion.

You've got it! Introduction grabs attention and conclusion provides a great exit line. Between, details are grouped logically. One section flows into another.

Detail   ×4=

I can't get a clear picture of you. Words are too general. Not enough specifics. Try again.

Some of your details made me see, hear, taste, smell, and feel. A few passages blur into generality. Work for consistent richness of detail.

This paper is so rich in sensory detail that it involved me completely. I like those sharp word choices.

Usage and Mechanics   ×2=

Let's schedule a conference. I'll show you how to use the Writer's Handbook.

Your paper is neat, and I find only a few problems with usage, punctuation, capitalization, or spelling. Have a classmate check it over, and consult the Writer's Handbook.

This is exactly how a paper should look! Handwriting, spelling, usage, capitalization, and punctuation are exemplary.

Realizing the Here and Now

. . . If you're going to write something that isn't going to be thrown out with the coffee grounds, you have to tell it like it is.

—*Rex Reed*

Chapter 4

Recording an Oral Documentary

The writing you did during Unit I was *self*-centered. Not only did you write *about* yourself; you wrote mainly *for* yourself as well. During this unit, you will move outward to write for and about others.

One reason for writing about people is to understand them better. Putting someone down on paper helps you sort out and clarify what you know and feel about that person. Maybe you are puzzled about the seemingly contradictory behavior of your mother: one minute she insists that you act like a responsible adult and the next treats you like a six-year-old. You sit down and write it all out. Soon you begin to see your mother's point of view. You may not like it, but you understand it better. The writing you did about your mother has served its purpose. No one else needs to see it.

Such thinking on paper is called *expressive* writing. The writing you did about yourself in Unit I was mainly expressive. Although you shared some of your pieces with your classmates, with your teacher, and perhaps with others, their greatest value was to you. In a sense, you were your own audience as well as your own subject.

In this unit, you will write primarily for others. Writing addressed to others for the purpose of getting something done is termed *transactional*. Most school writing is transactional. Sometimes, the purpose is to convince your teacher that you know a subject, as on an essay exam or in a book report. Transactional writing may be to explain or to persuade. It may be simply to pass on what you have seen or heard. In this chapter, it will help you to share some of your own encounters with interesting people.

You probably won't have to look too far for material. Many of the people who move through your daily life have stories just waiting to be told.

Professional writers find some of their best subjects in seemingly ordinary people. During his days as an apprentice writer, Truman Capote recalls filling his journals with notes about friends and acquaintances. He lists these items as staples: "Descriptions of a neighbor. Long verbatim accounts of overheard conversations. Local gossip." This habit of seeing, hearing, and recording real people has profoundly influenced Capote's mature work. He has forsaken the conventional novel ("where," he says, "facts are disguised as fiction") for what he calls *narrative journalism* or the *nonfictional novel*. This innovation allows Capote to return to his favorite source, real people.

Your pieces will not be as ambitious as Truman Capote's. They will not reach millions of readers. Even so, other people will be your audience as well as your subject.

Transcribing Spoken Language

For the next few days, tune in on the voices you hear around you. Listen for those that are particularly distinctive and particularly interesting. Practice jotting down some of the conversations you hear. Catch not only what the voices say but also how they sound.

**Getting
It
Down**

Start a new page in the **Idea Bank** of your Writer's Notebook. Use that page and the ones following to transcribe snatches of conversation you overhear. Possibilities include one side of a telephone conversation, lunchroom chatter, arguments taking place in school hallways, sales pitches in local stores, supermarket conversations between parents and small children, boys or girls arranging dates, excuses being offered in the attendance office, and pep talks before a big game. If you wish, supplement your real-life transcriptions with a few from television.

**Checking
It
Out**

After you have several transcriptions, try them out on some classmates. See whether they can sort out the voices. How authentic does each sound? Which conversations are the most interesting? Do any hold enough promise to extend into more ambitious pieces of writing?

Studs Terkel is an American writer who has traveled all over the country doing on-the-spot interviews with hundreds and hundreds of people. In a book titled *Working,* Terkel transcribes the voices of people who do all kinds of jobs. The result is an oral documentary of America at work. His book *American Dreams: Lost and Found* is based on interviews with a cross-section of people—some well-known and others obscure—about their hopes and expectations, and often their disappointments. Terkel always lets his subjects speak for themselves. The voices in the book are theirs, not his.

SPOTLIGHT

Sharon Fox has her say in the section of the book titled "Fantasia." Tune in on this speaker's voice as she shares her version of the American Dream. You may find it helpful to read the passage aloud.

> *She is one of Chicago's most assiduous collectors of autographs. She earns her daily bread as a messenger at the Board of Trade.*
>
> "It's very prestigious to work there, even if you're a messenger, 'cause it's the largest commodity house in the world. There are a lot of rich people who work there, and it's respected. Not everybody can get a job there. You have to know somebody. Not everybody can walk through the door. So when I do, I feel kind of proud, even though I'm just a messenger.
>
> "My father and mother are both retired. My father just worked in a factory. My mother worked years ago for Pepsodent Tooth Company. They're just laborers." *(She pauses, then softly)* "I shouldn't put it down."
>
> *She carries an impressively thick leather-bound book of signatures and photographs; there are scrawled phrases: "Best wishes" and "God bless" are among the most frequent.*

I'm just one of millions. A hundred years from now, I'll be just a name on a gravestone and that will be it, I won't be in libraries or records or movies that they watch on TV. It's kind of nice to stand out in a crowd and be remembered rather than being just a face in the crowd.

Someone famous, they're important. That's why you want to see them and get their autograph. It means that you may never see them again, but you've shared a few minutes. We're rather quiet dull people, and anything that has a little shine to it is exciting.

I met Prince Charles, and he kissed me for my birthday. He's important and he's also famous. When he came to the Board of Trade, everything just stopped. We were told not to even approach him, but it got so crowded, it was his idea to just come out and shake hands.

I happened to be there. He shook my hand and I said: "Today's my birthday." Which it was, it's no lie. I said: "Can I have a kiss?" He thought about it for a second and he said: "Why not?" He kissed me on the cheek, and I kissed him. Everybody at the Board saw it. I don't think my feet were on the ground.

I may never see him again and never have that opportunity, and he may be king of England some day. I wish I could get to know him. He seemed like he could be nice. It was just a few minutes between us, and there we were . . . I wrote him a letter and sent him a picture that I had taken. I said, "It's not every girl who can be kissed by a prince," and I wanted to thank him.

That keeps me happy. I'm not happy all the time at the Board of Trade, so I have this side project, which keeps me going: meeting celebrated people and getting autographs. (She opens her book of treasures.) Barbara Streisand, Presley, a lot of people in here. There's Sylvester Stallone, there is Jack Nicholson and Louise Fletcher. There's Jack Ford. The son of the president.

More pages of the book are turned; familiar faces appear and all manner of signatures. Let us now praise famous men: Tony Bennett. Yul Brynner. George Burns. Buster Crabbe.

I've grown up with these people, watching them on TV. I never had many friends, so it was a substitute. I decided to go one step further and meet these people instead of admiring them from afar. My mother has an autographed picture of Jean Harlow. So maybe it's in the genes somewhere. (Laughs.)

I live at home. I never liked hanging out on street corners or going to parties. I don't drink or smoke. We're a churchgoing family, Baptist. My parents are all I've got, and I'm all they've got. They never had any hobbies. They have no real outside interest, outside of me. They want to see me happy, and they're interested in what I'm doing. Whatever I do reflects on them. They're like living through me. This is one country where you can do anything, and they prove it every day.

Are you familiar with Brenda Starr? I can identify with her. She's glamorous, not what I am. She's got this great love in her life,

Basil St. John, which I don't have yet. She goes on all these exciting capers. (Laughs.) Dale Messick, the lady who draws her, drew me into Brenda's wedding a couple of years ago. She hardly knew me. I took pictures of her and looked her up. She said: "Brenda's getting married. Would you like to be at the wedding?" I said: "Sure." So she drew me while I was at her office. I would have to point out to people it was me 'cause there's an awful lot of people in the strip.

I keep up by following the gossip columns: Kup, Gold, Maggie Daly. I know them and they know me. Kup has mentioned me once or twice. So has Aaron. So has Maggie. In my own life group, I became a celebrity. People I work with and the brokers at the Board of Trade, even though they make more money than I do, respect me more because I got my name in the paper.

I put out my magazine on Elvis Presley. It was after he died. It cost almost my whole bank account, but I wanted to do it. I put in the article "He Touched My Life." It was one of Presley's hymns I played all the time. People wanted *my* autograph. They asked me to

sign the article that I didn't even write. My pastor asked me to sign the article. My pastor! (Laughs.) He was impressed that I get around and meet people, 'cause I look like a wallflower. They don't think I have it in me. They put it in the church bulletin, too.

My parents have everything they worked for. They have a house, they go to church. Whatever dreams they have now are through me. They can say: "My daughter got her name in the paper." Not every mother can say that. "Here's my daughter with Elvis Presley."

Her magazine lies open on the table. There are photographs of Elvis Presley. There is writing. She reads: "'Elvis was a gift from God. How else could you explain the sudden rise from humble beginning to becoming a national star? It would be best if we remembered his religious songs. He was, after all, a being with human frailties. Thank you, Elvis, for touching my life. Love, Sharon Fox.'" (She adds softly) "Adios, I'll see you again."

Do you believe in the hereafter?

Yes. Because there has to be more to it than autographs. (Laughs.) There's just so many people and so many planets, and this is only one little step. If I can leave something behind creative, that I've done, maybe I'll be important to somebody.

What would happen if you lost your autograph book?

There are worse things that could happen. *C'est la vie.*

Use the following questions to guide a review of the excerpt. Make brief notes to prepare for a class discussion based on these questions:

1. The words in italics are those of the author, Studs Terkel. In what ways do these italicized sections set the stage for the young woman's monologue? What would be lost if they were omitted?
2. What is Sharon Fox's dream? Find the sentences that state it most explicitly. Why do you think Terkel includes this particular version of the American Dream in the section titled "Fantasia"?
3. What questions do you think Studs Terkel might have asked to get Sharon to reveal so much about herself, particularly about her dream?
4. Though Terkel lets Sharon speak for herself, he has undoubtedly smoothed out her sentences and organized her comments into a

coherent piece. In other words, he has *shaped* his material. Why do you think the author chose to begin and end Sharon's voice profile as he did? What progression do you find within the body of the monologue?

5. Sharon's comments—like those of other subjects in Terkel's oral documentary—were spoken rather than written. To reproduce the informality of her speech, the author has retained forms such as "'cause," for "because" and the pattern of short sentences, often loosely spliced with "and" or "so." What other such colloquial features can you find in the passage?

6. This monologue is one of a hundred included in Terkel's book. The voices differ, as do the dreams. The form, however, remains the same as the author allows all characters to speak for themselves. Why do you think the author chose this form? How effective do you consider the oral documentary? Why?

Every day, you hear people talk. You also read what people have written. The English you hear is the same English you read—up to a point.

Have you ever stopped to consider how spoken language differs from written language? In the first place, talk is fleeting. Unless captured by a recording device, words are gone almost as soon as they are uttered. After all, speech is nothing but air. Writing, on the other hand, lasts. Words put on paper can be read hours, days, or even centuries later.

Because writing freezes language and holds it, writers can look back at their words and make changes. Readers of a much-revised piece need never suspect that the first attempt may have been rough or clumsy. Of course, speakers can backtrack, too. But they cannot erase what has already been said. They can only keep talking until what they want to say comes out right.

Conversations are full of false starts. They often make great leaps in thought and leave sentences dangling. Even so, people in face-to-face conversation usually understand each other. Facial expression, signs and gestures, pauses, and vocal inflections all telegraph meaning. Since writers cannot depend on these signals, they must choose their words carefully and use mechanical devices like capitalization and punctuation to signal how those words are meant to sound.

In the passage you just read, Terkel presented spoken language in a written medium. In Question 5 of the Spotlight exercise, you identified some of the features that give Sharon's comments the flavor of informal spoken English. Did you notice such slang as "hanging out"? Did you catch the faddish insertion of *like* in such sentences as "They're like living through me?" Terkel has transcribed these features carefully to let readers feel that they are eavesdropping as Sharon chats about what is important to her.

Not all authors re-create so *much* spoken language in their writing, but most re-create some. Reporters lace their news stories with quoted comments. Novelists weave dialogue into their stories. Playwrights put words into the mouths of their characters and make conversation carry the plot. An ear for spoken language and the ability to re-create it on paper are valuable assets to any writer.

You have already practiced transcribing snatches of conversation. During the next series of activities, you will continue to record what people say. You will also shape what you hear into a finished piece, and work with some of your classmates to compile several related pieces into a mini-documentary.

Getting It Started

As a class, brainstorm promising topics for an oral documentary. To get started, consider special interests, skills, and feelings of people you know. What topics would encourage certain people to open up and share what they know and feel? School athletes, for example, might have lots to say about competitive sports— what attracted them to a certain sport; what is involved in training; how they feel before, during, and after a big game; whether they intend to continue with the sport after high school; whether they ever feel exploited. There may be people in your school or community who make things who would like to tell you about their craft. In considering this subject, don't overlook older people, who are often eager to explain crafts like quilt-making; classmates who have specialties like ceramics; local business people who may be expert in crafts ranging from cabinet-making to leather-tooling. Another possibility might be travel; you undoubtedly know people who have visited or lived in fascinating places. Still other topics might tap feelings and ideas rather than special skills or knowledge. For example, students you know might have lots to say if asked what changes they'd make if they ran your school, what living person they think best qualifies as a genuine hero or heroine, or what current issue they'd like to sound off about.

After brainstorming with other members of the class a good list of potential topics—for example, "Inside Views of Sports," "Local Artisans," "People Who Have Been Places," "If I Ran the School . . . ," "Heroes and Heroines," and "Sound-off"—

choose *one* of those topics. Your choice of topic will depend on the special knowledge, skills, and feelings of the persons you might interview. Form a small group with other students choosing the same topic. Everyone in the group will conduct an interview on that general topic. Be sure, however, that each of you chooses a different person to interview.

Brainstorm with members of your group a list of questions to help a person open up about your topic. Keep in mind that you don't want to guide the person too firmly. You'll want to ask just enough questions to keep the person talking about that particular topic. Avoid questions that are too personal, that wander off the topic, or that can be answered with a dead-end "yes" or "no." Include open-ended questions that will allow the person being interviewed to offer information and comments he or she might not otherwise be able to include. For example, a concluding question might be, "What else do you think people should know about ___?"

Write these interview questions in your Writer's Notebook, leaving space between to note responses. Consider these questions tentative. During the actual interview, some questions may seem unnecessary, inappropriate, or redundant. Better questions may come to mind. The questions in your Writer's Notebook will at least give you a starting point and remind you of key points that need to be explored.

Before you conduct your interview, look over the following suggestions and plan to use them as a guide:

1. Make an appointment with the person to be interviewed. Explain what you want to talk about and why. Ask the person to suggest a convenient time and place.
2. Before the interview, learn all you can about the person you will be talking to. If you aren't well-acquainted, this background information can be used to put the person at ease and get the conversation going. Also learn all you can about your topic so that you can listen intelligently and follow leads of the person you are interviewing.
3. Be on time for the interview. Bring your Writer's Notebook and two or three pencils.
4. In conducting the interview, be courteous and let the person know you are genuinely interested in what he or she has to say. Let the conversation flow as naturally as possible. Ask follow-up questions to encourage the speaker to expand on interesting points and to go into greater detail. If the interviewee goes off on a tangent, look for an opening to ask a question that will get the conversation back on track. Never interrupt.
5. Take notes as unobtrusively as possible. You'll probably need to develop your own "shorthand" system. Transcribe as many of the speaker's exact words as possible. Listen not only to what the person says but to the way he or she says it. Also, try to discriminate between important and unimportant details. Don't be afraid to ask for clarification if you don't understand something. Get enough accurate information so that you will not have to ask for a second interview.
6. During the interview, observe the speaker's facial expressions, mannerisms, and gestures. Body language is important to the total message.
7. When you have finished, thank the person for the interview. Later, follow up with a thank-you note or call.

Following the preceding guidelines, conduct your interview. Then, as soon as possible, review your notes. While the interview is fresh in your mind, add details and fill in gaps. Reconstruct as much as you can of what was said.

Your next step will be shaping the raw material you have collected into its most readable form. Remember that the purpose of an oral documentary is to capture talk on paper so that it can be shared with other people. As you review your notes, find the comments that will be most interesting to the classmates who will be your readers. Consider ways of organizing those comments so that they will be easy to follow. Remember that your purpose is to bring the content of the interview to life for people who were not there. To do so, you must put the speaker's voice on paper.

Study your notes carefully. Underline parts that seem most interesting. Mark through any comments that seem trivial or unrelated to your subject. Also, find the major points that were covered during the interview. Since conversation sometimes rambles, details related to a certain point may be scattered. In the margin by each series of comments, jot down the major point of those comments. These marginal jottings will help you in grouping related details, the first and most important step in organizing any paper.

Before attempting a first draft, share highlights of your interview with the small group of classmates who conducted interviews on the same general topic. As you talk, try to organize what you report around the main points you identified in the margins of your notes. Be sure to stress all comments you underlined because they seemed especially interesting. Ask members of your group to identify details that *they* found most interesting. Ask also whether anything you reported seemed unclear. Finally, check to see how well your attempt to cluster related details worked. Was your account of what the speaker said easy to follow, or would another arrangement make for a smoother flow?

Now that you have tried out your material on a real audience, put it on paper. In compressing what was said into a monologue, try to reproduce the voice of the speaker. Include characteristic expressions. Keep sentences short enough to reflect the rhythms of natural speech.

**Getting
It
Down**

When you finish your first draft, read it aloud to yourself. Does it flow easily? Is it clear? Does it sound like the person you interviewed? Pencil in any changes that seem helpful and put your paper aside.

SPOTLIGHT

Writing an Introduction

So far in this chapter, you have concentrated on transcribing speech. In the process, you should have sharpened your ear for spoken language. You have also practiced reproducing speech on paper.

Now, you will turn your attention back to written language. A good starting point might be to review Terkel's introduction of Sharon Fox on page 69. Part of the difference between that introduction and the monologue that follows is the difference between the author's voice and Sharon's. An even greater difference is that between written and spoken language.

This difference is demonstrated even more dramatically in Terkel's preface to *American Dreams: Lost and Found*. The following excerpt summarizes the author's impressions of those dreams and the possibilities they represent for America during the 1980's.

> Something's happening, as yet unrecorded on the social seismograph
> . . . The eighties may differ from the seventies by a quantum jump.
>   The capacity for change is beyond the measure of a statistician
> or pollster. Among those I've encountered in the making of this book
> are: an ex-Klan leader who won his state's human relations award;
> the toughest girl on the block who became a social worker; the
> uneducated Appalachian woman who became the poetic voice of her
> community; the blue-collar housewife who, after mothering nine,
> says "I don't like the word 'dream.' I don't even want to specify it as
> American. What I'm beginning to understand is there's a human
> possibility. That's where all the excitement is. If you can be part of
> that, you're aware and alive. It's not a dream, it's possible. It's
> everyday stuff."
>   There are nascent stirrings in the neighborhood and in the field,
> articulated by non-celebrated people who bespeak dreams of their

fellows. It may be catching. Unfortunately, it is not covered on the six o'clock news.

In this book are a hundred American voices, captured by hunch, circumstance, and a rough idea. There is no pretense at statistical "truth," nor consensus. There is, in the manner of a jazz work, an attempt, of theme and improvisation, to recount dreams, lost and found, and a recognition of possibility.

Here, Terkel's words are eloquent. They are also precise and economical. The sentences are often longer than those in ordinary speech. Both language and sentence structure reflect deliberate choices by a careful writer.

As an apprentice writer, you will find it helpful to study the words chosen by professionals. By collecting unfamiliar words and defining them in a special section of your Writer's Notebook, you can make those words your own and thus stockpile additions to your own writing vocabulary. The exercise that follows will help you get started.

Writer's Workbench 1

Vocabulary

A. Find each of these words in the preceding excerpt from Terkel's preface:

seismograph	nascent
quantum	articulated
improvisation	

Using a dictionary, answer these questions:

1. What would be lost if the first sentence read "Something's happening as yet unrecorded on *instruments measuring social behavior*"? What kind of instrument is a seismograph? What does figurative use of the word imply about society?
2. What would the next sentence lose if *huge* were substituted for *quantum*? In what sense does the word *quantum* reinforce the effect of the word *seismograph*?
3. In the first sentence of the third paragraph, can you think of any word that could be successfully substituted for *nascent*?
4. In the same sentence, why is the word *articulated* more forceful than the word *expressed* would be?

5. Try substituting the phrase *spontaneous arrangement* for *improvisation* in the concluding sentence of the excerpt. Why doesn't it work as well?

B. Start a **Word Bank** section in your Writer's Notebook. As your first entry, write each of the five words explored in part A. Define and use each in an original sentence.

As you encounter unfamiliar words in your reading, add them to the **Word Bank** section of your Notebook. Periodically, review your list of entries. You may wish to incorporate newly acquired words into your writing.

As you worked through the preceding vocabulary exercise, you may have noticed that general words often say less than more specific ones. The word *seismograph*, for example, communicates more than the word *instrument*. You may also have noticed that a single precise word can say more than a whole phrase: *improvisation* is less cumbersome than *spontaneous arrangement*; it is also more explicit. In casual conversation, you have little time to consider such options. You just use the best word or phrase that occurs to you at that moment. As a writer, you have time to search for the word that is most exact and most direct.

As you write an introduction for the monologue based on your interview, word choice will be a major consideration. Your purpose will be to set the stage for the monologue—to identify and perhaps describe the speaker for your reader. Since the introduction should be brief, every word must do exactly what it is meant to do.

In writing this introduction, you will also want to consider various options of sentence structure. The way words are joined into sentences shows how one idea relates to another. Sentence structure also reflects emphasis, highlighting some ideas and pushing others into the background. Furthermore, written sentences are often longer than spoken sentences. They pack more meaning into a single unit. Notice, for example, the second sentence in Paragraph 2 of the excerpt from Terkel's preface. Notice also how this very long sentence is preceded by three short ones. Such variety adds interest.

You have already practiced sentence-combining as a means of producing richer, more interesting sentences. In the process, you have worked with sentence patterns seldom used in ordinary speech. By extending your repertoire of sentence patterns, you can become a more powerful writer. The next exercise will focus on the basic principles of coordination and subordination. By applying these principles, you can give prominence to sentence parts you want to stress and show exactly how one idea in a sentence relates to another.

Writer's Workbench 2

Coordination and Subordination

Part I

Coordinate means "of equal importance." Often, a sentence contains coordinate parts. These equally important parts may be words, phrases, or clauses. Usually, they are linked by words like *and, but,* and *or.* Such connectives are called coordinating conjunctions.

When a sentence contains two main clauses (strings of words that include a subject and predicate and stand alone to express a complete thought), the sentence is termed *compound.* Notice the different ways such clauses are joined in the following sentences from an introductory paragraph like the one you will be writing. Combine the sentences as indicated by the cues, and write them in paragraph form. (Remember that an asterisk signals the beginning of a new paragraph.)

A. 1. Frantic debators jammed Room 011.   (At 3:15,)
   Clattering typewriters jammed Room 011.   (,)
   Mounds of papers jammed Room 011.   (, and)
   Papers were <u>disheveled.</u>
   The forensics tournament was only one week away.   (;)
   The tournament was the <u>biggest of the year.</u>

   2. Andy Landon was one of the busiest debators.
   He had agreed to an interview.   (, but)

   3. "Hi, Dana," he said.
   He emerged from behind a bank of file cabinets.   (, -ing)
   He started toward the door.   (and -ing)

   4. "I'd like to get away all afternoon."
   "I'd better be back by 4:00."   (; however ,)

* 5. Thirty minutes would be enough.
   Andy is a fast talker.   (:)

   6. He is also full of ideas.
   Ideas are about how to increase student involvement.
   Involvement is in sports.
   Involvement is in clubs.   (,)

Involvement is in other extracurricular activities.　(, and)
Ideas are about how to combat campus littering and vandal-
ism.　(;)
Ideas are about how to make Bellaire an even better school.
(; and)

After checking your combined stentences against the model provided by
your teacher, review those sentences and notice the following:

    a. In Sentence 1, the two main clauses (often called *independent*
        clauses because they can stand alone) are joined by a semicolon
        rather than a conjunction. If this sentence were read aloud, it
        would sound like two sentences. The semicolon signals a distinct
        pause and keeps the two clauses from running together. By using
        the semicolon, the writer signals the reader that the ideas in the
        two clauses are related and lets the reader figure out exactly how.

    b. In Sentence 2, the two main clauses are connected by the
        coordinating conjunction *but*. Notice that it is preceded by a
        comma. When linking main clauses in this way, be sure to
        choose the conjunction that most accurately defines the relation-
        ship between them. What relationship does *but* show? *and? or?
        nor? for?*

    c. In Sentence 4, the two main clauses are again joined by a
        semicolon. Words like *however, consequently,* and *therefore* are
        conjunctive adverbs rather than conjunctions. If such words are
        used to show the relationship between two equally important
        clauses, they must be preceded by semicolons and followed by
        commas.

d. In Sentence 5, the two main clauses are linked by a colon rather than a semicolon. A colon not only separates the two clauses; it also indicates that the function of the second is to explain or extend the first. Can you see why it is appropriate in this sentence? Professional writers often use the colon in this way for stylistic effect. Remember that a colon is like an arrow pointing forward: it calls attention to what is to follow.

e. Several of the preceding sentences contain a series of words or phrases. Notice that items in a series are separated by commas—for example, *frantic debators, clattering typewriters,* and *mounds of disheveled papers* in Sentence 1. Notice also that these phrases are grammatically parallel. Each consists of a noun and its modifiers. The two coordinate phrases in Sentence 3 are also grammatically parallel. *Emerging from behind a bank of file cabinets* and *starting toward the door* are both participial phrases. In other words, they are verb forms used as adjectives, in this case to modify the pronoun *he.* Remember that coordinate words or phrases should be grammatically parallel. Otherwise, they do not seem balanced.

f. Sentence 6 is *not* a compound sentence. It contains only one main clause. The semicolons in this sentence are used to separate items in a series when one or more of those items contains commas. Can you see why the sentence would be confusing if commas were substituted for semicolons? This use of a semicolon is consistent with the use you noted earlier. Always, the semicolon partitions coordinate elements. In a way, it works almost like an equal sign to indicate that what precedes and what follows carry the same weight.

B. Now you will practice applying these coordinating techniques as you write some original sentences. Write these sentences about the interview you conducted earlier. You may focus on the person you interviewed or on the circumstances surrounding your conversation. These sentences are just for practice.

1. Write a compound sentence in which the two main clauses are joined by the coordinating conjunction *or.* (Don't forget the comma.)
2. Write a sentence containing a series of three items. Be sure that these items are grammatically parallel and appropriately separated by commas.
3. Write a compound sentence in which the two main clauses are separated only by a semicolon.

4. Write a compound sentence in which the two main clauses are appropriately separated by a colon.
5. Write a sentence including a series in which at least one item contains commas; use semicolons to separate items in the series.

Exchange completed sentences with a partner for checking. If any sentence seems questionable, consult your teacher for help.

C. Review Terkel's introduction to the Sharon Fox monologue on page 69. Also review the excerpt from the preface to his book on page 78. Find sentences containing coordinate parts. Justify use of punctuation, especially colons and semicolons.

Part II

Subordinate means "of lesser importance." Most sentences contain subordinate words, phrases, or clauses which modify words in a main clause. Such modifiers sharpen meaning. Notice how subordinate parts work in the following sentences. Combine the sentences as indicated by the cues; write them in paragraph form, and you will have another introductory paragraph of the kind you'll be writing.

A. 1. Claudio Catuzzi is accustomed to SOMETHING.
Claudio answers questions.   (-ing)
Claudio is Central High School's exchange student from Italy.   (, . . . ,)
Questions are <u>about his country.</u>

2. He grows impatient.
He is asked the same question.   (only when)
The question is <u>old.</u>
The question is about SOMETHING.
Rome is a very romantic city.   (whether)

3. Claudio would rather tell you about schools.
Claudio is a senior this year.   (, who . . . ,)
Schools are <u>Italian.</u>

4. He has attended classes five hours a day for six days a week.
(-ing)
He finds American schools more relaxed.   (,)

5. He takes subjects this year.   (Since)
The subjects are <u>six rather than thirteen.</u>

He finds plenty of time to SOMETHING.   (,)
He goes places with his friends.
Friends are <u>new.</u>

6. His friends are learning plenty about the land.   (Meanwhile ,)
    Land is <u>far-away.</u>
    Claudio <u>calls</u> home.   (that)

After checking your combined sentences against the model provided by
your teacher, review those sentences and notice the following:

  a. In Sentence 1, the main clause is "Claudio Catuzzi is accus-
      tomed to answering questions about his country." The fact that
      Claudio is Central High School's exchange student from Italy
      adds valuable information, but it is not the main point of the
      sentence. Notice how the information is slotted in as an
      appositive—that is, as a noun or noun phrase that explains or
      identifies the person or thing preceding it. Since the appositive
      "Central High School's exchange student from Italy" gives
      nonessential information, it is set off by commas.
  b. In Sentence 3, the main clause is "Claudio would rather tell you
      about Italian schools." The subordinate clause "who is a senior
      this year" gives background information about Claudio. The
      whole clause therefore functions as an adjective. The relative
      pronouns *who, whom, whose, which,* and *that* are used to link
      adjective clauses to the nouns or pronouns they modify. In this
      case, since the information in the adjective clause (also called a
      relative clause) is nonessential, the clause is set off by commas.
      Notice, however, the relative clause *that Claudio calls home* in
      Sentence 6. Since that clause is essential to restrict the meaning
      of the general word *land,* the clause is not set off by commas.
      (Later exercises will provide additional practice in punctuating
      restrictive and nonrestrictive elements. ● Meanwhile, if you need
      to brush up on this distinction, consult pages H-15–20 of the
      Writer's Handbook.)
  c. In sentence 2, the main clause is "He grows impatient." "When
      he is asked the same old question" is a subordinate clause. It
      modifies the verb *grows* by telling when, and therefore functions
      as an adverb. Such adverbial clauses are introduced by subordi-
      nating conjunctions like *when, as, although, because, since,* and
      while. Find the adverbial clause in Sentence 5. Notice that this
      clause comes at the beginning of the sentence and is therefore set
      off by a comma.

d. In Sentence 4, the main clause is "He finds American schools more relaxed." In this sentence, "Having attended classes five hours a day for six days a week" is a phrase rather than a clause. Since it is introduced by an -*ing* verb form functioning as an adjective and since the entire phrase tells more about the subject *he*, the phrase is classified as a participial phrase. Participial phrases coming at the beginning of a sentence are always set off by commas and always modify the subject of that sentence. This construction is more common in writing than in speaking. Participial phrases allow the writer to animate sentences with more verbs. Also, they are economical and lend variety of sentence structure.

B. Now you will practice applying these subordinating techniques as you write some sentences of your own. Again, write about the interview you conducted earlier. Keep in mind that the most important idea in the sentence goes in the main clause and that less important information is subordinated. As you write these practice sentences according to the specifications that follow, notice how subordinate elements enrich each basic statement.

1. Write a sentence containing an appositive that must be set off by commas.
2. Write a sentence with an adjective clause introduced by *who, whom, whose, which,* or *that*. Decide whether the clause is restrictive or nonrestrictive and punctuate accordingly.
3. Write a sentence with an introductory adverbial clause. Set that clause off with a comma.
4. Write a sentence with an introductory participial phrase. Be sure that the phrase modifies the subject of the sentence and that it is followed by a comma.
5. Write a sentence containing both an adjective clause and an adverbial clause. Punctuate appropriately.

Exchange your completed sentences with a partner for checking. Again, if any sentences seem questionable, consult your teacher for help.

C. Once more, review the excerpt from the preface to Terkel's book on page 78. Find subordinate parts in each sentence. Identify adjective clauses and adverbial clauses. Also find participial phrases. (In this excerpt, the author uses past [-*ed*] rather than present [-*ing*] participles.) As you study the use of subordinate elements, account for the use of punctuation.

During previous English classes, you have probably worked with all of the constructions included in this Writer's Workbench. You have learned to place commas between items in a series, to use conjunctions in a compound sentence, and to make an introductory participial phrase modify the subject of a sentence so that it will not "dangle." If you are like most students, you have spent lots of time on the structure and mechanics of English sentences. You have worked extensively with sentence parts, usually one part at a time.

The purpose of the preceding Workbench is to help you bring some of those parts together. As a writer, you need to see the big picture. You need to keep in mind some basic principles of how sentences work. One of the most basic is that the main idea in a sentence belongs in the main clause. If there are two equally important ideas, they *both* go in main clauses. Less important ideas are subordinated. Their relationship to the rest of the sentence is indicated by the position they occupy and the connectives used to splice them in.

In later chapters of this book, you will concentrate on specific sentence-building techniques. As you do so, keep the big picture in mind. The point is not to master each part of the sentence and then practice applying all the rules pertaining to that part. As a writer, you must learn to deal with all kinds of options at once.

You will want to consider various sentence options as you write the introduction for the piece you transcribed from your interview. First, however, you will want to write down your ideas for that introduction.

***

Getting It Down

Assume that the person you interviewed is a stranger to the classmates who will read your rendition of what he or she said. What do they need to know about that person? What will establish the speaker's credibility on the subject being discussed? Would the audience like to know how the speaker looks or sounds? Would the circumstances of the interview help put it into context?

After considering such possibilities, jot down details that you think would contribute most to a brief introduction. Cluster details that seem to belong together. Decide upon a tentative order for these details. Look over your notes to see whether you have the raw material for a good introduction. If not, keep jotting down ideas.

Now, write the first draft of your introduction, probably no more than a page. Remember that your purpose is to prepare readers for the comments you transcribed earlier. In doing so, try to stimulate interest and provide a point of identification with the speaker.

Checking It Out

When you have completed your first draft, read it over with these questions in mind.

1. Does the introduction do what it is intended to do—that is, generate interest and set the stage for the speaker?
2. Does the introduction create one dominant impression? Do all details contribute to that impression? Are details specific?
3. Does the introduction flow smoothly? Are details arranged in an order that is logical and easy to follow?

After you are satisfied with the content of the introduction, check word choice and sentence structure. What words could be improved? Are sentences clear and smooth? Are main ideas in main clauses? Have a variety of subordinating techniques been used? Try various options. Work for both richness and variety. Punctuate appropriately.

Compare the introduction you have just written with the monologue you shaped earlier from material gathered during your interview. Read each aloud. Does the monologue sound like spoken English? Without being stiff or contrived, does the introduction sound more like written English?

The project you have been working on throughout this chapter will culminate in the compilation of an oral documentary. During this final stage of the project, you will work with the classmates who investigated the same general topic you did. Together, you will polish your individual pieces and write a preface establishing the common theme. Then, you will share your mini-documentary with the rest of the class and perhaps others in your school.

Getting It Right

Have a round-robin reading of papers written by members of your small group. (Clip introductions to monologues so that they may be read together.) When everyone has completed all of the papers, discuss each briefly, citing passages that don't seem clear and making suggestions for improvement. Put individual papers aside to take home so that final drafts may be completed out of class.

~~~~~~

Meanwhile, brainstorm possible approaches to a preface for the collected pieces. Remember that a preface must generate interest and orient readers to what follows. Be sure that your preface announces the common theme of pieces comprising your oral documentary and comments on that theme. As group members suggest ideas for the preface, have a recorder take notes and read them back to the group. Try to reach consensus on what is to be included. Have a volunteer complete a first draft of the preface so that it may be considered and revised by the group the next day.

Getting It Down

~~~~~~

As the first draft of the preface is read aloud, listen for the overall effect. At this point, do not make notes. Discuss with the rest of the group how well the preface accomplishes its purpose. Does it bind together the pieces that will comprise the oral documentary? Make any changes that will help set the proper tone and improve the overall effect.

Next, have the preface read aloud sentence by sentence so that members of the group can suggest specific improvements in wording and sentence structure. Choose two or three people to serve as an editing committee to oversee the writing of a final draft. Have another committee decide upon the order of the pieces to be included in the oral documentary and make a table of contents. Still another might make an appropriate cover and put the booklet together.

Getting It Right

~~~~~~

Since the oral documentary you produced in this chapter was *for* as well as *about* other people, you will want to share your booklet with the rest of the class and get their reactions. If the booklets seem especially successful, you may wish to place them on display in the school library so that they may be read by a wider audience of students and teachers.

Chapter 5

Writing a Feature Story

Newspapers are full of stories about people. Thumb through the pages of any paper. Notice how many names you see in headlines, in lead sentences, and under pictures.

Almost every news story has a human element. An international treaty can't be signed without real people to do the negotiating and wield the pens. Earthquake casualties aren't just numbers: they are men, women, and children. A scientific breakthrough doesn't just happen; someone makes it happen.

Such news stories are also carried on radio and television. Even so, newspapers remain immensely popular. They can be tucked under the arm and taken anywhere. They don't have to be read at any particular time or in any particular order. Stories stand alone and can be read selectively. Most can also be read quickly.

Writing for a newspaper is very demanding. Since circulation determines whether a particular paper stays in business, writers and editors must be closely attuned to their audience. Every issue must be worth buying—and reading. Stories must rivet and hold attention. As Steve Lovelady of *The Philadelphia Inquirer* cautions his colleagues, "The reader is looking for an excuse to quit reading at the end of every sentence and every paragraph. Don't give him or her one."

You may never be a reporter or an editor. Even so, you can learn a great deal about writing by trying your hand at newspaper-style stories. You can develop a stronger sense of audience, a firmer grasp of here-and-now details, and a greater economy of expression. You can also learn more about collecting and shaping material, especially about people, and presenting that material from an appropriate point of view.

Observing and Reporting

Like all good writers, a newspaper reporter must first have something to say. Empty words don't make good reading. Roy Peter Clark stressed this point when he addressed a convention of the American Society of Newspaper Editors:

> My greatest lesson as a journalist . . . is the importance of reporting. Without it, there is no good writing. You may have facility with language. But if you don't have the interesting facts, the details, the quotations, the descriptions, the anecdotes, your writing will have all the substance of a Fanny Farmer nougat.

A reporter's job is to gather information and relate it to others. That information is gleaned from many sources: from interviews like the one you conducted during the previous chapter, from printed materials, and from personal observation.

Good reporters rely heavily upon their own eyes and ears. They pay attention to detail, as you did in collecting material for your oral documentary. You collected this material by close listening. The practice activities that follow will help you sharpen your other senses and thus become a keen observer.

Getting It Started

Complete Exercises 1 and 2 in class. Spend no more than five minutes on each.

1. Choose one feature of the classroom—for example, a certain section of the chalkboard, a bookcase, a particular window or wall, one of the corners, or the floor. Write at least ten phrases describing that feature as precisely and as vividly as possible. Most details will probably be visual, but try to use the other senses as well. Exchange lists of phrases with a classmate and see whether each of you can identify what the other has described.
2. Choose one person in the classroom. Write at least ten phrases describing that person. Again, involve as many of the senses as possible. Exchange lists of phrases with a classmate or read that list aloud to the class. Is your subject readily identifiable? What details are most revealing?

Complete Exercise 3 outside of class. The next day, share your description with a small group of classmates. Ask them to identify your sharpest and most interesting details.

3. Watch a person doing something. For example, you might watch an athlete practice pole-vaulting or diving, your mother

icing a cake, or at work in her office, a driver filling a car with gas
or changing a tire, a friend mowing the lawn or making a bed.
Without explaining what is going on, write several sentences
describing the person in action. See how clear, detailed, and
interesting you can make your account of this commonplace
activity. Use lots of verbs to catch the action.

SPOTLIGHT

Except for practice, you will seldom write description for description's
sake. Details like the ones you have just written are woven into almost
every kind of writing. They lend immediacy by engaging the reader's
senses and creating a you-are-there feeling.

This kind of involvement is more important in some stories than in
others. When you read the front page of a newspaper, you probably feel
somewhat detached. You realize that you will be affected by the spiraling
inflation rate, you regret the airplane crash that occurred in a distant
land, and you are pleased that local voters approved a bond issue for
renovating school buildings in your town. Even so, you see such news
stories mainly as information. You do not need to identify with the people
making the news or feel that you are part of the action.

The feature story is an altogether different matter. Such stories focus
on human-interest items, present news in an entertaining way, or explain
and interpret facts. Don Duncan of the Tacoma *News-Tribune* speaks of
features as "the wide screen, 3-D, technicolor side of the newspaper
business." To provide such dimension and color, feature stories must be
rich in descriptive detail.

Here is the opening paragraph of a feature story that appeared in a
school newspaper:

> Martin Clifford has been busy this fall. Since becoming Westches-
> ter's new principal, he has been everywhere, getting acquainted,
> questioning, listening, making decisions, and smiling. Slumped in a
> comfortable office chair on a recent Friday afternoon, Mr. Clifford
> looked like an oversized wind-up toy whose spring had wound down
> from hard use. His perpetually open door caught the three o'clock
> sound of liberated students.

This is not the kind of opener you would find on the front page of a paper under the headline "CLIFFORD APPOINTED PRINCIPAL OF WESTCHESTER HIGH." The ensuing story *does* contain news, and the reporter undergirds that story with facts. But the information is personalized. The writer invites the reader to see what she saw and hear what she heard while sitting in Mr. Clifford's office that Friday afternoon. The result is a human-interest story that closes the distance between reader and subject.

SPOTLIGHT

At age twenty-six, Cynthia Gorney of *The Washington Post* won the 1980 American Society of Newspaper Editors competition in feature writing. Here is a sample of her award-winning work:

LA JOLLA, Calif.—One afternoon in 1957, as he bent over the big drawing board in his California studio, Theodor Seuss Geisel found himself drawing a turtle.

He was not sure why.

He drew another turtle and saw that it was underneath the first turtle, holding him up.

He drew another, and another, until he had an enormous pileup of turtles, each standing on the back of the turtle below it and hanging its head, looking pained.

Geisel looked at his turtle pile. He asked himself, not unreasonably, What does this mean? Who is the turtle on top?

Then he understood that the turtle on top was Adolf Hitler.

"I couldn't draw Hitler as a turtle," Geisel says, now hunched over the same drawing board, making pencil scribbles of the original Yertle the Turtle drawings as he remembers them. "So I drew him as King What-ever-his-name-was, King" (scribble) "of the Pond." (Scribble.) "He wanted to be king as far as he could see. So he kept piling them up. He conquered Central Europe and France, and there it was."

(Scribble.)

"Then I had this great pileup, and I said, 'How do you get rid of this imposter?'

"Believe it or not, I said, 'The voice of the people.' I said, 'Well, I'll simply have the guy on the bottom burp.'"

Geisel looks up from his drawing board and smiles—just a little, because a man is taking his picture and he has never gotten used to people who want to take his picture.

Dr. Seuss, American institution, wild orchestrator of plausible nonsense, booster of things that matter (like fair play, kindness, Drum-Tummied Snumms, Hooded Koopfers, and infinite winding spools of birthday hot dogs), detractor of things that don't (like bullying, snobbery, condescension, gravity and walls), is 75 years old this year.

As usual, he is somewhat embarrassed by all the fuss.

"It's getting awful," Geisel says, "because I meet old, old people who can scarcely walk, and they say, 'I was brought up on your books.' It's an awful shock."

There is probably not a single children's book author in America who has matched the impact, popularity and international fame of the spare, bearded California prodigy who signs his books Dr. Seuss.

Since 1936, when Ted Geisel the advertising illustrator first wrote *And to Think That I Saw It on Mulberry Street*, his books have sold 80 million copies in this country alone.

Mulberry Street was an effort, he explained later, to expel from his brain the maddening rhythm of a ship engine he had heard during the whole of a transatlantic voyage (da da Da da da Da da da Da da da da).

The late Bennett Cerf—at a time when his Random House writers included William Faulkner and John O'Hara—is on record as having called Geisel the only genius of the lot.

The drawings, manuscripts, and half-formed doodles of Dr. Seuss (who did not officially become a doctor until 1956, when Dartmouth College made him an honorary Dr. of Humane Letters), are kept in locked stacks of the Special Collections division of the UCLA library. He won two Academy Adwards for his World War II-era documentary film and one for the cartoon "Gerald McBoing-Boing," which he created. His books are published in about 45 countries outside the United States, including Brazil, Japan, the entire British commonwealth and the Netherlands, where *There's a Wocket in My Pocket* translates to *Ik heb een Gak in Myn Zak*! . . .

Geisel has lived for 30 years in La Jolla, which is a coastal town just north of San Diego that has developed a flowery, almost Caribbean sparkle as the wealthy build homes up the side of the mountain. At the very top of one of the mountains, with the diminishing acres of wild land to the east and to the west the wide blue curve of the Pacific, Geisel and his wife Audrey share an old stucco observatory tower and the elegant, helter-skelter maze of rooms they have built around it. "It just grew," Audrey Geisel said, "Seuss-like."

They have a swimming pool, a small Yorkshire terrier whose front end is indistinguishable from the back at first glance ("I've been accused of having drawn him," Geisel says) and a gray Cadillac Seville with GRINCH license plates—which took them several years to obtain, because when they first applied they learned that an ardent Seuss-lover with four children had already put GRINCH on the license plates and both sides of his RV. He finally moved to Iowa City and released GRINCH back to the Geisels, with a note of apology for having hogged it so long. . . .

[Geisel] is a private, engaging, intensely driven man, with a lean and sharp-nosed look that gives him an air of severity at first. His house is scattered with his own paintings and busts of creatures unlike anything anybody ever saw before, and as he leads visitors through the halls he makes congenial introductions, as though presenting boarders: "This is a green cat in the Uleaborg, Finland subway . . . this is a cat who was born on the wrong side of town . . . this is my religious period. . . .

He will not wear conventional neckties—only bow ties. He reads paperback books—history, biography, detective novels—so voraciously that his wife makes regular bookstore runs (often to a certain store that saves new books for him in a special Geisel cubbyhole) and then stashes the paperbacks away so she can hand him new ones in the evening, one at a time. He reads for distraction. He needs it. When he is at work, the names, the verse, the story line, the colors, the shapes and sizes of his extraordinary characters all press upon him. He tapes the working drawings to the wall and stares at them, rearranging, reading aloud to himself, feeling the rhythm of the words.

In his new book, a volume of tongue twisters coming out in the fall, Geisel has drawn a green parrot. He has studied all the colors on the Random House art department printing chart—his usual procedure—looking for the printer's ink shade that most closely matches his working drawings in colored pencil. There are 60 different shades of green on the chart, and Geisel cannot find the right one. This one is too yellow, that one too red. He does not explain to the art department why each green is wrong—just not parrotty enough, or something.

They know better than to ask. They will have the printer make up the precise shade of green.

"His color sense," says Grace Clarke, executive art director of the Random House junior books division, "is the most sophisticated I've ever run into." Geisel had to completely relearn color during the last two years, after undergoing an operation for removal of a cataract. The right saw brilliant color, following the operation: "the other eye, which still has a small cataract, sees everything like Whistler's Mother." The second cataract is to be removed next year, after which, says Geisel, deadpanned, "They claim I'll be as good as Picasso."

Geisel does not read children's literature, unless he is editing it, which is part of his job as the founder and head of the special early readers Random House Division called Beginner Books. Then he is fierce in his judgment, dismissing instantly the noxious breed of children's books that coo and mince and pat little heads.

"Bunny-bunny books," he calls them. "Sugar plums, treacle, whimsy." . . . "I try to treat the child as an equal," Geisel has said, "and go on the assumption that a child can understand anything that is read to him if the writer takes care to state it clearly and simply enough." . . .

Geisel never set out to be a children's book writer. He was born in Springfield, Mass., the son of a German immigrant who had been, at various times, a brewer, a park superintendent, and a world champion rifle shot. Ted Geisel grew up in Springfield, graduated from Dartmouth, and spent a year at Oxford, during which time he is reported to have proposed (unsuccessfully) a new edition of *Paradise Lost*, which would include such illustrations as the Archangel Uriel sliding down a sunbeam with an oil can to lubricate his trip.

He lived in New York, selling drawings, stories and political cartoons to magazines of the day—*Judge, Vanity Fair,* the *Saturday Evening Post*—and for 15 years he worked in advertising for Standard Oil of New Jersey.

He drew insecticide ads, "Quick, Henry! The Flit!" That was Geisel's creation.

He illustrated two volumes of jokes, tried unsuccessfully to sell an alphabet book, and then in 1936 laid out the wonderfully paced mad fantasy of the boy named Marco in *And to Think That I Saw It on Mulberry Street.* Before a publishing friend of Geisel's took the book in at Vanguard Press, 20 publishers turned it down.

He had an easier time with the next one. "I was sitting in a railroad train, going up somewhere in Connecticut," Geisel says. "And there was a fellow sitting ahead of me, who I didn't like. I didn't know who he was. He had a real ridiculous Wall Street broker's hat on, very stuffy, on this commuting train. And I just began playing around with the idea of what his reaction would be if I took his hat off and threw it out the window."

Geisel smiles a small, slightly evil smile.

"And I said, 'He'll probably just grow another one and ignore me.'"

Which gave us *The 500 Hats of Bartholomew Cubbins.* Boy, confronted in castle by snooty royalty, cannot doff his hat because new hats keep appearing to replace it. . . .

Once in a while there is an echo of something like anguish in Geisel's accounts of the workings of his own imagination—some constant, furious homage to the 1902 rifle target, its bullseye perforated by his father's exacting shots, that Geisel keeps mounted on the wall.

"To remind me of perfection," he says.

He will sometimes work late into the night, or break off into an entirely different project, when some flaw in a book begins to gnaw at him. He spent a full year struggling over the smallish gopher-like creature called the Lorax. "Once he was mechanized. That didn't work. He was big at one point. I did the obvious thing of making him green, shrinking him, growing him."

And then? "I looked at him, and he looked like a Lorax."

But he was equally stumped by the story itself, a dismal tale about the Once-ler, who hacks down all the Truffula Trees to mass-produce Threeds, thereby driving away the Swomee-Swans, starving out the Brown Bar-ba-loots, and—as the wheezing, outraged Lorax cries—"glumping the pond where the Humming-fish hummed." It was the angriest story Geisel had ever written, and he could not figure out how to make sense of it, how to keep it from turning into a lecture—" a preachment," as Geisel says. Geisel has a horror of preachments. Audrey Geisel, who quite rightly believes that the best way to come unstuck is to stand on your head and try looking at things that way, suggested they go to Africa for a while, which they did.

"I hadn't thought of the Lorax for three weeks," Geisel says. "And a herd of elephants came across the hill—about a half mile away—one of those lucky things, that never happened since. And I picked up a laundry pad and wrote the whole book that afternoon on a laundry pad." . . .

He pulls from a file some typewritten pages from his new book. "You want to try reading one?" Geisel asks.

His visitor, reading slowly, makes a stab at it:

> One year he had a Christmas brunch
> With Merry Christmas Mush to munch.
> But I don't think you'd care for such
> We didn't like to munch mush much.

There is a rather bad moment of tongue-twisting at the end and Geisel looks delighted. "These things are written way over the ability of first grade kids, and I think it's going to work," he said. "They're stinkers (the tongue-twisters, not the children).

"I think one reason kids are not reading up to their potential is a lack of being urged—you can't urge them with a big stick, but you can urge them with competition."

Well now, demands his visitor, Geisel has to read one.

"Not wearing the right glasses," Geisel says quickly. "I can't."

The following questions will help you see how this feature story is put together. Discuss these questions with a small group of classmates:

1. Why do you think Ms. Gorney chose to begin with the anecdote about Yertle the Turtle? In what way does this incident establish the focus of the story? What other incidents offer insights into the way Geisel's imagination works?

2. Notice that the Yertle incident is recounted in the past tense, as are other anecdotes and facts from Geisel's earlier life. The rest of the feature story unfolds in the present tense. Why? In what way does this bring the reader closer to the action?

3. Much of the material comprising this story obviously emerged from the reporter's interview with the famous Dr. Seuss. Who else is quoted in the article? What information does each contribute? Can you find any information that could have been gathered from previous articles and other printed material?

4. Descriptive details in the story show that the reporter is a keen observer. Which seem most vivid and most interesting? Which make the distinguished author seem like a real person?

5. List the three adjectives that best describe Dr. Seuss as portrayed in this article. What details illustrate each trait?

6. Notice that this entire story is written in the third person. In other words, the reporter never uses the pronoun *I*. If she refers to herself at

all, it is as "the visitor." Why do you think Gorney chose to stay out of the picture and speak in the third person?

7. Although never expressed directly, the writer's attitude toward her subject is clear. How would you describe that attitude? What choices of words and details most clearly reflect it?

In talking about what it takes to be a good feature writer, Cynthia Gorney says this:

> You have to be passionately interested in everything. You have to want to learn . . . everything there is to know. You have to know five times as much as you're ever going to use in the story. The only really essential quality of a writer is crazed curiosity.

The "crazed curiosity" of a writer comes into play long before pencil ever touches paper. It impels the writer to notice things that others would miss, to see the potential for a good story in a seemingly ordinary situation or person. It prompts the writer to ask questions and to read widely, to squirrel away information on a variety of subjects.

There are probably people in your school or community who excite your curiosity and would thus make subjects for a feature story. Your first task will be to find such a person.

Identify at least three people you know who are worth writing about. Consider the following possibilities as starters:

Getting It Started

1. Someone who is extremely popular or well-known in your town—for example, a city official, a TV personality or some other entertainer, a teacher, the coach of a school or professional team, a sports hero, or an artist.
2. Someone with an interesting or challenging job such as a newspaper or TV reporter, legal secretary, doctor, architect, firefighter, veterinarian, computer programmer. (You might also consider people who hold such off-beat jobs as dog-groomers, billboard painters, and crop dusters, or such thankless jobs as garbage collectors and truant officers.)
3. Someone who does the unusual or unexpected—for example, a sixty-year-old who competes in marathons, the only boy in

a sewing class or the only girl in an auto mechanics course, a teacher who works in the same school he or she attended as a student.

Identify the most interesting potential subjects you know.

Before making a final choice among the three, consider available sources of information. Be sure that the person you choose will grant an interview. (You will also want to be sure that other students don't plan to write about the same person.)

Once you have chosen a subject for your feature story, take inventory of what you already know about that person. Jot down all the facts you can think of. Then jot down possible sources of further background information, including printed material. If you have chosen to write about a well-known person in your city—perhaps the mayor or a sports hero—the local newspaper provides a good starting point. Most have topically arranged files of clippings, as do many city libraries. If nothing has been written specifically about that person, read up on his or her area of special interest. For example, in preparing to interview a member of the school board, you would need to find out all you could about how board members are elected, what their major responsibilities are, and how they conduct business. You might even attend a school board meeting as an observer. In building background on a local marathoner, you would want to learn all you could about competitive running, perhaps by reading a book or several articles on the subject. As you conduct such background research on your subject, make careful notes. Also make notes of what you learn about your subject from other people.

One feature can't tell *everything* about a subject. Think about the Ted Geisel story. It did not begin with Geisel's birth in Springfield, Massachusetts, and trace in biographical detail the events of the next seventy-five years. The reporter was interested primarily in the man behind the Dr. Seuss books, in the way those books came to be. Her research into Geisel's work, her interview with the author, and the resulting story all focus on that topic.

As you gather background information for your feature story, be sure you have a clear focus. Begin with your main reason for choosing a particular person as the subject of your story. What sets that person apart? What has that person done that you really want to know about? The answer to such questions will help you find an appropriate focus.

Keeping the focal point of your feature story in mind, develop a list of questions to guide your interview with the subject of that story. Take a few minutes to review notes from the interview you conducted during the previous chapter. What kinds of questions seemed to work best? Also consider what you have learned in doing background research on your subject. This information should allow you to ask knowledgeable questions.

Following the guidelines on page 76, conduct the interview for your feature story. As soon as possible, review and expand your notes. Besides reconstructing as much as possible of what was said, jot down recollections of how the person looked, sounded, and moved. In jotting down first-hand observations, try to recall characteristic mannerisms, details of the person's dress or environment, points that struck you because they were unexpected. Make your notes as thorough and as detailed as possible. (Remember Gorney's statement about the reporter's

Getting It Started

needing five times as much material as will actually appear in the story!)

At this point, you may wish to conduct brief, informal back-up interviews with people who have special insight into the subject of your story. For example, during an interview with a teacher who works in the same school he or she attended as a student, that person might have mentioned a revered third-grade teacher, long-retired. You might like to see how that long-retired teacher remembers your subject as a third-grader. If you are writing about a doctor, you might like to see what insights a long-time receptionist or nurse can offer. As you gather such information, be careful not to pry. A feature story is not gossip. It is for public consumption and should not conflict with the individual's right to personal privacy. In asking questions, be guided by the projected focus of your story.

Before you start the first draft of your feature story, take a moment to consider audience. Your oral documentary was directed to a specific group of readers, your own classmates. When you began to write, you already knew a great deal about that audience. You knew that it was comprised of people who were about the same age, attended the same school, and shared certain broad interests. You could predict with some accuracy what they would want to know. In fact, you verified your hunches by trying out material on your audience and getting a response.

Your feature story will be directed to a more general audience, the readership of a local newspaper. Think of all the people who read that paper. What do you think the age range might be?—the range of educational background and occupations? Although it is hard to generalize about such a diverse readership, you *can* assume a common interest in local people and events.

You can also assume that most readers approach the newspaper casually. Few read it word for word from the first page through the last. Most scan the headlines and the opening sentences of articles that catch their eye. If your feature story is to hook readers, it must have a strong headline and an arresting lead.

Even if your feature story never goes beyond the bulletin board in your English classroom, you will find writing for a large and demanding audience a worthwhile challenge. In responding to that challenge, you should learn some valuable lessons about how to achieve both impact and clarity.

A well-defined point of view will help. In writing this piece, step back from your material. Write in your own voice, but don't clutter the story with references to yourself. Report in the third person. Avoid the pronoun *I*; use *he* or *she* instead. This point of view will keep the spotlight focused on the subject.

Also, plan to write your story in the present tense. After all, that story is about the here-and-now. Notice the use of present-tense verbs in the Dr. Seuss piece: "Geisel *looks* up . . .," "As usual, he *is* somewhat embarrassed . . .," "They *have* a swimming pool . . .," ". . . Geisel *says* sadly." These verbs catch the action as it is in progress, not after it is over. The reader feels almost like an eye witness as the story unfolds.

You probably have no difficulty recognizing and using present-tense verbs. You may need to brush up on the present-perfect tense. Consider the sentence "Geisel *has lived* for thirty years in La Jolla." *Has lived* is in the present-perfect tense. It indicates an action that began in the past and is still occurring right up to the present moment. You will probably need to use such verbs in your feature story. Just remember that the present-perfect tense is signalled by *have* or *has*.

Although you will be writing in the present tense, you should shift to the past tense for events that are being recalled from an earlier time. Notice the use of past-tense verbs in these sentences: ". . . Theodor Seuss Geisel *found* himself drawing a turtle," "He *lived* in New York . . .," "He *had* an easier time with the next one." These verbs relegate previous events to the past and make it clear that they are nothing more than historical background.

Again, you probably have little difficulty recognizing and using past-tense verbs. The following sentence will allow a quick review of the past perfect: "*Mulberry Street* was an effort, he explained later, to expel from his brain the maddening rhythm of a ship engine he *had heard* during the whole of a transatlantic voyage." Look at the verb *had heard*, which is in the past-perfect tense. In other words, it indicates an action that was completed at some time in the past. In this case, Geisel had heard the engine before he made the effort to expel the noise from his brain and certainly before he explained the writing of *Mulberry Street*. Remember that the past-present tense is signalled by the helping verb *had*.

Writers who understand verb tense can make it work for them. It is not coincidental that most essays are in the present tense and most fiction in the past. In either case, verb tense should be consistent. Any shift should be deliberate, not careless. Shifting into the past tense to distinguish what happened previously from what is happening now is effective. Careless shifts such as "He walk*ed* to the fireplace and pick*s* up the poker" are confusing. As you write your feature story, try to make verb tense work for you. Use the present tense to create a here-and-now perspective. Avoid unjustified shifts. When appropriate, use present-perfect or past-perfect tenses for precision.

Getting It Down

Now go back and review your notes. Underline highlights. Make marginal notes to flag main points. Number those points to indicate a tentative order.

Before you start writing, think about the focus you decided upon earlier. The material gathered during your interview may suggest a narrowing or slight shift of focus. You may have discovered a new angle. If so, keep it in mind as you begin to write.

To get started, think about your audience. Picture someone thumbing through the paper and pausing at your story. What headline would grab that reader's attention and lay the groundwork for the story to follow? After you have a tentative headline, ask yourself what opening sentences would strike the right tone for the story, make the browser want to keep reading, and lead smoothly into what you have to say. Think of the opening as a keynote. Remember that readers will be wondering "What's this all about?" Tell them right off, in the most interesting possible way.

When you finish the opening section, start a new paragraph. In journalistic writing, paragraphs are often short. Start a new paragraph when you bring in a new idea to move the story forward. As you do so, you will probably want to quote the person you are writing about. You may also wish to quote what others have said about that person. Rather than relying totally on transcribed speech as you did in your oral documentary, however, you will also want to include descriptive details, anecdotes, and background information.

When you finish developing one point and aren't sure what to say next, imagine a prospective reader's asking "And so?" or "What else?" Tell that reader more, being sure to include all the highlights underlined in your notes. Tell your story in the most vivid detail possible. Right now, just get it all down. Later, you can refine what you have written.

Try out your feature story on a small group of classmates. Read each other's papers as stand-ins for various subscribers to the local paper. Answer these questions about each story:

1. Would the headline grab my attention? Does it go with the story that follows?
2. Does the lead make me want to keep reading? Does it set the tone and establish the focus for the story as a whole?
3. Does the story show good reporting? Is it filled with facts, details, quotations, and anecdotes?
4. Does the story have human interest? Is it told in a way that brings the subject to life?
5. Is the story told in the third person? Are present-tense verbs used consistently except to recount previous events?
6. Does the story flow smoothly? Are related details grouped into paragraphs so that the body is logically organized? Does one paragraph lead smoothly into the next? Are connections clear?
7. Can you suggest specific ways of making the story more readable for a general newspaper audience?

As the group considers your paper and responds to these questions, make notes. Then put the story away for a day or two. A little distance will help you see your story more objectively and revise it more easily.

SPOTLIGHT

Tightening Up Sentences

If you chose a good subject and did some solid reporting, your first draft can undoubtedly be developed into a strong feature story. First, however, the draft may need some revision, perhaps even some rewriting.

Because of deadlines, reporters must work fast. They get a story down and then do whatever rewriting is necessary. In recounting her struggle over one particularly difficult paragraph, Cynthia Gorney said this:

> I talked it out, wrote it out, and wrote it over and over. I crumpled up pages and threw them away. It was a process of just paring down and paring down and just trying to make it as clear and as short and as strong as I could.

This statement captures the essence of good newspaper style. As you revise your feature story, you will want to make every paragraph "as clear and as short and as strong" as you can.

Study the opening sentences of a student's feature story:

> At the entrance to the large mansion stands an iron gate. The gate is covered with ivy. The fact is that no passerby would suspect what lies a mere half-mile beyond that gate. Few are allowed to travel up the winding lane, which is canopied by oaks, to the front door of the hundred-year-old house that it leads to.

You can see that this student has some good ideas. These sentences make the reader curious about the person who lives in the remote mansion. Details like the iron gate, the half mile of winding lane, and the age of the house bring the scene into focus. Figurative use of the word "canopied" is fresh and colorful. Despite this potential, the passage suffers from wordiness. It needs pruning.

The first problem lies in the phrase "large mansion," which is redundant. In other words, it says the same thing twice: a mansion is by definition large. Saying "large mansion" is as repetitious as saying "round circle," "new innovation," or "consensus of opinion."

The first two sentences could be compressed into one. The combined sentence might read "At the entrance to the mansion stands an iron gate, covered with ivy." In this version, notice how the second sentence has been reduced to a phrase. It *could* be reduced to a single word: "At the entrance to the mansion stands an ivy-covered iron gate." The same technique could be used in the last sentence. Here, the clause "which is canopied by oaks" could be reduced to "oak-canopied." The first part of that sentence would then read, "Few are allowed to travel up the winding, oak-canopied lane . . ."

Some phrases in the passage are just empty: they add no meaning. "The fact is that . . ." simply adds padding. Cutting that phrase allows the sentence it introduces to read more forcefully: "No passerby would suspect what lies a mere half-mile beyond that gate." "That it leads to" in the final sentence is another empty phrase that should be cut. By the time

this phrase appears, it is already obvious that the winding lane leads to the front door of the house.

After the preceding pruning, the opening of the feature story would read like this:

At the entrance to the mansion stands an iron gate, covered with ivy. No passerby would suspect what lies a mere half-mile beyond that gate. Few are allowed to travel up the winding, oak-canopied lane to the front door of the hundred-year-old house.

Isn't this version clearer, shorter, and stronger?

Later, you will learn other ways of pruning deadwood out of your writing. For the present, concentrate on these three:

1. Avoid redundant expressions.

2. Use the most economical construction possible. (When appropriate, reduce a clause to a phrase; a phrase to a single word.)
3. Omit words and phrases that add no meaning.

As you strive for conciseness in revising your feature story, be careful not to strip away detail. Writing can be both rich and concise. The point is to pack as much meaning into words as possible.

You'll want to be especially careful about words that do little more than leave blanks for readers to fill in. Words like "nice" can mean almost anything, depending upon context. A house can be nice. So can a person, a poodle, a new stereo, a party, and a day at the beach. Most words of vague praise or blame are really just place-holders in a sentence. What does a *lovely* dress look like? Is it long or short? Is it red? Is it made of wool? Does it have ruffles? The word *lovely* creates no word picture; it just editorializes. A lively writer would describe the dress in detail and let the reader conclude that it is indeed lovely.

Notice that *nice, lovely, terrible,* and *wonderful* are all adjectives; so are fad words like *neat, great,* and *cool.* But not all adjectives act as empty place-holders. Consider the adjectives used to describe Ted Geisel in a sentence from the feature story you read earlier: "He is a *private, engaging,* intensely *driven* man, with a *lean* and *sharp-nosed* look that gives him an air of severity at first." These adjectives do more than leave blanks for the reader to fill in. Furthermore, abstract words like *private, engaging,* and *driven* are amply illustrated by anecdotes and observations. The reporter shows as well as tells. Even words used to tell must pull their own weight.

You have already practiced sentence-combining as a technique for building rich, concise sentences. The following exercise will introduce another way of experimenting with sentence patterns you might not try otherwise.

Writer's Workbench

Sentence-Expanding

You have already learned that the most important idea in a sentence should be expressed in the main clause. You have also learned that words, phrases, and clauses subordinated to that main clause can bring it into sharper focus.

Here are three main clauses from the story about Dr. Seuss:

1. Theodor Seuss Geisel found himself drawing a turtle.
2. He drew another, and another.
3. Dr. Seuss is 75 years old this year.

All of these clauses say something important. All carry the main idea of the sentence in which they appear. The main clauses alone, however, don't have much dimension or color.

Now study the full sentences built around the clauses. Note the position of each main clause.

1. One afternoon in 1957, as he bent over the big drawing board in his California studio, *Theodor Seuss Geisel found himself drawing a turtle.*
2. *He drew another, and another,* until he had an enormous pileup of turtles, each standing on the back of the turtle below it and hanging its turtle head, looking pained.
3. *Dr. Seuss,* American institution, wild orchestrator of plausible nonsense, booster of things that matter (like fair play, kindness, Drum-Tummied Snumms, Hooded Koopfers, and infinite winding spools of birthday hot dogs), detractor of things that don't (like bullying, snobbery, condescension, gravity and walls), *is 75 years old this year.*

Can you see how much the subordinate elements sharpen each main clause? Notice also that the main clause can come at the beginning of the sentence, it can come at the end, or it can be split. (Occasionally, it also comes in the middle.) The position of the main clause helps determine emphasis.

Sentences are sometimes classified as either *loose* or *periodic*. A loose sentence is one that makes a complete statement and then adds details. Since the main clause comes early in the sentence, the sentence can be cut off at any subsequent point and still make sense. Sentence 2 is loose. It could be cut off at several points and still make sense. Both Sentence 1 and Sentence 3 are periodic. In other words, they do not complete the main clause until the end of the sentence, until they get close to the period (thus the name). Neither could be cut off earlier and make sense.

Most English sentences are loose, especially in speech and informal writing. Even in more formal contemporary writing, there is a strong trend toward more loose sentences. Such sentences often start generally and are sharpened by progressively finer details. Notice the honing that occurs in the second sample sentence. The sentence begins with the artist drawing one turtle and then another, pans to the resulting pileup of turtles, moves in on individual turtles that stand on each other's backs, closer in on the hanging heads, and still closer in on the pained looks. Such sentences move with an easy, natural rhythm. Most also have a clear progression as each detail becomes sharper than the last.

Since end position is considered climactic and thus the strongest position in an English sentence, periodic arrangement is most emphatic. Although used sparingly by modern writers, such sentences pack a punch. Notice how the first sample sentence builds momentum. By beginning with the afternoon in 1957 with someone bent over a drawing board, the writer gives the reader time to wonder a little. This anticipation builds a mild suspense that carries the reader along and gives extra emphasis to the fact that Theodor Seuss Geisel found himself drawing a turtle.

In Sentence 3, the main clause works like a sandwich to hold all the details in the middle together. Notice that the first two words in the sentence are the subject; the predicate is deferred until the very end. Anticipation of what is to be said about the subject propels the reader along, letting the intervening details fall into place along the way. Though such a sentence pattern is not commonplace, it is most effective.

One way to increase your repertoire of sentence patterns is to practice sentence-expansion. This time, you will expand base sentences by imitating models.

Example:

Base Sentence: ⎯⎯ heard thousands screaming his name.

Model Sentence: One afternoon in 1957, as he bent over the big drawing board in his California studio, Theodor Seuss Geisel found himself drawing a turtle.

Expanded Sentence: That Sunday at 4:32, when he broke for a new rushing record in the Houston Astrodome, Earl Campbell heard thousands screaming his name.

Notice how the expanded sentence follows the grammatical pattern of the model. Notice also that the blank in the base sentence has been filled in with the name *Earl Campbell*. Blanks in the base sentences will allow you to choose your own subjects and thus write about someone or something you know in detail.

Write expanded versions of the base sentences that follow, making each follow the grammatical pattern of the model sentence:

1. **Base Sentence:**   ⎯⎯ turns away from ⎯⎯ and scowls.
    Model Sentence: Geisel looks up from his drawing board and smiles—just a little, because a man is taking his picture and he has never gotten used to people who want to take his picture.

2. **Base Sentence:** ____ has (have) attracted 10,000 fans to only one ____ .

   Model Sentence: Since 1936, when Ted Geisel the advertising illustrator first wrote *And to Think That I Saw It on Mulberry Street*, his books have sold 80 million copies in this country alone.

3. **Base Sentence:** ____ and ____ found ____ and ____ .

   Model Sentence: At the very top of one of the mountains, with the diminishing acres of wild land to the east and to the west the wide blue curve of the Pacific, Geisel and his wife Audrey share an old stucco observatory tower and the elegant, helter-skelter maze of rooms they have built around it.

4. **Base Sentence:** The ____ are ____, ____ creatures.

   Model Sentence: He is a private, engaging, intensely driven man, with a lean and sharp-nosed look that gives him an air of severity at first.

5. **Base Sentence:** ____ has vacationed for two weeks in ____ .

   Model Sentence: Geisel has lived for 30 years in La Jolla, which is a coastal town just north of San Diego that has developed a flowery, almost Caribbean sparkle as the wealthy build homes up the side of the mountain.

Share your expanded sentences with a small group of classmates. Do all sentences follow the appropriate model? Do subordinate elements add sharp, interesting detail? Are all sentences clear?

Together, choose the best expansion of each base sentence. After reconvening as a class, compare the expansions chosen by each group for Base Sentence 1, Base Sentence 2, etc. Also decide which sentences are loose and which are periodic. What patterns seem especially effective?

This exercise has pushed you to work with sentence patterns that you might not discover otherwise. In the process, you have learned to handle some new constructions. Later, you will practice expanding sentences *without* a model, embedding subordinate details in any way you wish.

That, of course, is one thing you will do in revising your feature story. Find sentences that seem thin. Embed specific details that will give those sentences a rich texture and add body to the story as a whole. Remember journalist Roy Peter Clark's statement that a story has substance only if it has "the interesting facts, the details, the quotations, the descriptions, and the anecdotes." When you inject detail into your sentences, the effect is more than cosmetic.

Working Toward Independence

In revising your feature story, you will want to apply everything you have learned so far in this unit. A quick review will help you recall techniques you have practiced and see how they all fit together.

In this chapter and the previous one, you have concentrated on transactional writing—that is, on audience-centered writing that is intended to get something done. First, you recorded an oral documentary for an audience of your own classmates. Your purpose was to pass on what you had been told. Now, you are in the process of writing a feature story to inform and entertain a larger and more diverse audience, such as the readership of your local newspaper.

You have learned that writing is more demanding than face-to-face conversation because the audience is more remote. For that reason, you have worked on *shaping* your message. You have strained out trivial or irrelevant details that might distract, and you have highlighted details that help make key points. You have grouped details that go together so that your presentation will be logically organized. You have worked on beginnings that will hook the reader and establish the focus of the whole piece. You have also learned to write from a third-person point of view so that you will not come between reader and subject. You have learned to keep the sequence clear by using accurate and consistent verb tense.

Just as the major emphasis of Unit I was on pre-writing (collecting and developing material), the major emphasis of this unit has been on drafting (getting that material down on paper in full, preliminary form). The paper takes shape as it is drafted, but that shape is rough. In writing first drafts, you have considered focus, selection of details, organization, and point of view. But the big push at this stage has been to get idea down on paper and to explore those ideas fully.

Final shaping takes place as a paper is revised. Once words have been captured, they can be read critically. As a writer, you can look back and decide what needs to be added, deleted, substituted, and rearranged so that the piece will be as clear and interesting to its audience as possible.

In this unit, you have worked on both word choice and sentence structure. During revision, you have learned to spot words that are vague or empty and to substitute more explicit ones. You have learned to make sentences more concise by cutting out redundancy, by using the simplest possible constructions, and by omitting phrases that add no meaning. By practicing both sentence-combining and sentence-expanding, you have learned to pack lots of detail into each unit of thought. In the process, you have learned to put the most important idea of a sentence into the main clause and to subordinate less important ideas. You have also learned to link coordinate elements appropriately and to underscore the balance of such elements by making them grammatically parallel. By combining and expanding sentences according to prescribed patterns, you have practiced constructions that you probably don't use in everyday speech or writing, and that may add color and variety to your sentences.

Before revising your feature story, take a few minutes to scan this chapter and the preceding one. Turn to the section of your Writer's Notebook titled **Notes on the Writing Process** and add to the entries you made earlier. For example, under "Pre-writing Strategies" you might add *conducting interviews.* Since this unit has concentrated on how to shape material into a fully developed draft, most of your notes will probably go under "Guidelines for Drafting." Some will go under "Guidelines for Revision." By continuing to maintain this log of writing techniques, you will clinch your understanding of new approaches and fit them into context. Reviewing these notes will help prepare you for new writing tasks. Right now, updating your notes should refresh your memory on techniques to apply in revising your feature story.

Getting It Right

Reread the first draft of your feature story as if you were reading it for the first time in the pages of a local paper. Does it hold attention? Does it have substance? Look at the big picture and make any changes you think would help the overall effect. Review the suggestions made by the classmates who read your story. Follow the suggestions that seem helpful. Also apply the criteria comprising Checkpoint 2 on page 116. Make any changes that make your story meet those criteria; work with content and organization first. Then tighten individual sentences to eliminate wordiness, sharpen word choice, enrich detail, and increase variety. After you have pencilled in changes, read through the whole piece to check the overall effect.

As you make a final draft, remember to edit carefully. Newspapers can't afford too many lapses in usage, mechanics, or spelling. ● If you aren't sure about a word or sentence, consult a classmate, your teacher, or the appropriate section of your Writer's Handbook. Before you hand in your paper, you may wish to exchange stories with a friend for a final proofreading. Keep in mind that Checkpoint 2 on page 116 will be used to evaluate your work.

Once your paper has been evaluated and returned, you will probably want to share it. One possibility is a class bulletin board. Another is to submit your feature story to the school newspaper for possible publication or to save it for entry in a writing contest. Don't forget to make a copy for the person you wrote about.

CHECKPOINT 2

1	2	3	4	5

Reporting   ×4=

Your story doesn't say enough. Where are your facts, details, quotations?

You are getting there. Dig up a few more specifics to flesh out an essentially sound story.

Ace reporting! Solid story full of sharp observations, quotations, anecdotes, and facts.

Audience Appeal   ×4=

Headline and lead too bland. Not enough human interest. Try for some punch.

With a little work, headline and lead will hook most readers. Work human interest angle harder.

Wide appeal from headline to closing sentence. Strong in both clarity and pizzazz.

Organization   ×4=

Hard to follow. Try finding a natural starting point and then asking, "What comes next?" Number parts, and let's talk through paper.

Story flows fairly well. You've organized into logical parts. Check connections. Also check for sentences that seem out of place. Reading aloud will help.

Careful planning paid off. Every sentence and paragraph leads smoothly and logically to the next. What a well-wrought piece!

Point of View   ×2=

Use of "I" distracts. Stay out of picture and speak in third person.

Consistently third person. That's good. Check verb tense for accuracy and consistency.

You've got it! Third-person, present-tense perspective sharp and consistent.

Conciseness   ×2=

Too much padding. Look for wasted words and chop them out.

Good job. No redundancies; just a few empty phrases and unnecessarily long constructions. Tighten up a little and you'll have it.

Lean, muscular prose—just right for a newspaper where every inch counts.

Sentence Structure   ×2=

Sentences don't contain enough detail. Review last Workbench and try some expanding. Break up those monotonous patterns.

Sentences have the right emphasis; you've subordinated details well. Try packing in a few more and varying structure—for instance, a periodic sentence here and there.

Sentences are rich with embedded detail. Emphasis right. Lots of variety.

Usage and Mechanics   ×2=

Copy needs a clean-up. Let's schedule an editing session.

Story is almost ready to go public. Have a classmate help you check for the few lapses in usage, punctuation, capitalization, or spelling.

Ready to go to press! Form, spelling, capitalization, punctuation, and usage show thorough editing. Good clean copy.

Chapter 6

Recording Contemporary History

Has it ever occurred to you that the six-o'clock news is really history? Do you realize that the front page of your daily newspaper is also history? Actually, any chronological report of significant events is history. It doesn't matter whether those events happened yesterday or a thousand years ago.

Your generation is one of the first to grow up as eye-witnesses to history. In your own living room, you have watched rockets being fired ever deeper into space, presidents being inaugurated, and sometimes even wars being fought. To you, those events can never be reduced to one-liners in a history book. Whether you realize it or not, many of the sights, sounds, and feelings surrounding those events will remain with you.

Not all of the history unfolding around you each day makes the six-o'clock news. Events can be significant without being dramatic; obscure people quietly do things that make a little bit of difference. The difference may be positive or negative. It may be in medicine or education, fashion design or entertainment. Nothing stands still— including values and lifestyles. All of this is history in the making, and it is happening where you are.

One way to participate more fully in everyday history is to write about it. Some of America's most popular writers have become so engrossed in chronicling the here-and-now that they have given up fiction altogether. As you have seen in previous chapters, their writing is often called "new journalism;" *new* because it didn't appear until the 1960s and *journalism* because it involves the kind of factual reporting found in newspapers and magazines.

Actually, the new journalists go far beyond reporting. They probe beneath the surface of a subject. They fill their accounts with so many revealing and often dramatic details that the effect is much like fiction. The reader gets caught up with the people and events being described. Many times, characterizations of real people seem as vivid and as memorable as those in any novel.

In this chapter, you will borrow some writing techniques from the new journalists. You will also practice and extend some of the approaches you have already learned for gathering material, shaping it for an audience, and revising it into a polished piece. In the process, you will concentrate on establishing a strong point of view and maintaining a consistent tone of voice. If you impose your own slant and speak in your own voice, the resulting perspective will set your reports apart from all other accounts of the same events.

Striking the Right Tone

Tone is mainly a reflection of attitude toward the subject—whether the writer is earnest or flippant, whimsical or matter-of-fact, bitter or optimistic. It is also a matter of how formal or informal the writer sounds.

Tone is easier to recognize than it is to describe. Read the two passages that follow. Both describe the homecoming of astronauts after journeys into space. The first was written in 1968, just after the crew of Apollo 8 returned from the first flight around the moon. The second is a more recent retrospective account of an earlier event, the reception given John Glenn after his first orbital flight around the earth.

> Those who stayed behind, families and colleagues, neighbors and wide-eyed schoolchildren, greeted the returning Apollo 8 astronauts here early December 29 with a warm embrace of pride and awe.
>
> More than 3,000 people stood on the runway at the Ellington Air Force Base when the Air Force C-141 jet transport plane landed at 3:12 A.M., Eastern standard time, with the relaxed and smiling moon explorers—Colonel Borman, Captain Lovell and Major Anders.
>
> A reddish half-moon hung low over the dark horizon, as if waiting for the astronauts' safe return, before dropping out of sight for another night. It was cold and starry, but few noticed.

> Al Sheppard and Gus Grissom didn't know what was happening. Poor Gus—all he had gotten after his flight was a medal, a handshake, a gust of rhetoric from James Webb, out on a brain-frying

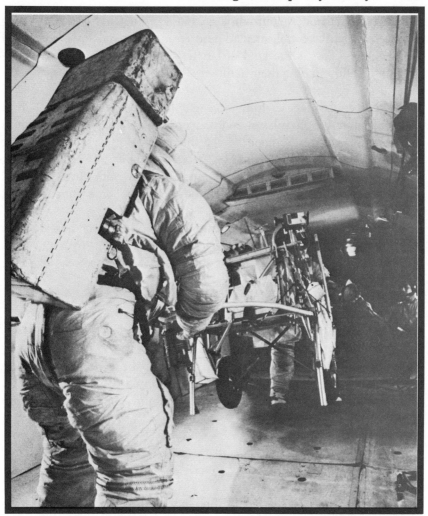

strip of asphalt at Patrick Air Force Base, plus a few attaboys from a
crowd of about thirty. For John—well, the mobs that had showed up
for the launch, for the fireworks, barely seemed to have thinned out
at all. Cocoa Beach was still full of the crazy adrenalin of the event.
Out-of-towners were still tooling around all over the place in their
automobiles and asking where the astronauts hung out. They didn't
want to miss a thing.

Although these two passages describe similar events, one is a great deal
more formal than the other. The first, which appeared in a commemora-
tive issue of *Look Magazine,* describes the homecoming scene with
dignity. The astronauts are referred to as Colonel Borman, Captain

Lovell, and Major Anders—not as Frank, Jim, and Bill. Sentence structure is fairly complicated. There is no slang and little novelty of word choice. This is the kind of language people speak when they are dressed up and minding their manners. It is not stiff or pompous, but it is careful and proper.

The second passage, from a recent book by new journalist Tom Wolfe, is much more relaxed and conversational. It calls the astronauts by their first names. Sentences have the rhythm of everyday talk. The account is peppered with slang like "attaboy," "hang out," and "tooling around." It uses contractions and doesn't shy away from novelty. This is the kind of language people use when they put on old blue jeans and relax with good friends.

Good writers have tact. They know when to be formal and when to be informal. Also, they know how to be consistent. Imagine for a moment that the opening sentence of the *Look* article had read like this:

> Those who stayed behind, families, and colleagues, neighbors and
> school *kids*, greeted the returning Apollo 8 astronauts here early
> December 29 with a warm *hug* of pride and awe.

Although synonyms for *children* and *embrace*, the words *kids* and *hug* jangle. They are much too colloquial for a formal context.

Imagine, on the other hand, that the third sentence of the Tom Wolfe piece had read like this:

> For John—well, the *multitudes* that had showed up for the launch,
> for the fireworks, barely seemed to have *dissipated* at all.

Here, the situation is reversed. Although *multitude* and *dissipated* have the same meaning as *mob* and *thinned out*, they seem much too heavy for such a breezy context.

As a writer, you need a good ear for both formal and informal language. Though you must be careful to avoid careless or inappropriate mixtures of the two, you must also realize that formality and informality are not absolutes. Teacher/writer Donald Hall explains the continuum this way: "We would write more easily if we could think of prose as either informal or formal, as if nothing existed between the poles. But most good prose lives in the temperate regions on either side of the equator."

Even so, it is a good idea to make some clear distinctions, especially in terms of vocabulary. The next exercise will provide practice in selecting words for their formality or informality and in using these words in an appropriate context.

Writer's Workbench 1

Levels of Diction

Diction (word choice) is basic for any writer. The fact that English offers a veritable supermarket of synonyms makes control of diction even more challenging—and more crucial—than it might be in other languages. Although synonyms carry almost the same meaning, they are not usually interchangeable. This may be due to different levels of formality. Study the fifteen word groups below. Each group consists of four synonyms ranging from formal to informal.

1. crowd
   mob
   host
   multitude

2. uproar
   tumult
   disturbance
   commotion

3. speech
   address
   oration
   talk

4. cry
   weep
   bawl
   sob

5. false
   fraudulent
   counterfeit
   fake

6. vow
   pledge
   promise
   oath

7. courage
   valor
   bravery
   pluck

8. top
   peak
   summit
   pinnacle

9. elaborate
   ornate
   embellished
   fancy

10. praise
    kudos
    accolades
    commendation

11. spectator
    viewer
    observer
    onlooker

12. tale
    narrative
    anecdote
    story

13. dirt
    soil
    earth
    loam

14. decay
    rot
    moulder
    decompose

15. humorous
    amusing
    comic
    funny

A. Draw a vertical line on a sheet of paper to make two columns. Head one column **Most Formal** and the other **Most Informal**. Down the left-hand margin, number 1–15. Opposite each number, write in the appropriate column the word from each set that you consider the most formal and the word you consider the most informal. When you have finished, compare your choices with those of your classmates. Discuss any discrepancies.

B. Using a very informal level of language, write several sentences about some event you have observed—perhaps a parade, a campaign rally, an awards ceremony, or a holiday celebration. Use at least five words from the preceding list that you identified as being most informal.

C. Rewrite your account of the special event using a very formal level of language. Substitute at least five of the words you identified as being most formal.

D. Share both accounts with a small group of classmates. See whether all words seem to fit. Does the informal account seem relaxed and conversational without being ungrammatical or careless? Do sentences sound like everyday speech? Do sentences in the formal account sound more like the written English you find in school textbooks? Does this account avoid contractions and slang?

Often, the origin of a word helps account for its level of formality. Many words that came into the language from Latin seem formal. Examples from the list on page 123 include *multitude, tumult, oration, fraudulent, valor, summit, elaborate, accolades, spectator, narrative,* and *humorous.* As you may know, Latin is a classical language that flourished in the days of the Roman Empire. Some Latin words—especially those related to religion and law—were absorbed into English very early when Roman missionaries came to the British Isles. The greatest infusion of Latin words came much later when the Norman invaders occupied England, beginning in 1066. Since the conquerers spoke French, which is a Romance (Latinate) language, and since they mingled for many years with the people they conquered, their effect upon the language was dramatic. Some linguists estimate that more than half of all English words have their roots in Latin.

Many less formal words date back to Old English, the language that evolved when Germanic tribes, especially the Angles and the Saxons, settled in what is now England more than fifteen hundred years ago. Compare these words originating from Old English to the words you just noticed were derived from Latin: *crowd, false, pluck, top, onlooker, dirt,* and *rot.* Such short, simple words are typical of Old English. They still comprise the basic word-stock of the language we speak and write in America.

Some informal words originate as slang or corrupted versions of more formal expressions. *Fake*, for example, was strictly slang until it gradually entered the mainstream of the language. *Mob* is a drastically shortened form of the Latin phrase *mobile vulgus*, meaning "vacillating crowd." *Kudos* is a corruption of an old Greek word (kydos); *funny*, a dialectal variation of the Middle English word *fond*, meaning "a fool."

Writers can choose words appropriately without the slightest acquaintance with etymology. On the other hand, insights into the background of words can heighten sensitivity to language. Whether the writer uses such insights or works just by intuition, the important point is to maintain a consistent level of diction in every piece of writing.

The choice between a formal and an informal level of diction usually depends upon subject, audience, and occasion. It also depends upon purpose. Both passages you read earlier were about astronauts returning from exploits in space. Both were for mass audiences. The article reporting the return of the Apollo 8 crew, however, was written for a special issue of *Look Magazine*. Because the purpose of that special issue was to celebrate as well as report America's accomplishments in space, the tone was formal. The account of the reception for John Glenn is from *The Right Stuff*, a book in which Tom Wolfe not only reports the exploits of the astronauts, but also explores their personalities and analyzes the way they were transformed into popular heroes. Because he focuses on the human story behind the headlines, he can afford to be informal.

Tone, of course, is more than a matter of whether diction is formal or informal. It is also a matter of attitude. The authors of the *Look* article treated their subject admiringly; Tom Wolfe treated his irreverently. Both formal and informal prose can be matter-of-fact, bitter, amused, nostalgic, or proud. It all depends upon the author's attitude.

SPOTLIGHT

The following excerpt from Tom Wolfe's *The Right Stuff* comes from a chapter about the physical and psychological testing required of prospective astronauts. This part of the book tells what went on behind the scenes just before the original astronauts were chosen for the Mercury project. As you read the account, notice how the author's attitude colors not only choice of words but also choice of details.

Pete Conrad, being an alumnus of Princeton and the Philadelphia Main Line, had the standard E.S.A. charm and command of the proprieties. E.S.A was 1950's Princeton club code for "Eastern Socially Attractive." E.S.A. qualities served a man well in the Navy, where refinement in the officer ranks was still valued. Yet Conrad remained, at bottom, the Hickory Kid. He had the same combination of party manners and Our Gang scrappiness that his wife, Jane, had found attractive when she met him six years before. Now, in 1959, at the age of twenty-eight, Conrad was still just as wirily built, five feet six and barely 140 pounds, still practically towheaded, and he had the same high-pitched nasal voice, the same collegiate cackle when he laughed, and the same Big Weekend grin that revealed the gap between his two front teeth. Nevertheless, people gave him room. There was an old-fashioned Huck Finn hickory-stick don't-cross-that-line-or-I'll-crawl-you streak in him. Unlike a lot of pilots, he tended to say exactly what was on his mind when aroused. He couldn't stand being trifled with. Consequently, he seldom was.

That was Conrad. Add the normal self-esteem of the healthy young fighter jock making his way up the mighty ziggurat—and the lab rat's revolt was probably in the cards from the beginning. . . .

At Wright-Patterson Air Force Base where they went for the

psychological and stress testing, psychiatrists were running the show. . . . They took notes in little spiral notebooks. Every gesture you made, every tic, twitch, smile, stare, frown, every time you rubbed your nose—there was some White Smock standing by jotting it down in a notebook.

One of the most assiduous of the monitors was a psychologist, a woman named Dr. Gladys J. Loring—as Conrad could tell from the nameplate on her smock. Gladys J. Loring was beginning to annoy him intensely. Every time he turned around she seemed to be standing there staring at him, without a word, staring at him with utter White Smock detachment, as if he were a frog, a rabbit, a rat, a gerbil, a guinea pig, or some other lab animal, scribbling furiously in her notebook. For days she had been watching him, and they had never even been introduced. One day Conrad suddenly looked her straight in the eye and said: "Gladys! What . . . are . . . you . . . writing . . . in . . . your . . . notebook!"

Dr. Gladys J. Loring looked at him as if he were a flatworm. All she did was make another notation of the specimen's behavior in her notebook. . . .

In one test the interviewer gave each candidate a blank sheet of paper and asked him to study it and describe what he saw in it. There was no one right response in this sort of test, because it was designed to force the candidate to free-associate in order to see where his mind wandered. The test-wise pilot knew that the main thing was to stay on dry land and not go swimming. As they described with some relish later on in the BOQ [Bachelor Officers Quarters], quite a few studied the sheet of paper and looked the interviewer in the eye and said, "All I see is a blank sheet of paper." This was not a "correct" answer, since the shrinks probably made a note of "inhibited imaginative capacity" or something, but neither did it get you in trouble. One man said, "I see a field of snow." Well, you might get away with that, as long as you didn't go any further . . . as long as you did not thereupon start ruminating about freezing to death or getting lost in the snow and running into bears or something of the sort. But Conrad . . . well, the man is sitting across the table from Conrad and gives him the sheet of paper and asks him to study it and tell him what he sees. Conrad stares at the piece of paper and then looks at the man and says in a wary tone, as if he fears a trick: "But it's upside down."

This so startles the man, he actually leans across the table and looks at the absolutely blank sheet of paper to see if it's true—and only after he is draped across the table does he realize that he has been had. He looks at Conrad and smiles a smile of about 33 degrees Fahrenheit. . . .

The next day, after the heat-chamber test, in which he spent three hours shut up in a cubicle heated to 130 degrees, Conrad was rubbing the sweat off the end of his nose when he looked up—and sure enough, Dr. Gladys J. Loring was right there, making note of the event in her spiral notebook with a ballpoint pen. Conrad reached into the pocket of his pants . . . and came up with a spiral notebook and a ballpoint pen just like hers.

"Gladys!" he said. She looked up. She was startled. Conrad started scribbling in his notebook and then looked at her again. "Aha! You touched your ear, Gladys! We call that inhibition of the exhibitionism!" More scribbling in the notebook. "Oh-oh! Lowering of the eyes, Gladys! Repressed hypertrophy of the latency! I'm sorry, but it has to go in the report!"

Word of how the flatworm turned . . . how the lab rat had risen up . . . how Pavlov's dog rang Pavlov's bell and took notes on it . . . oh, word of all this circulated quickly, too, and everyone was quite delighted. There was no indication, however, then or later, that Dr. Gladys Loring was amused in the slightest. . . .

Conrad was back home in North Town Creek, back at Pax River, when the letter from NASA arrived. He knew he had played it very smoothly during the testing . . . Still, he had spoken his mind before and it had never hurt him. His career in the Navy had gone up on a steady curve. He had never been left behind. So he opened the letter.

From the very first line he knew the rest. The letter noted that he had been among the finalists in the selection process and said he was to be commended for that. Alas, it went on, he had not been one of the seven chosen for the assignment, but NASA and one & all were grateful to him for volunteering and so forth and so on . . .

Not too long afterward, Conrad was told that across the master sheet on top of his file at Wright-Patterson had been written: "Not suitable for long-duration flight."

Before trying your own hand at writing some contemporary history in the manner of the new journalism, consider these questions:

1. On a scale of one (all-out informality) to ten (extreme formality), where would you place this piece? Why? (Consider word choice, sentence structure, degree of novelty, and anything else you think contributes.)

2. What word best describes the way Wolfe seems to feel about Pete Conrad? about psychiatrists/psychologists in general and Glayds J. Loring in particular? about Conrad's rejection as a candidate for the Mercury crew? Find words and details that reflect these feelings.

3. What word best describes the overall tone of the chapter? Explain, pointing to specific details and word choices.

4. In *The Right Stuff,* Wolfe brings recent history alive by piling detail upon detail.

    a. Look at the sentence "He had the same combination of party manners and Our Gang scrappiness that his wife, Jane, had found attractive when she met him six years before." Why is this sentence far more lively and more informative than "He had the same combination of gentility and aggressiveness that women had always found attractive"? Find other sentences with particularly striking details.

    b. When writers want to telegraph a great deal in few words, they sometimes use allusions—in other words, brief references to real or fictitious people, events, and places they expect their readers to know. The mention of Our Gang is an allusion. So are references to Huck Finn and Pavlov's dog. What does each contribute? In using such references, what is Wolfe assuming about the audience that will buy and read his book?

    c. This account comes from a chapter titled "The Lab Rat." Find other mentions of rats and other animals used as laboratory specimens. How does this repetition enhance unity? What else does it contribute?

5. *The Right Stuff* is based on six years' careful research including interviews with astronauts, review of official documents, and extensive background reading. The book rests upon a solid foundation of fact, but it reads like fiction. Wolfe doesn't hesitate to invent dialogue, flesh out scenes with imaginative details, and eavesdrop on the thoughts of his characters. Find examples of such embellishments. What do they add?

6. Wolfe reports in the third person. He refers to all characters, including Conrad, as *he* or *she.* Yet, the events at Wright-Patterson are so strongly slanted that the reader sees things through Conrad's eyes.

    a. Reread the paragraph beginning "One of the most assiduous monitors. . . ." How might this paragraph read if it were slanted to reflect Dr. Loring's point of view?

    b. In what other parts of the chapter does the reader assume Conrad's point of view?

Not all of the new journalists write like Tom Wolfe. Neither should you. But you can use some of the same techniques without resorting to imitation. The next series of activities will help you do just that.

～～～～～～～～～～～～～～～～～～～～～～～～～～～～～

Getting It Started

In the early 1980's, this tiny piece of contemporary history appeared in at least one American newspaper:

Charles' fiancee prepares to learn royal etiquette

LONDON (AP)—Lady Diana Spencer, who will marry Prince Charles after her 20th birthday this summer, got her first lesson in royal etiquette Wednesday over breakfast with Queen Mother Elizabeth, the prince's grandmother.

Spencer moved into Clarence House, the official London residence of the 80-year-old queen mother, after Buckingham Palace announced the royal wedding plans Tuesday.

A palace spokesman said the royal family chose Clarence House to be Spencer's pre-marriage home because she will be close to people who can instruct her in the dos and don'ts of the strict code of royal conduct. The residence is 200 yards from the palace, where the 32-year-old prince and heir to Britain's throne proposed to her a few weeks ago in his private sitting room.

A palace spokesman said Queen

Mother Elizabeth and Spencer spent "some time" talking about palace life and her summer wedding.

The queen mother, one of Britain's most popular royal figures, went through the adjustment of palace life 58 years ago, when as Lady Elizabeth Bowes-Lyon she married the prince who became King George VI.

Later, Spencer was driven by an armed Scotland Yard bodyguard to the apartment she shared with three girlfriends the past two years to gather some personal belongings.

She ignored a pack of reporters and photographers as she left the building. Her bodyguard toted a brown suitcase.

There was a scuffle between some newsmen and police officers guarding the apartment block and one photographer was arrested after he refused to move from a sidewalk. Hours before, the doorman had fought off muggers who demanded apartment pass keys but police said there was no indication they were specifically trying to gain entrance to Spencer's flat.

A wedding date has not been announced, but the couple said Tuesday it will probably be in late July. Spencer's birthday is July 1.

While Spencer assists in planning the wedding, Charles will be off on a five-week trip to the United States, Venezuela, New Zealand and Australia. He is to leave March 30.

Spencer did not see the prince Wednesday. He left Buckingham Palace early in the morning for a "private engagement."

Palace officials dismissed as "speculation" a report in London's Guardian daily that Queen Elizabeth II will appoint Charles governor-general of Australia after he marries.

The governor-general represents the monarchy in Australia. The post is held by 60-year-old Sir Zelman Cowen, recently appointed.

Study this story or find one you like better. (In selecting your own newspaper story, be sure to find one that includes details about the people involved.)

Since this piece of writing will be mainly for practice, you need not take time to do extensive research. Do take time to jot down details you happen to know about the people, places, and events mentioned in the story. In preparing to write about the above clipping, for example, you might jot down what you know from other sources about Prince Charles, Lady Diana, and Queen Mother Elizabeth. You might even find pictures of them in magazines. You might also jot down anything you know about the customs of British royalty and anything you can learn about Clarence House.

Decide how you feel about the events reported in the news story. For example, do you consider tradition important, or do you consider lessons in royal etiquette outmoded and trivial? If you have a deep respect for tradition, you might write about Lady Diana's preparation for marriage to Prince Charles in a serious, perhaps even admiring tone. In so doing, you would use a fairly formal level of language. On the other hand, if you consider royal etiquette superficial and silly, you might adopt a cynical or flippant tone. In this case, you might use informal language.

Finally, choose one segment of the news story to expand as one of the new journalists might. In preparing to write this brief episode, jot down details that will bring the scene alive. Try snatches of dialogue, sharp descriptive details, perhaps even an allusion or two. Remain faithful to fact, but fill in with details that give your account the rich texture of fiction.

**Getting
It
Down**

Using the notes you have just made, write a brief episode based upon the news story you selected. Build that episode upon a framework of fact, but fill in with imaginative details that are consistent with what you know about the people, places, and events in the story. Choose both words and details to reflect your own attitude. In other words, write in your own voice and in a distinct tone. Use the appropriate level of diction.

**Checking
It
Out**

Share your story with at least three classmates. Begin by having each read the clipping upon which your story is based. After your version has also been read, ask your classmates to respond to these questions:

1. Does the story show responsible reporting? In other words, is it consistent with fact?
2. Though essentially factual, does the story seem as compelling as fiction? What details do most to create a you-are-there immediacy? What parts need to be enriched with more such detail?
3. Does the level of diction seem appropriate? Is language formal or informal? Are there any jarring inconsistencies?
4. What is the overall tone of the piece? Where is the tone most distinct?

Unless your teacher directs otherwise, you need not take this paper into a final draft. Of course, you may have written such a promising story that you want it to go public. If so, you will undoubtedly find the comments of your classmates helpful as you revise. You may want to get more such help as you edit. Even if you leave the paper in rough form, it has served an important purpose. It has provided practice in recounting and interpreting current history, in controlling tone of voice and level of diction, and in fleshing out a factual account with vivid details.

In previous chapters, sentence-combining and sentence-imitation exercises have helped you practice packing sentences with detail. As you have tried new sentence patterns, you have noted the kind of punctuation required for each. Before beginning your next writing project, you will take a brief time-out to deal with a punctuation problem that many writers find particularly troublesome. This exercise will also illustrate control of tone in short pieces written by high school students about events in their own city and in their own school.

Writer's Workbench 2

Punctuating Restrictive and Nonrestrictive Elements

You have already learned that subordinate sentence parts sharpen the main clause of a sentence. Several kinds of subordinate elements can sharpen the meaning of nouns. Adjectives and prepositional phrases are among the most common. Fortunately, they pose few punctuation problems. Commas are required only when two or more adjectives precede the same noun or when an introductory prepositional phrase needs to be followed by a distinct pause.

Other subordinate elements used with nouns are harder to punctuate. There is, however, a simple rule of thumb that will tell you when commas are needed and when they are not. Study the alternate versions of these three sentences and see whether you can infer the rule:

> Houston, known as the Golden Buckle on the Sunbelt, has a problem.
> The city known as the Golden Buckle on the Sunbelt has a problem.

> Heavy traffic, which snarls freeways in all metropolitan areas, threatens to bring the nation's fifth largest city to a halt.
> The congestion which snarls freeways in all metropolitan areas threatens to bring the nation's fifth largest city to a halt.

Even Los Angeles, Houston's western counterpart, is not faced
with accommodating 375 additional cars each day.
Even Houston's western counterpart Los Angeles is not faced
with accommodating 375 additional cars each day.

Review the first sentence in each pair. If the phrase or clause set off by
commas in each is omitted, that sentence is still clear:

Houston has a problem.
Heavy traffic threatens to bring the nation's fifth largest city to a
halt.
Even Los Angeles is not faced with accommodating 375 additional cars each day.

In each case, the noun about which the phrase or clause gives additional
detail is specific enough to stand alone. No additional words are needed
to *restrict* meaning. The phrase or clause, though interesting and
important, is nonessential.

The opposite is true of the second sentence in each pair. If the phrase
or clause following the noun is omitted, each sentence seems vague and
unclear:

The city has a problem.

The congestion threatens to bring the nation's fifth largest city to a halt.

Even Houston's western counterpart is not faced with accommodating 375 additional cars each day.

In each case, the noun about which the phrase or clause tells more is very general. What city has a problem? What kind of congestion threatens that city? Which western city is considered its counterpart? Here, the words that have been omitted provide more than interesting sidelights. Those words are essential to *restrict* the meaning of the nouns they follow. For that reason, there is no comma to signal a slight pause. Read each pair of sentences aloud and note the difference.

The rule of thumb to help you punctuate such sentences is this: Use commas to set off nonrestrictive (nonessential) phrases or clauses telling more about nouns; do not use commas to set off restrictive (essential) phrases or clauses telling more about nouns.

Notice that this rule applies to adjectival clauses (often called relative clauses because they begin with a relative pronoun), participial phrases, and appositives. In the first example, *known as the Golden Buckle on the Sunbelt* is a participial phrase. In the second example, *which snarls freeways in all metropolitan areas* is a relative clause. In the third example, *Houston's western counterpart* is an appositive. (● If you need to review these constructions, see pages H-15–20 in the Writer's Handbook.)

A. Write each sentence that follows, inserting the phrase or clause in the position specified. Use commas to set off nonrestrictive elements.

1. The box was delivered last week.
    INSERT   *containing Rockport High School's newest teacher* after *box.*

2. Scarcely after being unpacked and plugged in, this electronic teacher was tagged with the appropriate nickname.
    INSERT   *Merlin* after *nickname.*

3. His wizardry goes beyond math.
    INSERT   *the subject he teaches more than sixty students a day* after *math.*

4. He recognizes every name.
    INSERT   *typed on his keyboard* after *name.*

5. He never loses his temper with students.
   INSERT   *who miss the same problem three times* after *students.*

6. His face remains benignly neutral as it flashes the words.
   INSERT   *a cathode ray tube* after *face.*
   INSERT   *"Try again!"* after *words.*

7. Even students report feeling relaxed with Merlin.
   INSERT   *who admit suffering severe math anxiety* after *students.*

8. More advanced students never become bored.
   INSERT   *pushing to see how far and how fast they can go* after *students.*

9. So far, this new teacher's only problem is that he doesn't have time for everyone.
   INSERT   *who wants tutoring* after *everyone.*

10. Rumor has it that more electronic teachers will be delivered to Rockport before next September.
    INSERT   *built to Merlin's specifications* after *teachers.*

Check your sentences against the models provided by your teacher. Get help with any examples that may have confused you. • If you need further explanation, consult pages H-15–20 of the Writer's Handbook.

B. Review both sets of student sentences used as examples in this exercise. Consider how well the writers controlled tone. The three sentences about traffic problems in Houston have a somber, almost urgent tone. What word choices convey this attitude? How would you describe the tone of the piece about computerized math instruction? In other words, how does the writer seem to feel about Merlin? How can you tell?

Assuming a Point of View

In the autobiographical writing you did earlier in this course, you undoubtedly used a first-person point of view. In other words, you spoke of yourself as *I* or *me*. Since you were your own subject, you offered the reader an insider's view.

When you write about others, as you have in this unit, you most often assume a third-person point of view. In other words, you speak of the people you write about as *he* or *she*. Yours is an outsider's view. Unless you choose to write yourself in as a first-person observer, you stay out of a story about other people. You have already learned that oral documentaries and feature stories, for example, assume a third-person *objective* point of view in which the narrator acts as an anonymous reporter, relating only what can be seen or heard.

New journalists like Tom Wolfe also write from a third-person point of view, but that point of view is not objective. Often, it borders on *omniscient*—in other words, all-knowing. Wolfe's account of the "lab rat's revolt" (page 125) goes beyond details that could have been observed by the most alert reporter visiting Wright-Patterson. (And remember: the story was constructed years later!) He interprets the motives and feelings of both doctors and astronauts. He tells exactly what Pete Conrad was thinking when he got his rejection letter. In fact, the entire account is slanted to reflect Conrad's view of events. It is the irrepressible Hickory Kid with whom the reader identifies throughout.

As you will see in the next unit, understanding how point of view works can help you become a better reader as well as a better writer. It is not enough to distinguish between first- and third-person points of view. Variations of each occur in both fiction and nonfiction. Learning to choose and maintain an interesting point of view in your own writing will give you a head start reading all kinds of literature.

One point of view you might like to try is *third-person limited omniscient*. At first glance, the words *limited* and *omniscient* seem contradictory. If *omniscient* means *all-knowing*, how can such a point of view be *limited*? The only limitation lies in filtering thoughts and observations through the consciousness of a single character. The concluding episode of *The Right Stuff* provides a good example. Here again, Wolfe assumes an all-knowing point of view, but he limits details to those that would be perceived by one person, a test pilot named Yeager. This slanting gives the episode a sharp focus and provides a strong point of identification for the reader.

SPOTLIGHT

The following passage recounts the near-tragic failure of Yeager's historic attempt to pilot an experimental aircraft to an altitude above 100,000 feet. Before reading this episode, you should know that Tom Wolfe considers Chuck Yeager the embodiment of "the right stuff" for which the book is named. Early in the book, he has identified the well-known test pilot as "the most righteous of all the possessors of the right stuff." As you read, look for qualities that might have earned Yeager this honor. Also notice how different the tone of this account is from that of the excerpt you read earlier.

Yeager hasn't bailed out of an airplane since the day he was shot down over Germany when he was twenty . . . I've tried A!—I've tried B!—I've tried C!—11,000 feet, 7,000 from the farm . . . He hunches himself into a ball, just as it says in the manual, and reaches under the seat for the cinch ring and pulls . . . He's exploded out of the cockpit with such force it's like a concussion . . . He can't see . . . *Wham* . . . a jolt in the back . . . It's the seat separating from him and the parachute rig. . . . His head begins to clear . . . He's in midair, in his pressure suit, looking out through the visor of his helmet . . . Every second enormously elongated . . . infinite . . . such slow motion . . . He's suspended in midair . . . weightless . . . The ship had been falling at about 100 miles an hour and the ejection rocket had propelled him up at 90 miles an hour. For one thick adrenal moment he's weightless in midair, 7,000 feet above the desert . . . The seat floats nearby, as if the two of them are parked in the atmosphere . . . The butt of the seat, the underside, is facing him . . . a red hole . . . the socket where the ejection mechanism had been attached . . . It's dribbling a charcoal red . . .

the remains of the rocket propellant . . . It's glowing . . . it's oozing out of the socket . . . In the next moment they're both falling, him and the seat . . . His parachute rig has a quarter bag over it and on the bag is a drogue chute that pulls the bag off so the parachute will stream out gradually and not break the chute or the pilot's back when the canopy pops open during a high-speed ejection. It's designed for an ejection at 400 or 500 miles an hour, but he's only going about 175. In this infinitely expanded few seconds the lines stream out and Yeager and the rocket seat and the glowing red socket sail through the air together . . . and now the seat is drifting above him . . . into the chute lines! . . . The seat is nestled in the chute lines . . . dribbling lava out of the socket . . . eating through the lines . . . An infinite second . . . He's jerked up by the shoulders . . . it's the chute opening and the canopy filling . . . in that very instant *the lava*—it smashes into the visor of his helmet . . . Something slices through his left eye . . . He's knocked silly . . . The jerk of the parachute had slowed his speed, but the seat kept falling . . . It had fallen out of the chute lines and the butt end crashed into his visor . . . 180 pounds of metal . . . a double visor . . . has smashed through both layers . . . He's burning! . . . There's rocket lava inside the helmet . . . The seat has fallen away . . . He can't see . . . Even with the hole smashed in the visor the helmet is full of smoke . . . He's choking . . . blinded . . . The left side of his head is on fire . . . He's suffocating . . . He brings up his left hand . . . He has on pressure-suit gloves locked and taped to the sleeve . . . He jams his hand in through the hole in the visor and tries to create an air scoop with it to bring air to his mouth . . . The flames . . . They're all over it . . . They go to work on the glove where it touches his face . . . They devour it . . . His index finger is burning up . . . But he doesn't move it . . . Get some air— . . . Nothing else matters . . . It's that or nothing, no two ways about it . . . He jams both hands underneath . . . It's a tremendous effort . . . It lifts . . . Salvation! . . . Like a sea the air carries it all away, the smoke, the flames . . . The fire is out. He can breathe. He can see out of his right eye. The desert, the mesquite, the motherless Joshua trees are rising slowly toward him . . . He can't open his left eye . . . Now he can feel the pain . . . bad . . . Nearly down . . . He gets ready . . . Right out of the manual . . . A terrific wallop . . . He's down on the mesquite, looking across the desert, one-eyed . . . He stands up . . . He's in one piece! . . . He can hardly use his left hand . . . The whole side of his head . . . He starts taking off the parachute harness . . . It's all in the manual! Regulation issue!

. . . He starts rolling up the parachute, just like it says . . . Some of the cords are almost melted through, from the lava . . . His head feels like it's on fire . . . The pain comes from way down deep . . . But he's got to get the helmet off . . . He doesn't dare touch his head . . . It feels enormous . . . Somebody's running toward him . . . It's a kid, a guy in his twenties . . . He's come from the highway . . . He comes up close and his mouth falls open and he gives Yeager a look of stone horror . . .

"You . . . look *awful!*" The Good Samaritan, A.A.D.! Also a Doctor! And he just gave his diagnosis! That's all a man needs . . . to be forty years old and to fall one hundred thousand feet in a flat spin and punch out and make a million-dollar hole in the ground and get half his head burned up and have his eye practically ripped out of his skull . . . and have the Good Samaritan, A.A.D., arrive to render a midnight verdict among the motherless Joshua trees while the screen doors bang and the pictures of a hundred head pilots rattle in their frames:

". . . You look awful."

A few minutes later the rescue helicopter arrived. The medics found Yeager standing out in the mesquite, him and some kid who had been passing by. Yeager was standing erect with his parachute rolled up and his helmet in the crook of his arm, right out of the manual, and staring at them quite levelly out of what was left of his face, as if they had had an appointment and he was on time.

Make notes on your responses to these questions. Then compare your responses to those of several classmates.

1. If Yeager embodies the meaning of the term "the right stuff," what do you think "the right stuff" is? What qualities does the phrase imply? Exactly how does Yeager demonstrate these qualities after he bails out of the doomed plane? What significant phrase is repeated throughout the account of this ordeal?
2. Although Wolfe recounts this episode in the third person, he gives details that only Yeager could know. In what parts is the third-person omniscient point of view the most obvious?
3. Notice that most of the events recounted here unfold in the present tense. How do present-tense verbs make the reader feel closer to the action? At what point do verbs shift to the past tense? What is the effect of this shift?

4. What word best describes the overall tone of this passage? Cite words and details that contribute to this tone.

5. The most common use of the ellipsis (. . .) is to show the omission of one or more words from a direct quotation. Wolfe's abundant use of the ellipsis for a different purpose is unusual. What do you think that purpose might be? What is unusual about sentence structure at points where the ellipsis is most common? Does the device seem to you effective? Why or why not?

In this climactic episode of his book about Amerca's early exploits in space, Tom Wolfe uses a technique basic to good writing of all kinds. He uses concrete detail to breathe meaning into an abstraction.

"The right stuff" is abstract. It is intangible. You can't reach out and touch it. You can't see it or hear it. Such abstractions are hard to grasp. Wolfe could have helped a little by explaining that "the right stuff" is partly cool courage, but courage is also an abstraction. Chuck Yeager, on the other hand, is concrete. Vicariously, you can see what he sees, hear the rush of air as he explodes out of his plane, feel the heat as he battles the flames inside his helmet. You can also stand back and watch the erect figure, helmet held in regulation position, wait calmly for a rescue helicopter. No longer is "the right stuff" an abstraction. You have seen it in action.

In so doing, you have noted an important writing technique—one that is useful not only in such narrative writing as the piece you have just read, but in descriptive, expository, and persuasive writing as well.

Moving Toward Independence

In this chapter, you have assumed the role of contemporary historian. You have taken lessons from one of the new journalists who write factually about the present. From him, you have learned more about rich use of imaginative detail. You have learned to choose and maintain an appropriate level of language and to write in a distinct tone of voice. Finally, you have extended previous work with point of view and use of concrete detail.

The final writing assignment in this chapter will give you a chance to practice all of these techniques. First, take a few minutes to review the chapter and add to the section of your Writer's Notebook reserved for **Notes on the Writing Process**. Under "Pre-writing Strategies," for example, you might add *newspaper clippings*. "Guidelines for Drafting" would be a good place for notes about tone and point of view. Since this chapter has provided no new suggestions for revision, you might review your previous notes on this part of the writing process. The important point is to consolidate what you have just learned with what you have learned previously and in so doing extend your personal repertoire of writing strategies. See how many of those strategies seem applicable to the writing assignment that follows.

This assignment again casts you in the role of contemporary historian. You have already noticed that contemporary historians like Tom Wolfe do more than write chronological summaries of events in their own lifetimes. They sift out what they consider most significant and comment on it. Like sociologists, they analyze and interpret. Wolfe, for example, uses Chuck Yeager as Exhibit A for what is admired not just by America's first astronauts or even by the whole fraternity of flyers. Yeager epitomizes what Americans considered heroic during the late fifties and early sixties as they rallied around the space program with patriotic fervor.

Getting It Started

Heroes provide a good index of social values. Although modern America has been called a nation without heroes, there are still public figures who attract huge crowds and extravagant admiration. Obscure people who exemplify some ideal are often called "unsung heroes." Because they have different values, different groups of Americans have different heroes. Beverly Sills, for example, reflects one set of values; the late John Lennon, another. Both have "unsung" counterparts.

Think of some person, famous or obscure, who might be considered a contemporary hero. Jot down the values that person represents.

What you have just jotted down is abstract. Consider how the person you have chosen has earned the respect of a group that shares his or her values. How, exactly, have these values been demonstrated in larger-than-life proportions? What has the person done that is out of the ordinary?

Choose one incident that sets your hero apart. Jot down details that you have heard or read about it. (If you are writing about an "unsung hero" you know personally, include your own observations.) Then invent and jot down details that you can use to flesh out the bare bones of the account and make it read like fiction.

Finally, decide how formal your level of diction should be in recounting events from the life of your hero. Also consider your own attitude toward the subject. What tone does it suggest? Also decide upon a point of view. Are the thoughts and feelings of your subject important and revealing? If so, you will probably want to use third-person limited omniscient. If not, third-person objective will work just as well.

~~~~~~

Pretend that you have been commissioned to write a short chapter for a book titled *American Heroes of the '80s.* Each chapter is to feature a narrative profile of someone who represents a certain set of current values.

    Recount some episode in which your hero demonstrates the qualities for which he or she is admired. In the style of the new journalism, bring the scene alive with abundant detail. Use the tone and point of view that lend the greatest intensity to your account.

    When you have finished your first draft, give it a title that identifies the heroic quality illustrated in the episode. That title may use abstract words.

**Getting
It
Down**

~~~~~~

Read your "chapter" aloud to a small group of classmates. Without any discussion, ask each member of the group to jot down the word that best captures the set of values or traits exemplified by your own hero. See how well interpretations mesh with each other and with the intention reflected by your title. Try to identify details that might have caused confusion. Ask for suggestions on how to make your point more clearly without resorting to abstract explanations.

    Ask also how your classmates would rate your "chapter" on each criterion comprising Checkpoint 3 on page 145. Take notes to be considered later as you revise your paper.

**Checking
It
Out**

~~~~~~

After reviewing the comments and suggestions of your class-mates, pencil on your rough draft the revisions you wish to make. Then put the paper aside for a while.

    Later, come back and read it for overall effect. Does it do what you intended it to do? Also, measure the paper as it now

**Getting
It
Right**

stands against the criteria by which it will be evaluated. Do you see other improvements that need to be made?

Incorporate these improvements into a final draft. Proofread and edit carefully before handing it in. Be especially alert for any problems with commas to set off nonrestrictive phrases and clauses.

After your teacher evaluates and returns papers, your class may wish to compile them into an anthology titled *American Heroes of the '80s*. If you and your teacher think it is good enough, this scrapbook of contemporary history may be put on display in the school library.

CHECKPOINT 3

1	2	3	4	5

Purpose   ×5=

I can't tell what this episode is supposed to illustrate. Let's talk.

Title tells me what you are trying to show, and you've chosen a good subject. Episode itself needs sharpening or reconsidering.

Even without your title, I could see what your hero stands for. And you didn't resort to abstract explanations!

Detail   ×5=

Your account of this incident is sketchy. Fill in details that show what an observer would have seen and heard. Don't just summarize.

You have the right idea. Most details are concrete and vivid. Add a few more. Would it help to simulate some dialogue?

Keep this up, and Tom Wolfe will see you as a rival! Your details are not only concrete and graphic; they are selected to dramatize what your hero represents.

Tone   ×4=

Read your piece aloud. Can you hear some words that are too formal or too informal? Also try to choose words that will show your attitude toward this person and what he (she) represents.

Level of language is consistent. Good! Read your account aloud in the tone of voice that best shows your attitude toward the subject. Can you insert some words that will show this attitude more distinctly to readers who haven't heard your rendition?

Tone is distinct, appropriate, and consistent. No good reader could have any doubt about your attitude toward this subject. Level of diction seems just right.

Point of View   ×4=

Using *I* makes the story confusing. Use only *he, she, they,* and other third-person pronouns. (See Writer's Handbook, page H-5.)

Third-person point of view remains consistent, but I can't tell whether you intend to be objective or omniscient. Review pages 137–138 and see me if you need help.

You chose just the right point of view and never wavered. Good job!

Usage and mechanics   ×2=

This paper needs a general clean-up. Start with the lines I've checked on your paper. Consult pages of the Writer's Handbook I've noted by each check.

Only a few lapses keep this paper from being a model of standard usage and mechanics. Work on the lines checked on your paper. Don't forget how much the Writer's Handbook can help.

Impeccable. Your attention to usage, form, and mechanics shows respect for your readers as well as pride in your own work.

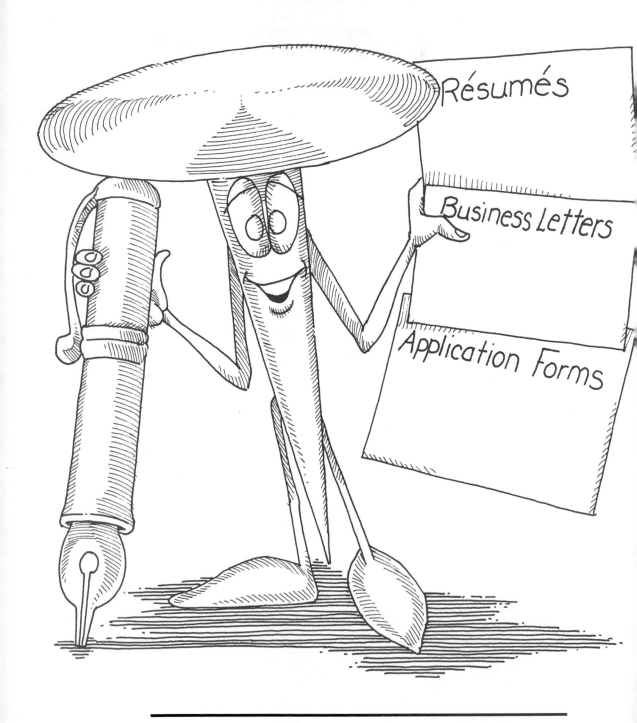

Chapter 7

Getting Down to Brass Tacks

This chapter is about practical writing. It will deal with such tasks as composing business letters, making résumés, and filling in application forms. Because such tasks get down to everyday business, they are sometimes called *brass-tacks writing*. This kind of writing is extremely important because it can help you get things done.

Actually, this entire unit has focused on writing to get things done. Every assignment has been audience-centered. Sometimes your audience has been as immediate and familiar as a group of classmates. At other times, it has been as remote and anonymous as the general leadership of a big newspaper. Sometimes, your purpose has been simply to transmit your own observations to that audience. At other times, your purpose has been persuasive as well as informative. You've tried to get your audience to share your attitudes as well as your observations. Always, you have worked to make connections with your readers. In other words, your writing has been transactional.

Oral documentaries, feature stories, and accounts of contemporary history are certainly not *impractical*. Indeed they are very useful. Practicality is a matter of degree. Letters and job applications get more immediate responses. There is less doubt of success or failure. Furthermore, success or failure of brass-tacks writing hits close to home. It makes a real-life difference.

Many of the skills you have learned in previous chapters are applicable to brass-tacks writing. In working through the assignments that follow, you will sharpen these skills. You will also learn some new techniques, especially techniques of writing plain English, cutting out unnecessary words, and proofreading.

Letters That Get Action

Since telephones have become so commonplace and long-distance rates so affordable, people don't write letters as often as they once did. Still, letters are far from obsolete. When you receive a gift, a note says thank you more convincingly than any telephone call. Written invitations still make a party seem special. Although your grandparents or other far-away relatives may enjoy an occasional long-distance chat, they probably read your letters over and over. Taking time to write shows that you really care. It is no coincidence that many people save letters the way they save photographs.

Although this chapter does not include practice in writing such letters, it may nudge you to catch up on notes to friends and relatives. • If so, you may review matters of form by consulting page H-20 in your Writer's Handbook. Remember that the form of a friendly letter differs in several ways from that of a business letter.

In this chapter, you will concentrate on business letters. Such letters are almost always intended to get action—for example, to get a refund for inferior merchandise, to receive a free booklet, to secure a job interview. Right now, you are getting ready to apply for college admission or for a job, perhaps both. Could there be a better time to practice writing letters that get action?

Though letters are much shorter than most of the pieces you've written during this course, they involve the same process. First, you collect your ideas. Then you shape your message. Finally, you revise and polish that message.

Your first exercise in letter writing will be a group effort. Get ready to participate by taking a couple of minutes to jot down actions that can be prompted by business letters. In each case, be very explicit about what the recipient might be urged to do—for example, vote against a bill in Congress, send a refund, remove an overcharge from a credit account, say "yes" to a speaking engagement. Pool your list of actions with those of your classmates as your teacher makes a composite list on the chalkboard. Identify the actions on the list that would require the most persuasive letters. Together, choose five or six situations for the class to use for practice.

**Getting
It
Started**

Join a small group of classmates interested in writing a practice letter based on *one* of the five or six situations selected by the class. (Other small groups will address the other situations.) First, reach agreement on the purpose of the letter. Exactly what will the recipient of the letter be asked to do?

Next, visualize the recipient of the letter. Put yourself in that person's shoes. What kind of opening line would make a good impression? What kind of opening line would put you off?

Remember that a good first sentence gets right to the point. It tells exactly what the writer is after, but it does so in a way that makes the request sound attractive to the reader as well as to the writer. To strike just the right tone, pretend that you are the recipient of the letter and think "What's in it for me?" For a merchant being urged to buy advertising space in a school yearbook, the benefit might be good will in the community and perhaps some new customers. For a business person being asked to correct an overcharge on a bill, it might be keeping a customer and avoiding the risk of bad public relations. For a city official being invited to visit a high school government class, it might be the opportunity to meet young people with fresh ideas—not to mention a vote in the next election. Of course, if such benefits are stated too quickly or too bluntly, the letter will sound presumptuous.

Keep these points in mind as you experiment with various opening lines. Have a group recorder get them down. Evaluate each and choose the one that does the most appealing job of getting right to the point of the letter.

To get ideas for the body of the letter, do some individual free writing. Begin with the opening line you agreed upon and write non-stop for five minutes. Be guided by only one question: "Why should the recipient of the letter do what he or she is being asked to do?" Write as many reasons as you can. Don't worry about form or even continuity. Just get your ideas down on paper.

When you finish, have a round-robin reading of free writings done by members of the group. Identify the strongest parts so that the recorder can write them down for possible inclusion in the group letter. Discuss ideas from the free writings that might be used in the closing of the letter. Consider especially direct questions and suggestions for immediate action that will get things moving in the direction you want.

SPOTLIGHT

Before drafting your practice letter, study the sample that follows:

```
                        1282 Sand Street
                        Harbor Town, Pennsylvania 16222
                        January 3, 198____


Ms. Alison Wiley
1043 Century Drive
Pittsburgh, Pennsylvania 15260


Dear Ms. Wiley:

    Ever since the filmmaking workshop you
conducted for our media club last spring, we
have been hoping you would return for another
```

session this year. That session is tentatively scheduled for the second Saturday in May, but we could adjust the date if another time would be more convenient for you.

This year, we would like to divide the workshop into two parts, one for beginners and the other for more experienced film makers. A repeat of what you did last year would be perfect for the first group. Those of us who worked with you last year would like you to view a short film we made after your visit and give us suggestions on how we might improve our techniques. If you are able to join us and agree to this arrangement, we would like to plan an all-day meeting. From 9:00—11:00 A.M. you could work with beginners and from 12:30—2:00 P.M. with the more experienced group.

We are extremely eager to have you with us. Would you let us know if we can expect you for our May workshop?

Thank you very much for your consideration.

Sincerely,

Claudette Gilbert

Claudette Gilbert
Program Chair
Shoreline High School Media
Club

Notice that this letter gets right to the point. Claudette links her request to a sincere compliment that will make the recipient realize how much her contributions to the club are valued. The tone is respectful without being stuffy. The writer's voice comes through. She wastes no words in making her case. That case is clear and persuasive. The letter ends with a direct question. Presumably, the recipient will want to respond to that question right away.

You may want to review the sample business letter for form. Although there are some variations of form, the basic parts of the letter are consistent. Unless the letter is typed on stationery with a letterhead, the heading always begins with the address of the sender. Even under a letterhead, the date follows. Next comes the inside address. The greeting, sometimes called the salutation, is followed by a colon. (In a friendly letter, you will remember, it is followed by a comma.) The body of the letter, like other pieces of writing, is organized into paragraphs. Unless the writer chooses to use block form—in which all letter parts including heading and closing are placed against the left-hand margin—paragraphs are indented as usual. In the business letter as in the friendly letter, the complimentary close is followed by a comma. A personal signature is needed even if the letter is typed.

Getting It Down

Collaborate with other members of your small group to draft a letter from the notes you made previously. Begin in a straightforward but appealing way. Tell the person addressed exactly what you want him or her to do and why. Organize what you say into paragraphs. Be persuasive but not presumptuous. Write in a natural, courteous tone. Clinch your letter by closing with a direct question, an appeal for a reply, or a suggestion for constructive steps that will get things moving. Be sure to observe appropriate form for a business letter.

Put your group letter aside for a while before considering possible revisions. In preparing to revise, you might consider the most common flaw that creeps into business correspondence.

That flaw is wordiness. In a misguided attempt at formality, some letter writers pad their sentences. For example, they write "if the suggestion meets with your approval" instead of "if you approve"; "make inquiry regarding" instead of "ask"; and "it has come to my attention" rather than "I notice" or "I see." Although such phrases are so common that they have become a kind of business jargon, plain English is much stronger. If you suspect that you have written a stiff, wordy sentence, read that sentence aloud. Ask yourself, "Is this what I would say if I were talking to someone face to face?" This question is the most reliable test for plain English.

Reconvene your group and check your practice letter for padding and pretentious wording. Pare any questionable sentences down to plain English. Then reconsider the letter in light of these questions: **Checking It Out**

1. Is the purpose of the letter clear? In other words, can the reader tell exactly what you want?
2. Is the tone of the letter right? Is it positive, natural, and courteous?
3. Does the first sentence make the reader want to keep reading? Does it make the request clear and relate that request to something that will interest or benefit the recipient?
4. Is the letter persuasive? Does the requested action seem mutually beneficial to the person writing the letter and the person receiving it?
5. Is the body of the letter well-organized? Are related ideas woven into paragraphs?
6. Does the letter end with a direct question or appeal for action?
7. Is the letter clear and concise? Has all padding been cut out?
8. Is the letter free of misspellings and problems of mechanics and usage?
9. Is the form appropriate for a standard business letter?

After making appropriate revisions, have one member of your group make a copy of the final draft. Have several people in the group proofread. **Getting It Right**

Your teacher may want you to share your letter with other groups in the class, perhaps on a bulletin board. You may even wish to copy some of the letters written by other groups and keep them in a special section of your Writer's Notebook. These letters could start a collection of model business letters for various occasions.

The Résumé

The kind of letter you have just learned to write can help you in applying for a job. Your letter to a prospective employer can set you apart from other applicants. At the very least, a good letter of application should get you an interview. The chances are even better if that letter is accompanied by a well-written résumé.

Résumé is a French word meaning "summary" or "short history." Actually, it is a highly condensed autobiography focusing on your job credentials. Since the form of the résumé may be new to you, study the following model written by a high school student.

SPOTLIGHT

RÉSUMÉ of Mala Como

ADDRESS:
　　420 Hyacinth Street
　　Golden, Colorado 80401
TELEPHONE:
　　(303) 555-2181
SOCIAL SECURITY NUMBER:
　　524-96-0303

OCCUPATIONAL GOAL:
　　To become a bookkeeper

PERSONAL DATA:
　　Born: August 21, 196___
　　Have lived in Colorado all my life, attending Jefferson County public schools. Interests include skiing, reading, and writing poems as well as short stories.

EDUCATION:

> Golden High School (pending graduation in June)
> Major: Business
> Grade average: A− (upper 10% of class)

> <u>Extracurricular activities:</u>
> Future Business Leaders of America. President, 1980–81. Fund-raising leader, 1979–80. 4-H Club. 6-year member. Champion, flower arranging, 1978. Blue ribbons, county fair, garden vegetables, 1976–77.

EXPERIENCE:

1979–present (part-time and summer)

> Jefferson County Department of Social Services
> > As assistant to accountant/bookkeeper, write receipts for approximately $75,000 per month paid by clients. Type bills, business letters, and state reports.
> Help balance county books with state books each month.

1978–79 (part-time and summer)

Casa Bonita Restaurant

> > As waitress for six months, took orders and served guests.
> > Assumed responsibility for answering telephones.

REFERENCES: (by permission)

> > Ms. Maria Fuente, Administrative Assistant for Jefferson County Department of Social Services; 8550 West 14th Avenue; Lakewood, CO 80215; phone 232-6941.
> > Ms. Naomi Brown, Business Teacher at Golden High School; 701 24th Street; Golden, CO 80401; phone 278-0726.
> > Mr. and Mrs. Kenneth Viburg, 6224 West 72nd Avenue; Arvada, CO 80005; phone 421-2888.

Before beginning work on your own résumé, consider these questions:

1. Notice how information is organized into categories, which are highlighted in the left margin. How does this format help the reader?
2. A résumé must be very concise. Notice that Mala has wasted no words. Even when elaborating about her personal background and job responsibilities, she has used brief sentence fragments. Notice that she has kept them grammatically parallel.

3. Notice that the listing of job experience begins with the most recent and works back in time. Why do you think such order is standard for résumés?

4. A résumé must be kept up-to-date. Suppose that it is two years after Mala wrote her original résumé. Where would each of the following fit into an updated résumé?

   a. During the two years since high school graduation, Mala has worked as a bookkeeper for the Evergreen Landscape Company of Denver. She has received special training in data processing and now uses a microcomputer.

   b. She has attended night classes at the University of Denver and earned a total of eighteen hours in bookkeeping and accounting. Her grade-point average is 3.5 (B+).

   c. In February, 198___, one of her college papers "Applications of Microprocessing to Bookkeeping in the Small Business" was

published in the Business Department newsletter at the university.

After deciding where and in what form each of these additions should be inserted, review the résumé. Is there anything that should be deleted in the updated version?

Now that you understand résumé form and have had some practice in compressing items and fitting them into the appropriate category, you should be ready to compose a résumé of your own.

You won't have much trouble beginning your résumé. Such details as address and social security number are easy to compile. More open-ended details of personal strengths and interests, academic highlights, extra-curricular activities, and responsibilities assumed on various jobs are less obvious. They take more thought.

Getting It Down

Make three lists of details for possible inclusion in your résumé. The first, which will provide material for the *personal data* section, might be headed "What am I good at?" Under this heading, jot down talents and abilities that set you apart. What do other people say you are good at? What special hobbies or activities allow you to extend various abilities or interests?

Head the next list "What about school?" Below, jot down the name of the school you attend. (If you have moved recently, also note the name of your previous school.) If you have concentrated on courses in a certain academic area, include that information. Have you earned any awards or honors? Have you engaged in special projects? What school organizations do you belong to? Do you hold any offices?

Head your last list "Where have I worked and what have I done there?" List any jobs you have held, beginning with the most recent and leaving room to jot down major responsibilities. Did any job teach you a special skill? Be sure to include the exact name of each employer, the dates you held the job, and whether it was part-time or summer.

**Getting
It
Down**

Some of the items you included on the lists you just made probably don't belong in your résumé. Go back and underline those that seem most important and therefore most appropriate in a résumé. As you review your lists, you may think of items you missed earlier. If so, add them. Using the résumé you studied earlier as a model, draft your own. Be sure that all information is accurate and complete.

The list of what you are good at should help you with the last part of the Personal Data section. Here, don't pad. Use parallel fragments to identify special interests and strengths that personalize you. Your list of items associated with school should help you with the Education section. Be sure to start with the name of the school and the date you expect to graduate. Present yourself favorably but realistically. Be sure to date extra-curricular activities, beginning with the most recent and moving back. Your list about work will help you with the Experience section. Again, start with your most recent job. Give the name of the employer and tell exactly what you did. Here also, use parallel fragments for conciseness. Instead of listing references, just add a note References Available upon Request. (Before actually *using* your résumé, you should start asking teachers, former employers, and other adults who know you well for permission to use them as references. You might also start collecting up-to-date addresses and telephone numbers for each.)

**Checking
It
Out**

Before making a final draft of your résumé, have it checked by a classmate, your teacher, or perhaps one of your parents. Does it present you favorably? Is information accurate and complete? Do extraneous details creep in? Is any information misplaced—that is, placed in the wrong category according to the headings in the left margin? Are spelling, punctuation, and usage correct?

Using the format illustrated earlier, make a typed final draft of your résumé. (If you cannot type, perhaps you can get a friend or relative to do it for you.) Proofread carefully. Remember that a résumé is often your ticket to a job interview, but only if it represents you well and is not marred by careless errors.

**Getting
It
Right**

In such brass-tacks writing as letters and résumés, you can't afford errors. Spelling errors are particularly distracting. In proofreading, you must be careful not to let a spelling error go uncorrected.

Although you no longer study spelling as a separate subject in school, you can still become a better speller. Since spelling is largely a matter of visual memory, reading widely and paying attention to the way words look in print will help. So will careful pronunciation of words. For example, if you mispronounce "February," you are likely to misspell it. If you say "revelant" instead of "relevant," you are likely to spell it that way. Still another way to improve your spelling is to keep a list of words that give you trouble. Review the list periodically and check for your own personal spelling demons when you proofread a paper.

Although English spelling does not always go by its own rules, there are a few major rules that are particularly helpful. Remember the old standby *"i* before *e* except after *c* or when sounded like *a* as in *neighbor* and *weigh"*? That rule can guide in spelling such words as *receive,* *relieve,* and *feigned.* ● See the Writer's Handbook, pages H-36–47 for additional help in spelling.

If you have trouble with spelling, you may wish to undertake your own systematic review of such spelling rules. Meanwhile, you can work to eliminate careless errors:

1. <u>Avoid omitting letters.</u>   Pronounce these words, taking care *not* to omit italicized letters:

accident*a*lly	gener*a*lly
ar*c*tic	ge*o*graphy
dor*m*itory	govern*m*ent
every*b*ody	laboratory
fur*t*her	len*g*th

2. <u>Avoid inserting extra letters.</u>   Pronounce these words, being careful not to add extra syllables or letters.

drowned	lightning
elm	mischievous
genuine	remembrance
height	umbrella

3. <u>Avoid changing letters.</u>   As you pronounce these words, take care not to change the sounds of letters in italics:

de*s*pair	prep*a*ration
existence	privi*l*ege
int*r*oduce	rest*a*urant

4. <u>Avoid transposing letters.</u>   In pronouncing this last set of words, be careful not to transpose italicized letters:

child*r*en	p*r*efer
hund*r*ed	p*r*eserve
pe*r*spiration	vill*ai*n

Careful pronunciation and proofreading can go a long way toward helping you avoid spelling errors. Be on the alert for letters that might have been omitted, inserted, changed, or transposed. When in doubt, check spelling in a dictionary or with another person.

Even good spellers sometimes confuse words that look or sound a great deal alike. The exercise that follows will help you distinguish words that are commonly confused.

Writer's Workbench

Spelling: Commonly Confused Words

A. Write an original sentence illustrating appropriate use of each word in the following list. If necessary, consult a dictionary.

1. accept	2. affect	3. altar
except	effect	alter

4. capital	5. complement	6. council
capitol	compliment	counsel
7. emigrant	8. principal	9. prophecy
immigrant	principle	prophesy
10. sight	11. stationary	
site	stationery	
cite		

B. Exchange sentences with a partner. Check each other's sentences for appropriate use of words in the list.

Even words that do not look or sound as much alike as those in the preceding exercise can cause confusion. Consider these examples: *farther* and *further*, *formerly* and *formally*, *incredible* and *incredulous*, *infer* and *imply*. Can you explain the difference in each of these pairs? Can you use each word appropriately in a sentence? You may wish to start a special section in your Writer's Notebook to collect frequently confused words. By alerting yourself to possible confusion, you can often avoid it. Nowhere is it more important to avoid careless use of the wrong word than in brass-tacks writing.

Moving Toward Independence

In this chapter, you have concentrated on the real-world tasks of writing business letters and résumés. You have gone about such writing in much the same way as you approached previous pieces. You collected material, organized it, and presented it in a way that would appeal to the reader. Because brass-tacks writing is usually read by busy people, you took special care not to waste words. Because you were eager to make a good impression, you used a business-like but natural tone of voice and paid careful attention to form. In an effort to keep that impression unmarred, you concentrated even more than usual on proofreading.

The final assignment in this chapter will allow you to apply what you have learned. It will also provide a dress rehearsal for seeking a job interview or admission into college.

~~~~~~

After reviewing guidelines for writing business letters to get things done, write a letter to a prospective employer or to an admissions officer in the college you would like to attend. Attach the résumé you wrote earlier. Before making a final draft of the letter with

**Getting
It
Right**

the attached résumé, check both according to criteria comprising Checkpoint 4 on page 163. Proofread and edit carefully before making a final draft.

When your letter and résumé are returned, put them away for later use. If they are well done, they will give you a head start in actually applying for that job or for college admission.

CHECKPOINT 4

1	2	3	4	5

Content   ×5=

Letter and résumé don't really *sell* you. Recipient probably wouldn't call. See me for suggestions.

You present yourself well. Check for key details that have been omitted. Beef up just a little.

This letter and résumé should get action. You include just the right details on your résumé and create just the right impression in your letter.

Organization   ×4=

Letter rambles and résumé seems loose. Try making notes on details that go together, then rewrite.

You're on your way. Résumé has just a couple of stray items, and letter could do with minor tightening.

Sharp! Résumé has all items in the right category. Flow of letter is smooth and logical. Beginning and ending unify and clinch.

Economy   ×4=

Check for wordiness. Saying things in a natural, straightforward way will help. Read aloud and prune.

Just a *little* inflated. Shrink down a few wordy passages and you'll have it.

Every word counts. Both résumé and letter get straight to the point.

Form   ×4=

Review form of business letter, page 150, and form of résumé, page 154. Work on both, getting help from a classmate if needed.

Basically, you have both forms. Check models on pages 150 and 154. Clear up just a few lapses.

Picture perfect! Both your letter and your résumé could be displayed as models.

Mechanics   ×3=

Oops! Proofreading must have been rushed. Take time and try again. Ask for help, especially in spelling.

Almost ready to mail. Check for the few errors that slipped through.

Just what employers and colleges are looking for—faultless spelling, usage, capitalization, and punctuation. Proofing pays!

Realizing Literature

"The urge to write is the child of the love of reading."

—John Hersey

Chapter **8**

Reader as Writer

Readers and writers are partners in creation. Both *realize* literature. The writer fills the page with words, but those words don't come alive until someone reads them. Readers and writers may be separated by oceans or centuries, but the printed page allows the thoughts and experiences of one to become real to the other.

You already know that reading can help you become a better writer, but has it ever occurred to you that writing can also make you a better reader? Consider the case of poetry. You have read lots of poems. You recognize the way lines are laid out on the page, the way words are arranged to sound musical, the way similes and metaphors work. But as long as poetry remains a spectator sport, you will never see it from the inside. Only by writing poems can you weigh decisions on where to break lines, how to choose words for their sound as well as their sense, and how to create comparisons that explode with meaning. Even a poor poet understands such matters better than a non-poet.

In this chapter, you will write some poems and stories of your own. Later in the unit, you will concentrate on responding to poems and stories others have written. Some of your responses will be personal. Others will be analytical. Throughout the unit, the emphasis will be upon writing about writing.

In earlier units, you have practiced both *expressive* and *transactional* writing. You began the course by writing mainly for self, to clarify feelings, to recapture experiences, to sort out ideas. Such expressive writing is "I-centered." Later, you moved to audience-centered-writing—that is, writing to inform or persuade others. Such transactional pieces are "you-centered."

Writing about literature can be expressive. You might, for example, log personal responses to a novel in your Writer's Notebook or simply jot down reflections prompted by a poem. More often, writing about literature is transactional, especially in school. In a book report, you explain to other readers your interpretation and opinion of *Brave New*

World. On an essay test, you seek to convince your teacher that you do indeed understand *Hamlet*.

Though you will do some expressive and transactional writing about literature in the chapters that follow, you will first try some *poetic* writing. Don't take this term too literally. It applies to prose as well as to poetry—in fact, to all form-governed writing. When writing is "it-centered" rather than "I-centered" or "you-centered," its purpose is termed *poetic*.

You already recognize the importance of form in literature. You know that certain conventions are observed in poetry, others in fiction, and still others in drama. Literature shares this reliance upon form with the other arts. Think, for example, of painting, sculpture, music, and dance. Without form, there is no art.

As you try your hand at literary art forms, you will expand your repertoire of writing techniques. In this chapter, you will extend your earlier work with comparison by concentrating on metaphor and simile. Since the artful use of language demands exactly the right word, you will also work further on diction, especially verbs. Throughout the chapter, you will concentrate on arranging words into rich sentences, and sentences into paragraphs or stanzas. In other words, you will concentrate upon shaping language according to the demands of a given form.

Shaping a Poem

Poetry is easy to recognize but hard to define. Even poets have trouble agreeing on a definition. Most resort to metaphor. Marianne Moore, for example, calls poets "literalists of the imagination" who present "imaginary gardens with real toads in them." According to Archibald MacLeish, "A poem should be palpable and mute/As a globed fruit"; it "should not mean but be." Edward Lueders writes that poetry depends upon "surprise and wild connections," upon linking "words that never knew each other until right now." At the very least, most would agree that poetry is language at its most intense. Most would also agree that much of this intensity comes from compression.

Poems are not just about spring, young love, and moonlight. They may be about almost anything, even about the mundane or the ugly. As you work through this chapter, you might like to sample some of the contemporary poets represented in books and magazines. Note the wide range of subjects.

Your first writing assignment will be based on some observations you may consider non-poetic. See whether you can shape those observations into a poem.

Here are some notes recording a spectator's observations at the scene of an automobile accident. Study those notes and try to recreate the scene in your mind. Imagine what you might see, hear, and feel.

> Ambulance approaches.
>> bell ringing
>> red light flashing
>> speeding down dark street past lighted buildings
>> making fast curve
>> slowing down to move into crowd
> Ambulance stops and loads victims.
>> doors thrown open
>> interior brightly lighted
>> injured placed on stretcher
>> stretcher rolled back into place
> Ambulance moves away.
>> rocking motion
>> doors closed
> Onlookers remain.
>> policemen sweeping glass, making notes, washing blood,
>>> hanging lanterns on wreckage clinging to iron pole
>> traffic beginning to move carefully
>> crowd milling around
>>> talking quietly
>>> questioning reason for injury, death

These notes could, of course, provide the makings of a short story. The events could be fleshed out with characters, plot, and even theme. The same notes could be developed into a play. There is plenty of potential drama. The material itself is neutral. Choice of form is strictly up to the writer.

This time, however, you will develop this raw material into a poem. The emphasis will be upon the images themselves and upon the ripple effect created by those images. (Think of the widening circles that ripple out when a rock is dropped into a pond.)

To get started, go back through the notes. As you again try to visualize the scene, jot down images that occur to you. *See* the ambulance careening down a dark street; *hear* the old-fashioned bell used as a warning signal before the day of sirens. Jot down phrases that capture what you see, hear, and feel. Use the most vivid words you can find. Don't try to connect images into sentences. Just fill in sensory detail. Try to make phrases as compact as they are vivid.

Getting It Down

When you are satisfied with your list of images, pretend that you are one of the spectators on the edge of the crowd. From that vantage point, recount the approach of the ambulance, the loading of the victims, the departure of the ambulance, and the aftermath of the accident. Try to end with the thoughts, questions, and feelings that the accident has created within you. Even in pondering the meaning of what has happened, don't lapse into abstract explanations. Try to reflect what you feel in images—that is, in sensory language.

Once you get the basic flow of the poem, go back and see where sentences should break into lines and lines into stanzas. Experiment by reading aloud, pausing ever so slightly at the end of a line. Remember that stanzas should be divisions of thought. Be sure to have some reason for dividing the poem into stanzas.

After you have at least a tentative form, go back and work on wording. Consider the sound as well as the meaning of words. Your poem need not rhyme—in fact, this poem *should* not—but you can still make sound work for you. If you are trying for a harsh effect, use harsh-sounding words. If part of the poem is meant to sound gentle, use softer words. Experiment with alliteration (words that begin with the same sound like "tried and true") and assonance (words that feature the same vowel sound like "free and easy").

Checking It Out

Finally, reread your poem for overall effect. Is it what you intended? Is it unified? Also, check for unnecessary words. Sometimes poets leave out connectives and telegraph their meaning. If your images are strong and clear enough, you should be able to do some compressing.

Put away the draft of the poem you have just completed and read the following accident poem by a well-known American poet.

SPOTLIGHT

Auto Wreck
Its quick soft silver bell beating, beating
And down the dark one ruby flare
Pulsing out red light like an artery,
The ambulance at top speed floating down
Past beacons and illuminated clocks   5
Wings in a heavy curve, dips down,
And brakes speed, entering the crowd.
The doors leap open, emptying light;
Stretchers are laid out, the mangled lifted
And stowed into the little hospital.   10
Then the bell, breaking the hush, tolls once,
And the ambulance with its terrible cargo
Rocking, slightly rocking, moves away,
As the doors, an afterthought, are closed.

We are deranged, walking among the cops   15
Who sweep glass and are large and composed.
One is still making notes under the light.
One with a bucket douches ponds of blood
Into the street and gutter.
One hangs lanterns on the wrecks that cling,   20
Empty husks of locusts, to iron poles.

Our throats were tight as tourniquets,
Our feet were bound with splints, but now
Like convalescents intimate and gauche,
We speak through sickly smiles and warn   25
With the stubborn saw of common sense.
The grim joke and banal resolution.
The traffic moves around with care,
But we remain, touching a wound
That opens to our richest horror.   30
Already old, the question Who shall die?
Becomes unspoken Who is innocent?
For death in war is done by hands,
Suicide has cause; and stillbirth, logic.
But this invites the occult mind,   35
Cancels our physics with a sneer,
And spatters all we know of denouement
Across the expedient and wicked stones.

Karl Shapiro

Working either independently or with a small group of classmates, consider the following questions:

1. The first seven lines of the poem are all one sentence. Notice how the momentum of the sentence propels the reader along just as the ambulance is propelled along the street. The subject of this first sentence does not come until Line 4. What is that subject? What three verbs (Lines 6–7) comprise the predicate?

2. Notice such words as "soft," "silver," "floating," "wings," and "dips" in the first sentence of the poem. Notice also such words as "hush" and "rocking" in Lines 11–14. What is the effect of these words? What impression of the ambulance do they convey?

3. How do the words you noticed in 2 contrast with "leap" and "mangled" in Lines 8 and 9? What similarly abrupt or harsh words do you find in the closing lines of the poem?

4. Who are "we" (Line 15 and following)?

5. Shapiro uses an abundance of similes and metaphors. You may already know that a simile is a comparison stated directly with the words "like" or "as." A metaphor is an *implied* comparison.

   a. Why are these similes so apt and powerful?

     1. red light *like an artery*   (Line 3)

     2. tight *as tourniquets*   (Line 22)

     3. *Like convalescents* . . . we   (Lines 24–25)

   b. What comparison is being implied in each of the following metaphors? Why is each so effective?

     1. wrecks that cling,/ *empty husks of locusts*   (Lines 20–21)

     2. feet *bound with splints*   (Line 23)

     3. we remain, *touching a wound*   (Line 29)

6. The final stanza of the poem is a reflection on what has happened. Exactly what does the speaker mean when he concludes that the accident "spatters all we know of denouement/ Across the expedient and wicked stones"?

The point of your reading Karl Shapiro's poem is *not* to demonstrate how much difference there is between the polished work of a professional poet and your own attempt. The point is to show you how a poet shapes material so that you can try some of the same techniques. What you learned from a close reading of "Auto Wreck" should help you improve your own poem. Before you start to revise, however, take another look at some of the words in the poem. The first word-study exercise will not only provide indirect help with diction in your own writing; it will also expand your reading vocabulary.

Writer's Workbench 1

Vocabulary: Words in Context

A. Consult a dictionary to find the meaning of each of the following words for the context in which it appears in the poem. Write down the word and its meaning.

deranged (Line 15)	banal (Line 27)
composed (Line 16)	occult (Line 35)
convalescents (Line 24)	physics (Line 36)
gauche (Line 24)	denouement (Line 37)
saw (Line 26)	expedient (Line 38)

B. Write an original sentence using each word in the same sense in which it is used in the poem.

C. Compare your dictionary definitions and original sentences with those of several classmates. Discuss what you think were Shapiro's reasons for choosing each of the words for a particular context. Do any words seem to be used figuratively rather than literally? Which words seem particularly well-chosen?

The second word-study activity will focus on Shapiro's use of verbs, especially in the first part of the poem where the sense of motion is particularly strong.

Writer's Workbench 2

Diction: Strong Verbs

A. What image is evoked by each of the following action verbs? (To get the whole image, you will need to consider the subject along with the verb.)

wings	(Line 6)
dips	(Line 6)
brakes	(Line 7)
leap	(Line 8)
tolls	(Line 11)

B. Notice that all of these verbs are in the active voice. In other words, in each case the subject of the verb does the acting. Only in Lines 9 and 10 does the poet use passive-voice verbs—verbs whose subjects receive action and do not act. Find the three passive voice verbs in those lines. Why are such verbs appropriate here?

C. A writer can increase verb density by using participles. As you probably know already, participles are -*ing* or -*ed* verb forms used as adjectives. In the first ten lines of the poem, find these participles: *beating, pulsing, floating, illuminated, entering,* and *mangled.* Which participles stand alone and which introduce participial phrases? What noun does each modify? Which precede the noun modified and which follow it? Which require commas? Which seem especially vivid? Why?

Now that you have studied Shapiro's poem and worked on word choice, get out the draft of the accident poem you wrote earlier.

~~~~~~

Considering the techniques you noted in "Auto Wreck," read over your own poem and see what improvements you can make. Try especially to insert powerful similes and metaphors, vivid action verbs (including participles), perhaps some contrast. Work on sound effects and try to heighten sensory language. See whether you can strengthen concluding lines so that they reflect your feelings and thoughts about what has happened.

Checking
It
Out

Before making a final draft, share your revised poem with at least three classmates. Ask each to respond to these questions:

Is what happened recounted clearly and vividly? Are there any passages that need clarifying?

What images are most effective in making the reader share the experience with his or her senses?

What comparisons are most powerful?

Do strong verbs re-create the action? Which are best?

Is the form of the poem appropriate? In other words, do line arrangement and use of stanza divisions enhance both sound and meaning?

What is the overall effect? How does the ending intensify that effect and suggest some significance?

~~~~~~

After considering the responses of your readers, make a final draft of your poem. Your teacher will probably ask you to read your poem aloud or display it so that it can be compared to those of your classmates.

Getting
It
Right

~~~~~~

Even though everyone in the class wrote from the same list of observations, poems undoubtedly vary. No one chose exactly the same images, exactly the same similes or metaphors, or exactly the same form. It is such choices that transform raw material into a poem. The more imaginative the choices and the greater the compression, the better the poem. The more experience you have in making such choices, the more sensitive you will be as a reader of poetry.

Before moving on to another literary form, try one more exercise that will help clinch what you have learned about reading and writing poems. This exercise is based on a poem written by a student. It will provide practice in choosing and interpreting similes, using stanza divisions to reinforce meaning, and drawing the threads of the poem together in the closing lines.

Writer's Workbench 3

Similes

A. Here is part of a poem expressing one high school student's frustration about classroom recitation. Complete this part of the poem by filling in your own comparisons. Use your Writer's Notebook.

> Question,
>   recite.
>   Funny mechanical voices
>   make me chuckle inside.
>   Their constant din rattles
>   as if . . . . . .
>
>   . . . . . .
>   . . . . . .
>   . . . . . .
>   . . . . . .
> Again, quickly.
>   Question,
>   recite.
>   The slogans fall into
>   place like . . . . . .
>
>   . . . . . .
>   . . . . . .
>   . . . . . .
>   . . . . . .
> Now faster.
>   Question,
>   recite.
>   Traffic jam voices crawl
>   through the air like
>
>   . . . . . .
>   . . . . . .
>   . . . . . .

Again.
  Try it
    again.
      The tiring mouths fade
      and run together like
      . . . . . .

Compare your similes with the ones in the original. Also, notice how the poem ends.

Recitation

Question,
  recite.
      Funny mechanical voices
      make me chuckle inside.
      Their constant din rattles
      as if small children
      had gathered up the
      sounds and rolled them
      down the street in a
      rusty tin can.

Again quickly.
   Question.
      recite.
         The slogans fall into
         place like programmed
         hands of a midnight
         assembly line performing
         feats of magic before
         wide-eyed Henry Fords.
Now faster.
   Question,
      recite.
         Traffic jam voices crawl
         through the air
         like the stumbling curses
         of a Main Street drunk.
Again.
   Try it
      again.
         The tiring mouths fade
         and run together like
         a painting in the rain.
I think I'll be silent for a while.
In time, the machines will rust,
slogans will give birth to more
slogans, drunks will fall asleep,
and paint will dry in the sun.

Kevin C.

B. In this student's poem, similes do more than create vivid images of how voices sound during class recitation. They also help structure the poem.

1. Why do you think the writer chose this particular pattern of line arrangement? Why do such phrases as "Question, recite" stand out while the word pictures containing similes are indented under these phrases?

2. Notice that the pattern changes in the last five lines. How? In what way do these concluding lines draw the poem together? (Note the change from simile to metaphor.) How do they show the speaker's attitude toward the scene he has re-created in the poem?

3. Review the similes you wrote in Part A of this exercise. Write your own five-line conclusion echoing those similes and showing how you feel about the classroom scene re-created in your version of the poem.

C. Share your version of "Recitation" with a small group of classmates. Discuss similarities and differences between poems written by members of the group and the original.

A famous poet once said "A poem begins in delight and ends in wisdom." This statement may be a bit ambitious for beginning efforts such as Kevin's. Nevertheless, it does say something important about how most poems move. They begin with images that delight—or at least stimulate—the senses. They end with the significance of those images. Good poems suggest that significance rather than state it bluntly.

"Auto Wreck" follows this pattern. It begins with a series of images re-creating the scene of an accident. The scene is rendered vivid by sensory language and powerful comparisons. The reader is expected to do no more than experience the sights, sounds, and feelings being described. At the end, however, the speaker in the poem becomes reflective. The reader confronts the question of significance. What does all this mean?

Understanding the flow from "delight" to "wisdom," seeing stanzas as thought divisions in a poem, and rubbing images against each other in the form of simile or metaphor can help you get started writing poems. Being even a fledgling poet gives you an advantage as a reader. You are at least beginning to think like a poet. You see poetry from the inside. This insider's view is sure to make you appreciate language at its most intense. That's just what poetry is.

Shaping a Story

Most of us read fiction for the same reason we go to movies. We enjoy it. We find pleasure in being amused, moved, or even frightened. For a while, we can forget who we are and be someone else. Vicariously, we can go places we've never been and participate in experiences we'll never have.

Although we read mainly for pleasure, a good story offers more. It offers insight. It brings us to a full understanding of ourselves and others. By dealing with imaginary people caught in imaginary conflicts, fiction offers us flashes of truth that go beyond mere fact. Such insights make us more human.

In order to offer insight as well as pleasure, a story must have more than plot. Of course, it *must* have plot. Otherwise, nothing happens. A story takes place only when a character is involved in conflict and that conflict somehow works itself out. But it takes interesting characters to bring a plot alive, to make the reader care what happens next.

Even the best short stories can be reduced to a simple plot summary and the best novel to a brief synopsis. Good fiction writers don't just tell a story; they dramatize it through the human beings involved. They flesh out each scene with graphic detail and have their characters talk to each other. They make the story seem so real that the reader suspends any realization that he or she is indeed reading something that didn't really happen.

There is no better way of learning the craft of fiction than to try writing some. The next activity will help you do so.

Getting It Started

Here is the plot summary of a short story by a writer who really mastered the craft. As you will see, the plot is mildly amusing but not really remarkable.

An aristocratic lady takes a train through the English countryside to visit a friend. At a station along the way, she leaves the train to make a cart driver stop mistreating his horse. The train continues without her. Almost immediately, a wealthy woman drives up and mistakes her for the governess she was expecting. The aristocratic lady, who delights in taking people at their word, plays along. Since she also delights in poking fun at pompous behavior, she does and says outrageous things in her role as governess. The next day, after being fired by the unsuspecting woman for practicing unconventional teaching methods on the children, the lady boards the train and completes her journey to visit the friend.

With a small group of classmates, brainstorm a few scenes that could bring this plot to life. Think of a name for the aristocratic woman, her employer, and the children. Discuss how they might look and talk. What might have been said at the station when the lady was assumed to be the governess? How might she have deliberately scandalized the family at dinner that night? What unconventional teaching method might have led to her dismissal? As you brainstorm details and scenes to develop this plot, take notes on particularly promising ideas.

Working solo, write a brief story based on the plot summary. Decide in advance what point of view you want to use. (For example, should you let the lady tell the story in the first person or simply recount events as they would be told by an anonymous third-person narrator?) Concentrate on a few fully developed scenes, which may be spliced together with summary sentences to indicate the passage of time. Be sure to include dialogue.

**Getting
It
Down**

SPOTLIGHT

Now put your story aside and read the original from which the plot summary was borrowed.

The Schartz-Metterklume Method

Lady Carlotta stepped out onto the platform of the small wayside station and took a turn or two up and down its uninteresting length, to kill time till the train should be pleased to proceed on its way. Then, in the roadway beyond, she saw a horse struggling with a more than ample load, and a carter of the sort that seems to bear a sullen hatred against the animal that helps him to earn a living. Lady Carlotta promptly betook her to the roadway, and put rather a different complexion on the struggle. Certain of her acquaintances were wont to give her plentiful admonition as to the undesirability of interfering on behalf of a distressed animal, such interference being "none of her business." Only once had she put the doctrine of noninterference into practice, when one of its most eloquent exponents had been besieged for nearly three hours in a small and extremely uncomfortable May tree by an angry boar-pig, while Lady Carlotta, on the other side of the fence, had proceeded with the water-color sketch she was engaged on, and refused to interfere between the boar and his prisoner. It is to be feared that she lost the friendship of the ultimately rescued lady. On this occasion she merely lost the train, which gave way to the first sign of impatience it had shown throughout the journey, and steamed off without her. She bore the desertion with philosophical indifference; her friends and relations were thoroughly well used to the fact of her luggage arriving without her. She wired a vague noncommittal message to her destination to say that she was coming on "by another train." Before she had time to think what her next move might be, she was confronted by an imposingly attired lady, who seemed to be taking a prolonged mental inventory of her clothes and looks.

"You must be Miss Hope, the governess I've come to meet," said the apparition, in a tone that admitted of very little argument.

"Very well, if I must I must," said Lady Carlotta to herself with dangerous meekness.

"I am Mrs. Quabarl," continued the lady, "and where, pray, is your luggage?"

"It's gone astray," said the alleged governess, falling in with the excellent rule of life that the absent are always to blame; the luggage had, in point of fact, behaved with perfect correctitude. "I've just telegraphed about it," she added, with a nearer approach to truth.

"How provoking," said Mrs. Quabarl; "these railway companies are so careless. However, my maid can lend you things for the night," and she led the way to her car.

During the drive to the Quabarl mansion Lady Carlotta was impressively introduced to the nature of the charge that had been thrust upon her; she learned that Claude and Wilfrid were delicate, sensitive young people, that Irene had the artistic temperament highly developed, and that Viola was something or other else of a mold equally commonplace among children of that class and type in the twentieth century.

"I wish them not only to be *taught*," said Mrs. Quabarl, "but *interested* in what they learn. In their history lessons, for instance, you must try to make them feel that they are being introduced to the life stories of men and women who really lived, not merely committing a mass of names and dates to memory. French, of course, I shall expect you to talk at mealtimes several days in the week."

"I shall talk French four days of the week and Russian in the remaining three."

"Russian? My dear Miss Hope, no one in the house speaks or understands Russian."

"That will not embarrass me in the least," said Lady Carlotta coldly.

Mrs. Quabarl, to use a colloquial expression, was knocked off her perch. She was one of those imperfectly self-assured individuals who are magnificent and autocratic as long as they are not seriously opposed. The least show of unexpected resistance goes a long way towards rendering them cowed and apologetic. When the new governess failed to express wondering admiration of the large newly purchased and expensive car, and lightly alluded to the superior advantages of one or two makes which had just been put on the market, the discomfiture of her patroness became almost abject. Her feelings were those which might have animated a general of ancient

warfaring days, on beholding his heaviest battle-elephant ignominiously driven off the field by slingers and javelin throwers.

At dinner that evening, although reinforced by her husband, who usually duplicated her opinions and lent her moral support generally, Mrs. Quabarl regained none of her lost ground. The governess not only helped herself well and truly to wine, but held forth with considerable show of critical knowledge on various vintage matters, concerning which the Quabarls were in no wise able to pose as authorities. Previous governesses had limited their conversation on the wine topic to a respectful and doubtless sincere preference for water. When this one went as far as to recommend a wine firm in whose hands you could not go very far wrong Mrs. Quabarl thought it time to turn the conversation into more usual channels.

"We got very satisfactory references about you from Canon Teep," she observed; "a very estimable man, I should think."

"Drinks like a fish and beats his wife, otherwise a very lovable character," said the governess imperturbably.

"My *dear* Miss Hope! I trust you are exaggerating," exclaimed the Quabarls in unison.

"One must in justice admit that there is some provocation," continued the romancer. "Mrs. Teep is quite the most irritating bridge player that I have ever sat down with; her leads and declarations would condone a certain amount of brutality in her partner, but to souse her with the contents of the only soda-water siphon in the house on a Sunday afternoon, when one couldn't get another, argues an indifference to the comfort of others which I cannot altogether overlook. You may think me hasty in my judgments, but it was practically on account of the siphon incident that I left."

"We will talk of this some other time," said Mrs. Quabarl hastily.

"I shall never allude to it again," said the governess with decision.

Mr. Quabarl made a welcome diversion by asking what studies the new instructress proposed to inaugurate on the morrow.

"History to begin with," she informed him.

"Ah, history," he observed sagely; "now in teaching them history you must take care to interest them in what they learn. You must make them feel that they are being introduced to the life stories of men and women who really lived—"

"I've told her all that," interposed Mrs. Quabarl.

"I teach history on the Schartz-Metterklume method," said the governess loftily.

"Ah, yes," said her listeners, thinking it expedient to assume an acquaintance at least with the name.

"What are you children doing out here?" demanded Mrs. Quabarl the next morning, on finding Irene sitting rather glumly at the head of the stairs, while her sister was perched in an attitude of depressed discomfort on the window seat behind her, with a wolfskin rug almost covering her.

"We are having a history lesson," came the unexpected reply. I am supposed to be Rome, and Viola up there is the she-wolf; not a real wolf, but the figure of one that the Romans used to set store by—I forget why. Claude and Wilfrid have gone to fetch the shabby women."

"The shabby women?"

"Yes, they've got to carry them off. They didn't want to, but Miss Hope got one of father's fives bats and said she'd give them a number nine spanking if they didn't, so they've gone to do it."

A loud, angry screaming from the direction of the lawn drew Mrs. Quabarl thither in hot haste, fearful lest the threatened castigation might even now be in process of infliction. The outcry, however, came principally from the two small daughters of the lodge-keeper, who were being hauled and pushed toward the house by the panting and disheveled Claude and Wilfrid, whose task was rendered even more arduous by the incessant, if not very effectual, attacks of the captured maidens' small brother. The governess, fives bat in hand, sat negligently on the stone balustrade, presiding over the scene with the cold impartiality of a goddess of battles. A furious and repeated chorus of "I'll tell muvver" rose from the lodge children, but the lodge mother, who was hard of hearing, was for the moment immersed in the preoccupation of her wash-tub. After an apprehensive glance in the direction of the lodge (the good woman was gifted with the highly militant temper which is sometimes the privilege of deafness) Mrs. Quabarl flew indignantly to the rescue of the struggling captives.

"Wilfrid! Claude! Let those children go at once. Miss Hope, what on earth is the meaning of this scene?"

"Early Roman history; the Sabine women, don't you know? It's the Schartz-Metterklume method to make children understand history by acting it themselves; fixes it in their memory, you know. Of course, if, thanks to your interference, your boys go through life thinking that the Sabine women ultimately escaped, I really cannot be held responsible."

"You may be very clever and modern, Miss Hope," said Mrs.

Quabarl firmly, "but I should like you to leave here by the next train. Your luggage will be sent after you as soon as it arrives."

"I'm not certain exactly where I shall be for the next few days," said the dismissed instructress of youth; "you might keep my luggage till I wire my address. There are only a couple of trunks and some golf clubs and a leopard cub."

"A leopard cub!" gasped Mrs. Quabarl. Even in her departure this extraordinary person seemed destined to leave a trail of embarrassment behind her.

"Well, it's rather left off being a cub; it's more than half grown, you know. A fowl every day and a rabbit on Sundays is what it usually gets. Raw beef makes it too excitable. Don't trouble about getting the car for me, I'm rather inclined for a walk."

And Lady Carlotta strode out of the Quabarl horizon.

The advent of the genuine Miss Hope, who had made a mistake as to the day on which she was due to arrive, caused a turmoil which that good lady was quite unused to inspiring. Obviously the Quabarl family had been woefully befooled, but a certain amount of relief came with the knowledge.

"How tiresome for you, dear Carlotta," said her hostess, when the overdue guest ultimately arrived; "how very tiresome losing your train and having to stop overnight in a strange place."

"Oh, dear, no," said Lady Carlotta; "not at all tiresome—for me."

Saki

Before comparing this story to the one your wrote, consider these questions:

1. How does the anecdote about Lady Carlotta's "noninterference" when her friend was treed by the angry boar prepare the reader for her going along with Mrs. Quabarl's statement "You must be Miss Hope, the governess"? How does Lady Carlotta again take Mrs. Quabarl literally on the kind of education she insists upon for her children?
2. Notice that the author's language is formal, sometimes even quaint. Find examples. Why has he chosen such a stiff style? What would the story lose if told in a more breezy, conversational way?
3. Both characters and plot in this story are painted with a broad brush. There is no attempt at subtlety or even realism. How do names contribute to this kind of broad humor? What else seems exaggerated to add to the fun?

4. Read some of the dialogue aloud. How should Mrs. Quabarl's lines sound? Lady Carlotta's? Which lines seem most amusing?
5. The author obviously uses the Quabarls to satirize extremes of upper-class manners as well as extremes of educational fads. In each case, what does he seem to be holding up to ridicule?

"The Schartz-Metterklume Method" was written early in this century by one of England's finest satirists whose pseudonym was "Saki." As you undoubtedly see, there is much more to the story than plot.

There is, of course, a plot. The eccentric Lady Carlotta, who takes people at their word when she can deflate them that way, is mistaken for a governess. Since the reader already knows that she is a titled aristocrat as well as a headstrong woman, this situation creates a little dramatic irony: the reader knows more than the other characters. Almost immediately, a conflict develops between the pretentious Mrs. Quabarl and her new governess. This conflict, which is mainly verbal, builds as Lady Carlotta practices her one-upmanship at dinner and promises to teach her young charges by the Schartz-Metterklume method. Her antagonist is so intimidated that she loses every round. The climactic episode comes the next morning when the children are engaged in an over-zealous reenactment of history. When Lady Carlotta is fired and sent on her way, Mrs. Quarbarl thinks only momentarily that she has triumphed. The reader knows better. The protagonist has had the fun of cutting her high-brow employer down to size and continues her journey as she had planned all along.

Most stories share such a plot structure. There is a protagonist (the main character with whom the reader's sympathies lie) joined in conflict with some antagonist, either an opposing character or some force such as nature or fate or society. Sometimes, the primary conflict is even *inside* the main character. In a novel, there may be conflicts of all these kinds. In any case, there is some inciting incident that sets off the conflict. The conflict then builds through a series of complicating incidents to a climax. At this moment of decision, the conflict is resolved one way or the other.

As the plot develops, so does character. Usually, the main character is most fully developed. This development comes not only through direct description but through dramatization—what the character does, says, and even thinks. The best authors show more than they tell.

They also use both character and plot to embody some insight into human nature or into society. Such an implied comment is called *theme*. Think about "The Schartz-Metterklume Method." What comment is Saki making about the excesses and foibles of his day?

Now that you have read a story by a professional author and analyzed some of the techniques used to make that story come to life, look back at the draft you wrote from the same plot summary. Again, the point is not to compare. The point is to learn from a fine craftsman.

**Checking
It
Out**

Look back at your story and see whether it contains at least the essential elements of plot. Do you develop a conflict between your central character and the other characters? Does this conflict build to a climactic episode? Is the climax followed by some sort of resolution that rounds out the story?

Do your characters come through? Is your aristocratic lady developed in some detail by her actions and her dialogue? Is she consistent? Is she amusing?

Is the point of view in your story consistent? (You may have noticed that Saki used an anonymous third-person narrator. The point is that he did not shift.) Do you sustain a consistent tone—perhaps light or satiric?

After you fill in any gaps and refine your story, share it with a small group of classmates. Find out what they like best about your version and how they think it might be improved.

**Getting
It
Right**

Using the responses of your classmates and any techniques you learned from Saki, make a final draft of your story. Give it an appropriate title.

Think for a moment how the same material about deflated snobbery might have been used in a poem or a play. Think how it might have been developed into a novel. Each would be vastly different. Form does indeed shape the message.

Although your stories and poems may never break into print, the experience of writing in different literary forms has its own rewards. It stretches the imagination. It heightens awareness of words. It demands a grasp of form. Imagination, awareness of words, and grasp of form pay big dividends in writing. They also pay big dividends in reading. The reader who is also a writer becomes a full partner in realizing literature.

Chapter 9

Reading and Responding

© 1959 United Feature Syndicate, Inc.

THERE'S A LESSON TO BE LEARNED HERE SOMEWHERE, BUT I DON'T KNOW WHAT IT IS.

This cartoon may make you smile, or it may make you sigh, "How true!" If you are with someone else, you may want to share the cartoon and talk about it. If you are in the right mood, you might even do some writing, perhaps a reflection on that lesson Linus knows is in there somewhere.

Poems, stories, plays, and even cartoons call for some kind of response. They aren't like recipes or directions for assembling stereo components. With recipes or directions, attention is focused primarily upon what you will have after the text is discarded—a chocolate cake or a stereo system. But the value of literature comes from living through the text itself.

Good readers often continue to live through a text long after the book has been closed. References to a novel or poem crop up in their conversation, perhaps even in letters or diary entries. Sometimes, literature inspires readers to create pieces of their own as you did during the previous chapter.

In this chapter, you will explore different ways of responding to literature. Sometimes a response will be oral or visual; more often, it will be written. Sometimes, you'll stay close to a text by performing or even imitating it. At other times, your response will move away from the text and assume a form of its own. Whatever the response, it will allow you to participate more fully in literature, both as a reader and as a writer.

Reading—A Performing Art

One response to a text is to perform it. Musicians respond this way all of the time. They read the notes from a sheet of music and play them on a guitar or a trombone; singers lift words as well as notes from the score.

Actors respond to a dramatic script in much the same way. They perform the play with their voices and their bodies. A good performance is more than a reading of the script. Every line and every gesture reflects the actor's own response to the playwright's words as well as to those of the director.

Many pieces of fiction contain enough drama to be performed. Has one of your English teachers ever selected a short story with lots of dialogue, assigned roles, and had a different student read the lines of a certain character? If so, you may have found yourself reading dialogue with more expression than usual, projecting yourself into a role almost as if you were on stage. Readers' theater heightens personal response by allowing direct participation in a piece of literature.

Poems are naturals for oral interpretation. Some poems are, in fact, mini-dramas. In the activity that follows, you will try performing one such poem.

Oral Response Activity

Performing a Poem: Ensemble

For this activity, you will need to team with two other classmates. Your first task will be to read the following poem. As you do so, try to sort out the voices.

Countdown

T minus 60 seconds
and counting
marbles on 4th Street
which Joey collected
since age 5½
years ago the
buildings were new
but now they're
falling down
to T minus 50
on the Cape
and all systems are go
up the street
to Stuyvesant which
is the end of the
world and beyond
it are monsters breathing
jet propulsion fuel
now disconnected from
the pad at T minus 40
all systems are green
light at the corner
by the delicatessen
where meat is grown
in white wax paper
and milk is made in
bottles like the ones
Daddy brings home to the
pad now cleared at
T minus 30 while voice

communications with
the world through the
welfare worker are not
proceeding at T minus
20 and now removed
from the launching room
are 2 dead rats and
Mammy is screaming
10, 9, 8, 7 days till
the next check comes for
6, 5, 4, 3, dollars or even
2, 1, zero, ignition, Lift-off
to buy a pair of brand
new shining rockets

Ron Penoyer

Do you distinguish three different voices? One, of course, is that of the flight controller as he counts down the final sixty seconds before liftoff. The other two voices comment on other things, one in much more general terms than the other. Try to decide where one voice leaves off and the other begins. There will be some overlap since the words ending one comment often begin the next.

Assign parts so that one member of your group will read the lines spoken by a single voice. Since comments of various speakers overlap, some words and phrases should be read in unison. (You might even try reading these parts slightly out of sync rather than strictly in unison to heighten the effect.) Practice reading the poem aloud several times, working on timing and appropriate delivery for each voice. Because the poem gets more complicated as it progresses, you will probably need to concentrate much of your practice on the ending.

Perform your version of "Countdown" for the rest of the class. Listen closely as other groups perform their renditions. Discuss any differences.

If time permits, you might tape record your reading. You might also clip pictures from magazines and make a collage illustrating the images juxtaposed in the poem.

Think back to your first reading of "Countdown." What was your initial response?—frustration? curiosity? admiration?—maybe a little of all three?

As you discussed the poem with your two classmates, did you begin to see it more clearly? Did you notice things you hadn't noticed before? As you began to practice reading it aloud, did you start to *feel* the words?

Now that you have made the poem your own by performing it, do you respond even more fully?

"Countdown" is clearly a mini-drama as well as a poem. The dramatic element in other poems may be more subtle. Usually, there is just one speaker. Try performing such poems as monologues. Responding with your own voice to the words of the poet will deepen both your understanding and your enjoyment of those words.

Talking Back to an Author

Have you ever been so perplexed or so moved by a piece of literature that you wished you could talk to the author? Though a person-to-person conversation is seldom possible, you can always talk to the author on paper. Writing a letter is a satisfying response—even if the letter is never mailed.

Henry David Thoreau, an American essayist who has been dead

more than a hundred years, continues to evoke strong responses from
modern readers. Here is an excerpt from *Walden*, his best-known work:

> I went to the woods because I wished to live deliberately, to front
> only the essential facts of life, and see if I could not learn what it
> had to teach, and not, when I came to die, discover that I had not
> lived. I did not wish to live what was not life, living is so dear; nor
> did I wish to practice resignation, unless it was quite necessary. I
> wanted to live deep and suck out all the marrow of life, to live so
> sturdily and Spartanlike as to put to rout all that was not life, to cut
> a broad swath and shave close, to drive life into a corner, to reduce
> it to its lowest terms, and, if it proved to be mean, why then to get
> the whole and genuine meanness of it, and publish its meanness to
> the world; or if it were sublime, to know it by experience, and be
> able to give a true account of it in my next excursion. For most
> men, it appears to me, are in a strange uncertainty about it . . .
> Still, we live meanly, like ants . . . Our life is frittered away by
> detail. An honest man has hardly need to count more than his ten
> fingers, or in extreme cases he may add his ten toes, and lump the
> rest. Simplicity, simplicity, simplicity! I say, let your affairs be as two
> or three, and not a hundred or a thousand; instead of a million
> count half a dozen, and keep other accounts on your thumbnail.

Can you see why such a philosophy would have so much appeal in
today's complex technological society? Thoreau's sublime confidence in
the power of the individual and in each individual's ability to know
spiritual truth directly by divine intuition—a philosophy known as
Transcendentalism—has appealed to previous generations as well.

Almost a half-century ago, another distinguished American writer
responded to Thoreau's *Walden* in the form of an open letter to its author:

Walden (June 1939)

Miss Nims, take a letter to Henry David Thoreau:
Dear Henry: I thought of you the other afternoon as I was approach-
ing Concord, doing fifty on Route 62. That is a high speed at which
to hold a philosopher in one's mind, but in this century we are a
nimble bunch . . .

I may as well admit that I was journeying to Concord with the
deliberate intention of visiting your woods; for although I have never
knelt at the grave of a philosopher nor placed wreaths on moldy

poets, and have often gone a mile out of my way to avoid some
place of historical interest, I have always wanted to see Walden
Pond. The account which you left of your sojourn there is, you will
be amused to learn, a document of increasing pertinence; each year
it seems to gain a little headway, as the world loses ground. We may
all be transcendental yet, whether we like it or not. As our common
complexities increase, any tale of individual simplicity (and yours is
the best written and the cockiest) acquires a new fascination; as our
goods accumulate, but not our well-being, your report of an existence without material adornment takes on a certain awkward
credibility . . .

I knew I must be nearing your woodland retreat when the
Golden Pheasant lunchroom came into view—Sealtest ice cream,
toasted sandwiches, hot frankfurters, waffles, tonics, and lunches.
Were I the proprietor, I should add rice, Indian meal, and molasses
—just for old time's sake. The Pheasant, incidentally, is for sale: a
chance for some nature lover who wishes to set himself up beside a
pond in the Concord atmosphere and live deliberately, fronting only
the essential facts of life on Number 126. Beyond the Pheasant was a
place called Walden Breezes, an oasis whose porch pillars were made
of old green shutters sawed into lengths. On the porch was a

distorting mirror, to give the traveler a comical image of himself,
who had miraculously learned to gaze in an ordinary glass without
smiling. Behind the Breezes, in a sun-parched clearing, dwelt your
philosophical descendants in their trailers, each trailer the size of
your hut, but all grouped together for the sake of congeniality.
Trailer people leave the city, as you did, to discover solitude and in
any weather, at any hour of the day or night, to improve the nick of
time; but they soon collect in villages and get bogged deeper in the
mud than ever . . .

Before I quit I walked clear round the pond and found the place
where you used to sit on the northeast side to get the sun in the fall,
and the beach where you got sand for scrubbing your floor. On the
eastern side of the pond, where the highway borders it, the State has
built dressing rooms for swimmers, a float with diving towers, drinking fountains of porcelain, and rowboats for hire. The pond is in fact
a State Preserve, and carries a twenty-dollar fine for picking wild-
flowers, a decree signed in all solemnity by your fellow-citizens
Walter C. Wardwell, Erson B. Barlow, and Nathaniel I. Bowditch.
There was a smell of creosote where they had been building a wide
wooden stairway to the road and the parking area. Swimmers and
boaters were arriving; bodies plunged vigorously into the water and
emerged wet and beautiful in the bright air. As I left, a boatload of
town boys were splashing about in mid-pond, kidding and fooling,
the young fellows singing at the top of their lungs in a wild chorus:
"Amer–ica, Amer–ica, God shed his grace on thee,
And crown thy good with brotherhood
From sea to shi–ning sea."

E. B. White

Notice the warm conversational tone White uses in his letter. He writes
as if speaking to a respected companion who shares his knowledge of
Thoreau and his gentle—if sometimes irreverent—sense of humor.
Notice also how White slips in phrases from *Walden*. Apparently he
responds deeply and directly to the text, but he also projects its ideas into
a world Thoreau never knew. White's talking back to this essayist he so
greatly admires results in a response that is itself a fine essay.

**Getting
It
Started**

Think about what you would like to say in your own open letter
to Thoreau. (If you have not already studied *Walden*, you may
wish to read other excerpts.) Imagine what the famous Transcen-
dentalist might think of your life-style and that of people around

you. Consider also how your life might be enriched by practicing some of the simplification Thoreau advocated.

If you prefer, think what you might say to E. B. White in response to his letter. Remember White's major point in 1939: Thoreau's book, *Walden*, was gaining in popularity each year as the world steadily lost ground. If White worried about materialism then, what would he think now? In Thoreau's terms, how much ground has the world lost since 1939? Reread White's letter and think how you'd like to respond.

Prepare to write an open letter to the writer who arouses in you the stronger response. Jot down key words and phrases used by that writer. Consider applications the writer's beliefs and concerns seem to have in your life. How does it make you feel to read what he or she wrote? Are you moved to make any changes in your attitude or even in your life-style? Jot down notes on these points.

Draft an open letter to the author you chose. Focus on your own experience with a particular text and what it means to you. Begin by placing yourself in a situation that makes you recall the author's words, and look at those words in a new way. Make your response to that piece come alive with specific illustrations. Tie it firmly to the text itself. Write in your own voice, using a natural conversational tone. Address your remarks to Thoreau or White, but think of your real audience as other readers with whom you share a common background and a lively sense of humor.

**Getting
It
Down**

For the moment, lay aside the letter you have just drafted and take a closer look at White's. Notice first the way the letter flows. After an introduction about the situation prompting the author to think back through his reading of *Walden*, the letter moves chronologically and spatially. It reports in sequence the various landmarks of the journey and the new response to Thoreau's words each conjures up.

Your letter is probably not organized around a journey. It should, however, have a smooth flow. Beginning with a real-life situation that gives you a new perspective on the text should help insure that smooth flow. Such a situation places your response in a personal context and provides a unifying frame.

Notice also the tone of White's letter. His voice is relaxed, but not careless or overly colloquial. He never talks down to his reader or strains to be cute. White writes as if talking to a respected, literate friend. But because he is writing, he can take time to polish his language and organize his ideas for conciseness and interest.

White's style is smooth. His sentences roll along easily, taking the reader with them. Such long sentences would be almost impossible to follow if they weren't expertly punctuated to keep ideas from running together. Since punctuation guides pauses and even helps signal tone, it allows the reader to "hear" the sentences. White is a master at making punctuation work for him.

Throughout this course, you have practiced such techniques as sentence-combining and sentence imitation. The point of such practice is to write richer sentences of your own. Since rich sentences are often longer and more intricate, they require careful punctuation. This is a good time to review punctuation guidelines you've already studied and to learn some new ones. ● See your Handbook if you need to check any particular points.

Writer's Workbench 1

Punctuation

A. Commas.   Your ear can often tell you where to put commas. Read a sentence aloud and listen for any light natural pause. A comma probably goes in that spot. Even so, it is a good idea to know a few rules. To brush up on rules you've studied before and should be applying automatically, account for the commas in these sentences from E. B. White's letter:

1. That is a high speed at which to hold a philosopher in one's mind, but in this century we are a nimble bunch.
2. As our common complexities increase, any tale of individual simplicity . . . acquires a new fascination.
3. The Pheasant, incidentally, is for sale . . .
4. Beyond the Pheasant was a place called Walden Breezes, an oasis whose porch pillars were made of old green shutters sawed into lengths.
5. On the eastern side of the pond, where the highway borders it, the State has built dressing rooms for swimmers, a float with

diving towers, drinking fountains of porcelain, and rowboats for hire.

Check your explanations with those of your classmates. ● If you need further review of basic comma usage, consult pages H-13–20 in your Writer's Handbook.

B. <u>Semicolons and Colons.</u>   You have already learned to use semicolons between clauses of a compound sentence when there is no conjunction. Such linkage saves words and often heightens contrast or balance. The semicolon simply couples equally important clauses; it doesn't tip the balance toward either. It signals the reader to pause and get ready for another idea, but not to stop because that idea belongs with the preceding one and is closely related to it.

You have also learned that a semicolon is used *with* a conjunction to separate clauses in a compound sentence when that sentence contains other commas. In this case, the semicolon signals a slightly longer pause than the comma and shows graphically where one clause leaves off and the other begins.

1. Find two sentences in White's letter in which semicolons alone link compound sentences.
2. Find another sentence in which a semicolon appears before a coordinating conjunction to partition clauses containing other commas.

You already know that a colon follows the greeting of a business letter. You may have noticed the colon after "Dear Henry" in White's letter and realized that it lends a slight formality to get the letter started. You may have also noticed several commas and been uncertain why they were used.

As you know, the colon always points ahead. It calls attention to what is to follow. For that reason, it is sometimes used like a semicolon in a compound sentence, but with one important difference: it primes the reader for the next clause. It signals that the preceding clause is just introductory, that it will be explained or illustrated or completed by the clause that follows. Because a colon points forward, it is also used to introduce long quotations or a list.

3. Explain the colon that follows "Miss Nim, take a letter to Henry David Thoreau."
4. Find two sentences in which the colon is used to partition the clauses of a compound sentence. In each case, explain why the colon is used instead of the semicolon.
5. Find the colon used to introduce a quotation consisting of several lines.

C. <u>Dashes and parentheses.</u>   The dash usually indicates a sudden break in thought. For that reason, it is more at home in informal prose than in formal discourse. The dash is rather bold. It not only signals a break in the flow of a sentence; it emphasizes that break. Though the dash should be used sparingly, it can invigorate style.

White used the dash for conversational flavor. (It can be used for more staid purposes such as setting off nonrestrictive elements containing their own commas or highlighting an appositive.)

Parentheses also allow a writer to break the flow of a sentence, but in a low-key manner. Just as a dash calls attention to the idea that breaks in, parentheses slip incidental ideas quietly into the background.

1. Find the two sentences in which White uses dashes to indicate an abrupt break in thought. In what way do the words following the

dash break away into a detour? Why do you think White chose to emphasize each?

2. Find the sentence using parentheses to tuck in an interrupting element. Explain the use of parentheses rather than dashes.

3. Write two original sentences, one illustrating effective use of the dash and the other of parentheses.

By taking White's sentences apart and second-guessing his choice of punctuation, you have done more than review commas, semicolons, colons, dashes, and parentheses. You have explored style. Although there is much more to style than dropping in commas and dashes, punctuation does contribute. As you go back to work on the letter you wrote earlier, consider punctuation a means of signalling your reader how you want that letter to sound.

Checking It Out

Before getting down to the job of refining your paper, take time to reread the text to which you are responding. Let the words work on you. Do you see anything you didn't see before? Has writing about the text changed or deepened your response in any way?

With the author's words fresh in your mind, return to the first draft of your letter to the author. Does it say what you want to say? Does it capture your real thoughts and feelings about the text?

When you are satisfied that it does, check the letter for focus. Do you begin by placing yourself in a situation that triggers thoughts of Thoreau's or White's words? Do you hold the letter together by responding within that situation? Does one idea lead logically and smoothly to the next? Do you weave in echoes of the text itself?

Finally, check tone. Read the letter aloud. Does the voice sound like yours? Is it straightforward, warm? Do you enliven that tone with a little humor? Do sentences roll along smoothly rather than being chopped up? Do you make punctuation work for you?

After you ask yourself these questions and refine your letter accordingly, exchange papers with a classmate. Check each other on the same points and make suggestions, preferably by making pencil notes in the margin.

Getting It Right

Considering the suggestions of your partner, make a final draft of your letter. If you cannot type, write the letter neatly on unlined paper so that it will look like a letter.

Letter-writing is not the only way to talk back to an author. It is, however, a direct way to crystallize your responses. When you read something special, you might write short notes to the author. Such letters may even be mailed to contemporary writers in care of their publishers. Another possibility for talking back includes inventing simulated dialogue with an author about a particular story or poem. You will undoubtedly think of other ways.

Imitating Literature

It has been said that imitation in writing has a bad reputation but an honorable history. Some of the world's greatest writers profess to have learned their craft by copying and then imitating favorite passages from authors they admired.

Those writers were doing more than seeking to absorb style through osmosis. They were *responding* to passages that were special in some way. By copying what the author had written, they retracted the creative process and felt at least a hint of what the author might have felt. To imitate models, they had to think as the author had thought. Such activity is one form of response to literature. It is a way of getting closer to a piece, indeed of becoming part owner.

You have already tried imitation as a way of mastering new sentence patterns. The next activity will have the same benefit. But extending your control of sentence structure is not the main point. The main point is to get inside a piece of literature and respond to it more fully.

Getting It Started

The following paragraph from Ralph Ellison's *Invisible Man* introduces the protagonist of the novel. Most of us—regardless of race—can identify with the black man who feels that people look straight through him without really seeing him. Read the paragraph several times, at least once aloud.

I am an invisible man. No, I am not a spook like those who haunted Edgar Allen Poe; nor am I one of your Hollywood movie ectoplasms. I am a man of substance, of flesh and bone, fiber and liquids—and I might even be said to possess a mind. I am invisible, understand, simply because people refuse to see me. Like the bodiless heads you see sometimes in circus sideshows, it is as though I have been surrounded by mirrors of hard, distorting glass. When they approach me, they see only my surroundings, themselves, or figments of the imagination—indeed everything and anything except me.

Notice the progression of the paragraph. It starts with stark simplicity, the unlikely statement "I am an invisible man." It continues by countering the reader's expectation for some kind of supernatural being out of Poe or some horror movie. In other words, the speaker tells what he is *not*. He then continues to tell what he is. In doing so, he moves from the least important to most important, from body to mind. Then he resolves the apparent contradiction by explaining the sense in which he is invisible—first in the metaphoric images of the grotesque house of mirrors, then in literal terms.

The more closely you read the text, the more you should be able to respond to it. Try to get still closer by writing your own version. If you wish, you may begin with Ellison's sentence "I am an invisible man [or woman]" and develop that sentence in your own way. If you prefer, begin with a different sentence—for example, "I am a living anachronism" or "I am really two people." In either case, follow the grammatical pattern of Ellison's sentences as exactly as possible. Those patterns along with the progression explained above will help generate details. Be sure that all details develop your first sentence. (As you create your imitation of this model, you might notice the punctuation and relate it to what you learned in the previous Writer's Workbench.)

Getting It Down

Share your imitation with a small group of classmates. First, ask whether the content of the paragraph is clear and interesting. Do all details develop the opening sentence? Do the ideas and images

Checking It Out

hang together? Next, have your classmates follow the model as you read your paragraph again. Do all sentences fit Ellison's pattern? If not, how can they be rearranged, expanded, or otherwise changed to fit? Are there any word choices that might be improved?

~~~~~~

Getting It Right

Make a final draft of your imitation and display it with those of your classmates. As you compare your imitation with the others, notice how the model sparked different approaches and different images. Which imitations seem best to you?

~~~~~~

Although imitation is only one form of response, it can be an important one. Develop the habit of keeping your Writer's Notebook handy when you read. Copy passages that you find especially striking. Later, try using each passage as a model for your own piece. Do you feel that copying and imitating part of a piece makes it your own? Many readers do. You too may find imitation a satisfying response to literature.

Something Old, Something New

Most readers find it easier to respond to modern writing than to stories, poems, and plays of the past. Since good literature deals with timeless themes, it wears well. The barrier is language, not ideas.

As you may know, English is a relatively new language, scarcely more than 1500 years old. Even so, that language has changed a great deal. Old English—the parent language spoken by the Anglo Saxons— bears so little resemblance to modern English that it can be studied as a foreign language. Only students of Old English would be able to read this sentence from the Anglo-Saxon epic *Beowulf*:

Fyrst forð gewāt; flota wæs on ýđum, bāt under beorge.

Yet the epic about the primitive hero who slew monsters appears in translation in most high school literature books. All generations respond to a hero.

Modern heroes, of course, do not slay monsters who embody the nameless fears of a superstitious people. Even though today's readers take

Beowulf's conquest of the horrible Grendel less literally than the Anglo Saxons did, such exploits are not altogether foreign. The same kind of bigger-than-life, good-guys-vs.-bad-guys conflict remains popular in comic books and movies.

The epic has so captured the imaginations of some writers that they have responded with literary creations of their own. Poet Richard Wilbur, for example, wrote a poem titled "Beowulf." John Gardner wrote a whole novel inspired by the epic.

This darkly comic novel is told from the point of view of the monster Grendel, who finds life senseless and absurd. In disillusionment, he year after year breaks into the castle and slaughters the sleeping noblemen. This passage illustrates the tone of Gardner's novel:

> I plunge into the silent, hearth-lit hall, with a laugh that I wouldn't much care to wake up to myself. I trample the planks that a moment before protected the hall like a hand raised in horror to a terrified mouth (Sheer poetry, ah!) . . .

Even Middle English is hard to read except in translation. You can probably catch the gist of these familiar lines that open Chaucer's *Canterbury Tales*:

> Whan that Aprill with his shourës sootë
> The droghte of March hath perced to the rootë . . .

Even so, you have to work so hard at unlocking meaning that you can't really respond. Again, the problem is language rather than content. Once the language has been updated, modern audiences respond to *Canterbury Tales*. The popular stage version attests to that response.

By the time of Shakespeare, English had entered its modern period. Though the language doesn't sound like the language you hear every day, it is understandable. In fact, practiced readers respond to Shakespeare's language as deeply as they respond to his insights into human nature.

The next exercise is designed to help you respond to language of the past. It is based on a scene from Shakespeare's *Hamlet*, a tragedy about a young Danish prince charged with the responsibility of avenging his father's murder and thus restoring the honor of his kingdom. If you know the play, you will recognize this slightly abridged scene. It comes at the end of the play when Hamlet has finally killed his father's murderer. His mother, who has faithlessly married the murderer of her first husband, has drunk poison and Hamlet has been fatally wounded by a poisoned sword. He knows that he is dying. Horatio is Hamlet's best friend and Fortinbras another prince whom Hamlet considers noble enough to name King of Denmark.

Writer's Workbench 2

Paraphrasing Language of the Past

Hamlet: Horatio, I am dead;
      Thou liv'st; report me and my cause aright
      To the unsatisfied.
Horatio: Never believe it.
      I am more an antique Roman than a Dane.   5
      Here's yet some liquor left.
Hamlet: As th'art a man,
      Give me the cup. Let go! By heaven, I'll have't.
      O good Horatio, what a wounded name
      (Things standing thus unknown) shall live behind me!   10
      If thou didst ever hold me in thy heart,
      Absent thee from felicity awhile,
      And in this harsh world draw thy breath in pain,
      To tell my story.   [March afar off, and shot within.]
               What warlike noise is this?   15

Osric: Young Fortinbras, with conquest come from Poland,
To the ambassadors of England gives
This warlike volley.
Hamlet: O, I die, Horatio!
The potent poison quite o'ercrows my spirit.   20
I cannot live to hear the news from England,
But I do prophesy the election lights
On Fortinbras. He has my dying voice.
So tell him, with th' occurrents, more and less,
Which have solicited—the rest is silence.   25
Horatio: Now cracks a noble heart. Good night, sweet prince,
And flights of angels sing thee to thy rest!

                                     [March within.]

Why does the drum come hither?

[Enter Fortinbras and English ambassadors, with drum,
    Colors, and attendants.]

Fortinbras: Where is this sight?

Horatio: What is it you would see?   30
    If aught of woe or wonder, cease your search.

Fortinbras: This quarry cries on havoc, O proud Death,
    What feast is toward in thine eternal cell
    That thou so many princes at a shot
    So bloodily hast struck?   35

Ambassador: The sight is dismal;
    And our affairs from England come too late.
    The ears are senseless that should give us hearing
    To tell him his commandment is fulfilled . . .
    Where should we have our thanks?   40

Horatio: Not from his mouth . . .
    But since you are here arrived, give order that these bodies
    High on a stage be placed to the view;
    And let me speak to the yet unknowing world
    How these things came about. So shall you hear   45
    Of carnal, bloody, and unnatural acts . . .

Fortinbras: Let us haste to hear it,
    And call the noblest to the audience.
    For me, with sorrow I embrace my fortune.
    I have some rights of memory in this kingdom,   50
    Which now to claim my vantage doth invite me.

Horatio: Of that I shall have also cause to speak,
    And from his mouth whose voice will draw on more.
    But let this same be presently performed,
    Even while men's minds are wild, lest more mischance 55
    On plots and errors happen.

Fortinbras: Let four captains
    Bear Hamlet like a soldier to the stage;
    For he was likely, had he been put on,
    To have proved most royally; and for his passage   60
    The soldiers' music and the rites of war
    Speak loudly for him.
    Take up the bodies. Such a sight as this
    Becomes the field, but here shows much amiss.
    Go, bid the soldiers shoot.   65

        [Exeunt marching, after the which a peal of
            ordnance are shot off.]

A. Before writing a paraphrase of an excerpt from this scene, consider these questions:

1. Shakespeare used verb forms that are now archaic. What is the modern equivalent for *liv'st, didst, doth,* and *hath?* He also used the archaic pronouns *thee, thou,* and *thy.* What are their modern equivalents? Where else have you found such verbs and pronouns?

2. Sometimes Shakespeare made statements that would have been clear to well-educated audiences of the early 1600's but are not so clear today even though the words sound familiar enough. The line "I am more an antique Roman than a Dane" is a case in point. Elizabethans with a classical education probably knew that Roman noblemen showed ultimate loyalty to their fallen king by dying with him. Look at the context of this line. How do Horatio's next sentence and Hamlet's response help make this point clear?

3. Although some words in the passage are obsolete, context and structure strongly suggest their meaning. Take the word *o'ercrows* in Line 20. What must it mean? In other instances, spelling is different, but the word is still recognizable. The word *occurrents* in Line 24 is such a word. Still another difficulty occurs when a word like *solicited* (Line 25) is used in an unexpected way. Here, it means "evoked or brought about [these happenings]."

B. After you can read the scene through without much effort, using such insights into Shakespeare's language as suggested in the previous questions, choose any passage of at least ten lines and write a prose paraphrase—in other words, a "translation" into your own language. (Retain the form of the script.)

Once attuned to Shakespeare's language, most readers and theatergoers respond to tragedies like *Hamlet* and comedies like A *Midsummer Night's Dream.* Besides making generations of people laugh and cry and ponder human nature, Shakespeare's plays have inspired all kinds of written responses. Among the best-known is the popular musical *West Side Story* modeled after *Romeo and Juliet.*

Moving Toward Independence

The first two chapters in this unit have involved you in reading as well as writing. You have tried your hand at creating your own literary pieces—pieces that are form-centered rather than speaker-centered or audience-centered. You have done some close reading and responded in a variety of other ways. In the process, you have practiced several important writing techniques.

Take a few minutes to review these two chapters. Look especially for pointers on writing. Jot down key techniques in the section of your Writer's Notebook reserved for **Notes on the Writing Process**. For example, you might add "Fleshing-Out a Plot Summary" to your list of pre-writing strategies. Under "Guidelines for Drafting," you might make notes on how to write a conclusion that draws a piece together by echoing previous images and then commenting on significance.

After you have reviewed the unit so far, complete the following assignment. It will help you apply independently what you have learned in the last two chapters.

Getting It Down

Choose a piece of literature to which you respond strongly. You may choose a novel, a short story, a poem, or a play. Think for a few minutes about the way you respond and why. (Reread at least a part of the piece and keep it before you as you write.) What stands out to you in the selection and what feelings or thoughts does it evoke? Write a brief short story or poem reflecting this response. (Before beginning, study the Checkpoint on page 215. Besides letting you know how your paper will be evaluated, these criteria will help guide you as you write. When you hand in your final draft, provide your teacher with a copy of the story, poem, or play you were responding to.)

CHECKPOINT 5

1	2	3	4	5

Response to literature   ×5=

I can't see much connection between what you wrote and the piece that inspired it.

Response is clear and fairly well developed. Try building in more echoes of the work itself.

Your response comes through loud and clear. I can see exactly how you relate to this piece of literature.

Form   ×4=

Neither clearly a poem nor clearly a short story. Review characteristics in Chapter 8.

You almost have it.
a. Poem: Sharpen layout of lines and stanzas.
b. Story. Make events build to a peak. Also fill out character development. Work on tying ends together and getting to significance in conclusion.

Bravo! Masterful control of your chosen form.

Word choice   ×4=

Go back and mark generalities in paper. Substitute words that appeal to senses. Use more verbs to make piece move.

Most images are sharp, and I can see you're working on verbs. Try adding a few participles.

Exact as well as original. Images graphic and verbs abundant.

Similes and metaphors   ×4=

Where are your comparisons? See me if you'd like help there.

You have the right idea. Try compressing a few of those similes into metaphors. Reconsider any that border on triteness.

Similes and metaphors both apt and fresh. They say a great deal in few words.

Punctuation   ×3=

Big problems. Review Workbench 1 on pages 200–203. Then get a classmate to help you proofread and correct.

Accurate enough for clarity, but you don't make signals like dashes and colons work for you stylistically. Review Parts B and C of Workbench 1 on pages 200–203.

E.B. White would be proud of you. Punctuation not only guides reader through your sentences. It lends stylistic flair.

Chapter 10

Interpreting and Analyzing Literature

So far, you have written about literature as a participant. Now you will step back and become a critic. Fortunately, literary critics aren't just people who find fault. They are perceptive readers who analyze texts for greater insight into both meaning and craft.

To write literary criticism, you need not give up personal response. In fact, you *must* not. Response precedes analysis. Get inside a text and let it work on you. Experience the words in your own way. Only then are you qualified to step back and ask "Why do I respond like this? "How does the writer pull it off?" Critical analysis begins with such *why* and *how* questions.

This kind of writing about literature involves the same basic process as other kinds of writing you have done. You begin by discovering something interesting and worthwhile to say. This raw material will come largely from the text you are analyzing, but it will be colored by the experiences and feelings you bring to that text. You will continue by shaping your material, this time into the form of an expository essay. In organizing essays about literature, you will think in terms of an introduction, a body, and a conclusion. You will pay careful attention to coherence, arranging your ideas in an order that makes sense and providing careful transition from one idea to the next. In proofreading, you will check to be sure that tense is consistent and sentences aren't garbled by unclear pronoun references.

SPOTLIGHT

An Approach to Analysis

Although analyzing a James Joyce novel is much more complicated than analyzing a simple short story, the basic approach is no different. It is best to practice this approach first on something fairly easy, like this vignette by Gwendolyn Brooks:

Maud Martha Spares the Mouse

There. She had it at last. The weeks it had devoted to eluding her, the tricks, the clever hide-and-go-seeks, the routes it had in all sobriety devised, together with the delicious moments it had, un-doubtedly, laughed up its sleeve—all to no ultimate avail. She had that mouse.

It shook its little self, as best it could, in the trap. Its bright black eyes contained no appeal—the little creature seemed to understand that there was no hope of mercy from the eternal enemy, no hope of reprieve or postponement—but a fine small dignity. It waited. It looked at Maud Martha.

She wondered what else it was thinking. Perhaps that there was not enough food in its larder. Perhaps that little Betty, a puny child from the start, would not, now, be getting fed. Perhaps that, now, the family's seasonal housecleaning, for lack of expert direction,

would be left undone. It might be regretting that young Bobby's education was now at an end. It might be nursing personal regrets. No more the mysterious shadows of the kitchenette, the uncharted twists, the unguessed halls. No more the sweet delights of the chase, the charms of being unsuccessfully hounded, thrown at.

Maud Martha could not bear the little look.

"Go home to your children," she urged. "To your wife or husband." She opened the trap. The mouse vanished.

Suddenly, she was conscious of a new cleanness in her. A wide air walked in her. A life had blundered its way into her power and it had been hers to preserve or destroy. She had not destroyed. In the center of that simple restraint was—creation. She had created a piece of life. It was wonderful.

"Why," she thought, as her height doubled, "Why, I'm good! I am *good*."

She ironed her aprons. Her back was straight. Her eyes were mild, and soft with a godlike loving-kindness.

Now that you have read the story through, think about Maud Martha and her mouse. What details from the story float to the surface of your mind? Jot down those details.

Then reread the story. Do you notice things that you didn't notice before? What sticks with you this time? Add to your jot-list. Quote exactly any phrases that seem especially striking.

Next, look back at the beginning of the story and then at the end. What change has occurred between these two points, especially in the main character? Consider what brought it about. Summarize that change in your notes.

If there are thirty students in your English class, there are probably thirty different sets of notes on "Maud Martha Spares the Mouse." That is because each of you brought to the text a different set of personal experiences and feelings. Whose reading of the story is best? Nobody's is necessarily best. A good story is rich enough to allow varied interpretations.

One set of notes might look like this:

> mouse in trap—described as person
> determination to get mouse
> Maud Martha and mouse looking at each other
> mouse family—Betty, Bobby
> mouse does housecleaning too
> Maud Martha talking to mouse

mouse enjoyed game of chase?
Maud Martha felt clean
ironed aprons
seemed godlike
mouse played game, "laughed up its sleeve"
"air walked in her"
happier because had had a chance to destroy life but created
      instead

Another list might look like this:

had mouse at last
little mouse shook—expected no mercy
Maud Martha thinks of mouse as person with family
sympathy for children, small things
feels power to destroy or save
felt good after saving mouse
felt godlike
"fine small dignity"   (mouse)
"height doubled"   (Maud Martha)
changed because had used power to create, not destroy

Notice that these two jot-lists share some common items. Both readers, for example, notice Maud Martha's thinking the mouse may have a family and the word *godlike* at the end of the story. Both attribute the change in Maud Martha to her choosing to save a life rather than destroy it. Almost any good reader would agree.

Despite these basic similarities, the lists are different. The same details don't stand out for both readers. One responds to the phrase "air walked in her" and the other to the statement that Maud Martha's "height doubled." The phrases you noted on your own list may be different still. That's fine. The point is to capture the details and images that mean most to you.

After skimming off the details and images that are particularly important to you as a reader, the next step is to move back and study those notes. Which details are related? In other words, which seem to go together? What recurring patterns can you see?

Take the first list on page 219 as an example. The student who made these notes might see a connection between Maud Martha's determined efforts to rid her house of mice, the way she thinks of the mouse as doing seasonal housecleaning, and the fact that she irons her aprons at the end of the story. All of these details sound domestic. They show Maud

Martha to be a practical woman who values a clean house. The student might also see another pattern, one that doesn't quite fit with the first. A practical woman doesn't go around looking mice in the eye, talking to them, and inventing imaginary mouse families with children named Betty and Bobby. The reader had also noted the fact that Maud Martha thought maybe the mouse shared her enjoyment in the game of chase. These details seem to be connected. Besides showing a lively imagination, they show empathy. Maud Martha identifies with the mouse and assumes that it has feelings just as she does.

Not every detail in this list fits into one of the two categories. Some have little to do with either the practicality or the empathy of the main character. But enough do fit to make these groups of details seem significant. The reader might begin to wonder how and why. What do these two sides of the same person have to do with the way she feels at the end of the story? What does it all mean? In considering such questions, that reader is well on the way to writing a good critical analysis.

Now look back at the list of details that stand out to the second reader. The student who made these notes might review the list and realize that he or she has jotted down several details containing the word *small* or its synonym: "*little* mouse shook—expected no mercy," "sympathy for children, *small* things," " 'fine *small* dignity.' " This recurring image of smallness must mean something. Certainly, the mouse seemed tiny and helpless as it waited in the trap. Are there any other patterns? The reader might notice that the word *power* has been jotted down twice. Power certainly fits with *godlike*. Could it have anything to do with the way Maud Martha felt that her "height doubled" after she spared the mouse? Size does go with power. After a little thought, the reader might recognize a contrast between the two groupings of details that have emerged from the list. The mouse is tiny and helpless; Maud Martha, many times larger and more powerful. What does it mean that she feels even larger and more godlike after she has spared the tiny creature who had blundered into her power? In asking such questions, this reader, like the first, is well on the way to writing a good critical analysis. The two papers will be different, but not because one reader is right and the other is wrong. Remember that a good story is rich enough to allow more than one approach to interpretation.

Until now, the emphasis has been upon collecting details from the text and seeing how those details fit together. The next step is to begin drafting the critical analysis.

In order to get started in the right direction, there are several things to remember. First, a critical analysis is *not* a plot summary. An analysis of "Maud Martha Spares the Mouse" should not begin, "In this story, a woman starts looking at a mouse she has trapped and can't go through with killing it." Your job is not to rehash plot; it is to interpret and explain. Assume that your audience is a well-informed reader who is interested in getting a new slant on a familiar piece of literature.

That new slant should be your own. Take a stand about what is important in the story. Use your own insight into the piece to help your reader understand it more fully. Taking a stand about a piece of literature may seem risky. But as novelist Sloane Wilson once said, "A writer's job is sticking his neck out."

Before beginning to shape an essay from your notes on a piece of literature, write down in one sentence the main point you hope to make. State that point as clearly and precisely as possible. It is your thesis—in other words, your controlling idea. Every sentence you write must advance that point. Otherwise, it does not belong in your paper.

Don't announce your thesis in the very first sentence of your analysis. If you do, everything that follows will seem anti-climactic. Besides, such an opening sounds abrupt. Pique your reader's interest and point him or her in the right direction. Build your case gradually, supporting your interpretation with plenty of textual details. Include some direct quotations. Lead your reader carefully toward a conclusion that summarizes and clinches your point.

The student who was especially intrigued with Maud Martha's conflict between practicality and empathy might begin an analysis like this:

> Sometimes, the heart and the head send mixed messages. When they do, people like the protagonist of Gwendolyn Brooks' "Maud Martha Spares the Mouse" must choose sides . . .

Notice that the student takes an immediate stand about the conflict in the story: it is an inner struggle between the head and the heart. The first sentence makes a broad statement with which almost any reader could identify. The second applies that statement to a particular piece of literature, which is identified by title and author. The stage is now set to explore in detail how this conflict is developed and why it is so significant to the overall meaning of the story. The body of the paper does just that. It explains the two sides of the character and cites details from the text to illustrate each. Only then does the student summarize and clinch the thesis toward which the paper has been directed:

> Having listened to her heart, Maud Martha feels "a new cleanness." Without taking the imaginative leap of seeing the mouse in human

terms, she would have missed the joy of creating life rather than destroying it. It is with this sense of being "godlike" that she returns to the work-a-day world of ironing aprons—a practical woman still, but one with a big heart.

Notice that this conclusion echoes key words of the introduction and thus ties the whole piece together. The reader gets a sense of having arrived where he or she set out to go. Also note that quoted words from the story have been woven smoothly into the analysis and that the best line has been saved for last.

The introduction and conclusion of this critical analysis illustrate two other important points. Notice the absence of such phrases as "I think" or "in my opinion." In the first place, such phrases are superfluous. If the writer says something, he or she must think it. The analysis is assumed to reflect the writer's own opinions. Furthermore, phrases like "it seems to me" are wordy. They weigh the piece down with verbiage. Finally, first-person comments are intrusive. The spotlight is on the piece of literature being analyzed, not upon the person who is analyzing it. Third-person pronouns help keep the focus where it belongs.

The sample introduction and conclusion also illustrate a point about verb tense. Notice the use of present rather than past tense. Almost all critics find present tense more appropriate than past. After all, literature is enduring and dynamic. It is not read and discarded. Maud Martha, for example, is not a relic of the past. She comes alive each time the vignette is read. For that reason, it is more accurate to say "she is" than "she was."

Before attempting a literary analysis on your own, you might want to review the basic approach just illustrated. Here is a recap:

Pre-writing

1. *Collect details that leave the strongest impression.*   After a careful reading of the piece, spend a few minutes thinking about what you have just read. Don't force. Just be open to impressions the work leaves behind. Jot down details that you remember best and those that you relate to most strongly. Review the piece and see what else you notice. Add to your jot-list. Reread the first and last paragraphs of the story. Ask yourself what has changed. Add to your notes a few words summarizing that change.

2. *Group details that seem to be related.*   Study your jot-list and look for possible connections among details. Try to fit at least most of the items into two or three categories.

3. *Look for meaning.*   Consider the patterns you have found among

details and ask yourself "So what?" What do groupings of details add up to? What is their significance to the story as a whole?

Drafting

1. Assume a well-informed audience that shares your reading background.

2. Let your pre-writing notes guide you toward a well-defined thesis. Express that thesis in a clear, concise sentence. Be sure that everything you write supports that controlling idea.

3. In writing your introduction, concentrate on getting your reader hooked and pointing that reader toward your thesis. Be sure to mention the title and author of the literary piece being analyzed.

4. Develop the body of your paper fully, building a case for your interpretation of the piece. Support everything you say with textual evidence. Slip in direct quotations.

5. Conclude your analysis by drawing everything together and commenting on its significance. Heighten unity by echoing key words from the introduction and body of the paper. Make your thesis explicit. Clinch it with a good closing line.

6. Write in the third person, using present-tense words.

Explicating a Poem

Analyzing a poem is much like analyzing a story. The same basic approach applies. You begin by reading and responding to the text. Only after getting a sense of the whole do you begin taking the text apart and examining various pieces to see how they work. (Taken literally, the word *analyze* means *to take apart*.) You think about how the parts fit together and how each contributes to the whole. In the process, you gain new insight into the text.

You have already learned that poetry is highly compressed language. Every word counts. A poet never uses part of a word and throws the rest away. Sound counts as well as sense. Because of the way language works in poetry, analyzing a poem requires the closest possible attention to word choice. The next exercise will provide practice in weighing words for their effect in a poem.

The exercise is based on Dylan Thomas's poem "Do Not Go Gentle into That Good Night." Later, you will write an analysis of this poem. By first playing poet and reaching for exactly the right word, you will get to know the text from the inside.

Writer's Workbench 1

Choosing the Right Word

Mark Twain once said that the difference between the right word and *almost* the right word is the difference between lightning and the lightning bug. Few poets would disagree. Since every word in a poem must count to the utmost, near misses won't do. Poets weigh their words carefully, considering not only denotation (what the word means literally) but also connotation (What the word suggests by association). Besides evaluating each word separately, poets consider the way words fit together to create unified images. They also consider sound.

In composing "Do Not Go Gentle into That Good Night," Dylan Thomas undoubtedly weighed word choices carefully. Of course, we have no way of knowing what options he considered. Some of the options he *could* have considered are enclosed between colored bars in this otherwise unaltered copy of the poem. One of the words in each group is the poet's actual choice. After reading the poem and considering the options, see whether you make the same choices.

Begin by reading the poem through at least twice. Don't pause to consider which word is best. Any one of the three will make sense in a given context. Get a feel for the poem as a whole. Then go back and select the word you think fits best:

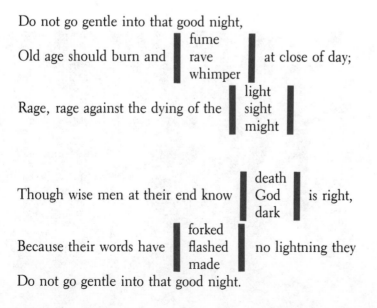

Do not go gentle into that good night,

Old age should burn and | fume / rave / whimper | at close of day;

Rage, rage against the dying of the | light / sight / might |

Though wise men at their end know | death / God / dark | is right,

Because their words have | forked / flashed / made | no lightning they

Do not go gentle into that good night.

Good men, the last [chance / wave / tide] by, crying how bright

Their frail deed might have danced in a [green / blue / stormy] bay,

Rage, rage against the dying of the light.

[Brave / Real / Wild] men who caught and sang the sun in flight,

And learn, too late, they [missed / grieved / offended] it on its way,

Do not go gentle into that good night.

Grave men, near death, who see with [blinding / brilliant / failing] sight

Blind eyes could blaze like [stars / suns / meteors] and be gay,

Rage, rage against the dying of the light.

And you, my father, there on the | sad / final / lofty | height,

Curse, bless, me now with your | salty / fierce / hot | tears, I pray.

Do not go gentle into that good night.
Rage, rage against the dying of the light.

Compare your word choices with those of several classmates. Discuss any differences. Be sure to consider meaning (both denotative and connotative), sound, and unity of image. Try to reach consensus.

Check your group's word choices against the original text supplied by your teacher. As a class, discuss probable reasons for each choice. Then make your own copy of the poem on notebook paper, being sure to get the poet's words exactly right. Also be careful to transcribe form and punctuation accurately. (Keep this copy of the poem to use in subsequent activities.)

By now, you should have a feel for the way words work in "Do Not Go Gentle into That Good Night." Before writing your own analysis of the poem, try two other activities that will help you examine the poem from other angles.

**Getting
It
Started**

Slowly and thoughtfully, read through the copy you made of the Thomas poem. Read primarily for meaning. Think hard about what the poet is saying and apparently feeling. When you finish reading, think of questions the poem raises in your mind. For example, you might wonder why the poet refers to death as "that *good* night" and then urges his father to rage against its dreaded approach. If death is good, why resist it? You might wonder about other apparent contradictions like the poet's seeing his father's tears as a blessing and a curse. How can they be both? You might wonder about certain words like *grieved* in the second line of Stanza 4. How and why might the sun be grieved? You might even wonder why the poet keeps repeating the lines "Rage, rage against the dying of the light" and "Do not go gentle into that good night."

In the margin of the paper upon which you copied the poem, jot down such questions. Place each question by the line that prompts it. Write overall questions at the bottom of the page.

Share your questions with a small group of classmates. Together, see where those questions lead. Make notes on any new insight reached.

Still working with the same small group, work out plans for a choral reading of "Do Not Go Gentle into That Good Night." Try reading in unison only the first and last stanzas plus the last line of intervening stanzas. Assign each stanza in the body of the poem to be read solo by a different person. Ensemble reading will give weight to the opening and closing stanzas and make repeated lines sound like a refrain. Solo voices will sharply differentiate the wise men, good men, wild men, and grave men—all of whom resist death for different reasons. A carefully arranged choral reading can dramatize the structure of the poem.

After you decide exactly how to arrange your reading, talk about the tone of voice in which various passages should be read. Are there places that should be louder or softer, faster or slower than others? Why?

After practicing several times, perform your choral reading for the class. Discuss any differences in oral interpretations by various groups and any insights you gained by participating in the choral reading.

Finally, go back to your handwritten copy of the poem and take stock. What is the most interesting question the poem raises in your mind? What images seem most striking and significant. (Mark them.) What relationship do you see among key images? What is the most satisfying discovery you have made about the poem?

After considering these questions, decide how to approach your analysis. In other words, frame a thesis. Here are some possibilities.

> "Do Not Go Gentle into That Good Night" uses images of light and darkness to express the poet's feelings about living and dying.

> In this poem, paradox is central to meaning.

> The poem is more an affirmation of life than a lament of death.

> "Do Not Go Gentle into That Good Night" reflects a reluctant acceptance of death.

After you have your thesis, list the best points you can think of to develop it. Under each major point, jot down some details from the poem that illustrate that point. Be sure to include some direct quotations.

The points you just listed will help you organize the body of your paper. Presumably, each will be discussed in a separate paragraph. Now think how you can best stimulate interest in this kind of analysis and how you can lead your reader into it. Jot down a possible approach.

Finally, think how you might conclude your paper. Remember that a good paper has forward motion. Everything propels the reader toward the end. A good ending puts the pieces that have been analyzed back together and comments on their significance. Your thesis sentence will help you here. Jot down anything else you might include in the culminating paragraph of your paper.

～～～～～～～～～～～～～～～～～～～～～～～～～～～～～

Using the notes you just made as an informal working outline, draft your analysis of "Do Not Go Gentle into That Good Night." (Don't be constrained by those notes; writing is a process of discovery, and you will get some of your best ideas after you get started.) Begin with an introductory paragraph that will spark interest and orient the reader to your approach. Develop each of your major supporting points into a full paragraph. Illustrate each point with abundant textual detail. Close the paper with a paragraph that draws your previous points together, shows the importance of those points to the poem as a whole, and underscores your thesis.

As you write, keep in mind that your audience is comprised of well-informed readers who are not complete strangers to Dylan Thomas or his poem. Write in your own voice. Use third person and present tense. Try to weave quoted details smoothly into your sentences.

**Getting
It
Down**

～～～～～～～～～～～～～～～～～～～～～～～～～～～～～

Since a first draft always needs a little time to cool before revision, put away the critical analysis you have just written. Use this time to consider some techniques that are especially important in writing about literature, indeed in all kinds of expository writing.

Although coherence is important in all kinds of writing, it is particularly crucial in exposition. If an explanation is to be clear, ideas must be arranged and presented in an order that makes sense. The reader must be able to move easily and without confusion from one idea to the next. One way of making sure a piece of writing is easy to follow is to build in appropriate transitions.

Transitions are the glue to hold sentences and paragraphs together. Fortunately, sentences and paragraphs that flow naturally, each emerging logically from the one before, don't need much. Using too much transition is like using too much glue; the result is a rough surface with seams that bulge and call attention to themselves. When transitions *are* needed, they should be used tactfully. Often, they can be tucked unobtrusively into the sentence rather than being placed conspicuously right up front.

Also, some transitions are implicit. Consider, for example, how pronouns help bind sentences together. If you mention the name Dylan Thomas in one sentence and begin the next with *he*, the linkage is automatic.

There are other simple ways to insure the same kind of linkage. Suppose you mention the name Dylan Thomas in one sentence and begin the next "This famous Welch poet." This phrase points back to its referent in the previous sentence just as the pronoun *he* did.

Often, however, implicit transitions aren't enough to insure continuity, especially between paragraphs and within paragraphs developed by several subpoints. A good writer knows when to use overt transitions like "in the next place" or "on the other hand."

Since transitions signal specific relationships, they can't be used interchangeably. Study the following transitions and identify the kind of relationship signalled by those in each group:

on the other hand	similarly
however	in the same vein
yet	along the same line
in contrast	
on the contrary	first
	next
besides	finally
then too	
furthermore	to illustrate
moreover	for instance
in addition	for example
also	such as
meanwhile	again

immediately	as has been noted
later	in other words
soon	in fact
afterward	
	therefore
to sum up	consequently
on the whole	for this reason
in short	hence
	thus

Notice that some transitions in each group sound heavier than others. *Consequently*, for example, sounds more imposing than *for this reason*. Your ear will tell you which transitional word or phrase blends most smoothly with the style of a particular paper. Try for a firm but deft touch.

Since pronouns make it unnecessary to repeat nouns and do double duty as transitional devices, they figure prominently in expository writing. Keep in mind that pronouns work *for* you only if the reader knows what they stand for. Be sure that every pronoun has a clear antecedent.

Writer's Workbench 2

Pronoun Reference

Problems with pronoun reference usually come in two forms: One is ambiguity; the other, vagueness.

Suppose that your critical analysis included this sentence:

The poet begs his dying father to bless
and curse him with his tears.

The first *his* in the sentence works. It points back to the word *poet*. Clearly, *his* dying father is the *poet's* dying father. But what about *his* tears? The sentence contains two possible referents, *poet* and *father*. Since both are singular and both masculine, either goes with *his*. The pronoun is ambiguous, and the reader can't be sure *whose* tears. One way to resolve this ambiguity is to use a direct quotation: " 'Curse, bless, me with your fierce tears,' the poet begs his dying father." Now there are three pronouns in the sentence: *me*, *your*, and *his*. All are clear.

The other common problem with pronouns is vagueness. Often the culprit is the personal pronoun *it* or the relative pronoun *which*. These words seem to invite being considered catch-alls. Here is an example that might creep into a critical essay:

> Wise men recognize that death is right, which offers some comfort.

There is no specific noun in the sentence for *which* to point back to. Rather, it refers vaguely to the whole idea expressed in the preceding main clause. To eliminate this flaw, the sentence could be rewritten to omit the relative pronoun: "Wise men's recognition that death is right offers some comfort."

For practice in spotting and correcting pronoun reference problems, rewrite the following sentences as directed:

1. Thomas repeatedly exhorts his father not to approach his death meekly. (Find the ambiguous pronoun and simply omit it.)
2. At the end of their lives, wise men realize that "their words have forked no lightning," but it does them no good. (Rewrite to eliminate the vague pronoun *it*.)
3. Good men remember their frail deeds and realize how they could have "danced" in the "green bay" of life. (Rewrite to eliminate the ambiguity in the pronoun *they*.)
4. Grave men have "blind eyes;" they blaze like meteors. (Rewrite to eliminate the ambiguity of the pronoun *they*.)
5. Wild men recall at the moment of death how they caught and celebrated the life-giving sun, which grieved it. (Rewrite to eliminate the vague pronoun *which*.)

As you revise your analysis of "Do Not Go Gentle into That Good Night," be especially conscious of coherence. Keep in mind that logical arrangement of ideas is even more important than transition. You will probably need to work on both.

Checking It Out

After looking back over your first draft and making any improvements that seem obvious, try it out on a group of classmates. Read your paper aloud and ask your listeners to jot down what they consider the main point—the thesis—of the paper. If there is confusion or disagreement, try to find out what caused it and how it might be eliminated. Next, ask group members whether they were convinced of your point. Did you support it adequately? Where might you need to provide more evidence from the text? Finally, ask for a response to your introduction and conclusion. Do they hold your paper together? Does the introduction chart a clear direction for the paper and lead the reader into the analysis without making everything else seem anticlimactic? Does it arouse interest and tell the reader just enough? What about the conclusion? Does it weave together all threads of the paper and answer the question "So what?"

By focusing on the big issues, your classmates should have given you a good starting point for revision. You know whether you got through to your readers, whether the paper succeeded in making its point clearly and convincingly. Making it do so should be your first priority in revision.

Make coherence your second priority. Be sure that your paper has a well-defined beginning, middle, and end. Also be sure that every sentence advances your thesis and that points are arranged in an order that makes sense. Check to be sure transitions have been inserted where they are needed.

When you get to the point of proofreading, check especially for clear pronoun reference. Also check to be sure you maintained a third-person point of view and used present-tense verbs.

In this chapter, you have concentrated on the basics of critical analysis. In doing so, you have been guided by your own responses to a story or poem. But you have gone beyond personal response. You have stepped back from the literary work and asked how the writer elicited such a response. You have also asked why. By exploring the answers to such questions, you have sharpened your insight and deepened your capacity for response to literature. By explaining your analysis on paper, you have allowed other readers to do so as well.

Chapter **11**

Writing a Comparative Analysis

For generations, children have gazed into the night sky and recited "Twinkle, Twinkle, Little Star." If you were one of those children, this two-line rhyme will sound vaguely familiar:

> Firefly, airplane, satellite, star—
> How I wonder which you are.

William Coles, who wrote these lines, was counting on that familiarity. Through deliberate imitation, he evokes the memory of the childhood rhyme. At the same time, he shatters the wonderment associated with that memory. To a space-age child, the airplanes and satellites that sparkle routinely against the night sky lack the ancient mystery of a distant star.

Without the reference point of "Twinkle, Twinkle, Little Star," this two-liner wouldn't work. The little poem has impact only if the reader relates it to the childhood rhyme and then notes the difference. In other words, meaning depends upon the reader's comparing and contrasting the poem with one he or she already knows.

This is an extreme example of how understanding of one text can be enriched by comparison to another. Usually, comparisons are less obvious and less direct. Even so, good readers often see relationships among poems and stories. A character in one novel seems reminiscent of a character in another; yet each is distinctive. Poems that bear little resemblance in form or tone may comment on the same theme. Good readers draw such parallels and note such contrasts. Indeed one way of understanding a piece of literature more fully is to compare it to a related piece. That is exactly what you will do in this chapter as you learn to write a comparative analysis.

In the process, you will apply everything you learned in the previous chapter. You will begin by arriving at your own interpretation of a literary piece. Only then will you explore that piece in relation to another. Once you have found common elements, you will explain in an essay how those elements are alike, how they are different, and how they contribute to the piece as a whole.

Although a comparative analysis is usually longer and more involved than the kind of interpretive essay you wrote earlier, it follows the same basic pattern. Writing such an analysis will help extend your organizational skills. It will also give you a chance to practice controlling proportion and emphasis. Both are important in a well-wrought essay.

Practicing Analysis of Comparison/Contrast

To find comparisons and contrasts worth analyzing, you need not look beyond a single story or poem. Significant similarities and differences emerge *within* as well as *among* texts. Examining related elements within a single piece will allow you to practice basic techniques underlying the full-scale comparative analysis. Read this story by African writer Nadine Gordimer.

SPOTLIGHT

The Train from Rhodesia

The train came out of the red horizon and bore down toward them over the single straight track.

The stationmaster came out of his little brick station with its pointed chalet roof, feeling the creases in his serge uniform in his legs as well. A stir of preparedness rippled through the squatting native vendors waiting in the dust; the face of a carved wooden animal, eternally surprised, stuck out of a sack. The stationmaster's barefoot children wandered over. . . . The flushed and perspiring west cast a reflection, faint, without heat, upon the station, upon the tin shed marked "Goods," upon the walled kraal, upon the gray tin house of the stationmaster and upon the sand, that lapped all around, from sky to sky, cast little rhythmical cups of shadow, so that the sand became the sea, and closed over the children's black feet softly and without imprint.

The stationmaster's wife sat behind the mesh of her veranda. Above her head the hunk of a sheep's carcass moved slightly, dangling in a current of air.

They waited.

The train called out, along the sky; but there was no answer; and the cry hung on: I'm coming . . . I'm coming . . .

The engine flared out now, big, whisking a dwindling body behind it; the track flared out to let it in.

Creaking, jerking, jostling, gasping, the train filled the station.

Here, let me see that one—the young woman curved her body further out of the corridor window. Missus? smiled the old boy, looking at the creatures he held in his hand. From a piece of string on his gray finger hung a tiny woven basket; he lifted it, questioning. No, no, she urged, leaning down toward him, across the height of the train, toward the man in the piece of old rug; that one, that one, her hand commanded. It was a lion, carved out of soft dry wood that looked like spongecake; heraldic, black and white, with impressionistic detail burnt in. The old man held it up to her still smiling, not from the heart, but at the customer. Between its Vandyke teeth, in

the mouth opened in an endless roar too terrible to be heard, it had a black tongue. Look, said the young husband, if you don't mind! And round the neck of the thing, a piece of fur (rat? rabbit? meerkat?); a real mane, majestic, telling you somehow that the artist had delight in the lion.

All up and down the length of the train in the dust the artists sprang, walking bent, like performing animals, the better to exhibit the fantasy held toward the faces on the train. Buck, startled and stiff, staring with round black and white eyes. More lions, standing erect, grappling with strange, thin, elongated warriors who clutched spears and showed no fear in their slits of eyes. How much, they asked from the train, how much?

Give me penny, said the little ones with nothing to sell. The dogs went and sat, quite still, under the dining car, where the train breathed out the smell of meat cooking with onion.

A man passed beneath the arch of reaching arms meeting gray-black and white in the exchange of money for the staring wooden eyes, the stiff wooden legs sticking up in the air; went along under the voices and the bargaining, interrogating the wheels. Past the dogs; glancing up at the dining car where he could stare at the faces, behind glass, drinking beer, two by two, on either side of a uniform railway vase with its pale dead flower. Right to the end, to the guard's van, where the stationmaster's children had just collected their mother's two loaves of bread; to the engine itself, where the stationmaster and the driver stood talking against the steaming complaint of the resting beast.

The man called out to them, something loud and joking. They turned to laugh, in a twirl of steam. The two children careered over the sand, clutching the bread, and burst through the iron gate and up the path through the garden in which nothing grew.

Passengers drew themselves in at the corridor windows and turned into compartments to fetch money, to call someone to look. Those sitting inside looked up: suddenly different, caged faces, boxed in, cut off, after the contact of outside. . . . What about that chocolate? It wasn't very nice . . .

A young girl had collected a handful of the hard kind, that no one liked, out of the chocolate box, and was throwing them to the dogs over at the dining car. But the hens darted and swallowed the chocolates, incredibly quick and accurate, before they had even dropped in the dust, and the dogs, a little bewildered, looked up with their brown eyes not expecting anything.

—No, leave it, said the girl, don't take it.

—Too expensive, too much, she shook her head and raised her voice to the old boy, holding up the lion. He held it up where she had handed it to him. No, she said, shaking her head. Three-and-six? insisted her husband loudly. Yes baas! laughed the boy. *Three-and-six?*—the young man was incredulous. Oh, leave it—she said. The young man stopped. Don't you want it? he said, keeping his face closed to the boy. No, never mind, she said, leave it. The old native kept his head on one side, looking at them sideways, holding the lion. Three-and-six, he murmured, as old people repeat things to themselves.

The young woman drew her head in. She went into the coupé and sat down. Out of the window, on the other side, there was nothing; sand and bush; a thorn tree. Back through the open doorway, past the figure of her husband in the corridor, there was the station, the voices, wooden animals waving, running feet. Her eyes followed the funny little valance of scrolled wood that outlined the chalet roof of the station; she thought of the lion and smiled. That bit of fur round the neck. But the wooden buck, the hippos, the elephants, the baskets that already bulked out of their brown paper under the seat and on the luggage rack. How will they look at home? Where will you put them? What will they mean away from the places you found them? Away from the unreality of the last few weeks? The man outside. But he is not part of the unreality; he is for good now. Odd . . . somewhere there was an idea that he, that living with him, was part of the holiday, the strange places.

Outside, a bell rang. The stationmaster was leaning against the end of the train, green flag rolled in readiness. A few men who had got down to stretch their legs sprang on to the train, clinging to the observation platforms, or perhaps merely standing on the iron step, holding the rail; but on the train, safe from the one dusty platform, the one tin house, the empty sand.

There was a grunt. The train jerked. Through the glass the beer drinkers looked out, as if they could not see beyond it. Behind the flyscreen, the stationmaster's wife sat facing back at them beneath the darkening hunk of meat.

There was a shout. The flag drooped out. Joints not yet coordinated, the segmented body of the train heaved and bumped back against itself. It began to move; slowly the scrolled chalet moved past it, the yells of the natives, running alongside, jetted up into the air, fell back at different levels. Staring wooden faces waved drunkenly, there, then gone, questioning for the last time at the windows. Here, one-and-six, baas!—As one automatically opens a hand to catch a thrown ball, a man fumbled wildly down his pocket, brought up the shilling and sixpence and threw them out; the old native, gasping, his skinny toes splaying the sand, flung the lion. . . .

The stationmaster went slowly in under the chalet.

The old native stood, breath blowing out the skin between his ribs, feet tense, balanced in the sand, smiling and shaking his head. In his opened palm held in the attitude of receiving, was the retrieved shilling and six-pence.

The blind end of the train was being pulled helplessly out of the station.

The young man swung in from the corridor, breathless. He was shaking his head with laughter and triumph. Here! he said. And waggled the lion at her. One-and-six!

What? she said.

He laughed. I was arguing with him for fun, bargaining—when the train had pulled out already, he came tearing after . . . One-and-six, baas! So there's your lion.

She was holding it away from her, the head with the open jaws, the pointed teeth, the black tongue, the wonderful ruff of fur facing her. She was looking at it with an expression of not seeing, of seeing something different. Her face was drawn up, wryly, like the face of a discomforted child. Her mouth lifted nervously at the corner. Very slowly, cautious, she lifted her finger and touched the mane, where it was joined to the wood.

But how could you, she said. He was shocked by the dismay on her face.

Good heavens, he said, what's the matter?

If you wanted the thing, she said, her voice rising and breaking with the shrill impotence of anger, why didn't you buy it in the first place? If you wanted it, why didn't you pay for it? Why didn't you take it decently, when he offered it? Why did you have to wait for him to run after the train with it, and give him one-and-six? One-and-six!

She was pushing it at him, trying to force him to take it. He stood astonished, his hands hanging at his sides.

But you wanted it! You liked it so much!

—It's a beautiful piece of work, she said fiercely, as if to protect it from him.

You liked it so much! You said yourself it was too expensive—

Oh *you*—she said, hopeless and furious. *You* . . . She threw the lion onto the seat.

He stood looking at her.

She sat down again in the corner and, her face slumped in her hand, stared out of the window. Everything was turning round inside her. One-and-six. One-and-six. One-and-six for the wood and the carving and the sinews of the legs and the switch of the tail. The mouth open like that and the teeth. The black tongue, rolling, like a wave. The mane round the neck. To give one-and-six for that. The heat of shame mounted through her legs and body and sounded in her ears like the sound of sand pouring. Pouring, pouring. She sat there, sick. A weariness, a tastelessness, the discovery of a void made her hands slacken their grip, atrophy emptily, as if the hour was not worth their grasp. She was feeling like this again. She had thought it was something to do with singleness, with being alone and belonging too much to oneself.

She sat there not wanting to move or speak, or to look at anything, even; so that the mood should be associated with nothing, no object, word or sight that might recur and so recall the feeling

again . . . Smuts blew in grittily, settled on her hands. Her back remained at exactly the same angle, turned against the young man sitting with his hands drooping between his sprawled legs, and the lion, fallen on its side in the corner.

The train had cast the station like a skin. It called out to the sky, I'm coming, I'm coming; and again, there was no answer.

Nadine Gordimer

Before going further, consider the way Gordimer uses comparison and contrast in this story. Use the following questions as a guide:

1. In what ways are the opening and closing sentences of the story similar? How do these sentences establish a time-frame and a space-frame for the intervening events?
2. In what ways do the train and its passengers contrast with the village and its people? List specific details characterizing each.
3. Notice how most of the passengers remain on the train and the village people remain in the dust outside. How do they communicate and exchange goods? Notice also how the beer drinkers fail to see beyond the window glass. How does the resulting sense of alienation heighten contrast?
4. The central characters in the story seem at least superficially alike. Besides being comfortably affluent and sharing a common back-

ground, the young woman and the young man are newly married. Yet they are also different. At what point in the story and under what circumstances do the differences begin to become apparent? How does each feel about the carved lion that is the crux of the conflict? Why is the woman angry about the purchase of the carving? Why is the man surprised at his wife's anger?

5. At the end of the story, the young woman feels sickened by "the discovery of a void." Find in the text other images of emptiness. How might the quality of life in the countryside beyond the windows of the train contribute to the feeling of emptiness? What realization about her marriage might deepen this feeling?

6. Does the story offer any promise that village life will become less barren or that the woman will become less alienated? Reread the last sentence of the story. Does the clause "there was no answer" suggest more than the literal silence of the sky? What broader implications might it carry?

Imagine that you had been asked to write a critical analysis of "The Train from Rhodesia." The questions you just considered would have provided a shortcut through the pre-writing steps you practiced in the previous chapter. Those questions helped you think back through the story and collect details that seem especially noteworthy. The way the questions were organized automatically grouped those details so that you could see connections easily. The last three questions helped you decide what all the details add up to and thus draw your own conclusions about the story as a whole.

Now suppose that you were beginning to draft a critical analysis based on your reading of the story. You already know that you wouldn't start by summarizing plot. You know enough to assume that your reader is familiar with the story and willing to analyze it further.

Your first job would be to formulate a thesis—that is, a controlling idea for your paper. Suppose that in mulling over the story and your own responses to the questions, you keep returning to the contrast between the natives' way of life and that of the tourists on the train. Yet you decide that this contrast is mainly background for the more subtle differences between individuals and their values. To you, the point of the story is the young woman's sinking back into isolation after she finds herself incapable of communicating her values to her new husband. From such a reading, you might formulate this thesis: "In 'The Train from Rhodesia,' Nadine Gordimer brings her characters into a collision of cultures and values in order to dramatize personal alienation."

Once you have decided on a thesis, you are ready to begin drafting your paper. Remember that a good critical analysis rarely begins with a direct statement of thesis. Such an opener would be too abrupt. The reason you frame your thesis and write it down before beginning the paper is so *you* will know where the paper is going. You'll lead the reader there gradually.

During the last chapter, you learned how to organize a critical analysis. You learned how to open with an introduction that will hook your reader and point in the direction of your thesis. You learned how to organize the body of your paper around key points that support your interpretation and to support each of those points with plenty of evidence from the text. You also learned that you should conclude by drawing everything in the paper together and commenting on its significance to the story or poem as a whole.

With all this in mind, go back to the hypothetical task of writing an analysis showing how comparison and contrast work in "The Train from Rhodesia." Remember that the sample thesis proposed earlier includes more than one set of contrasts. It includes the broad contrasts between two ways of life as well as the more explicit—and more important—contrasts between two individuals. A critical analysis developing this thesis would explain and illustrate both, but it would place greater stress upon the latter.

In writing about literature—indeed in almost any kind of writing—it is important to control emphasis. In other words, it is important to push lesser points into the background and to focus upon those that have greater significance. There are two basic ways of doing so. One is by making the proportion of the essay reflect the appropriate emphasis. The other is by placing the point that is to receive greatest emphasis in a climactic position—that is, at the end.

Think about how you would control proportion in a critical analysis developing the thesis proposed earlier. Since the contrast between the harsh life of the natives and the privileged life of the travelers is subordinate to the more important contrast between the young man and the young woman, it would be developed in less detail. Perhaps one good solid paragraph would be enough. The more crucial conflict of values between husband and wife would warrant fuller development, perhaps in two or even three paragraphs. Remember that the more important the point, the more fully it should be developed. The amount of space devoted to an idea is directly proportional to its importance in the essay.

Think also about the order in which you would arrange parts of the same essay. Since the broad contrast between the primitive life of the village people and the highly civilized life of the travelers is considered background, it should be explained and illustrated first. Since the clash of values that alienates the young woman is the focal point of the analysis, it should be saved for last. Remember that the end position is climactic. Reserve that position for your most important point. In an essay of critical analysis, that point will almost always relate to the theme of the selection being analyzed.

In writing a critical essay exploring contrasts in "The Train from Rhodesia," you would apply the same general organizational techniques you practiced during the last chapter. You would write an introduction, a body, and a conclusion. The body would be organized topically so that each paragraph explained and illustrated a major point.

Within this basic framework, however, comparison and contrast require special handling. Within each paragraph, you could consider two organizational options. Suppose for a moment that you were writing a paragraph showing how Gordimer contrasts life in the barren African countryside with life on the train. Here is one way of organizing illustrative details:

> Inside the train, the tourists drink beer in the dining car while half-starved dogs lack energy to compete with chickens for the candy tossed through windows. The train breathes out the rich aroma of meat cooking with onion for the well-fed tourists; among the villagers, only the stationmaster's family can afford the luxury of bread to go with the mutton that hangs on the veranda. The rest share the plight of the old artist who has thin toes and whose ribs are covered only by skin. On the train, the vacationers run casually back to their compartments to replenish their supply of money; outside, native artists grovel in the dust for the few coins their wares might bring.

Notice the alternating pattern of details. Each detail illustrating the affluence of the tourists is followed by a contrasting detail illustrating the harshness experienced by the villagers. This kind of organization allows sharp juxtaposition, careful balance, and tight structure.

Sometimes, however, you might prefer another method of organizing comparison or contrast. Here is another possibility:

> Inside the train, tourists drink beer in a dining car which "breathes out the smell of meat cooking with onion." They laugh and joke as they run back to their compartments for more money with which to buy more souvenirs for their bulging shopping bags. Meanwhile, outside the train, both villagers and animals struggle to survive a barren environment where such affluence is unknown. Dogs watch hopelessly as chickens gobble up the few hard candies tossed from

the train window. Only the stationmaster can afford bread to go with
the darkening sheep carcass hung unrefrigerated on the veranda.
Children with nothing to sell beg for pennies. Desperately, an old
man runs beside the train until his breath is "blowing out the skin
between his ribs" so that he can sell a carving for a mere pittance.

Notice that this version does not alternate details about the train with
details about the village. All details illustrating life on the train are
clustered together as are details illustrating life in the village. Notice that
the two parts of the contrast are carefully linked with this sentence:
"Meanwhile, outside the train, both villagers and animals struggle to
survive a barren environment where such affluence is unknown." When
details are organized in contrasting blocks rather than alternated, transition is especially important. This kind of organization has one advantage
over alternating arrangement. It allows the writer to control proportion
and arrangement so that one part of the contrast receives greater emphasis
than the other. When you are comparing or contrasting elements in
literature, you have the option of using block or alternating arrangement.
Use the one that seems best for a particular situation.

Thinking through the process of writing a critical analysis focusing on
comparison and contrast in "The Train from Rhodesia" should provide a
good rehearsal for the task of writing a comparative analysis showing how
two literary pieces are alike and how they are different. As you do so at the
end of this chapter, you will want to keep in mind what you have just
learned about using proportion and arrangement to control emphasis and
organizing according to alternating or block arrangement of details.

You will also want to remember all that you have learned in this
course about revision. Like other kinds of transactional writing, literary
analysis is intended to go public. Before it does, it should be carefully
revised and polished. As you revise the full-scale comparative analysis
assigned at the end of this chapter, keep in mind the four big questions to
ask yourself during revision:

1. What needs to be added?
2. What needs to be deleted?
3. What needs to be substituted?
4. What needs to be rearranged?

These questions can be especially helpful in revising a long and relatively
complicated piece of expository writing like a comparative analysis.

In editing, you will want to be sure your sentences are free of faulty
comparison. The following Writer's Workbench will help alert you to this
pitfall of comparative writing.

Writer's Workbench

Avoiding Faulty Comparison

A. The following sentences from various student essays contain faulty comparison. Correct each sentence by rewriting it according to directions enclosed in parentheses.

1. The sensitivity of the young husband seems less keen than his wife. (Insert the words *that of* after *than*.)
2. The woman begins to feel an emptiness as great as back in England. (Insert *she had felt* before *back*.)
3. At the end of the story, she appears lonelier than anyone on the train. (Insert *else* after *anyone*.)
4. Of the two, it was hard to tell which was saddest and most bewildered. (Change *saddest* to *sadder* and *most* to *more*.)
5. As the story closes, the young man is sadder but just as indifferent as his fellow tourists. (Change *as his fellow tourists* to *than his fellow tourists*, and move the phrase so that it follows the word *sadder*.)

B. Notice that the problem in each of the first three sentences is caused by omitting words. The result is an illogical comparison. Explain the problem of logic in the incorrect version of each sentence.

C. The problem in Sentence 4 stems from the writer's using the superlative rather than the comparative degree of an adjective and an adverb. As you have learned in earlier English courses, the comparative degree is used to apply to a comparison of two persons or things, and the superlative degree is used to apply to three or more. Many comparative forms (like *sadder*) end in *-er*, and many superlative forms (like *saddest*) end in *-est*. Such words as *more, less, better,* and *worse* are comparative; such words as *most, least, best,* and *worst* are superlative. Make two original sentences illustrating the appropriate use of comparative degree and two illustrating the appropriate use of superlative.

D. The uncorrected version of Sentence 5 carelessly uses *as* to complete the comparison begun by both *sadder* and *as indifferent*. The implied phrase *sadder as* doesn't work; the correct form is *sadder than*. Can you see how the substitution of *than* for *as* and the rearrangement of the sentence eliminate the problem?

As you draft and then revise your comparative analysis later in this chapter, be careful not to commit such errors. You will need a great deal of practice in writing accurate comparisons.

Extending Techniques of Comparison/Contrast

By thinking through a comparative analysis of setting and character in "The Train from Rhodesia" and by practicing some related writing techniques, you have laid a solid foundation for analyzing similarities and differences in two pieces of literature. In other words, you have laid the groundwork for writing a full-scale comparative analysis.

The story that you will read next shares some common elements with "The Train from Rhodesia." Both are set in exotic places; though not to the same degree, both settings are primitive. Both stories juxtapose characters who are native to such an environment with characters transplanted from more advanced and affluent countries. Other shared elements include lack of communication between characters and a conflict of values.

SPOTLIGHT

Across the Bridge

"They say he's worth a million," Lucia said. He sat there in the little hot damp Mexican square, a dog at his feet, with an air of immense and forlorn patience. The dog attracted your attention at once, for it was very nearly an English setter, only something had gone wrong with the tail and the feathering. Palms wilted over his head, it was all shade and stuffiness round the bandstand, radios talked loudly in Spanish from the little wooden sheds where they changed your pesos into dollars at a loss. I could tell he didn't understand a word from the way he read his newspaper—as I did myself, picking out the words which were like English ones. "He's been here a month," Lucia said. "They turned him out of Guatemala and Honduras."

You couldn't keep any secrets for five hours in this border town. Lucia had only been twenty-four hours in the place, but she knew all about Mr. Joseph Calloway. The only reason I didn't know about him (and I'd been in the place two weeks) was because I couldn't talk the language any more than Mr. Calloway could. There wasn't

another soul in the place who didn't know the story—the whole story of the Halling Investment Trust and the proceedings of extradition. Any man doing dusty business in any of the wooden booths in the town is better fitted by long observation to tell Mr. Calloway's tale than I am, except that I was in—literally—at the finish. They all watched the drama proceed with immense interest, sympathy and respect. For, after all, he had a million.

Every once in a while through the long steamy day, a boy came and cleaned Mr. Calloway's shoes; he hadn't the right words to resist them—they pretended not to know his English. He must have had his shoes cleaned the day Lucia and I watched him at least half a dozen times. At midday he took a stroll across the square to the Antonio Bar and had a bottle of beer, the setter sticking to heel as if they were out for a country walk in England (he had, you may remember, one of the biggest estates in Norfolk). After his bottle of beer, he would walk down between the moneychangers' huts to the Rio Grande and look across the bridge into the United States; people came and went constantly in cars. Then back in the square till lunchtime. He was staying in the best hotel, but you don't get good hotels in this border town; nobody stays in them more than a night.

The good hotels were on the other side of the bridge; you could see their electric signs twenty stories high from the little square at night, like lighthouses marking the United States.

You may ask what I'd been doing in so drab a spot for a fortnight. There was no interest in the place for anyone; it was just damp and dust and poverty, a kind of shabby replica of the town across the river; both had squares in the same spots; both had the same number of cinemas. One was cleaner than the other, that was all, and more expensive, much more expensive. I'd stayed across there a couple of nights waiting for a man a tourist bureau said was driving down from Detroit to Yucatan and would sell a place in his car for some fantastically small figure—twenty dollars, I think it was. I don't know if he existed or was invented by the optimistic half-caste in the agency; anyway, he never turned up and so I waited, not much caring, on the cheap side of the river. It didn't much matter; I was living. One day I meant to give up the man from Detroit and go home or go south, but it was easier not to decide anything in a hurry. Lucia was just waiting for a car going the other way, but she didn't have to wait so long. We waited together and watched Mr. Calloway waiting—for God knows what.

I don't know how to treat this story—it was a tragedy for Mr. Calloway, it was poetic retribution, I suppose, in the eyes of the shareholders he'd ruined with his bogus transactions, and to Lucia and me, at this stage, it was pure comedy—except when he kicked the dog. I'm not a sentimentalist about dogs, I prefer people to be cruel to animals rather than to human beings, but I couldn't help being revolted at the way he'd kick that animal—with a hint of cold-blooded venom, not in anger but as if he were getting even for some trick it had played him a long while ago. That generally happened when he returned from the bridge: it was the only sign of anything resembling emotion he showed. Otherwise he looked a small, set, gentle creature with silver hair and a silver mustache, and gold-rimmed glasses, and one gold tooth like a flaw in character.

Lucia hadn't been accurate when she said he'd been turned out of Guatemala and Honduras; he'd left voluntarily when the extradition proceedings seemed likely to go through and moved north. Mexico is still not a very centralized state, and it is possible to get round governors as you can't get round cabinet ministers or judges. And so he waited there on the border for the next move. That earlier part of the story is, I suppose, dramatic, but I didn't watch it and I can't invent what I haven't seen—the long waiting in anterooms, the bribes taken and refused, the growing fear of arrest and then the flight—in gold-rimmed glasses—covering his tracks as well as he could, but this wasn't finance and he was an amateur at escape. And so he'd washed up here, under my eyes and Lucia's eyes, sitting all day under the bandstand, nothing to read but a Mexican paper, nothing to do but look across the river at the United States, quite unaware, I suppose, that everyone knew everything about him, once a day kicking his dog. Perhaps in its semi-setter way it reminded him too much of the Norfolk estate—though that too, I suppose was the reason he kept it.

And the next act again was pure comedy. I hesitate to think what this man worth a million was costing his country as they edged him out from this land and that. Perhaps somebody was getting tired of the business, careless; anyway, they sent across two detectives, with an old photograph. He'd grown his silvery mustache since that had been taken, and he'd aged a lot, and they couldn't catch sight of him. They hadn't been across the bridge two hours when everybody knew that there were two foreign detectives in town looking for Mr. Calloway—everybody knew, that is to say, except Mr. Calloway, who couldn't talk Spanish. There were plenty of people who could have told him in English, but they didn't. It wasn't cruelty, it was a sort of awe and respect: like a bull, he was on show, sitting there mournfully in the plaza with his dog, a magnificent spectacle for which we all had ringside seats.

I ran into one of the policemen in the Bar Antonio. He was disgusted; he had had some idea that when he crossed the bridge life was going to be different, so much more color and sun, and—I suspect—love, and all he found were wide mud streets where the nocturnal rain lay in pools, and mangy dogs, smells and cockroaches in his bedroom, and the nearest to love, the open door of the Academia Commercial, where pretty mestizo girls sat all morning learning to typewrite. Tip-tap-tip-tap-tip—perhaps they had a dream, too—jobs on the other side of the bridge, where life was going to be so much more luxurious, refined and amusing.

We got into conversation; he seemed surprised that I knew who they both were and what they wanted. He said, "We've got information this man Calloway's in town."

"He's knocking around somewhere," I said. . . .

"Could you point him out?"

"Oh, I don't know him by sight," I said.

He drank his beer and thought awhile. "I'll go out and sit in the plaza. He's sure to pass sometime."

I finished my beer and went quickly off and found Lucia. I said,

"Hurry, we're going to see an arrest." We didn't care a thing about Mr. Calloway, he was just an elderly man who kicked his dog and swindled the poor, and who deserved anything he got. So we made for the plaza; we knew Calloway would be there, but it had never occurred to either of us that the detectives wouldn't recognize him. There was quite a surge of people round the place; all the fruit-sellers and bootblacks in town seemed to have arrived together; we had to force our way through, and there in the little green stuffy center of the place, sitting on adjoining seats were the two plainclothesmen and Mr. Calloway. I've never known the place so silent; everybody was on tiptoe, and the plainclothesmen were staring at the crowd looking for Mr. Calloway, and Mr. Calloway sat on his usual seat staring out over the money-changing booths at the United States.

"It can't go on. It just can't." Lucia said. But it did. It got more fantastic still. Somebody ought to write a play about it. We sat as close as we dared. We were afraid all the time we were going to laugh. The semi-setter scratched for fleas and Mr. Calloway watched the USA. The two detectives watched the crowd, and the crowd watched the show with solemn satisfaction. Then one of the detectives got up and went over to Mr. Calloway. That's the end, I thought. But it wasn't, it was the beginning. For some reason they had eliminated him from their list of suspects. I shall never know why.

The man said, "You speak English?"

"I *am* English," Mr. Calloway said.

Even that didn't tear it, and the strangest thing of all was the way Mr. Calloway came alive. I don't think anybody had spoken to him like that for weeks. The Mexicans were too respectful—he was a man with a million—and it had never occurred to Lucia and me to treat him casually like a human being; even in our eyes he had been magnified by the colossal theft and the worldwide pursuit.

He said, "This is rather a dreadful place, don't you think?"

"It is," the policeman said.

"I can't think what brings anybody across the bridge."

"Duty," the policeman said gloomily. "I suppose you are passing through."

"Yes," Mr. Calloway said.

"I'd have expected over here there'd have been—you know what I mean—life. You read things about Mexico."

"Oh, life," Mr. Calloway said. He spoke firmly and precisely, as if to a committee of shareholders. "That begins on the other side."

"You don't appreciate your own country until you leave it."

"That's very true," Mr. Calloway said. "Very true."

At first it was difficult not to laugh, and then after a while there didn't seem to be much to laugh at; an old man imagining all the fine things going on beyond the international bridge. I think he thought of the town opposite as a combination of London and Norfolk—theaters and cocktail bars, a little shooting and a walk round the field at evening with the dog—that miserable imitation of a setter—poking the ditches. He'd never been across, he couldn't know that it was just the same thing over again—even the same layout; only the streets were paved and the hotels had ten more stories, and life was more expensive, and everything was a bit cleaner. There wasn't anything Mr. Calloway would have called living— no galleries, no bookshops, just *Film Fun* and the local paper, and *Click* and *Focus* and the tabloids.

"Well," said Mr. Calloway, "I think I'll take a stroll before lunch. You need an appetite to swallow the food here. I generally go down and look at the bridge about now. Care to come too?"

The detective shook his head. "No," he said, "I'm on duty. I'm looking for a fellow." And that, of course, gave *him* away. As far as Mr. Calloway could understand, there was only one "fellow" in the world anyone was looking for—his brain had eliminated friends who were seeking their friends, husbands who might be waiting for their wives, all objectives of any search but just the one. The power of elimination was what had made him a financier—he could forget the people behind the shares.

That was the last we saw of him for a while. We didn't see him going into the Botica Paris to get his aspirin, or walking back from the bridge with his dog. He simply disappeared, and when he disappeared, people began to talk, and the detectives heard the talk. They looked silly enough, and they got busy after the very man they'd been sitting next to in the garden. Then they too disappeared. They, as well as Mr. Calloway, had gone to the state capital to see the Governor and the Chief of Police, and it must have been an amusing sight there too, as they bumped into Mr. Calloway and sat with him in the waiting rooms. I suspect Mr. Calloway was generally shown in first, for everyone knew he was worth a million. Only in Europe is it possible for a man to be a criminal as well as a rich man.

Anyway, after about a week the whole pack of them returned by the same train. Mr. Calloway traveled Pullman, and the two policemen traveled in the day coach. It was evident that they hadn't got their extradition order.

Lucia had left by that time. The car came and went across the bridge. I stood in Mexico and watched her get out at the United States Customs. She wasn't anything in particular but she looked beautiful at a distance as she gave me a wave out of the United States and got back into the car. And I suddenly felt sympathy for Mr. Calloway, as if there were something over there which you couldn't find here, and turning round I saw him back on his old beat, with the dog at his heels.

I said, "Good afternoon," as if it had been all along our habit to greet each other. He looked tired and ill and dusty, and I felt sorry for him—to think of the kind of victory he'd been winning, with so much expenditure of cash and care—the prize this dirty and dreary town, the booths of the money-changers, the awful little beauty parlors with their wicker chairs and sofas . . . that hot and stuffy garden by the bandstand.

He replied gloomily, "Good morning" and the dog started to sniff at some ordure and he turned and kicked it with fury, with depression, with despair.

And at that moment a taxi with the two policemen in it passed us on its way to the bridge. They must have seen that kick, perhaps they were cleverer than I had given them credit for, perhaps they were just sentimental about animals, and thought they'd do a good deed, and the rest happened by accident. But the fact remains—those two pillars of the law set about the stealing of Mr. Calloway's dog.

He watched them go by. Then he said, "Why don't you go across?"

"It's cheaper here," I said.

"I mean just for an evening. Have a meal at that place we can see at night in the sky. Go to the theater."

"There isn't a chance."

He said angrily, sucking his gold tooth, "Well, anyway, get away from here." He stared down the hill and up the other side. He couldn't see that that street climbing up from the bridge contained only the same money-changers' booths as this one.

I said, "Why don't *you* go?"

He said evasively, "Oh—business."

I said, "It's only a question of money. You don't *have* to pass by the bridge."

He said with faint interest, "I don't talk Spanish."

"There isn't a soul here," I said, "who doesn't talk English."

He looked at me with surprise. "Is that so? he said. "Is that so?"

It's as I have said; he'd never tried to talk to anyone, and they respected him too much to talk to him—he was worth a million. I don't know whether I'm glad or sorry that I told him that. If I hadn't, he might be there now, sitting by the bandstand having his shoes cleaned—alive and suffering.

Three days later his dog disappeared. I found him looking for it, calling it softly and shamefacedly between the palms of the garden. He looked embarrassed. He said in a low angry voice, "I *hate* that dog. The beastly mongrel," and called "Rover, Rover," in a voice which didn't carry five yards. He said, "I bred setters once. I'd have shot a dog like that." It reminded him, I *was* right, of Norfolk, and he lived in the memory, and he hated it for its imperfection. He was a man without a family and without friends, and his only enemy was that dog. You couldn't call the law an enemy; you have to be intimate with an enemy.

Late that afternoon someone told him they'd seen the dog walking across the bridge. It wasn't true, of course, but we didn't know that then—they'd paid a Mexican five pesos to smuggle it across. So all that afternoon and the next Mr. Calloway sat in the garden having his shoes cleaned over and over again, and thinking how a dog could just walk across like that, and a human being, an immortal soul, was bound here in the awful routine of the little walk and the unspeakable meals and the aspirin at the *botica*. That dog was seeing things he couldn't see—that hateful dog. It made him mad—I think literally mad. You must remember the man had been going on for months. He had a million and he was living on two pounds a week, with nothing to spend his money on. He sat there and brooded on the hideous injustice of it. I think he'd have crossed over one day in any case, but the dog was the last straw.

Next day when he wasn't to be seen I guessed he'd gone across, and I went too. The American town is as small as the Mexican. I knew I couldn't miss him if he was there, and I was still curious. A little sorry for him, but not much.

I caught sight of him first in the only drugstore, having a Coca-Cola, and then once outside a cinema looking at the posters; he had dressed with extreme neatness, as if for a party, but there was no party. On my third round, I came on the detectives—they were having Coca-Colas in the drugstore, and they must have missed Mr. Calloway by inches. I went in and sat down at the bar.

"Hello," I said, "you still about?" I suddenly felt anxious about Mr. Calloway. I didn't want them to meet.

One of them said, "Where's Calloway?"

"Oh," I said, "he's hanging on."

"But not his dog," he said, and laughed. The other looked a little shocked, he didn't like anyone to *talk* cynically about a dog. Then they got up—they had a car outside.

"Have another?" I said.

"No, thanks, We've got to keep moving."

The man bent close and confided in me, "Calloway's on this side."

"No!" I said.

"And his dog."

"He's looking for it," the other said. . . .

I don't think Mr. Calloway was looking for his dog, but his dog certainly found him. There was a sudden hilarious yapping from the car and out plunged the semi-setter and gamboled furiously down the street. One of the detectives—the sentimental one—was into the car before we got to the door and was off after the dog. Near the bottom of the long road to the bridge was Mr. Calloway—I do believe he'd come down to look at the Mexican side when he found there was nothing but the drugstore and the cinemas and the paper shops on the American. He saw the dog coming and yelled at it to go home—"home, home, home," as if they were in Norfolk—it took no notice at all, pelting toward him. Then he saw the police car coming and ran. After that, everything happened too quickly, but I think the order of events was this—the dog started across the road right in front of the car, and Mr. Calloway yelled, at the dog or the car, I don't know which. Anyway, the detective swerved—he said later, weakly, at the inquiry, that he couldn't run over a dog, and down went Mr. Calloway, in a mess of broken glass and gold rims and silver hair, and blood. The dog was onto him before any of us could reach him, licking and whimpering and licking. I saw Mr. Calloway put up his hand, and down it went across the dog's neck and the whimper rose to a stupid bark of triumph, but Mr. Calloway was dead—shock and a weak heart.

"Poor old geezer," the detective said, "I bet he really loved that dog." and it's true that the attitude in which he lay looked more like a caress than a blow. I thought it was meant to be a blow, but the detective may have been right. It all seemed to me a little too touching to be true as the old crook lay there with his arm over the dog's neck, dead with his million between the money-changers' huts, but it's as well to be humble in the face of human nature. He had come across the river for something, and it may, after all, have been the dog he was looking for. It sat there, baying its stupid and mongrel triumph across his body, like a piece of sentimental statuary. The nearest he could get to the fields, ditches, the horizon of his home. It was comic and it was pitiable; but it wasn't less comic because the man was dead. Death doesn't change comedy to tragedy, and if that last gesture was one of affection, I suppose it was only one more indication of a human being's capacity for self-deception, our baseless optimism that is so much more appalling than our despair.

Graham Greene

As you respond to the following questions, make brief notes. If time permits, compare your responses to those of two or three classmates.

1. The main character in the story is British fugitive Joseph Calloway. Yet the reader is never allowed to know Mr. Calloway intimately. Why do you think Greene filters the story through a narrator who is more a spectator than a participant—not only in this story but apparently in life itself? What is the narrator doing in the Mexican town? What comments make him seem world-weary but accurate in his reporting of the human scene?
2. Why does Mr. Calloway go for months without talking to residents of the Mexican town? Why don't the residents talk to him? In what ways

does the resulting isolation of the main character contribute to the story?

3. What details in the story help the reader reconstruct Mr. Calloway's previous way of life in England? Why would the Mexican border town be particularly depressing to a person accustomed to London and Norfolk?

4. The narrator mentions repeatedly how people on one side of the bridge idealize the town on the other side. Find examples. Then compare and contrast the Mexican town with its American counterpart. Why is it ironic that people want to be on the opposite side of the bridge?

5. What happens to Calloway is tragic. Yet the narrator often sees these events as comic. How does this sense of the absurd contribute to the tone and the theme of the story?

6. Calloway's dog plays a major part in the story. How do you think Calloway felt about the animal? Why? Consider especially the ambiguity of the dying man's gesture as he raised his hand to caress or strike the dog. Which do you think he intended to do? Also, why do you think Greene leaves this final scene so ambiguous?

7. Reread the last sentence of the story. How has "Across the Bridge" illustrated "a human being's capacity for self-deception" and "base-less optimism"? Why might the narrator feel that self-deception and optimism are "more appalling than . . . despair"?

Only stories with common elements provide a worthwhile basis for comparative analysis. Contrasts become significant only when they are thrown into sharp relief by a pattern of similarities. Since "Across the Bridge" and "The Train from Rhodesia" are both alike and different, they are good candidates for comparative analysis. Remember that the whole point of comparing and contrasting such stories is to understand both more fully—not to force artificial connections or to engage in an academic exercise.

Before undertaking an analysis of the two stories you have read in this chapter, take a few minutes to consider organization. Basically, you will follow the guidelines you learned in the previous chapter and extended in the first section of this chapter. Remember what you learned about alternating, and block arrangement of comparison and contrast. You may need to use both in your comparative analysis.

Suppose, for example, you were comparing and contrasting the use of setting in the two stories. You might have one paragraph explaining and illustrating how the two settings are alike. In that paragraph, you would illustrate each parallel with one or more details from each story. In other words, you would use alternating arrangement.

On the other hand, suppose that later in the same paper, you were explaining how each author uses setting for a distinctly different thematic purpose. Here, you would probably write a full paragraph explaining and illustrating how *setting* in "Train from Rhodesia" underscores *theme*. You would then write another full paragraph exploring the same relationship in "Across the Bridge." In other words, you would use block arrangement.

Since a comparative analysis is both longer and more intricate than other papers you have written, careful organization will be especially important. The same is true for transition. Remember that transition makes the paper read more clearly and more smoothly. It helps your audience follow twists and turns in your train of thought without ever getting off the track.

Moving Toward Independence

This chapter has prepared you to write a comparative analysis. It has done so by building upon the foundation established in the preceding chapter. The sample principles apply to all kinds of critical writing about literature. The comparative analysis is just longer and more involved because it explores similarities and differences in two or more literary pieces. Like other kinds of interpretive writing, the critical analysis is a means of sharpening, deepening, and extending insights into literature.

Before applying independently what you have learned in these two chapters, take a little time for review. Use the section of your Writer's Notebook titled **Notes on the Writing Process** to jot down pre-writing, drafting, and revising techniques that are especially helpful in writing a critical analysis. Don't forget to include pointers for dealing with comparison and contrast.

After you have reviewed these chapters, complete the following assignment. First, study the criteria comprising Checkpoint 6 on page 261. Besides letting you know how your paper will be evaluated, these criteria will help guide you as you write.

**Getting
It
Started**

**Getting
It
Down**

Write a comparative analysis in which you show how Nadine Gordimer's "The Train from Rhodesia" and Graham Greene's "Across the Bridge" use foreign settings and transplanted characters to comment on human values.

**Getting
It
Right**

To help you revise and polish your analysis, go over the Writer's Workbench on page 247. See also the "four big questions" on page 246.

As you have worked through this unit, have you begun to think of reading and writing as reciprocal processes—as reverse sides of the same coin? As you move on to work with writing about subjects other than literature, continue to read as many good books and poems as you can. Try to absorb style as well as ideas. In the process, you will indeed realize literature more fully, both as a reader and as a writer.

CHECKPOINT 6

1	2	3	4	5

Content   ×7=

You write generally about both stories but never get to a point-by-point comparison and contrast. Try listing likenesses of setting and characters, then differences. See me about where to go from there.

Paper is on the track. You define parallels and contrasts but need more illustrative details from both texts. Check also for balanced treatment of the two stories.

Masterful piece of analysis. You've done quite a job of explaining and illustrating similarities as well as differences. Paper creates fresh insights into both texts.

Organization   ×6=

Hard to follow. Review sections on introduction, body, conclusion; alternating and block arrangement. Then try revising your paper to follow the pattern of good exposition.

Fairly strong. Check to be sure introduction hooks reader and conclusion summarizes, then clinches thesis. Also check body paragraphs for details that don't quite fit and gaps that need transition.

All pieces fit neatly into the whole. Super introduction and conclusion. Deft handling of comparison. Use of alternating arrangement strong. Flow smooth and clear.

Emphasis   ×4=

I can't tell what point you want to emphasize. Devote more space to that point and put it last.

You are almost there. Make proportion reflect emphasis a little more distinctly. Give more importance to bottom line of how author treats values.

You did it! You chose to stress the points most crucial to theme, made proportion and climactic arrangement work for you.

Form, Usage, and Mechanics   ×3=

This analysis needs lots of polishing before it's ready to go public. Start by correcting problems marked on returned paper.

Only a few lapses keep this paper from being a model of form. Get a reliable classmate to help you find and correct trouble spots.

Picture perfect! Paper is neat and free of errors in spelling, usage, and mechanics. Verb tense is consistent. You avoided pitfall of faulty comparison.

Researching and Reporting the Future

*My interest is in the future because I'm
going to spend the rest of my life there.*
—*Charles F. Kettering*

Chapter 12

Giving Credit Where Credit Is Due

Most writing is not truly original. That may come as a surprise to you, since you may assume, as many do, that writing is creative and that all creative activity must be absolutely original. But think for a moment about how much creative work is not completely original.

Painters often belong to a "school" in which artists share similar techniques. Novelists often use relatively similar plot structures. Poets, especially of a century and longer ago, usually used what contemporary readers would consider copied structures—the sonnet, the ballad stanza, and iambic pentameter, to name a few. But they were still creative within the forms they shared.

Writers tend to follow somewhat similar structures when writing for given audiences, probably as much because audiences expect commonality than for any other reason. News stories, for example, often seem similar to one another (only the names have been changed, as the old saying goes). In professional publications, writers even follow stylebooks prescribing structures which must be followed if an article is to be published in a particular journal.

Beyond the similar structures which occur in articles written for a given audience and purpose, there is also an expectation that a writer will use and refer to material written by others. Scientists and members of other professions keep up to date by reading large numbers of articles written by their colleagues. Through reading what others have done, they learn of progress in their profession. Knowing the findings of other members of a profession can save considerable effort in "re-inventing the wheel."

There is yet another reason for including the discoveries of others in your writing. When you refer to a particular article or study, you are telling your readers that you are familiar with a particular piece of research and that you are placing your work in the same category. When a reader has read the viewpoints of the other authors you have included in your writing, it is easy for him or her to understand your position. You have created a context for your writing, and you have associated yourself with them and their writing.

All this is by way of saying that writers often rely on the writing of others. They get ideas from them; they use their work to support positions and conclusions; they criticize them. It is important to note that however they use them, *they always give them recognition.*

SPOTLIGHT

Giving Credit

There are many ways of giving credit to another for material you use in your writing. Journalists often give credit directly in an article, as in the following news story.

Heat Treatment on Cancer Tumor Shows Promise

DAYTONA BEACH, Fla.—The use of heat to roast inoperable cancer tumors appears to hold promise as a new cancer treatment, a Los Angeles cancer researcher says.

"It appears particularly effective in larger tumors, where we have the least to offer," says Dr. Frederick K. Storm, assistant professor of surgery at the University of California, who spoke with reporters at an American Cancer Society seminar here.

Storm acknowledges, however, that heat therapy still is experimental and shouldn't be used in lieu of other potentially effective standard methods.

"The idea of using heat to attack cancerous tumors has been around since the turn of the century," he says, "but there has never been a safe way of heating a human cancer tumor."

Now, using radio waves to make cells vibrate and thus generate heat, researchers are able to heat tumors at temperatures as high as 122 degrees Fahrenheit without damaging normal tissue.

"Previously we had no effective and safe way to induce hyperthermia," Storm says. "At 108 degrees tumors appear to begin regressing."

In tests, patients with serious skin cancer that had spread to the liver had a median survival of four months when chemotherapy was used alone. When the drug treatment was joined with hyperthermia, survival rose to a median of one year.

In colon cancer that has spread to the liver, Storm says, only 15 percent to 20 percent of patients ordinarily have a remission and it lasts only a few months. But of 11 patients with that condition who received combination drug-and-heat therapy, one has shown a complete response that so far has lasted 15 months; another has shown a partial response after seven months, and seven more still have the disease after five months but show no signs of further deterioration.

In four cancer patients treated with heat after the best known chemotherapy failed, Storm says, three showed some improvement.

Although controlled studies of the radio wave technique have yet to be performed, Storm says, the early evidence is very promising.

"Our preliminary results suggest that hyperthermia will become a fifth treatment for cancer," he says—joining surgery, chemotherapy, radiation and immunotherapy.

Storm notes that hyperthermia's greatest potential may be in combination with other therapies. In some cases, he says, there is hope that heat could render inoperable tumors operable.

"Since heat seems to enhance the effects of chemotherapeutic drugs and radiation therapy," Storm says, "reduced doses of these agents might be possible with less normal tissue injury."

Notice how the writer gives Dr. Storm credit in the story. The doctor is identified in the second paragraph, not only by name, but also by rank (assistant professor of surgery) and institution (University of California). The writer uses only information from Dr. Storm in the article, information which was probably obtained from a discussion at the American Cancer Society seminar in Daytona Beach, Florida.

Writers of articles in magazines tend to use the same technique. The following article represents an interview style which was popular in the early part of the twentieth century and has resurfaced recently in popular publications.

As you read this article, notice how like the "new journalism" it is. (Remember Chapter 6?) The article was first printed in *Cosmopolitan Magazine* in 1911. (Note the use of "man" to indicate "people" as well as the use of masculine pronouns when referring to people in a general way.)

THE WONDERFUL NEW WORLD AHEAD OF US

*Some Startling Prophecies of the Future As Described
by Thomas A. Edison and Reported by Allan L. Benson*

I ASKED Thomas A. Edison to talk to me about inventions. And he did. Inventions now remake the world every twenty years. I wanted Edison's forecast of what inventions are coming next. I wanted his views instead of those of anyone else, because I believed he was likely to know more than anyone else. I recalled particularly a remark that he once made to me.

"When I am trying to make a thing," he said, "I always play my blue chips first. I try to think of the biggest thing that could be done, and then do it.''

In other words, he lets his imagination go as far as it can. Such a man might appear to be an unreliable forecaster. Think a minute. Edison meant only that he tries to bring out full-fledged inventions. Yet, see how far even his great imagination falls short of developments. He put all his imagination into the phonograph—and produced a machine, turned with a crank, that nobody would buy to-day at any price. He played his blue chips into the incandescent electric light—and produced a light for which no one would to-day pay a white chip. The point is that Edison's imagination really is not great. It is great only in comparison with our small imaginations. It is small in comparison with the things it sees. It has never been great enough to see any of his own inventions as

they were destined to be.

Edison ought to know a good deal about transportation, so I asked him what improvements were probable in the means of transportation. Would electricity always be used only for short hauls? Was nothing better than steam in sight for long hauls? Should we always travel by steam to Chicago, to Denver, to San Francisco? Should we never travel by air?

Edison answered the aeroplane question first. He answered it by telling a story. Ten years ago he was sitting in front of his winter laboratory in Florida. Not a cloud was in the sky. The air, bathed in sunshine, was still. The smoke from a neighboring chimney went straight up—straight up for a thousand feet. Almost as high as the pillar of smoke soared a buzzard. Minute after minute, as Edison watched, the bird lazily described great circles. Sometimes it would slide down the air

a hundred feet and then climb back again. But whether the bird circled, slid, or climbed, it never flapped a wing. Always its wings were like the hands of a clock at a quarter to three.

Edison marveled. With no wind blowing, with no wing flapping, what kept the bird aloft? What enabled it to climb after it had slid down the air? Again and again, he asked himself these questions, but the answers did not come. Nine years later, the answers came.

"I think I know what kept that bird in the air," he said to me. "It traveled on sound-waves, and the little pin-feathers on the insides of its wings made the waves."

What he meant was this: Any agitation of the air makes a wave. Agitate the air rapidly enough and the waves come to us in the form of sound. Then the waves are called sound-waves.

"The air, when struck with sufficient quickness," continued Edison, "is as rigid as steel. Touch a match to a stick of dynamite on a five-ton rock and nothing will happen—the dynamite will merely burn up. Set off a charge of gunpowder and the dynamite will be exploded, but not rapidly enough to shatter the rock. But explode the dynamite with a fulminate of mercury cap and the explosion will come so quickly that the air cannot yield. The rock will be split, because it is less rigid than the air."

Edison believes the buzzard kept aloft by causing the pin-feathers on the insides of its wings to beat the air with tremendous rapidity. He believes the buzzard traveled on sound-waves, precisely as the bumblebee travels on sound-waves. The bumblebee derives its name from the fact that, in flying, it makes sound-waves.

Edison has a high regard for the bumblebee as a flier. He says its wings are exceedingly small in proportion to the size and weight of its body. It flies so well only because it uses its wings so well; beats the air until the air becomes like metal stilts. Moreover, he believes we shall have to learn wisdom from the bumblebee before we shall travel in the air very far, very fast, or very safely. He would apply the bumblebee principle to lifting the flying-machine, and the present propeller system to driving it ahead. In his opinion, flying-machines should be able to go straight up. Aeroplanes can go up only as they go ahead. "Suppose you had four million trained bumblebees," he said, "attached to wire wickerwork on which was seated a man. Can't you understand that if the bumblebees were signaled to fly, they would lift the man? I believe mechanical bumblebees could be so attached to a flying-machine that they would lift it straight up. By 'mechanical bumblebees' I mean inclined planes revolving upon perpendicular shafts at tremendous speed. Once in the air, ordinary propellers could be used to drive the machine ahead."

Edison believes the present type of aeroplanes will soon be discarded, and that "bumblebee fliers" will carry passengers at the rate of a hundred miles an hour, or more.

Meanwhile, transportation upon land, he declares, will be revolutionized. The steam-locomotive is blowing its last blasts for millions of people. The next generation of New-Yorkers and New-Englanders will first hear at school of steam-locomotives, and never will see them unless they go to some state that has neither much water power nor much population. Water-wheels will make electricity to run all the railroads that traverse regions in which there is abundant water power. Whole systems like the Great Northern will be thus operated. In densely populated states, electric locomotives will displace steam, regardless of whether water power is available. The New York Central will be electrified from end to end. Nor will there be, says Edison, in all New England or New York, a railroad operated by steam power.

There is great potential for a movement to substitute steel for wood in the making of furniture. It will occur because of the increasing cost of wood. Edison says one New York firm is already making steel office-furniture. No tubing is used. The various parts of chairs, tables, and desks are stamped out of sheet steel, and then bent into shape. The legs, arms, and backs of chairs are cut out as rapidly as the big wheels of stamping-machines can revolve.

"All furniture will soon be made of steel," said Edison. "The steel required for a given piece of furniture costs only one-fifth as much as the wood would cost for the same piece of furniture. Steel furniture is light, because only a little steel is required. And polished steel takes a beautiful finish. It can be stained in perfect imitation of mahogany, walnut, cherry, maple, oak, or any other wood. The babies of the next generation will sit in steel high-chairs and eat from steel tables. They will not know what wooden furniture is."

Edison had a good deal to do with the bringing out of the telephone. Perhaps he could conceive of something better than the telephone; better than the telegraph; better even than the Marconi wireless—something that would utilize a new force of which mankind is not yet conscious."

He could conceive of such a force. "So far as I know," said he, "there is no quality of the ether that will permit us to send wave-impulses in other than the electrical form, but I have no doubt that wave-impulses can be sent in other and, perhaps, better forms. I do know, however, that the present telephone is very imperfect. If you want to know how imperfect it is, read the drug market to a stenographer at the other end of the wire and see how much of it she will get. The success of the telephone is due to human imagination. A man is rung up on the 'phone. He gets a clue to the identity of the person who is calling him, and, if the subject broached is one with which he is familiar, the rest is easy. But mention a name that the other man did not expect to hear and see

how quickly he will break in with 'What's that?' 'Repeat that name,' and, finally, 'Spell it.'"

Edison believes the day will come when the telephone will leave little or nothing to the imagination; when it will shout out proper names, or whisper the quotations from the drug market. He depends upon Mr. Vail, the new head of the American Telegraph and Telephone Company and of the Western Union, to bring this day quickly.

"Mr. Vail is a big man and a very smart business man," said Edison. "Until his day, the telegraph business was in the hands of little men. Vail will encourage inventions. He is something of an inventor himself."

If Mr. Vail shall have as hard a time improving the telephone as Edison had improving the phonograph, he will be quite busy for two years after he begins. Edison's first phonograph couldn't say "sugar." The cylinder failed to deliver the "sh" sound. Edison undertook to remedy the defect. He did everything he could think of, but everything he could think of did no good. After he had toiled at the task eighteen hours a day for two years, he did something that he didn't think of that did good. To this day, he does not know what he did. All he knows is that his phonograph suddenly barked out "sugar" without a letter missing. Unconsciously he had remedied the defect that he could not remedy consciously.

"Do you know," he said, "I believe men do lots of things unconsciously. Sometimes these things help them, as the thing I did to the phonograph helped me; sometimes they bother them, as an ore experiment once bothered me. I was trying to reduce iron ore by a new process. I selected some ore for a test. The test showed twenty per cent iron. The regular runs of the mill showed only sixteen per cent. Again and again I selected samples and the tests continued to show twenty per cent. As persistently, the mill refused to give anybody else more than sixteen per cent. Finally, I shut my eyes when I picked out the pieces of ore to test, and then I got sixteen per cent, the same as the others. Unconsciously, you see, I had been picking out better samples than I should have taken. A lot of subconscious business was working in spite of me."

"There will be no poverty in the world a hundred years from now," said Edison. "There is no limit to the cheapness with which things can be made. The world will soon be flooded with the cheap products of machinery —not the poor products; the cheap products."

The world flooded with food, clothing, shelter, and luxuries! No half-starved children, no overworked mothers, no poverty-worried fathers, no disease-breeding, cheerless tenements or houses. The world flooded with food, clothing, shelter, and luxuries!

Impossible? Read on:

"Why should we expect poverty to continue?" asked Edison. "Poverty was for a world that used only its hands. When men used nothing but their hands, poverty was most intense. Now that men have begun to use their brains, poverty is decreasing. Poverty

is decreasing though we have been using our brains only a little while. Think how long the world has stood, and then recall that practically everything we know to-day that is worth while we have learned within a hundred years. Look about you and see how many things that were worth while were known a hundred years ago. And we have only just begun to use our brains. What we know is but an atom of what there is to know. But we are learning how to control the forces of nature. As we learn, we shall transform the world. The most wonderful changes are coming—changes about which no one can to-day do more than dream."

What a flashlight of the future! What a future in the flashlight! What a privilege to live in such a world! What privilege could be greater? Only one. The privilege of laying the foundations of such a world. Therein is our mighty opportunity. We live in a time when building operations worth while are still going on. All of us may not be here to see the specter of poverty laid away, but, according to Edison, a few of the youngest will hear the rattle of musketry over its grave.

This article is included for two reasons. First, it is an excellent example of one use of information from another source working in combination with an author's information. Second, it introduces a major thrust of the unit—The Future.

In the article you just read, you were given Mr. Edison's views of future happenings. The interviewer, Allan L. Benson, had questions in mind as he went to interview Edison, but he also knew about Edison's discoveries and opinions. Because he *knew about* Edison, he could frame questions during the interview which would make it a good one. The good interview, then, resulted in a good article. The key to this good interview (and the resulting good article) was a set of questions which focused on what Mr. Benson was concerned about—the future. In addition, the author systematically built the interview and the article so that it moved steadily toward the conclusion:

What a privilege to live in such a world! What privilege could be greater? Only one. The privilege of laying the foundations of such a world.

〜〜〜〜〜〜〜〜〜〜〜〜〜〜〜〜〜〜〜〜

Getting It Started

Think about the future for a few minutes. In your Writer's Notebook, write a few notes to yourself relating to your personal concerns for the future and what you feel will be important then. You might consider your own personal life, your aspirations and goals, your potential career. You might also consider things which have world-wide importance, such as world hunger, the exploration of space, problems of aging, or over-population. Jot down just a few words to remind you of your thoughts.

Now, arrange to interview a classmate, using a style similar to the one used by Mr. Benson as he interviewed Edison. As you begin the interview, find out what your classmate's concerns are—both personal and general.

As you conduct the interview, probe as deeply as you can into your classmate's concerns; at the same time, try to find solutions in your source's experience. Ask for opinions; ask for facts; ask for speculation.

During the interview, take notes so that you will get down the essence of what was said. Use a tape recorder if one is available.

〜〜〜〜〜〜〜〜〜〜〜〜〜〜〜〜〜〜〜〜

Getting It Down

When you finish the interview, write out your notes as quickly and completely as possible. Then begin a short article entitled, "The Wonderful (or Frightening or Exciting or Catastrophic, or some other adjective) World Ahead of Us." Write your article as an interview for possible publication in your school newspaper. Be sure to give full credit to your classmate in your article.

〜〜〜〜〜〜〜〜〜〜〜〜〜〜〜〜〜〜〜〜

Checking It Out

When you have completed your preliminary draft, share your work with the classmate you interviewed so that he or she can check the accuracy of your reporting. Then find another classmate who will act as a critic/audience. Go through your draft carefully with your critic, being sure you get helpful feedback.

〜〜〜〜〜〜〜〜〜〜〜〜〜〜〜〜〜〜〜〜

Using the feedback you received from the individual you interviewed and your critic, put your article in final form. Remember to keep your audience (readers of your school newspaper) in mind as you revise. Also, keep in mind your school newspaper's expectations for form and style.

Getting
It
Right

SPOTLIGHT

More on Crediting a Source

People who write and do research generally allow use of written material by others, with one restriction—the user must give the original author credit if his or her work is quoted. This gives recognition and honor to the original developers of the material. The fact that recognition must be given also discourages writers from plagiarizing.

Most of all, using the material of others saves "re-inventing the wheel" every time a writer starts out on a project. Think of the advances which have been made in scientific fields because researchers used the results of other research as a basis for their own!

The following writing presents a beginning on which you might build a statement of your own. The writer has summarized several important points from Paul Osterman's book, *Getting Started: The Youth Labor Market*. Think of ideas you might have which you could use together with this information.

Youth Unemployment: Is There a Cure?

Youth unemployment has moved to the forefront of national concerns in recent years, yet there is still very little agreement on its causes or consequences.

In a new book, *Getting Started: The Youth Labor Market*, Paul Osterman, an assistant professor of economics at Boston University, takes a searching look at the possible causes and proposed cures for this complex social problem.

Osterman stresses that some barriers to youth employment have not come about accidentally, but have been deliberately created to protect jobs for adults. Policies such as the minimum wage, compulsory education, and a variety of child labor laws have made it difficult and expensive for employers to hire young people. In addition, many jobs formerly reserved for young people have been automated.

Automation of farm jobs dealt a double blow to youth employment. Agriculture had generally been a youth-intensive industry; thus, many jobs traditionally done by youths disappeared. In addition, with so many agricultural workers left without jobs, competition for factory jobs intensified.

During the depression of the 1930s, many adult workers and their unions feared that young people would be preferred to older workers because they would work for lower wages; thus, compulsory education laws were strengthened. High schools gained more students during the first years of the depression than during any previous times.

The actual and long-term consequences of youth unemployment remain unknown. Many unemployed young people are enrolled in school, so they are not completely idle. Most unemployed young people do seem to get jobs eventually. On the other hand, some sociologists argue that youths rejected by the job market will develop destructive attitudes, ranging from self-hate to social anger. Many youths need jobs in order to supplement family incomes, since 51% of unemployed youths come from families with low incomes.

Osterman believes that reducing youth unemployment substantially will require serious intervention in the labor market structure. Policy decisions should not focus on those young people who may be expected to move into the central part of the economy but rather on those who are likely to stagnate in marginal jobs. This latter group consists of young people who experience much unemployment because of personal problems, and those who are essentially ready for a job, but face unemployment because of discriminatory practices.

The author describes a variety of approaches that have been tried for reducing unemployment, such as government-subsidized on-the-job training or govenment-sponsored employment programs, but these approaches have not been outstandingly successful, and Osterman labels his survey "quite pessimistic." Thus, *Getting Started* raises more questions than it answers, but it does provide a basis for understanding youth unemployment and so may lead to effective remedies.

Osterman, Paul, *Getting Started: The Youth Labor Market*, Cambridge: The MIT Press, 1980.

Does this material give you some ideas for writing? Did you know, for instance, that compulsory education grew largely as a result of the influence of labor? Does that provide you with an idea?

Does the writing raise questions in your mind about future employment, especially for young people? By introducing these concepts, has the writer caused you to think about your own employment? Do you have a solution to the problem of youth unemployment?

Jot down thoughts you have gained from this writing concerning youth unemployment. Share your jottings with your classmates; see if you have similar ideas.

After your discussion, think about writing a paper on youth unemployment in the future. When you have an idea that seems interesting to you, identify an audience and a purpose for your writing. For example, will you write a letter to a member of Congress suggesting a change in governmental policies concerning youth employment? Will you write a paper in which you support curriculum changes for your school so that youth can be better prepared to face problems in getting employment? Will you write a paper on the history of youth unemployment?

Discuss your ideas for papers with your classmates. See how many ideas for writing come out of this single writing of only seven paragraphs!

After you have talked about ideas for writing, think about the process you used in order to arrive at your position. Jot down some specifics about the process you used. If possible, be as specific as, "First I ___ , then I ___ ." Use a page of your Writer's Notebook for this purpose.

Now discuss the processes with your classmates. You may find as many processes as you have members of your class! Try to improve your process by using some techniques your classmates find useful. After your discussion, go back to your Writer's Notebook and revise your process statement if you received some helpful ideas from your classmates.

Remember in future assignments to use this process for getting ideas from the writing of others.

Getting
It
Started

SPOTLIGHT

Crediting Sources in Science

Scientists are probably best known for including the work of other researchers in their studies. It seems that every researcher wants to assure his or her readers that what is being reported in the article is a part of a larger body of research. Scientists usually show their readers not only that they are not "re-inventing the wheel," but also that their work is a part of a large "wheel" which has been in the process of development for some time.

The following introduction to an article in *Environment International* illustrates a scientific strategy to show that what is reported is part of a larger body of related research.

Introduction

The environmental impact of airborne particulates is becoming a matter of considerable concern (National Research Council, 1979). Several studies have been undertaken to determine the relative contributions of particulate emission sources (Friedlander, 1973a; 1973b;

Gartrell and Friedlander, 1975; Gordon *et al.*, 1971; Heisler *et al.*, 1973; Kowalczyk, *et al.*, 1978; Rahn, 1971). These studies are important in order to provide data which can be used to predict the effects of regulatory and other changes in emission source characteristics, and also to monitor the efficiency of such changes. In order to place the results of these studies in perspective, we have reviewed past efforts to use trace element data for source apportionment purposes. This report describes the evidence supporting assignment of tracers to various anthropogenic and natural sources. In addition, techniques are described that have been used to estimate the contribution of sources to the ambient total suspended particulate (TSP) loading. Strengths and weaknesses of the several approaches are compared.

Kleinman, Michael T., Merril Eisenbud, Morton Lippman, and Theo. J. Kneip, "The Use of Tracers to Identify Sources of Airborne Particles," *Environment International*, vol. 4 (1980), pp. 53–62.

Later in the article, the authors note the relationship of their *findings* to those of other researchers. The following paragraphs illustrate this technique for reporting data.

The concentrations of 29 elements in aerosols from the San Francisco Bay area have been used to estimate the importance of man-made particulates to the overall pollution problem in the area (John *et al.*, 1973; Martins *et al.*, 1973). Rahn *et al.* (1971) studied diurnal variations in aerosol trace element concentrations in the Livermore Valley and attempted to use the data to determine the impact of smog "imported" from the San Francisco—Oakland area. No definitive correlations of trace element concentrations with those of CO, NO_2, or "oxidant" were found.

The area-wide distribution of lead, copper, and cadmium in airborne particulates was studied in Chicago and Northwest Indiana and it was estimated that there was a significant contribution of airborne particulates to the trace metal content of Lake Michigan (Harrison and Winchester, 1971; Harrison *et al.*, 1971). Winchester and Nifong (1971) have estimated that the aerosol contributions of Cu, Mn, Ni, Pb, Ti, V, and Zn to the metal burdens of Lake Michigan equal or exceed those from streams. Klein (1975) suggested that aerosol deposition accounts for about one-fifth of the observed input of trace elements to Lake Michigan (except for Al, Co, La, Si, and Th, which are most likely due to mobilization of soil and sediment components).

Analysis of seasonal variations in TSP and vanadium concentrations have been used, after corrections for seasonal differences in atmospheric dispersion, to estimate the contribution of space heating to the New York City aerosol. Extending this technique further, it was demonstrated that increased levels of TSP and V could be attributed to the burning of high sulfur fuels during the oil embargo which occurred during the 1973/1974 winter (Kleinman *et al.*, 1977).

The following article provides another kind of beginning. After reading these paragraphs, an author might be tempted to discuss in some detail the way organisms respond to danger in the environment. Do you see some potential for plants helping mankind by providing early warning systems against environmental problems?

Environmental Sentinels:
Flowers That Spot Pollution

Biological warning systems for air pollution are nothing new. Coal miners long used the "canary in a cage" technique for detecting the build-up of dangerous gases in coal mines. If a bird stopped chirping, it was time to leave.

Over the years, scientists have searched for other animals and organisms that might also serve as environmental sentinels. Among all the plants tested, a hybrid of *Tradescantia*, more commonly known as the spiderwort, has generated the most scientific interest.

"When exposed to a mutagen (any substance capable of causing changes in genetic structures or functions of organisms) just before it blooms, mutated cells in the hairs of the *tradescantia* stamen turn from blue to pink," says Shahbeg Sandhu, a research biologist with the U.S. Environmental Protection Agency. These mutations, called "pink events," are visible under a microscope. Although the mutations are not positive indications of harmful effects on humans, it is at least a possibility that a mutagen capable of causing changes in plant cells might also affect human cells.

EPA, the National Institute of Environmental Health, and the Brookhaven National Laboratory collaborated on preliminary field trials of the spiderwort in 1976. Plants exposed to the air in industrial cities showed many instances of color changes, while plants exposed to the "clean" air of the Grand Canyon showed little change. "*Tradescantia* is useful for detection of the presence of known harmful substances in the air, as well as detection of damaging effects of a combination of ordinarily innocuous compounds. It is especially promising as a monitoring tool because of its simplicity," says Sandhu.

A California company, already convinced of *Tradescantia*'s usefulness, is now marketing the plant. Protech Products, Inc., of Santa Barbara, relying on the research of Japanese scientist Sadeo Ichikawa, claims that the spiderwort will turn pink after exposure to roughly 100 millirems of radiation annually. Ichikawa calls the plant "the most excellent test system ever known for low-level radiation." Besides detecting air pollution and nuclear radiation, says Protech, other research appears to indicate that the spiderwort will also turn pink in reaction to pesticides, fungicides, herbicides, and sulfur dioxide.

Scientific interest in biological warning systems doesn't stop with the spiderwort. Since no single plant can detect all harmful chemicals, says Sandhu of EPA, "our goal is to develop a battery of mutagen-sensitive bioassays, including plants, for monitoring environmental quality." EPA has already contracted with universities around the U.S. to study corn, barley, and *Arabidopsis*, a member of the mustard plant family.

How do these paragraphs influence your thoughts on this subject? Would you consider writing a technical explanation of how the spiderwort responds to mutagens? Would you consider the multitude of possibilities for using sensitive organisms to detect industrial hazards? Would you consider the potential for having house plants which detect mutagens so that warning could be given if mutagens were present in your home?

Discuss possibilities with your classmates. Then think of your own processes for getting ideas for writing. You wrote of your processes earlier in this chapter. Now consider the roles the following play in helping you decide what to write:

1. your own interests
2. your knowledge of the subject
3. your purpose for writing
4. your audience

Share your thoughts with your classmates about what shapes your writing. Then add notes about your discussion to your Writer's Notebook. You have seen how authors use the material of others as they present information. You have observed how a study or article is placed in the company of similar studies to enable the reader to know where the author is "coming from," and how the writing of others is used to show the need for the material being reported. You have also explored the possibility of using the writing of others as a stimulus for your own writing.

~~~~~~

Getting It Started

Look back over the material presented in this chapter. Find instances in which authors have used material from other writings in each of the following situations:

1. to place a study in the company of a larger group of somewhat similar research
2. to support a point an author wishes to make
3. to present the findings or opinions of others

Discuss these uses with your classmates. Then go to your school library and look for magazine articles which use similar techniques. If your school library does not contain research and academic journals, ask some of your teachers who may subscribe to them, or visit your public library. If you live near a college or university, you might try their library.

The news story and the interview article at the beginning of the chapter provide one way to strengthen writing using the words of other writers. The excerpts from research studies show other ways. Later chapters will present more techniques for incorporating information and words from other sources into your writing. Two points are important to remember: authors regularly use material from the work of others, and when they do, they give credit to the original source for what they have borrowed.

• If you want to get a head start on procedures for giving credit, refer to pages H-29–31 in your Handbook. Instructions are given there for citing the work of others.

Chapter 13

Data for Deciding

In Chapter 12, you learned how information helped people in several professions show how their research, practices, and ideas fit into studies that others had already made. You also read examples of writing in which authors used information from others to provide foundations for their own work. You saw how data from studies, books, and other writing were used to give authors ideas for their own writing. What you witnessed was people using information developed by others so that they would not have to begin at the very beginning each time they decided to write.

Writing about things you have done or discovered can help others as they consider actions of their own. Successful people in all professions read about how others solve problems. By carefully reading about the successes and failures of others, they can apply appropriate information to their own situations and attack their problems from an enlightened perspective. Of course, these same individuals have an obligation to share their own experiences with the other members of their professions. Generally, they do this through writing.

Stating a Position

Most writers are really problem-solvers. Even writers of fiction fit this description. A good story contains a conflict; resolving that conflict is a major task for the author. A writer of non-fiction will usually pose a problem fairly early in an article and spend the remainder providing a solution. Some writers, of course, provide both the problem and the solution early, and then support the solution in the remaining words.

An important point to remember is that writers usually identify problems as a starting point for their work. Then the solutions to those problems often make up the substance of what they write.

SPOTLIGHT

Read the following passage which introduces *The Global 2000 Report to the President*. See if you can identify the problem which underlies the writing of this document.

Major Findings and Conclusions

If present trends continue, the world in 2000 will be more crowded, more polluted, less stable ecologically, and more vulnerable to disruption than the world we live in now. Serious stresses involving population, resources, and environment are clearly visible ahead. Despite greater material output, the world's people will be poorer in many ways than they are today.

For hundreds of millions of the desperately poor, the outlook for food and other necessities of life will be no better. For many it will be worse. Barring revolutionary advances in technology, life for most people on earth will be more precarious in 2000 than it is now—unless the nations of the world act decisively to alter current trends.

This, in essence, is the picture emerging from the U.S. Government's projections of probable changes in world population, resources, and environment by the end of the century, as presented in the Global 2000 Study. They do not predict what will occur. Rather, they depict conditions that are likely to develop if there are no changes in public policies, institutions, or rates of technological advance, and if there are no wars or other major disruptions. A keener awareness of the nature of the current trends, however, may induce changes that will alter these trends and the projected outcome.

Barney, Gerald O., *The Global 2000 Report to the President*, Volume One, Washington, D.C.: U.S. Government Printing Office, 1980.

Would you agree that the problem which gave rise to this study was probably, "What will the future hold for the world?" or "What, specifically, can we expect the world to be like in 2000?"

Look again at the three paragraphs. Paragraph one presents a classic use of cause-effect reasoning. The author says, "If . . . ,then" in his first statement: "If present trends continue, (then) the world in 2000 will be. . . ." *Present trends* represents the *cause*; the remainder of the paragraph represents the *effects*.

That first paragraph is a kind of summary of the entire report. However, in the second paragraph, the author holds out some hope: ". . . —unless the nations of the world act decisively to alter current trends." That theme is continued in paragraph three: "They do not predict what will occur. Rather, they depict conditions that are likely to develop *if there are no changes in public policies, institutions, or rates of technological advance, and if there are no wars or other major disruptions. A keener awareness of the nature of the current trends, however, may induce changes that will alter these trends and the projected outcome.*"

Even in the "hopeful" section of the report we see the authors using the cause-effect technique. By inference, we are led to believe that if changes in public policies, institutions, or rates of technological advance occur, there is some hope that their forecast will not come true.

Take a few minutes and write several "If . . . , then" statements about the future. You may find yourself using ideas from these statements later in this unit, so take some care in preparing them. When you finish, share them with your classmates and discuss your use of the cause-effect process.

**Getting
It
Started**

SPOTLIGHT

In 1977, President Carter directed the Council on Environmental Quality and the Department of State to prepare the report which appears on page 284. The following paragraphs are from the Preface of the document. They illustrate the concerns which caused the study to be ordered.

Preface

Environmental problems do not stop at national boundaries. In the past decade, we and other nations have come to recognize the urgency of international efforts to protect our common environment.

As part of this process, I am directing the Council on Environmental Quality and the Department of State, working in cooperation with the Environmental Protection Agency, the National Science Foundation, the National Oceanic

and Atmospheric Administration, and other appropriate
agencies, to make a one-year study of the probable changes
in the world's population, natural resources, and environment through the end of the century. This study will serve
as the foundation of our longer-term planning.

President Carter issued this directive in his Environmental Message to the Congress on May 23, 1977. It marked the beginning of
what became a three-year effort to discover the long-term implications of present world trends in population, natural resources, and
the environment and to assess the Government's foundation for
long-range planning.

Government concern with trends in population, resources, and
environment is not new. Indeed, study of these issues by Federal
commissions and planning boards extends back at least 70 years. The
earlier studies, however, tended to view each issue without relation
to the others, to limit their inquiries to the borders of this nation and
the short-term future, and to have relatively little effect on policy.
What is new in more recent studies is a growing awareness of the
interdependence of population, resources, and environment. The
Global 2000 Study is the first U.S. Government effort to look at all
three issues from a long-term global perspective that recognizes their
interrelationships and attempts to make connections among them.

The Global 2000 Study is reported in three volumes. This
Summary is the first volume. Volume II, the Technical Report,
presents the Study in further detail and is referenced extensively in
this Summary. The third volume provides technical documentation
on the Government's global models. All three volumes are available
from the U.S. Government Printing Office. (Barney, 1980, p. vii)

The total report which resulted from this directive includes three volumes
filled with information. It is clearly one of the most important reports to
come from the U.S. Government in recent years.

The introduction, which appears on page 284, is a brief summary of
the total report. The next section, "Principal Findings and Conclusions"
provides information (still broad and somewhat non-specific) which
shows the bases on which the statements in the introduction were formed.

As you read the next section of *The Global 2000 Report to the
President*, look for ways in which the author supports the position taken
in the introduction (page 284).

Principal Findings

Rapid growth in world population will hardly have altered by 2000. The world's population will grow from 4 billion in 1975 to 6.35 billion in 2000, an increase of more than 50 percent. The rate of growth will slow only marginally, from 1.8 percent a year to 1.7 percent. In terms of sheer numbers, population will be growing faster in 2000 than it is today, with 100 million people added each year compared with 75 million in 1975. Ninety percent of this growth will occur in the poorest countries.

Population Growth

While the economies of the less developed countries (LDCs) are expected to grow at faster rates than those of the industrialized nations, the gross national product per capita in most LDCs remains low. The average gross national product per capita is projected to rise substantially in some LDCs (especially in Latin America), but in the great populous nations of South Asia it remains below $200 a year (in 1975 dollars). The large existing gap between the rich and poor nations widens.

Economics

World food production is projected to increase 90 percent over the 30 years from 1970 to 2000. This translates into a global per capita increase of less than 15 percent over the same period. The bulk of that increase goes to countries that already have relatively high per capita food consumption. Meanwhile per capita consumption in South Asia, the Middle East, and the LDCs of Africa will scarcely improve or will actually decline below present inadequate levels. At the same time, real prices for food are expected to double.

Food Production

Arable land will increase only 4 percent by 2000, so that most of the increased output of food will have to come from higher yields. Most of the elements that now contribute to higher yields—fertilizer, pesticides, power for irrigation, and fuel for machinery—depend heavily on oil and gas. . . .

Conclusions

At present and projected growth rates, the world's population would reach 10 billion by 2030 and would approach 30 billion by the end of the twenty-first century. These levels correspond closely to estimates by the U.S. National Academy of Sciences of the maximum carrying capacity of the entire earth. Already the populations in sub-Saharan Africa and in the Himalayan hills of Asia have exceeded the carrying capacity of the immediate area, triggering an erosion of the land's capacity to support life. Unless this circle of interlinked

Present Reality as a Predictor

problems is broken soon, population growth in such areas will unfortunately be slowed for reasons other than declining birth rates. Hunger and disease will claim more babies and young children, and more of those surviving will be mentally and physically handicapped by childhood malnutrition.

Hopeful
Signs

Indeed, the problems of preserving the carrying capacity of the earth and sustaining the possibility of a decent life for the human beings that inhabit it are enormous and close upon us. Yet there is reason for hope. It must be emphasized that the Global 2000 Study's

projections are based on the assumption that national policies regarding population stabilization, resource conservation, and environmental protection will remain essentially unchanged through the end of the century. But in fact, policies are beginning to change. In some areas, forests are being replanted after cutting. Some nations are taking steps to reduce soil losses and desertification. Interest in energy conservation is growing, and large sums are being invested in exploring alternatives to petroleum dependence. . . . Water supplies are being improved and waste treatment systems built. High-yield seeds are widely available and seed banks are being expanded. Some wildlands with their genetic resources are being protected. Natural predators and selective pesticides are being substituted for persistent and destructive pesticides. . . .

    With its limitations and rough approximations, the Global 2000 Study may be seen as no more than a reconnaissance of the future; nonetheless its conclusions are reinforced by similar findings of other recent global studies that were examined in the course of the Global 2000 Study (see Appendix). All these studies are in general agreement on the nature of the problems and on the threats they pose to the future welfare of humankind. The available evidence leaves no doubt that the world—including this Nation—faces enormous, urgent, and complex problems in the decades immediately ahead. Prompt and vigorous changes in public policy around the world are needed to avoid or minimize these problems before they become unmanageable. Long lead times are required for effective action. If decisions are delayed until the problems become worse, options for effective action will be severely reduced.

                                   (Barney, 1980, pp. 1–5)

A Call to Action

Titles were added in the left-hand margins to illustrate the major elements of each supporting statement. Look at the marginal titles and see if the paragraphs under "Principal Findings" and "Conclusions" provide a strong support base for the statement made in the introduction.

    Discuss the approach which this author used to support the major point of the paper. Then jot down some ideas in your Writer's Notebook for organizing a report such as this.

    As you consider your own approach, look carefully at how this author forms generalizations from sets of specific data. See how the information in the "Principal Findings" and "Conclusions" sections of the paper seems almost automatically to point to the statements made in the introduction.

As indicated earlier, this document is huge—three volumes full of data collected by many agencies of the U.S. Government from many sources. What you have read so far is truly the tip of the iceburg. The next information you will read includes somewhat more specific support for the first paragraph under "Principal Findings"—the paragraph concerning population growth.

Table 1 Population Projections for World, Major Regions, and Selected Countries

	1975	2000	Percent Increase by 2000	Average Annual Percent Increase	Percent of World Population in 2000
	Millions				
World	4,090	6,351	55	1.8	100
More-developed regions	1,131	1,323	17	0.6	21
Less developed regions	2,959	5,028	70	2.1	79
Major regions					
Africa	399	814	104	2.9	13
Asia and Oceania	2,274	3,630	60	1.9	57
Latin America	325	637	96	2.7	10
U.S.S.R. and Eastern Europe	384	460	20	0.7	7
North America, Western Europe, Japan, Australia, and New Zealand	708	809	14	0.5	13
Selected countries and regions					
People's Republic of China	935	1,329	42	1.4	21
India	618	1,021	65	2.0	16
Indonesia	135	226	68	2.1	4
Bangladesh	79	159	100	2.8	2
Pakistan	71	149	111	3.0	2
Philippines	43	73	71	2.1	1
Thailand	42	75	77	2.3	1
South Korea	37	57	55	1.7	1
Egypt	37	65	77	2.3	1
Nigeria	63	135	114	3.0	2
Brazil	109	226	108	2.9	4
Mexico	60	131	119	3.1	2
United States	214	248	16	0.6	4
U.S.S.R.	254	309	21	0.8	5
Japan	112	133	19	0.7	2
Eastern Europe	130	152	17	0.6	2
Western Europe	344	378	10	0.4	6

Source: Global 2000 Technical Report, Table 2-10 (Barney, 1980, p. 9)

Comparable supporting information exists for each major point. It is presented in several more detailed sections of the report.

As you look at this instance of information being used to form generalizations, you might be reminded of a pyramid somewhat like this:

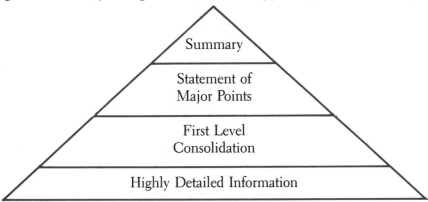

Some form of combining information occurs at each level; generalizations are formed each time one moves to a higher level.

How do you determine the amount of detail that you should include in a report? Your audience and purpose will probably give you a basis for that decision. Whatever you decide, however, you will probably always include material from the top down, that is, you will probably always include a summary. If your audience is not interested in anything more than that, and if you can satisfy the purpose with only that, perhaps that will be all that is necessary. Reread the introduction (page 284) to *The Global 2000 Report to the President.* Can you think of situations in which that would have been sufficient for a given audience and purpose? Think of that as the equivalent of the "summary" section of the pyramid.

Would there be instances when the introduction, together with the "Principal Findings" and "Conclusions" sections of the report would be sufficient? Think of those sections as representing the "summary" and "statement of major points" sections of the pyramid.

The "first level consolidation" would be represented by the table on page 290. The "highly detailed information" would be represented by the material in the other volumes of the document.

Inductive Reasoning

The author of this report has used a technique for building generalizations which is common among non-fiction writers—an inductive approach.

To understand the inductive technique, assume that we took 1,000 students from the high schools in Cleveland and compared their height and weight with that of 1,000 students from the high schools of Seattle. If we discovered the average height and weight of the groups to be similar, we could infer that the height and weight of high school students in Cleveland and Seattle were similar.

Now, suppose you had two friends, one from Cleveland and one from Seattle. If one were taller than the other, would you automatically believe that all citizens of his or her city would be taller than those from the other city?

Both situations involve inductive reasoning. The first uses a large sampling of students from each city. If the sample is representative of the total population, we can trust our conclusion. Of course, if we purposely selected basketball centers from one city and midgets from another, we would have good reason to doubt our conclusions.

In the second instance, we can be reasonably sure that one person cannot be representative of an entire population, and even though we might like to draw a generalization from the sizes of our friends, we know it would be incorrect.

We form generalizations by examining specifics. If the specifics, working together, tell us something, we call that a generalization. Each time we move up the pyramid, we are forming generalizations.

Unfortunately, we can never investigate all possible specifics of most situations. For instance, we might go to a restaurant and have a good meal. We could say, "We went to restaurant X and had a good meal." But we could not say with any degree of confidence, "We will always have a good meal at restaurant X," because we had not had enough experience with restaurant X to make that statement.

If a friend were to ask us for our recommendation concerning restaurant X, after only one visit we would probably say, "We had a good meal," and let it go at that. Our friend would be left to his or her own devices. But if we had been there on ten occasions and each time had a fine meal, we might say, "I've been there ten times and had exceptional food each time. I feel certain you will have a fine dining experience there."

While making recommendations about the restaurant to our friend, we have taken a set of specifics (our feelings about the quality of food each of the times we have eaten at the restaurant) and formed a generalization. In this case, our generalization is a speculation, just as are most generalizations. We speculate that, since we have consistently enjoyed good meals at restaurant X, our friend will have the same experience.

The problem with making generalizations based on a sample (when you are not able to consider every possible instance) is that you cannot be sure your speculation will always be true. But imagine what it would take to be absolutely sure about a restaurant! You would have to eat there regularly for years. You would have to eat there at times when the chef was ill and an assistant had to manage the kitchen. You would have to eat there when deliveries were slow, or not even made.

Another problem to be aware of in using inductive reasoning is the "loaded" sample. Let's say that we are in a state where there is serious public concern about athletic injuries. With the advent of more and more girls' sports, the members of the state girls' athletic council decide that they will not let girls' athletics become as injury-prone as boys' has become. So they decide to establish strict rules, carefully enforced by trained referees, to cut down on the number of injuries.

After two years, the council decides to check on the effect of its new rules. They compare the number of injuries to girl athletes in the current year to the number in the year before the new rules were put into effect. Surprisingly, there are more injuries a year after the rules than there were the year before.

What could account for such an occurrence? In this instance, substantially more girls were engaged in athletics one year after the rules were put into effect than in the year before they were enacted. The number of injuries is closely related to the number of persons participating in athletics, and the council, rather than looking at the percentage of athletes injured in each year, looked at the total number of injuries. Because their populations were different, they obtained inaccurate results.

This same error is often made by authors as they choose facts to support their positions. It is easy to ignore facts that do not support your opinion, while selecting only those that do.

Getting It Started

Look back at the paper from *The Global 2000 Report to the President*. First read the introduction (page 284) and then read the remainder of the excerpts from the paper on pages 285–289. Do the specifics lead you to agree with the author's introductory statement? Has the author moved up the pyramid in what appears to be a logical, well-supported way?

Make lists of those marginal titles which label items you feel are 1. most supportive, 2. somewhat less supportive, and 3. not very supportive. Share your ideas with your classmates and discuss why some elements are more effective than others in supporting the point of the paper. Discuss whether the problems with items in categories 2 and 3 relate to improper generalization, insufficient proof, or some other problem. Then, consider what it is that makes the items in category 1 so effective.

Jot down feelings about things which make inductive processes work well and problems which you might encounter as you use them. In your Writer's Notebook, combine these jottings with the other comments you have made about your writing process.

Forming Generalizations About the Future

Getting It Down

On the next pages, you will find parts of several articles which relate to the future. Using information from these articles, attempt to form a generalization you could support with the material given. Use only the information provided. Do not go to the library for additional material. Do not search your personal experience for helpful data. Just use what is presented.

Jot down the generalization once you have formed it.

Then write down the bits of information which you used to form your generalization. Do not attempt to write out each sentence from the source documents which you used. Merely give a word or two to remind yourself of each information bit which supports your generalization.

Do not feel you must use every article in building your generalization.

"It is People Who Use Energy," by Kingsley S. Davis

Between 1955, the last time we produced as much energy as we consumed, and 1978, our energy consumption rose 99 percent. More than a third (38.3 percent) of that increase was due to population growth—52.6 million in the 23-year period—the rest being due to rising per capita consumption. Since very little manpower is required to produce energy (less than half of 1 percent of the labor force), the growth of population contributed nothing to the production of energy but did contribute greatly to its consumption. According to the Census Bureau's medium projection, our population in 2000 will be 38 million greater than it is now. In that case, our energy supply will have to rise by 17 percent in two decades just to maintain per capita consumption, or per capita use will have to be cut by one-sixth to hold total consumption to the present amount.

The entire world's population is growing more rapidly than

ours—currently about 75 million annually. By the year 2000, the
projected human population will be 2.3 billion greater than it is
today.

Davis, Kingsley S., "It Is People Who Use Energy," *Science*, Jan. 30, 1981, p. 1.

The National Science Foundation Looks to the Future

In the United States, industry is responsible for almost 40 percent of
total energy consumption. A significant fraction of this energy is used
in separating and processing materials. Because we now have so
many new materials, chemical pathways, and end products, the old
engineering approach of case-by-case evaluation and experimentation
is no longer sufficient for selection of the optimum process. More
general and fundamental theories and models must be developed to
compare the efficiencies and energy requirements of distillation, ex-
traction, membrane transport, absorption, and other separation processes.

The search for substitute materials or those offering entirely new
combinations of properties is a particularly exciting area. Molecular
alignment of polyethylene can produce a polymer with a tensile
strength that exceeds that of glass or steel on a weight-for-weight
basis. By means of an "ultradraw" technique, an organic polymer
filament 1/8-inch thick can support a weight of almost 3700 pounds.
This pioneering work is now being scaled up to produce insulation
for superconducting magnets.

Metallic glasses are another case in point. These are produced
when molten metallic alloys are "splat-cooled" at rates of 100,000 to
1 million degrees per second. Because such rapid cooling prevents
crystallization in the resulting solid, its molecules are arranged in
essentially amorphous, random patterns like those in glass. Glasses
can be produced that have yield strengths far in excess of those of
commercial steels and are more corrosion-resistant than stainless steel
and lighter and stronger than aluminum. The potential for these and
other new glasses is enormous, perhaps rivaling the impact on modern society of the semi-conductor technologies born a little more
than three decades ago.

International comparisons are of considerable interest here, too.
Between 1963 and 1977 Japan awarded approximately as many degrees to engineers as did the United States, even though Japan's
population is only about half the size of our own. In Japan, about 20
percent of baccalaureates and 40 percent of master's degrees are in

engineering, compared with 5 percent for each degree level in this country. Interestingly, only about half of Japan's engineers actually enter the engineering professions; the rest become civil servants or managers of industry. In fact, about half of Japanese senior civil servants and industrial directors have engineering qualifications. The fact that Japan almost doubled its share of world trade between 1963 and 1977, while the U.S. share declined about 25 percent, may owe much to the engineering skills of managers of the Japanese national enterprise.

Peter Drucker, in an article in *Fortune* magazine last November, quoted a Japanese official who said: "You in the United States have in the last ten years doubled the number of people in law schools, while you barely even maintained the number of people in engineering schools. We in Japan have not increased the number of lawyers but have doubled the number of engineering students. Lawyers are concerned with dividing the pie, engineers with making it larger."

I am aware that attempts to forecast future needs for scientists and engineers are fraught with uncertainties. But I am impressed with the forecast of the Bureau of Labor Statistics that opportunities in science and engineering occupations will grow by about 40 percent at all degree levels between 1978 and 1990. This growth would create 180,000 new jobs in the mathematical, physical, life, and social sciences, 250,000 new engineering jobs, and 480,000 jobs in the computer professions over the 12-year period. In addition, there is evidence of a high degree of mobility among scientists and engineers in terms of their ability to shift to "hot" fields. For example, in a survey of 1977 engineering and science baccalaureates, it was found that almost three times as many were working in the computer professions in 1979 as had obtained bachelor's degrees in that field 2 years earlier. The trend is even more marked at the doctoral level; in 1979 it was found that three and a half times as many Ph.D.'s were working as computer professionals as had *ever* earned degrees in the field.

Slaughter, John B., "The National Science Foundation Looks to the Future," *Science*, March 13, 1981, pp. 1134–1136.

Will They Feed the World's People?

Two thirds of the world's population live in a region known as the equatorial "hunger belt"—a region encircling our globe where the land is simply too poor to produce enough food for all its inhabitants. Unusually bad weather, crop failures, or political and economic problems can swiftly deplete food supplies even in more fertile areas. And when food becomes scarce, everyone suffers. In rich countries, though, people can afford to pay more for their food. But in less developed nations—especially the impoverished Third World nations of Africa and Asia—people starve. When prices skyrocket as the world's citizens compete for a limited food supply, nations like these are unable to import food. And their populations are just too high to be fed—adequately—by wealthier countries.

Scientists are always trying to develop grains that will produce more food per acre. Grains alone, though, usually can't supply an adequate variety and amount of protein to "build" young bodies and—later—to keep them fit. And *protein deficiency is the most damaging form of malnutrition* suffered in underdeveloped nations today. In young children, protein deficiency stunts growth and—worst of all—leads to permanent brain damage that affects intelligence, behavior, language and motor skills. The challenge now is to discover new methods to raise food *and* to provide protein. And scientists are beginning to face that challenge.

In the future, the oceans may be turned into huge "farms"—where shrimp and fish are raised like vegetables.

Mariculture—the scientific farming of the sea—is already underway. In Spain, for example, fishermen are raising mussels—a kind of shellfish—by planting their young on long ropes attached to rafts. In eight to ten months, the baby mussels are ready for harvest and ocean farmers haul up the ropes.

In the Philippines, fish are being raised in underwater bamboo-and-net cages.

Dr. Mark Strahmann—professor of biochemistry at the University of Wisconsin—has already found a way to make protein-rich alfalfa edible for humans. Ordinarily, alfalfa has so much of a chewy material called cellulose that only animals equipped with multiple stomachs—like cows—can digest it properly. But Dr. Strahmann has invented a machine that breaks alfalfa down for us.

Dr. Strahmann's machine turns the tough alfalfa cells into a green juice that is 25 to 35 percent protein. When the juice is heated, it changes into something that looks like cottage cheese. After it is dried, it becomes a dark green powder that Dr. Strahmann calls "Leaf Protein Concentrate," or LCP.

LCP can be used in breads, cereals, sausage—and even cookies. And an area a little bigger than Texas, says Dr. Strahmann, could supply enough LCP to give every human presently living a generous helping of LCP protein per day.

Microbes in certain plants, and some kinds of bacteria, fungi, and yeasts can also yield protein. The trick is to turn the bacteria living in trees, vines, grasses, and straw into a powder called Single Cell Protein, or SCP. Pigs and poultry are already eating SCP.

The search for food is making some scientists look for protein in plants we have previously ignored. For example, the 12-foot-high Tetra is an amazingly protein-rich plant that grows in New Guinea. The tetra is 34 to 37 percent protein. Compare that to a greasy hamburger—which, by the way, is mostly fat and contains 22 percent protein not counting the roll.

One day we may even be eating insects! The Australian Aborigines and some primitive peoples have eaten, and, perhaps, even enjoyed, protein-rich bugs. And as the world population soars and its food supply shrinks, we may learn to enjoy them, too.

Grasshoppers may become the new peanut butter and jelly sandwich of the future. They contain 60 percent protein. Termites, also, may become an important food source. They can be baked into casseroles or tossed into salads.

Other new foods of the future will be imaginative blends of foods we already eat. Ricetein tastes and looks like rice—but it's a far more nutritious mix of rice and soy protein. Soy protein comes, of course, from soy beans.

Naglin, Nancy, "Will They Feed the World's People?" *Science World*, April 3, 1980, pp. 6–8.

Wood: Fuel of the Future?

Given the near-catastrophic state of deforestation in many of the developing nations, and the sheer immensity of the energy demand in the industrialized states, it is a bit disconcerting to hear someone tout old-fashioned wood as a potentially important source of energy. But that is exactly what senior researcher Nigel Smith of the Worldwatch Institute in Washington, D.C., does in the Worldwatch report released on 31 January ("Wood: An ancient fuel with a new future"). The report outlines a number of trends that lead him to believe that the worldwide use of wood will increase at least 50 percent by the end of the century.

Wood's potential contribution to the energy budget of the United States is even greater than that, adds Smith. In 1980, the United States used roughly 1.5 quads (quadrillion British thermal units) of wood energy, mostly in the wood products industry. This compares to an estimated total U.S. energy consumption of some 80 quads in 1980. He quotes a study by the Office of Technology Assessment which suggests that wood could supply about 10 quads by the turn of the century without disrupting the flow of raw material to the wood products industry; depending on the effect of energy conservation measures on the growth of demand, says Smith, this could represent some 10 percent of the total.

Smith, who came to Worldwatch after 4 years at the Brazilian Institute for Amazonian Research in Manaus, notes that proper management of wood resources is especially critical in the poorer nations; approximately half the families in the world still cook their food and heat their homes with wood. In most of the Third World, in fact, the ever-rising cost of kerosene and other fossil fuels leaves them with little other choice.

But proper management is in terribly short supply at the moment. The desperate need for firewood has led to massive deforestation in many parts of Asia and in sub-Saharan Africa during the last decade. Yet Smith thinks that the process can still be reversed. Development agencies such as the World Bank have greatly stepped up the funding of forestry projects in recent years. More important, Smith finds that some of the developing nations are beginning to look at their forests not as impediments to progress, but as an energy resource. Some recent reforestation programs have gone quite well; during the last decade in South Korea, for example, villagers established 643,000 hectares of trees, about half as much area as the country has in rice.

In the United States and other industrialized nations, events since the 1973 oil embargo have made a return to wood look attractive for reasons other than aesthetics. Prior to 1973 fewer than 200,000 wood stoves were sold in the United States, Smith says; in 1980 that figure climbed to well over 1 million. "Seven percent of the homes in the country are now entirely or partly heated with wood stoves or furnaces, and the proportion is steadily increasing," he says.

A similar pattern of conversion to wood is apparent in industry, Smith writes. In the middle 1960's, sales of wood-fired industrial boilers were a negligible percentage of the U.S. total; by the middle 1970's, they had climbed to 5 percent. The U.S. pulp and paper industry now provides half its own energy from waste products. The Swedish paper industry obtains 60 percent.

Industrial use of wood is receiving a boost from the availability of wood in more convenient forms. Machines have been developed that shred trees into matchbox-sized chips, for example. Burlington, Vermont, plans to build a 50-megawatt wood-chip furnace that will generate electricity for 20,000 city residents. Wood waste is also being bound together into small pellets that can be used directly in coal furnaces. Pellets are denser and drier than wood chips, so they are more economical to transport.

An increased reliance on wood is not without its environmental hazards, however. Aside from deforestation in the Third World, there is the problem of air pollution. Woodsmoke haze is already quite thick over certain New England villages in winter. Vail, Colorado, has limited new houses to one wood stove apiece. In London, wood fires are banned.

"None of these environmental problems is insurmountable," says Smith. "Small precipitators installed in chimneys can reduce harmful effluents and more efficient stoves designed for short-lived, intense fires would emit fewer noxious compounds."

One important advantage of growing trees for energy is that woodlots need not compete directly with land needed for growing food, says Smith. Land that is marginal for agriculture—erosion-prone hillsides, for example—may be perfectly suitable for trees. In the United States, for another example, the Tennessee Valley Authority may soon establish trees for firewood production on some of the barren land under its power lines. The spread of woodlots is also unlikely to provoke the kind of public ire drawn by other energy developments, Smith points out; for once, the production of energy would actually enhance the scenery.

M. Mitchell Waldrop, "Wood: Fuel of the Future?" *Science*, Feb. 27, 1981, p. 914.

When you have a generalization written out and you also have notes which remind you of the bits of information you used to form that generalization, discuss your material with your classmates.

    Consider these questions as a start:

1. Is the generalization a logical one, given the information you have?
2. Have you chosen appropriate points to support the generalization?
3. Have you cited enough information to support your generalization? Are there other points you could have included to make the support stronger?
4. Does the generalization make sense?

You may decide to have a classmate work with you as you form your generalization and determine support for it. Be sure, whatever you do, that you understand this process.

    Talk about the process you followed in forming your generalization. When did you form your generalization—early in your reading or after you had read most of the material? Did the information lead you to a conclusion or did you force the information to fit your generalization?

    What role did the following play in your choice?

1. your own interests
2. your feelings about audience
3. your knowledge of the subject
4. your purpose for writing

Checking It Out

In your Writer's Notebook, write notes to yourself about this process. Write about the process that was most successful in forming generalizations. Write about how you selected items to support and develop your generalization. React to processes that other members of your class used, and either incorporate them into your strategy or reject them and write why you think they are inappropriate.

Getting It Down

Chapter 14

Working It Through

In the last two chapters, you will read several examples which use inductive reasoning to build generalizations, and you have attempted that process yourself as well. You have probably identified several problems which can result when some part of the process is inadequate or incorrect.

This chapter introduces a related process for reasoning: the deductive process. Deductive reasoning is commonly used in everyday life, just as inductive processes are. It also often forms the basis for the introduction or conclusion of a paper.

You will have an opportunity in this chapter to work with both deductive and inductive processes; you will study both when they work well, and you will have a chance to repair generalizations and conclusions made when the processes are faulty for some reason.

Remember—*inductive* reasoning involves starting with a specific body of information and attempting to see some pattern in it. That pattern, then, becomes a generalization, made on the basis of the information.

Deductive Reasoning

Deductive reasoning starts with a broad statement known to be true; given that statement, we try to find specific conclusions or other instances of the subject of the investigation. The broad statement is usually referred to as an *assumption*.

The classical presentation of deductive reasoning is in a formula which is called a *syllogism*. The syllogism is made up of a *major premise*, a *minor premise*, and a *conclusion*. Look at the following syllogism:

Major Premise: All humans will die.
Minor Premise: John and Mary are humans.
Conclusion: John and Mary will die.

The following diagram illustrates the relationship of the premises.

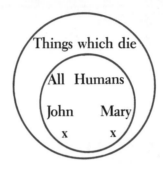

The conclusion is based on the following logic: If John and Mary are humans, whatever is common to all humans will be common to them; if humans are a part of the class of things which die, then John and Mary, because they are humans, will die.

Consider another example:

Major Premise:	All birds have feathers.
Minor Premise:	My pet is a bird.
Conclusion:	My pet has feathers.

The conclusion is obvious. But check this example:

Major Premise:	All birds can fly.
Minor Premise:	My pet ostrich is a bird.
Conclusion:	My pet ostrich can fly.

But ostriches cannot fly. What is the problem with the syllogism? Do you see that there is an error of fact in the major premise? The fact is that all birds *cannot* fly. Flying is not a characteristic common to all birds. The ostrich is one example of a non-flying bird.

See if you can discover the problem with this syllogism:

Major Premise:	All good football players get bruises.
Minor Premise:	I have bruises.
Conclusion:	I am a good football player.

The assumption that all good football players get bruises is probably in error. Some may not, and even bad football players get bruises. But there is a problem with the minor premise, too. The fact that I have bruises does not necessarily put me in the company of good football players. My bruises may have been caused by a fall down the stairs.

A deduction is reliable only when the premises are true and the conclusion logically follows the premises.

Writer's Workbench 1

Writing Logically

A. Write conclusions for the following premises:

1. Major Premise: All dogs are mammals.
   Minor Premise: Fido is a dog.
   Conclusion:

2. Major Premise: All scholarship winners are honor students.
   Minor Premise: Susan is a scholarship winner.
   Conclusion:

3. Major Premise: Population is increasing.
   Minor Premise: As the population increases, quality of life decreases.
   Conclusion:

4. Major Premise: A strong industrial base helps a country advance.
   Minor Premise: Lesser developed nations wish to advance.
   Conclusion:

5. Major Premise: If population growth exceeds the growth of the food supply, starvation occurs.
   Minor Pemise: Population growth in country x exceeds the growth of its food supply.
   Conclusion:

B. Write syllogisms for each of the following passages. Use this example as a guide:

We know from past experience that if a country can get control of its population growth, its development will move more rapidly than if it fails to limit population. Country X, to the amazement of many international observers, has taken control of population growth, and it is now moving rapidly toward developed status.

Syllogism:

Major Premise:	Countries which control population growth develop more rapidly than those which do not.
Minor Premise:	Country X has taken control of its population growth.
Conclusion:	Country X is moving rapidly toward developed status.

1. World Bank loans, when carefully used to establish strong trade-oriented activities in developing countries, contribute much to speeding development. Country Y has made prudent use of recent World Bank loans by using them to support indigenous industries such as lumbering, rice farming, and light manufacturing of exportable products. We can expect country Y to move quickly to a more developed condition.

2. It seems generally true that all developed countries have strong industrial trade bases. The developed countries of Western Europe, for example, engage in active manufacturing and trade, not only among themselves, but with the entire world. However, Middle Eastern countries, even with their substantial wealth in oil, still are not well developed, even though their average income is among the highest in the world. They have no strong industrial base.

3. A key to real development in a country seems to be the distribution of substantial amounts of the country's wealth to large numbers of its citizens. In countries where wealth is concentrated in the hands of a few, one can almost be assured that the country will be either poorly developed or underdeveloped.

4. The process of photosynthesis in plants of the earth contributes substantially to the removal of carbon dioxide and replenishing of oxygen in the earth's air. Massive deforestation is taking place in the equatorial jungles and rain forests of the world. Unless these trees are replaced, a change in the amount of oxygen available for supporting combustion and even for breathing could occur.

5. When smallpox was eradicated, a major killing disease was eliminated. In many countries, cultures were conditioned to expect many deaths each year, especially among children, from smallpox. The culture, anticipating many infant deaths, encouraged large families so that at least some of the children could live to adulthood. Now that smallpox has been eradicated, more children are living and populations are growing more rapidly in many areas of the world.

C. Now, write short paragraphs for each of the following syllogisms.

Provide an appropriate conclusion unless one is given.

1. Major Premise: Education is not readily available in most less developed countries.

   Minor Premise: John is a citizen of a less developed nation.
   Conclusion: John may find it difficult to get an education in his country.

2. Major Premise: Wood is the only source of heat for rural citizens in country Z.

   Minor Premise: If present rates of consumption continue, the wood supply of country Z will be gone in ten years.

   Conclusion:

3. Major Premise: If the wood supply of country Y is consumed, rural residents will have no source of heat.

   Minor Premise: The wood supply of country Y will be completely used up in five years.

   Conclusion:

4. Major Premise: For a strong, industrial base to operate, a country must have natural resources, plentiful labor, and financial support.

   Minor Premise: Country M has natural resources and a plentiful labor supply, but no financial support.

   Conclusion:

5. Major Premise: You cannot have your cake and eat it too.
   Minor Premise: You have eaten your cake.
   Conclusion:

~~~~~~

**Checking
It
Out**

Discuss this Workbench with your classmates. Be sure you understand how the deductive process works: how to identify major and minor premises, how to form conclusions, how to spot logic that doesn't seem to work. You will have an opportunity to explore problems with logical operations later; however, get a sense now of what works for you and what does not.

~~~~~~

**Getting
It
Started**

Think of some everyday situations in which you use deductive reasoning. Think about problems with your car—"It sounds as if it's either an ignition problem or it's getting too much gas. It doesn't seem to be getting too much gas, so it must be the ignition." If you prefer, think about deciding on where to go on a date—"All the other kids are going to the dance, but we'd rather be by ourselves, so we'll go to a movie instead." Can you spot the premises and conclusions in those statements?

Write out at least three examples of situations in which you used deductive reasoning during the last week. Write each in syllogism form, including Major Premise, Minor Premise, and Conclusion.

~~~~~~

Writer's Workbench 2

Building Syllogisms

The following tables contain information which you can use to build syllogisms. Using the data, generate at least three syllogisms, including conclusions. Then write a short paragraph for each syllogism.

Table 1 Total Population in the Older Ages and Decennial Increases: 1950 to 2040

(Numbers in thousands. Estimates and projections as of July 1. Figures refer to the total population of the 50 States and District of Columbia. A minus sign (−) denotes a decrease. See text for explanation of Series I, II, and III)

Year	65 years and over			70 years and over			75 years and over			85 years and over		
	Number	Increase in preceding decade		Number	Increase in preceding decade		Number	Increase in preceding decade		Number	Increase in preceding decade	
		Amount	Percent		Amount	Percent		Amount	Percent		Amount	Percent
ESTIMATES												
1950	12,397	(X)	(X)	7,348	(X)	(X)	3,904	(X)	(X)	590	(X)	(X)
1960	16,675	4,278	34.5	10,394	3,046	41.5	5,621	1,717	44.0	940	350	59.3
1970	20,087	3,412	20.5	13,065	2,671	25.7	7,600	1,979	35.2	1,432	492	52.3
1976	22,934	(X)	(X)	14,654	(X)	(X)	8,741	(X)	(X)	1,966	(X)	(X)
PROJECTIONS[1]												
1980	24,927	4,840	24.1	16,227	3,162	24.2	9,434	1,834	24.1	2,294	862	60.2
1990	29,824	4,897	19.6	19,803	3,576	22.0	12,021	2,587	27.4	2,881	587	25.6
2000	31,822	1,998	6.7	22,630	2,827	14.3	14,386	2,365	19.7	3,756	875	30.4
2010	34,837	3,015	9.5	23,211	581	2.6	15,060	674	4.7	4,575	819	21.8
2020	45,102	10,265	29.5	29,126	5,915	25.5	16,975	1,915	12.7	4,776	201	4.4
2030	55,024	9,922	22.0	37,936	8,810	30.2	23,170	6,195	36.5	5,681	905	18.9
2040 . . . . . . (II)[3] (III)[4] Range . . . (I)[2]	54,925	−99	−0.2	40,774	2,838	7.5	27,907	4,737	20.4	7,980	2,299	40.5

(X) Not applicable.
[1] Base date of projections is July 1, 1978.
[2] High estimate
[3] Middle estimate
[4] Low estimate

Source: U.S. Bureau of the Census, *Current Population Reports*, Series P-25, Nos. 311, 519, 614, 643, and 704.

**Table 3. Percent Distribution of the Population
65 Years Old and Over, by Age: 1950 to 2020**

Age	1950	1960	1970	1976	Projections				
					1980	1990	2000	2010	2020
65 years and over.......	100.0	100.0	100.0	100.0	100.0	100.0	100.0	100.0	100.0
65 to 69 years	40.7	37.7	35.0	36.1	34.9	33.6	28.9	33.4	35.4
70 to 74 years	27.8	28.6	27.2	25.8	27.3	26.1	25.9	23.4	26.9
75 to 79 years	17.4	18.5	19.2	17.7	17.3	18.4	20.1	17.0	16.8
80 to 84 years	9.3	9.6	11.5	11.9	11.3	12.2	13.3	13.1	10.2
85 years and over.......	4.8	5.6	7.1	8.6	9.2	9.7	11.8	13.1	10.6

Source: U.S. Bureau of the Census, *Current Population Reports,* Series P-25, No. 311, 519, 614, 643 and 704.

Table 4. Sex Ratios of the Population, by Broad Age Groups: 1950 to 2020
(Males per 100 females. Estimates and projections as of July 1. Figures include Armed Forces overseas)

Age and projection series	1950	1960	1970	1976	Projections				
					1980	1990	2000	2010	2020
All ages .... II[2]					95.0	94.8	94.6	94.4	93.8
I[1]	99.3	97.0	94.8	94.8	95.1	95.2	95.4	95.7	95.7
Range.......... III[3]					94.9	94.5	94.0	93.5	92.4
Under 15 years	103.8	103.4	103.9	104.2	104.5	105.1	105.2	105.1	105.1
15 to 29 years......	98.7	97.7	97.8	100.3	101.3	101.3	102.1	102.1	102.1
30 to 44 years......	97.4	95.5	95.2	95.8	96.6	97.2	96.7	96.8	97.3
45 to 59 years......	99.8	96.9	93.4	94.8	95.3	95.1	95.9	95.4	95.3
60 to 64 years......	100.4	91.2	87.7	87.9	87.9	98.8	89.9	91.1	90.9
65 to 69 years......	94.0	87.8	80.7	79.3	79.7	80.5	82.4	82.4	83.2
70 to 74 years......	91.3	85.3	73.9	73.5	72.4	72.9	74.6	74.8	75.9
75 to 84 years......	85.0	77.4	65.9	61.0	60.3	59.6	59.9	60.7	61.4
85 years and over ...	70.0	63.8	53.2	47.0	44.7	40.9	39.4	38.8	38.5
65 years and over ...	89.5	82.6	72.0	69.0	68.2	67.3	66.6	67.0	69.3
75 years and over ...	82.6	75.0	63.3	57.7	56.2	54.7	54.0	53.4	54.2

[1]high estimate
[2]middle estimate
[3]low estimate
Source: U.S. Bureau of the Census, *Current Population Reports,* Series P-25, Nos. 311, 519, 614, 643, and 704.

Table 11. Comparison of Estimates and Projections of Populations 65 Years and Over and 70 Years and Over: 1975 to 2000 (Numbers in thousands. Estimates and projections as of July 1)

Age group and projection	1975			2000		
	Population	Difference from current estimate		Population	Difference from latest projection[1]	
		Amount	Percent		Amount	Percent
65 YEARS AND OVER						
Current estimate[2]	22,420	(X)	(X)	(X)	(X)	(X)
Projections (P-25 *report number and date of issue*):[3]						
704 (July, 1977)	(X)	(X)	(X)	31,822	(X)	(X)
601 (Oct., 1975)	22,330	-90	-0.4	30,600	-1,222	-3.8
493 (Dec., 1972)	22,170	-250	-1.1	28,842	-2,980	-9.4
470 (Nov., 1971)	21,859	-561	-2.5	28,839	-2,983	-9.4
448 (Aug., 1970)	21,503	-917	-4.1	28,837	-2,985	-9.4
381 (Dec., 1967)	21,160	-1,260	-5.6	28,184	-3,638	-11.4
286 (July, 1964)	21,172	-1,248	-5.6	28,199	-3,623	-11.4
187 (Nov., 1958)	21,872	-548	-2.4	(NA)	(NA)	(NA)
123 (Oct., 1955)	20,665	-1,765	-7.9	(NA)	(NA)	(NA)
78 (Aug., 1953)	20,689	-1,731	-7.7	(NA)	(NA)	(NA)
70 and OVER						
Current estimate[2]	14,319	(X)	(X)	(X)	(X)	(X)
Projections (P-25 *report number and date of issue*):[3]						
704 (July, 1977)	(X)	(X)	(X)	22,630	(X)	(X)
601 (Oct., 1975)	14,233	-86	-0.6	21,577	-1,053	-4.7
493 (Dec., 1972)	14,484	165	1.2	20,310	-2,320	-10.3
470 (Nov., 1971)	14,169	-150	-1.0	20,226	-2,404	-10.6
448 (Aug., 1970)	13,983	-336	-2.3	20,306	-2,324	-10.3
381 (Dec., 1967)	13,690	-629	-4.4	19,859	-2,771	-12.2
286 (July, 1964)	13,688	-631	-4.4	19,866	-2,764	-12.2
187 (Nov., 1958)	14,089	-230	-1.6	(NA)	(NA)	(NA)
123 (Oct., 1955)	13,117	-1,202	-8.4	(NA)	(NA)	(NA)
78 (Aug., 1953)	13,131	-1,188	-8.3	(NA)	(NA)	(NA)

X Not applicable. NA Not available.
[1]*Current Population Reports*, Series P-25, No. 721, April 1978.
[2]Latest projection is 31,822,000, published in *Current Population Reports*, Series P-25, No. 704, July 1977.
[3]Base date may be a few months to one and a half years prior to publication date and final death statistics used may relate to a calendar year two to three years before the publication date.

Table 5. Life Expectancy at Birth and at Age 65, by Race and Sex: 1900 to 1976

Race and year	At birth				At age 65			
	Both sexes	Male	Female	Difference	Both sexes	Male	Female	Difference
ALL RACES								
1900-02 . . .	49.2	47.9	50.7	2.8	11.9	11.5	12.2	0.7
1939-42 . . .	63.6	61.6	65.9	4.3	12.8	12.1	13.6	1.5
1954	69.6	66.7	72.7	5.0	14.4	13.1	15.7	2.2
1968	70.2	66.6	74.0	7.4	14.6	12.8	16.3	3.5
1976	72.8	69.0	76.7	7.7	16.0	13.7	18.0	4.3
WHITE								
1900-02 . . .	49.7	48.2	51.1	2.9	11.9	11.5	12.2	0.7
1939-41 . . .	64.9	62.8	67.3	4.5	12.8	12.1	13.6	1.5
1954	70.5	67.4	73.6	6.2	14.4	13.1	15.7	2.6
1968	71.1	67.5	74.9	7.4	14.7	12.8	16.4	3.6
1976	73.5	69.7	77.3	7.6	16.1	13.7	18.1	4.4
BLACK AND OTHER RACES								
1900-02 . . .	33.8	32.5	35.0	2.5	10.9	10.4	11.4	1.0
1939-41 . . .	53.9	52.3	55.6	3.3	13.0	12.2	13.9	1.7
1954	63.4	61.0	65.8	4.8	14.6	13.5	15.7	2.2
1968	63.7	60.1	67.5	7.4	13.7	12.1	15.1	3.0
1976	68.3	64.1	72.6	8.5	15.8	13.8	17.6	3.8
WHITE-BLACK DIFFERENCE								
1900-02 . . .	15.9	15.7	16.1	(X)	1.0	1.1	0.8	(X)
1939-41 . . .	11.0	10.5	11.7	(X)	−0.2	−0.1	−0.3	(X)
1954	7.1	6.4	7.8	(X)	−0.2	−0.4	–	(X)
1968	7.4	7.4	7.4	(X)	1.0	0.7	1.3	(X)
1976	5.2	5.6	4.7	(X)	0.3	−0.1	0.5	(X)

(X) Not applicable.

Source: National Center for Health Statistics (U.S. Public Service) and the U.S. Bureau of the Census. For 1976, "Advance Report-Final Mortality Statistics, 1976," *Monthly Vital Statistics Report*, Vol. 26, No. 12, Supplement (2), March 1978.

Checking It Out

Did you form your syllogisms around a common Major Premise (a typical response to this assignment), or did you stay with one theme through all your syllogisms, centering all your data on the effects of increasing longevity on population, or some other idea?

Share your syllogisms and paragraphs with a classmate. Have him or her check your logic, just to be sure you have a legitimate statement. Also, have your classmate check to be sure your paragraphs actually reflect the statements you have made in your syllogisms. Have your classmate or your teacher help you if there are any problems.

With a group of your classmates, discuss the process you used in extracting data, building syllogisms, and writing paragraphs. See what processes they used and compare them with your own. You may find some helpful techniques by listening to other members of your class describe their processes.

When you have had an opportunity to review the processes you used, change them, based on successful strategies used by your classmates. Then, in your Writer's Notebook jot down some notes about your modified process. Next do one more syllogism, and write a paragraph based on it to be sure the process works for you. Share your work with a classmate (perhaps a different one from the one you worked with in the last activity) so you can be sure it is complete, accurate, and appropriate.

**Getting
It
Started**

When you are sure your process works, write out the procedures in your Writer's Notebook under the heading, "How I Handle Deductive Logic."

**Getting
It
Down**

Writer's Workbench 3

Problems with Logic

It is easy to make errors as we draw conclusions. A number of common fallacies, or sources of error, are listed next, along with brief illustrations of each. Do not attempt to memorize the names of each fallacy. Rather, try to sense when something is wrong with a statement and use common sense to find the cause of the problem. Use these illustrations to polish your common sense.

1. Begging the question.   This occurs when one or more of the premises which we assume to be true are either false or unproven. Read the following paragraph and see if you can see the error.

> Everyone knows how important hard work is to success, and when the individual citizens of a country work hard, their country prospers. That's the problem with the people in most less developed countries today. They don't work. They just lie around all day doing nothing. If they would just get to work, great things would happen to their nations.

Write out the premises represented in this paragraph and see if you can find the problems.

Another example of begging the question involves a kind of circular reasoning. Read the following paragraph and see if you can spot the problem.

> People who live in less developed countries are lazy and don't want to work. We know they're lazy because if they had any get-up-and-go, they wouldn't be living in countries like that.

2. Red Herring.   This label comes from a time when hunting dogs were led away from the scent of the fox because someone had dragged food with a very strong scent (perhaps a dried, salted fish) across the trail. The hounds would be diverted to a stronger scent, thus losing the scent of the fox.

Sometimes writers and speakers drag red herrings across a nice clean, logical trail in order to avoid an embarrassing discovery. Red herrings in writing are usually false issues which, on their own, appeal to the reader, but really do not speak to the topic.

Here is an example of a red herring.

> The problems which an aging population presents for a society are immense. The financial burden which individuals unable or unwilling to work because of their age place on the resources of a country make it important that careful planning be undertaken at the family, the community, and the national levels.
>
> But what about the young who refuse to work? They are the real culprits.

The issue of "youth" was inserted into the argument to avoid dealing with the difficult issue of the problems of the aged in a society. Red herrings are often used to divert attention from difficult and unpopular issues and to place the burden on a scapegoat. In the preceding paragraph, unemployed young people were used to divert the argument.

3. <u>Argumentum Ad Hominem.</u>   In this error of logic, the writer attacks the person (usually the source of information) rather than the information itself. The following paragraph illustrates the fallacy of *Argumentum ad hominem*.

> Michael Jeremy has written that we must think of the future, that we must conserve energy, that we must limit consumption of goods. Yet here is a man who lives in conspicuous consumption. His home is a mansion. He has a staff to serve him. Mr. Jeremy certainly writes a good game. I challenge him to live the game before he expects others to do so.

Jeremy's arguments may have been forceful and quite legitimate; however, this author attacks Jeremy, the man, rather than the issues he raises.

4. <u>Hasty Generalization.</u>   This problem usually involves coming to a conclusion too quickly, without adequate evidence. Writers often make this error when they are in a hurry and have little time to research their subject. They will often base a generalization on one or two sources and hope for the best. Unfortunately, luck will not always be with them, and they will sometimes make generalizations which are not substantiated by the available information. Just because a person says or writes something does not mean that it is true. Look for other evidence as well; when you find several sources which complement one another and support your position, you will not have made a hasty generalization.

5. <u>The Either-Or Problem.</u>   People who believe the old saying, "There are two sides to every problem," often make this error. In reality, there are generally many more than two sides to any issue. When a writer so simplifies a situation as to present an "either-or" issue, the reader should question what has been written. When a writer finds an issue which appears to have only two sides, he or she should be concerned that the information on which the writing is based is inadequate. Here is an example of an either-or error.

> Mr. Jones has raised the question of what to do about the population explosion in developing countries. The answer is really quite simple. Either we leave things as they are and the population continues to grow or we insist that the countries limit population by law. In order

to put teeth in our actions, we need to withhold grain and other food products from any country which does not pass population control laws.

This writer has ignored the many possibilities which exist for population limitation. He is reflecting the simple thinking which we all long to hear—there are two sides, and only two sides, to an issue. He needs to look at both, and decide which is better. The problem, of course, is that almost nothing is that simple. Use great care as you investgate options for your writing. There are almost always more than two.

6. <u>Faulty Analogy.</u>   Read the following paragraph and see if you find the problem.

> Everyone knows you can't teach an old dog new tricks. Now, the Governor is trying to shut down twenty regulatory commissions because he thinks they are not needed. But there is one problem he has not confronted: what to do with all the employees of these commissions. The average age of commission employees is 57, and they have been working for the commissions for an average of 31 years. All of these people are on civil service, so they are guaranteed jobs. They know little else but commission business. Frankly, we do not want them in the other branches of the state government, because they won't be able to learn new procedures. It will be cheaper to keep the commissions in operation than to try to transfer these old dogs into jobs where new tricks are needed.

Did you spot the problem—using an old saying and applying it to a situation where it may not fit? The writer may really be arguing to continue the commissions, and this may be a kind of "red herring" to drag across the trail of legitimate argument on the issue. But he has applied an old cliché to support an argument, and the support is weak. The relationship between old dogs and experienced people is certainly a questionable one.

7. <u>Inadequate Cause.</u>   Humans often look for easy causes—especially when they are trying to lay blame on someone or something. Students who fail classes in school sometimes claim genetic influence from their parents who had difficultly with the same classes. It is rare to hear someone say, "I did poorly in that class because I just didn't study enough."

As you look for indications of inadequate cause in writing, it is easy to reject the simple, straightforward explanation. Try not to do that. There is nothing automatically better about complex arguments than about simple arguments. The simple answer will often be the right one. As you provide support for your statements, just be sure that your evidence is strong and that your logic makes sense.

There are many more kinds of problems with logic, and you may want to study them in some detail. Your library probably contains several good books on logic and fallacy (errors in logic). However, what is important for a writer is not to know all the possible errors in logic, but rather to have the sense to know when an argument is weak or incorrectly supported. Writers develop this sense through experience and by being constantly on the alert against problems in logic.

Go back to the section entitled "Problems with Logic" which begins on page 313. Take each of the kinds of error listed and write a short paragraph for each in which you purposely make the error. Then give your paragraphs to a classmate and ask him or her to find the errors and rewrite your paragraphs to make the logic more sound.

Getting It Started

When your paragraphs have been modified, see if your classmate caught the errors and made appropriate changes. The chances are good that your reader will catch some errors which crept in, in addition to those you planned. Be prepared for some surprises.

Talk about your writing with your classmate. Discuss the errors you made, both purposely and unintentionally.

Discuss the whole matter of logic as a class. What are some ways you can use logic to develop and support a position? What are things you must avoid?

Now find some instances in which inductive and deductive logic have been used in articles, textbooks, and other material easily available to you. Share your examples and discuss the techniques the writers used. As you look for these, see if you can find situations in which writers have made errors in logic. Share those instances of error with your classmates.

Checking It Out

Chapter 15

Writing an Informational Report

The informational report is probably the most common form of professional writing. Business letters are often less formal, shortened forms of the informational report. The following examples show a few instances when informational reports might be required in everyday situations.

A. Jane Maxwell, department manager for records and tapes in a discount store, asked one of her clerks, Jerry Kahn, to visit the stores of four competitors to get price information on the seven price-levels of records they all sell.

"Write up a little summary of what you find, Jerry," Ms. Maxwell directed.

B. The owner of an automobile service station was considering adding another service bay. He contacted an architect to begin preliminary plans. As they discussed possible design, the architect asked whether the station owner had considered the possibility of building a bay dedicated to some specialty such as inspecting and repairing anti-pollution equipment.

The owner's response was to call over one of his attendants. "John, do you know how to use a library?"

"Sure, I guess I could manage," the attendant responded.

"How about taking the rest of the day and going over to the library to see if you can find out if anybody is building specialty bays in stations these days. If they are, see if you can find out what they're into, like anti-pollution repair or things like that. Write up what you find so I can show it to the architect."

C. Paul's car failed the safety inspection because his tires were bald. It was clear he needed new ones. As he was about to start searching the paper for tire sales, he remembered hearing one of his friends say she had gotten some information on tires in the reference area of the library.

Paul checked several references, jotted down comparative information about various brands of tires, and made a list of tires with their good and bad qualities. Then, he began looking for sales and kept looking until he found the best tire for the money.

D. Joan's father usually took a handful of vitamins every day, never paying much attention to dosage—a few from this bottle, a few from that. Joan felt uncomfortable with what her father was doing, so one day when she saw him take ten vitamin A tablets, she said, "Dad, you shouldn't take so many of those. I've heard that too much vitamin A can be really bad for you."

Her father replied, "Come on. Vitamins are good for you. If a little bit is good, more must be better."

Joan made a trip to the library that afternoon. She found information on maximum doses of many vitamins, and she also found evidence of the danger of taking too much vitamin A. She wrote it up, complete with references, and gave it to her father.

Informational reports are useful. Unfortunately, too many people fail to write down the information they find, relying on their memories to recall it when needed. It is best to write out information, complete with references. This method produces accurate reports.

Informational reports are sometimes called research papers or term papers. Sad to say, the research report or term paper has acquired a bad name. Students have looked on these papers as a form, rather than as something which could help them learn about an interesting topic. "If you get all the footnotes right, you'll get an A," is a common feeling. Form is important, but only because it helps the reader of the paper.

SPOTLIGHT

Read the following informational report by Albert Rosenfeld, a specialist in the field of gerontology (aging). The excerpt has been extracted from his book, *Prolongevity*. He uses an inductive approach, combining information on the control of aging from many sources. Here is his conclusion:

I will venture to predict that by the year 2025—if research proceeds at reasonable speed—most of the major mysteries of the aging process will have been solved, and the solutions adopted as part of conventional biomedical knowledge; and that some of the solutions will by then already have come into practical use to stave off the ravages of senescence.

Prolongevity: The Extension of the Human Life Span

In ancient Greece, the average life expectancy was something like 22 years. Individuals did live to ripe old ages, but their number was small enough to render them an elite group in most ancient societies, where their seasoning was rare and their wisdom prized. A Greek who reached the age of 70 in the fifth century B.C. had just as many years to live—perhaps more, since he had to be tougher to have survived so long under such conditions—as does the 70-year-old

of today, who has merely reached his average life expectancy.

Sophocles wrote *Oedipus Rex* when he was 75, and won the last of his many dramatic prizes at 85, still going strong. . . . This is not to say that vigorous longevity such as Sophocles' goes unmatched today, but simply that it is still rare. The maximum life span has *not* been extended. And our contemporaries who reach 70, 80, and 90 probably have just as many aches and failings as the ancients did, though there may be a few more medications available to ease their more troublesome pains.

The fact that so many of us do reach 70 and beyond is what makes us more aware than ever how universal are the ravages of the aging process—ravages that made even Sophocles, for all his honors and amours, a thoroughgoing pessimist in his declining years. Observing the inexorable nature of these changes, their variety, their sheer multiplicity, and their interlocking complexity, most traditional gerontologists have maintained an unshakable conservatism despite the boldness of their stated goals. The prevailing view, understandably, has been that, considering the multifaceted nature of the aging process, it would be foolish to count on any significant progress toward final answers until countless further generations of painstaking experimentation shall have passed.

Typical of this cautious outlook, even among scientists not reputed as especially conservative, is the conclusion of a 1962 paper in *Proceedings of the Royal Society*. Its author, anatomist P. L. Krohn of the University of Birmingham, after describing a brilliantly original series of experiments designed to study the effects of transplantation on aging tissue, finally appends his demurrer: "Nothing has been said to imply that problems of old age are likely soon to be solved by this approach. . . . The solution will probably come as slowly and insidiously as the aging process itself."

Control of Aging May Begin Soon

Gerontologist Bernard Strehler of the Univeristy of Southern California represents a spirited avant garde of scientists who vigorously dispute the cautious, pessimistic views of the medical traditionalists. They believe that significant progress can be made toward the control of aging, perhaps in our own lifetimes or within the current century. The more confident gerontologists are hopeful of buying a little extra time for themselves personally while waiting for the larger advances to be accomplished—much as a leukemia victim might hope for the larger breakthroughs to occur while he is in remission.

Scientists who a few years earlier would have deplored such speculations as being in the realm of the quack and the con man are now distressed that the general public just won't give serious credence to the new possibilities. If people begin to believe in them, progress will certainly occur more rapidly. Gerontologist Alex Comfort is convinced not only that a project to slow down aging is feasible but that it could be carried out for relatively modest sums of money.

In any case, because the older explanations of aging leave so much still unexplained, interest in the avant garde view has been growing in research laboratories all over the world. This view is easy to summarize. Though even avant garde gerontologists differ in the details of their schemes and their persuasions, they are clearly coming together in the common convictions:

(1) that there does exist within ourselves an identifiable "clock of aging," a genetically determined program which dictates that we will age and die, and the rate at which this will occur;

(2) that we have an excellent chance of discovering the location (there may be more than one) of the clock of aging, as well as the nature of its operating mechanisms—and how to interfere with them to our own advantage;

(3) that, moreover, all this can begin to happen, not centuries from now, but *now*, if only the research can be carried out;

(4) that senescence may thus be started on its way to obsolescence.

Research on Aging: Many Promising Approaches

Let us assume that gerontological research does hold out a valid promise of additional good years of life. In that case, each of us is bound to wonder whether the hoped-for advances will occur in time to add good years to our own lives—and to the lives of those we wish to share ours with; and, further, what we might meanwhile do to enhance the probability that we will be on hand to take advantage of whatever breakthroughs may occur.

It is impossible to set forth a timetable of upcoming gerontological achievements with any assurance that these events will occur on schedule. This is true even for a given theory or a given investigator. Suppose, as one example, that researcher Donner Denckla succeeds in his quest for the thyroid-blocking hormone, and it turns out to be *the* death hormone, as theorized. How long would it take for the results to start doing us any good? Denckla has recently made some careful calculations, considering each painstaking step along the way: isolating and purifying the hormone (if indeed only one hormone is involved), discovering its structure, synthesizing it, devising some molecular means to inhibit its action; perhaps identifying its releasing factor in the hypothalamus—the smaller molecule that induces the pituitary to release the larger one—and going through the same sequence of procedures with it; getting a sufficient supply of the inhibiting agent to test it on animals; carrying out the necessary animal trials; then—with Food and Drug Administration approval and the informed consent of the subjects—conducting some preliminary human experiments, followed by broader and more conclusive human trials; and finally getting the new drug on the market. Denckla figures that, even with good luck, going at his present maximum pace it will take him 40 years to complete the work. With stepped-up funding and expanded facilities, he feels he might do it in 20. Thus it is not preposterous for Denckla, who is now only 40, to maintain a reasonable hope that he could become a direct beneficiary of his own research.

Most gerontologists doubt that substantial advances will be made within their own lifetimes. But many do not share this skepticism, and they encourage a cautious optimism in others. Modest progress —much more modest than that envisioned as the finale of Denckla's overall program—might still offer a slowed-down rate of deterioration, enhanced vigor and enjoyment in the later years, some alleviation or even reversal of overt aging symptoms—in a word, a significant postponement of old age as it is customarily experienced (and feared in advance). Human beings who are very young today may hope that, if they remain in reasonably good health through, say, their middle years, they may become the first people in history to have their life spans extended by artificial means—by how many years, no one can say. Gerontologists such as Comfort and Strehler have held out a long-shot hope that, if you can hang on a little longer, and then a little longer, perhaps helped in each case by some of the smaller breakthrough events, it is just barely possible you could still be here and a candidate for further prolongevity when the larger breakthroughs arrive.

The pace of progress in gerontology should quicken as the National Institute on Aging begins to support programs on a broader scale. Within the next decade or so, I believe we will see the proving out of some of the potential anti-aging substances known at this time as well as others yet to be discovered. At least a few should prove to be effective, with acceptably minimal side effects.

A number of antioxidants are already at hand, and some are safely ingestable—among them Vitamin E. Vitamin C is also an antioxidant, though less so; and it is supposed to amplify the effects of Vitamin E. A much more powerful antioxidant than either is the element selenium. Traces of it are present in many of our foods, and perhaps we already get all of it that we need—or is good for us. More is not necessarily better. But "supernutrition," as Richard Passwater calls it, the administration of unusually large doses of vitamins and minerals, is a popular trend among biological investigators, and some purely dietary aids to age resistance may well be developed. Selenium will undoubtedly be among the substances studied for that purpose.

The usefulness of antioxidants will depend on the validity of the free radical theory of aging. This does not mean free radicals will have to be shown to be *the* cause of aging, only that they represent an important factor in wear-and-tear damage. We have at least indirect proof that this is so. As researcher Richard Hochschild reminds us, "Animal studies show that deficiency of vitamin E in the diet leads to damage of exactly the kind predicted. Age pigments pile up faster. Mitochondria, the power houses of the cell, swell and eventually disintegrate, knocking out the energy generating ability of the cell. And lysosomes break open, releasing their digestive chemicals to digest the entire cell. Thus a small amount of free radical damage is multiplied into a devastating sequence of pathological events."

Much of this damage is prevented or repaired by the body's own self-protective mechanisms as well as by antioxidants naturally present. But, as the studies cited by Hochschild—including those of A. L. Tappel—indicate, an antioxidant deficiency clearly reveals extensive free radical damage. When there is such a clear-cut deficiency, antioxidant therapy can definitely reverse the damaging trend. Moreover, substituting one equally effective antioxidant for another will accomplish the same result, proving that it *is* the antioxidant function at work.

Other good bets for such availability are hormone preparations (such as thymosin), lipofusein inhibitors (such as centrophenoxine), and lysosome membrane stabilizers (such as the DMAE with which Hochschild has been getting such encouraging results). The same is true of cross-link inhibitors. Robert Kohn, for example, has—in collaboration with F. S. LaBella of the University of Manitoba—had some success with a substance called betaaminoproprionitrile. Kohn has investigated other possibilities, too, as has Johan Bjorksten. Even though the prevention or reversal of cross-linkages may (like antioxidant therapy to combat free radical damage within cells) fail to get at the basic cause of aging, such an outcome could still prolong the good years of life through "symptom relief." If a drug were to appear that could do no more than uncross-link collagen molecules in the connective tissue outside the cells, the benefits could be considerable.

Collagen makes up some 30 to 40% of the body's protein. Its universal presence in the body's framework is what has led scientists of Kohn's stature to suggest that the aging of collagen could be a primary factor in the overall aging of the organism. Nutrients going from the bloodstream to the cells must pass through collagen in order to get there. The same is true of waste materials going in the other direction. If collagen becomes dense and rigid, it also becomes less permeable (perhaps even impassable in some cases); hence the cells have a harder time getting their food and getting rid of their wastes, and heart and lungs probably have to work correspondingly harder. Changed collagen molecules could also invite autoimmune attack.

So it is clear that the loosening up of collagen via uncross-linking (or preventing cross-linkage in the first place) could help keep the body younger longer. This would probably be true of appearance as well, since much of the skin's aging and wrinkling could be due to collagen changes. It is even conceivable, as Hochschild further suggests, that it could slow down the graying and falling out of hair. The next decade could be an exciting one, then, in terms of the first visible steps toward anti-aging medications.

Many substances under investigation, such as the temperature-lowering agents of Rosenberg and Kennedy, will undoubtedly take much longer to test because so much is still unknown about the effects of chronic cooling on living organisms. But it is possible that, within two decades, we would know whether such medications are feasible or not—and, if they are, we should by then also have a good idea when we might expect our physicians to be able to prescribe them for us. During this same 20-year period I think we will also be getting close to arriving at some effective enzyme mixtures and other compounds that would supply substances that were running short and counteract substances that were in damaging oversupply.

During this 20 to 30 years, a multitude of lines of investigation will be followed simultaneously, and surely some of them will bear fruit. Work such as Denckla's is problematical, depending on good luck and adequate funding. But I am more optimistic than most

about seeing significant progress in hormonal research, in understanding the hypothalamo-pituitary role in aging, in understanding and controlling the on-off switching of genes, and in the general area of genetic engineering. I will venture to predict that by the year 2025—if research proceeds at reasonable speed—most of the major mysteries of the aging process will have been solved, and the solutions adopted as part of conventional biomedical knowledge; and that some of the solutions will by then already have come into practical use to stave off the ravages of senescence.

Albert Rosenfeld

Rosenfeld begins by putting the aging process in perspective. He does not state his conclusion in the early paragraphs; rather, he introduces the topic by hooking his reader at a point of interest—his or her own aging as it relates to history. His major introductory point is that even though more of us are living longer, the *maximum* age has remained constant for much of recorded history.

The author could have taken another approach. One, perhaps more common than the one he took, would be to begin with a paraphrase of the statement he makes in the conclusion. He might have begun as he did and then, after the introduction, said something like the following:

> A large body of research points to the distinct possibility that we will understand the biological mechanisms of aging in the next 30–50 years, and by the year 2050 medical control of the aging process will be possible.

Had he done this, he would have taken away the possibility of unfolding his evidence gradually, bringing the reader along with him on his discovery process. Rosenfeld may have felt that this discovery process was important for the reader to go through. His information is so revolutionary, so contrary to common expectation, that announcing the conclusion in the opening paragraphs might well put off some readers.

The Planning Process

Rosenfeld led his readers through an inductive process to help them understand, a little at a time, what he would conclude. He understood his audience to be somewhat skeptical. His purpose was to inform his readers of new research and then lead them to his conclusion.

As you plan an informational report, you, too, must be aware of your purpose and your readers. You must also be aware of yourself and your own knowledge and interest.

As writers approach the informational report, they consider the following things as part of the planning, pre-writing stage:

> Their own interest in and knowledge about the subject
> The purpose of the report
> The readers: their knowledge of the subject
>   their attitudes toward the subject
>   their need for information
> Accessibility of information

The Writer's Interest in and Knowledge About the Subject

There may be times when you will have to write an informational report about something you have little interest in and less knowledge about. However, informational reports, most often, are related rather directly to one's job or to classes one is taking. Clearly, most writers will do informational report assignments in a field in which they have some background.

A good rule of thumb for selecting topics for informational reports, is to write about something which you find interesting and which you want to learn more about. If you can follow this rule, you will not only write good reports, but you will be learning about areas you find interesting.

~~~~~~~~~~~~~~~~~~~~~~~~~~~~~~~~~~~~

What ideas about the future interest you? In this text you have read material about the future—population, energy, longevity, and other subjects. Did any of them interest you?

Jot down some ideas about the future which you find interesting enough to use as a topic for an informational report. Talk with your classmates about possible topics, as well. You may find space travel and colonization interesting. You may find future world food supplies something you would like to know more about. You may wish to learn more about energy in the future, including some of the options available. You may be intrigued by the attitudes people have about the future—whether they think things will improve or not, whether they think the world will move in the direction of peace or toward more conflict, whether political changes will take place in response to changes which occur.

If necessary, go back for ideas to some of the material in previous chapters. Some of the charts presented in Chapter 14 may give you ideas. Some of the excerpts from research articles in Chapter 12 may also suggest topics.

**Getting
It
Started**

~~~~~~~~~~~~~~~~~~~~~~~~~~~~~~~~~~~~

When you have a subject which interests you, discuss it with a classmate. Explain what specifics interest you. See if your classmate finds the topic interesting.

**Checking
It
Out**

~~~~~~~~~~~~~~~~~~~~~~~~~~~~~~~~~~~~

After your discussion, make changes in your subject if necessary. When you are satisfied with it, write a brief statement about your subject and why you are interested in it. Place your writing in your Writer's Notebook.

**Getting
It
Down**

~~~~~~~~~~~~~~~~~~~~~~~~~~~~~~~~~~~~

Preparing Informational Reports

Now that you have identified an area which interests you, it is time for a major assignment. You and the other members of your class will prepare informational reports on various areas of the future. Each of you will research and write about a specific subject of interest to you. When your papers are finished, they will be brought together into a single volume entitled, "Dimensions of the Future," and placed in your school library. Your readers will be the other members of your class and the general student body of your school. The purpose of the volume and each of the reports in it is to provide members of your student body with information about the future which they may not now have.

This chapter will lead you, step by step, through the process of writing your report. While you may work somewhat more quickly or slowly than some of your classmates, be sure to follow the sequence presented here. When you finish your report, you will have an opportunity to consider short-cuts and other revisions you might make in the process.

Getting It Started

Accessibility of Information

Before you go too far in pursuing your topic, you need to check to see whether information is available on it. An information report is *not* a paper in which you merely express your own opinions. Such a report assumes that you will bring together a considerable amount of information from many sources. For this particular assignment, you should have at least five different sources. If you were to use only a single source—the book *Prolongevity* by Rosenfeld, for example—it might be better if the reader were to go directly to the book itself and not even bother reading your report. *The informational report should not be a summary of a book or article. It should be a collection of information from many sources, all focused on a single topic.*

Your first stop should probably be the card catalogue of your school library. If some of the authors you have encountered in the material printed in this and previous chapters seem to have something to say on your topic, you might look for them by name. However, you will probably find the most information in the subject section of the card catalogue. Look under words which seem to relate to your subject—words like future, population, medicine, hunger, energy, and the like. Search each subject heading for sub-headings which might lead you to material which is more specifically related to your subject.

When you find a helpful book, prepare a bibliography card for it. • Refer to pages H-54–62 in the Handbook for specific suggestions for completing these cards. At this stage, you should write the call number of the book on the back of the card so that you can find your reference in the library when you are ready to examine your sources.

Your second stop should be the *Readers' Guide to Periodical Literature.* This publication indexes many magazines commonly found in school and public libraries. As you did with the card catalogue, look first for authors' names, then for subjects. Since the *Readers' Guide* is published frequently, you will have to look in several volumes to be sure you have found what material is available on your subject. Usually, you should go through a minimum of five years of the *Guide,* although your topic may dictate that you go back further or that you use only the most recent publications. The *Readers' Guide* is an extremely useful tool.

When you find sources which you think may be helpful, prepare bibliography cards for them, just as you did for your book sources. • Refer to the Handbook (page H-62) for specific directions on the preparation of cards for magazines.

Your library may have indexes other than the *Readers' Guide.* If your topic is psychological, there is an index called *Psychological Abstracts*; if it is medical, consult *Index Medicus.* There is an index for nearly every major field of study. Ask your librarian whether these indexes are available, and, if so, how to use them. Most are similar to the *Readers' Guide* in format and are easy to use.

Do not stop your search until you have found at least ten sources which you think will be helpful. The chances are good, since you have looked only at titles in this search, that half of your material will not be too helpful. If you must discard half of ten references, five will still remain as sources.

If your school library does not have sufficient information, visit your public library, or, if you have a college or university close by, visit its library. Check with professional people— doctors, psychologists, lawyers, teachers—in the field which you are researching to see whether they have journals which might be helpful. Look through magazines and books which you have at home; you may find something useful in them.

If, through all your searching, you cannot find at least ten useful sources, reconsider your topic. It may be so current that nothing has been reported on it. Or it may be that your resources are simply inadequate.

Go through the same process for identifying a new topic that you used before. Your search for information should have given you some additional ideas about where to find available information. Use those ideas, combined with other interests you have, and develop a new thrust for your report.

~~~~~~~~~~~~~~~~~~~~~~~~~~~~~~~~~~~~~~

Determining Purpose

Getting It Started

When you have finished your report, what need will it satisfy for your readers? Since your report is meant to inform your fellow students, that clearly is its major purpose. But do you have other purposes for writing this report? Does your subject lend itself to promoting a positive view of the future?—a negative view? Will your reader understand a particular view of the future after having read your report? Will your report not only inform, but also encourage your reader to take some action? Will you expect your reader to want to learn more about your subject as a result of having read your report?

In your Writer's Notebook, write a clear statement of purpose for your report. Share this statement with a classmate, get reactions, and revise it as necessary. Take great care in preparing, since your statement will be a major guide for your writing.

~~~~~~~~~~~~~~~~~~~~~~~~~~~~~~~~~~~~~~

Analyzing Your Readers

Getting It Started

When you write an informational report, you must carefully analyze your readers along at least three dimensions: knowledge, interests, and opinions.

Knowledge: How much do your readers already know about the topic? How technical should your language be?

Interests: Are your readers already interested in the topic or will you have to use a "hook" to get their interest? How much detail will they want to see in the paper?

Opinions: Will your readers accept the information in your report without question, or do they already have strong opinions contrary to the information you will present? Do your readers think the topic of your report is important? Do your readers accept you as a reliable person who will give them honest, important information?

Your perceptions of the nature of your readers will influence the way you write your report.

In your Writer's Notebook, write answers to each of the preceding questions. Your answers, along with your statement of purpose, should form an important basis for the information you include in your report. It should also have a major impact on how you approach your topic.

When you finish the analysis of your readers, discuss it with a classmate. Is it appropriate? Are your judgments correct?

It may be necessary to discuss the nature of your readers with the entire class. Sometimes individuals make judgments about their readers on the basis of a very small sample, comprising only those whom they know well. Discuss the student body of your class as potential readers. Try to develop judgments which are consistent throughout your class.

As you form your judgments about your potential readers, think about how their nature will influence the way you present information in your paper. Since all of your reports will be gathered into a single volume, each should reflect a common understanding of who the audience is and what that group of readers expects in an informational report.

When you are satisfied that you have a solid sense of your readers, revise your comments in your Writer's Notebook. Then, write a few brief notes to yourself in which you suggest some things you might do to suit your writing to your readers.

Getting It Down

Gathering Information and Shaping the Topic

You have selected a topic in which you have some interest; you have what appears to be an ample number of sources of information for your report; you have a purpose outlined; you have analyzed your readers and have some sense of an approach

Checking It Out

which you will take to appeal to them. Your next step is to get the information.

Begin by reading one good source. As you read, try to identify useful pieces of material. Remember how Rosenfeld led his readers through an inductive process to a conclusion? Try to let what you read, bit by bit, shape your report.

When you are convinced that the source has worthwhile information which speaks to your subject, begin taking notes. ● Follow the procedures outlined on pages H-53–57 of the Handbook. Use your plans for your subject, your purpose, and your knowledge of your readers to assist you in deciding which material to use.

When you have your "bearings," go to several other sources. As you read the material, let your sense of what the paper will eventually look like begin to evolve. Will you begin with a statement that makes your position strong and clear at the beginning of your report, or will you let the paper unfold, waiting until the end to reveal your conclusion?

As you consider how the paper will take shape, think, too, about your subject. Is it so broad that you could write a book about it, or is it so narrow that you can find almost no help in your sources? Think about modifying your subject, if necessary. Your information will tell you whether your subject needs narrowing or broadening.

Checking It Out

Ask a classmate or your teacher to review your subject, your purpose, your sense of your readers, and your early notes from your sources. Ask for help in modifying your subject if necessary. Check with another individual you trust to be sure your judgment about your subject is correct.

If you need more sources and more information to round out your topic, look for bibliographies at the ends of the articles and books which are your sources. Many times bibliographies will lead you to other useful sources. Be sure to make bibliography cards for these, just as you did with your other sources.

Shaping the Report

You have already given some thought to the shape your report will take. As you continue to take notes, make structure a major consideration. As you find material, see if it will fit into groupings or categories.

Go back to chapter 13, page 284, and read the material from *The Global 2000 Report to the President*. See how the paragraphs in the "Principal Findings" and "Conclusions" sections point to the statement the author makes in the "Introduction." Will your report have many elements, as that did? Does your information tend to group more like that in the article (page 323) by Albert Rosenfeld, or does your information suggest some other kind of structure?

Some writers like to work from an outline. However, unless you know your subject rather well, it is nearly impossible to develop an outline until you have surveyed your sources fairly completely. If at this point you feel comfortable deciding on a structure and building an outline which will guide the remainder of your notetaking, do so. You may find that you need to wait until you have been through all of your source material very carefully before you decide on the organization you will use for the report.

You must base the structure of your report on at least four things:

1. Your perception of the subject
2. Your purpose
3. Your readers
4. Your information

As your feel for the subject improves, and if you have been considering possible structures as you have taken notes from your information sources, you will probably develop a good sense of how the paper should be organized. Once that sense is solid enough to give you a basis for sketching out an approach, do so. If more than one approach seems possible, sketch out as many as you wish.

~~~~~~

**Checking
It
Out**

As soon as you have sketched out a possible approach for your paper, check it out with a classmate or your teacher. Discuss why you intend to take your particular approach, and see whether your resource person agrees that you have made a good choice.

If several members of your class are at this point at the same time, it might be good for you to get together to discuss your approaches. Sometimes fresh ideas come out of such discussions that would not occur to you individually.

~~~~~~

Whatever your decision, make sure that it is tentative. There is always opportunity to change, right up to the time when you submit your final copy. Of course, the sooner you get an approach decided on, the easier taking notes and writing will be. A decision about approach will help shape your decisions about the material you will use and that you will omit.

If you want to make an outline, sketch out topics that will fit with your chosen approach. This will help you even more in deciding which information to include in your notes.

~~~~~~

Writing the First Draft

**Getting
It
Down**

Some writers simply must have an outline to guide them as they write informational reports. Others prefer to write a preliminary draft and use it to experiment with different approaches. Often writers who take this approach develop an outline after the draft is completed; their outlines then help them to revise. Whatever strategy you use, when you get your notes written on cards and when you have your approach generally decided upon, it is time to write your first draft.

Keep the following in mind as you write:

1. Be sure your report is logical. If you have used inductive processes, be sure you have sufficient evidence to support your conclusions. If you have used a cause-effect technique, be sure the logic of that relationship holds up. If you have used a form of deductive reasoning, identify the syllogism and check it to be sure you have drawn an appropriate conclusion.

2. Be sure your report is written in such a way that your readers can understand it. Avoid language unfamiliar to your reader.

3. Avoid the use of the word "you" in your report. Informational reports are usually written in a more formal style, usually in the third person, although some use an "I" (first person) approach.

4. Use the active voice whenever possible. Passive constructions (For example: The discovery was made by Smith) are awkward and do not flow well.

5. Use numbers, titles, and headings if necessary to make the report clear and easy to read.

6. Use tables to summarize information in your report whenever possible.

7. Use charts and graphs to illustrate points that might be less clear written in prose.

8. Be sure to give credit to your sources for material you have quoted directly and also for that which you have paraphrased. ● See pages H-54–62 in the Handbook for information on crediting sources.

9. Remember that this is an informational report. You are expected to gather information from numerous sources, each of which points to a common subject. Use the information from your sources to make your point, not information from your memory or experience.

When you finish your preliminary draft, you may find that you now know how you want the report to be structured. If necessary, rewrite your preliminary draft in such a way as to fit the approach you have decided on. (You may find it necessary to go back to your sources for additional information, especially if your change in approach is drastic.)

Revising the Draft

When you are satisfied that your first draft is structured approximately the way it should be and that you have at least the beginnings of a report, have one of your classmates read your draft carefully and give you suggestions for revision. You may find it helpful at this time to have a classmate outline your paper to see whether he or she perceives its structure in the same way you do.

Checking
It
Out

Talk with your classmate about necessary changes. You may have too much material in some areas, not enough in others. Some of your information may contradict other things you have said.

Also, have your classmate check the accuracy of your citations—those situations in which you gave credit to a source for material you used. Give him or her your notecards and bibliography cards so that a careful, complete check for accuracy can be made.

Ask your classmate to read the paper as a member of the student body of your school. Have him or her check the language you used and the approach you took from the perspective of your potential readers. Does the approach work? Is the language right? If not, how can it be changed to make it more appropriate? Use the scales in the evaluation Checkpoint (page 341) to help you in this assessment, if necessary.

Make changes based on your classmate's feedback and your own evaluation.

~~~~~~

Putting the Paper in Final Form

After you have completed the revision of your report, prepare your bibliography. ● Pages H-54–62 in the Handbook provide guidance for you in this area. Be sure to cite all references you have used, even if you have not quoted material from all of them.

When you are satisfied with your report, prepare a title page (● See pages H-49–50 in the Handbook) and type the report. Since you will be putting this report on file in the library for others to read, it is important that it be as neat as possible. ● Follow the format indicated on pages H-49–51 of the Handbook as you type the paper.

Getting It Down

~~~~~~

Recapping the Process

You have been led through a relatively structured process as you wrote this informational report. You have found a topic of interest; you have looked for material; you have determined a purpose for your report; you have analyzed your readers; you have gathered information and modified your topic based on the information you found; you have shaped the structure of the paper; you have written a draft; revised that draft; and put the paper in final form. Now is the time to reflect on that process.

Getting It Right

In your Writer's Notebook, write a reaction to the process you followed. Identify the parts of the process which were especially useful and those which were not helpful. Identify areas that should have been included but were not.

Discuss the process with your classmates. Are there things which most of you think should be added? Are there items that should be omitted? Are there specifics in some categories which should be changed, eliminated, or added?

Now write a step-by-step process for writing an informational report. Make it as detailed as possible. Be sure to include all the things which are peculiar to you—things others may not even consider, but which are important as you write reports.

When you have finished your statement, share it with the

other members of your class. Then keep your statement as a guide to follow when you are asked to write papers like this in college or in some other setting.

You will be evaluated according to Checkpoint 7 which follows.

CHECKPOINT 7

1	2	3	4	5

Topic   ×2=

Your topic is unclear in the report. You seem to be writing on many different topics at the same time.

Your topic has fairly good focus in the report, but it lacks specificity.

This report is well focused and specific.

Purpose   ×2=

It is hard to see a purpose in your report. We need to discuss the problem.

Your purpose is fairly clear, but you have not chosen material to advance your purpose

Your purpose and material blend well and produce a powerful report.

Readers   ×2=

Have you directed this report to an audience? It seems to be a hodge-podge of words which do not fit your readers.

Some of your words are poorly chosen and do not fit the audience. Your approach may not be quite on target, either.

The words you use and the approach you take fit your audience well.

Material   ×4=

Some of your material fits your topic, but much does not.

Several quotes and other items seem not to fit your topic or your readers very well.

You have chosen material well to support your topic.

Logic   ×4=

The paper does not seem to fit any logical pattern. I have difficulty coming to the same conclusions you did.

Several instances of faulty logic make this report less effective than it might have been.

Your logic holds up well, and the approach you chose seems to be an outgrowth of the logic you use.

Form   ×4=

There are real problems with form in your report. Review the Handbook for help.

You have made several errors in the form of your report, but none are serious.

You followed form very precisely in this paper.

Overall Effect   ×2=

This paper does not inform effectively.

You inform your reader, but the impact of the report is not as strong as it might be.

This is a powerful paper which clearly accomplishes its purpose.

Acknowledgments

Grateful acknowledgment is made to the publishers, authors, or copyright holders for permission to use and adapt the following materials in this book:

American Association for the Advancement of Science: "The National Science Foundation Looks to the Future," Slaughter, J.B., *Science* Vol. 211, pp. 1131–1136, 13 March 1981; "It Is People Who Use Energy," Kingsley, D.S., *Science* Vol. 211, p. 1, 30 January 1981; "Wood: Fuel of the Future?" Waldrop, M.M., *Science* Vol. 211, p. 914, 27 February 1981. Copyright 1981 by the American Association for the Advancement of Science.

The Associated Press: "Charles' fiancee prepares to learn royal etiquette." Reprinted with the permission of the Associated Press.

The Bobbs-Merrill Company, Inc.: From *Gemini*, copyright © 1971 by Nikki Giovanni. Used with permission of the publisher, The Bobbs-Merrill Company, Inc.

Doubleday & Company, Inc.: From *Looking Back* by Joyce Maynard. Reprinted by permission of Doubleday & Company, Inc.

Farrar, Straus and Giroux, Inc.: Reprinted by permission of Farrar, Straus and Giroux, Inc. Selection adapted from *The Right Stuff* by Tom Wolfe. Copyright © 1979 by Tom Wolfe.

Harper & Row Publishers, Inc.: "Maud Martha Spares the Mouse" from *The World of Gwendolyn Brooks* by Gwendolyn Brooks. Copyright 1953 by Gwendolyn Brooks Blakely. Reprinted by permission of Harper & Row Publishers, Inc. "Mirror" from *Crossing the Water* by Sylvia Plath. Copyright © 1963 by Ted Hughes. Originally appeared in *The New Yorker* and reprinted by permission of Harper & Row Publishers, Inc. "About Myself" from *The Second Tree from the Corner* by E.B. White. Copyright 1945 by E.B. White. Originally appeared in *The New Yorker* and reprinted by permission of Harper & Row, Publishers Inc. Abridged from "Walden" (pages 80–87) in *One Man's Meat* by E.B. White. Copyright 1939 by E.B. White. Reprinted by permission of Harper & Row Publishers, Inc.

Nancy Naglin: "Will They Feed the World's People?" by Nancy Naglin. Used with permission of the author.

New Directions: "Do Not Go Gentle into That Good Night." *The Poems of Dylan Thomas*. Copyright 1952 by Dylan Thomas. Reprinted by permission of New Directions.

Newhouse News Service: "Heat Treatment." Used with permission of Newhouse News Service.

Ronald J. Penoyer: "Countdown" by Ronald J. Penoyer, from *Inside Outer Space*, edited by Robert Vas Dias, Doubleday Anchor Books, 1970. Reprinted by permission of the author.

Pergamon Press, Ltd: Reprinted with permission from *Environment International*, Volume 4, Kleinman, Michael T., Merril Eisenbud, Morton Lippman, and Theo. J. Kneip, "The Use of Tracers to Identify Sources of Airborne Particles," copyright 1980, Pergamon Press, Ltd.

Random House Inc.: "Auto Wreck," copyright 1942 and renewed 1970 by Karl Shapiro. Reprinted from *Collected Poems: 1940–1978* by Karl Shapiro, by permission of Random House Inc. From *American Dreams: Lost and Found* by Studs Terkel, copyright © 1980 by Studs Terkel. Reprinted by permission of Pantheon Books, a division of Random House Inc.

Charles Scribner's Sons: From Thomas Wolfe, "Circus at Dawn" (copyright 1934, 1935 by Modern Monthly Inc.; copyright renewed 1962, 1963 by Paul Gitlin) in *From Death to Morning*. Copyright 1935 by Charles Scribner's Sons; copyright renewed 1963 by Paul Gitlin. Reprinted with the permission of Charles Scribner's Sons.

Times Books: "Apollo 8" Copyright © 1974 by Richard S. Lewis. Reprinted by permission of *Times Books*, a division of Quadrangle/The New York Times Book Co., Inc. from *Voyages of Apollo:The Exploration of the Moon*. By: Richard S. Lewis.

University of Notre Dame Press: "Barrio Boy" by Ernesto Galarza. Copyright 1971, University of Notre Dame Press, Notre Dame, Indiana 46556.

Viking Penguin Inc.: "The Train from Rhodesia" from *Selected Stories* by Nadine Gordimer. Copyright 1962 by Nadine Gordimer; reprinted by permission of Viking Penguin, Inc. "Across the Bridge" from *Nineteen Stories* by Graham Greene. Copyright 1947, renewed 1975 by Graham Greene. Reprinted by permission of Viking Penguin, Inc. "Funeral" from Gordon Parks, *Whispers of Intimate Things*. Copyright 1971 by Gordon Parks and reprinted by permission of Viking Penguin, Inc. "The Schartz-Metterklume Method" from *The Complete Short Stories of Saki* (H.H. Munro). Copyright 1930 by the Viking Press, Inc. Renewed 1958 by the Viking Press, Inc. Reprinted by permission of Viking Penguin Inc.

The Washington Post: Cynthia Gorney. From "Dr. Seuss: Wild Orchestrator of Plausible Nonsense for Kids," © *The Washington Post*.

The World Future Society: "Environmental Sentinels: Flowers That Spot Pollution," February, 1981; "Prolongevity: The Extension of the Human Life Span" by Albert Rosenfeld, February, 1977; "Youth Unemployment: Is There a Cure?" February 1981; *The Futurist*, published by the World Future Society, 4916 St. Elmo Avenue, Washington, D.C. 20014.

Writer's Handbook

Special Problems in Writing

Most writers operate with a "first-things-first" method. They get their ideas down on paper and then worry about following the conventions of spelling, punctuation, and usage. We certainly suggest you do the same. The sections which follow are here to help you with problems you might encounter when you revise your rough draft. There are several sections, each serving a special purpose.

The following table of contents indicates the areas covered and the pages on which assistance may be found.

Usage

USE OF PRONOUNS

The following examples provide models which should guide you in the proper use of pronouns. Refer to the sample sentences and find one which is similar to the sentence you are concerned about. Then see how the pronouns have been used and make sure that your sentence uses the pronouns similarly.

Subject

___ liked the movie.	___ and ___ liked the movie.	
I	I	I
We	We	we
You	You	you
He	He	he
She	She	she
They	They	they
It	It	it

Direct Object

The kangaroo chased ___.	The kangaroo chased ___ and ___.	
me	me	me
us	us	us
you	you	you
him	him	him
her	her	her
them	them	them
it	it	it

Predicate Pronoun

The winner is ___.	The winners are ___.
was	were
I	we
you	you
she	they
he	

Object of the preposition

The fight was with ___.   The fight was between ___ and ___.

me	me	me
us	us	us
you	you	you
her	her	her
him	him	him
them	them	them
it	it	it

Possession

___ running impressed the judges.

My
Your
His
Her
Their
Its

Indirect Object

The faculty sent ___ the book.

me
us
you
him
her
them
it

The faculty sent ___ and ___ the book.

me	me
us	us
you	you
him	him
her	her
them	them
it	it

SUBJECT-VERB AGREEMENT

A verb must agree in number with its subject. A singular subject takes a singular verb; a plural subject takes a plural verb.

That *man owns* the store.   (singular subject and singular verb)
Those two *women own* the store.   (plural subject and plural verb)

Past tense verbs are the same in singular and plural except for forms of the verb "be."

it *missed*, they *missed*   I *looked*, we *looked*
he *shared*, they *shared*   he *was*, they *were* (changes for
                                  a form of the verb "be")

Compound subjects joined by *and* take a plural verb, whether the subjects are singular, plural, or mixed:

Sue and her father *cook* delicious family meals.
The actors and actresses *need* more rehearsals.
Only three students and one teacher *want* to come along.

The number of the verb is not affected by words or phrases between the verb and its subject:

A *resolution* of these problems *is* vital.
Diplomacy, as well as intelligence, *is* crucial.
The *construction* of more skyscrapers *is* unavoidable.

The following pronoun subjects use a singular verb: anybody, anyone, each, either, everybody, everyone, neither, one, no one, someone, somebody:

Does anybody want to learn? *Each* of the boys *has* money.
No one cares enough. *Someone has* to accept the responsibility.

The following pronoun subjects use a plural verb: both, few, many, several:

Both Larry and Tony *are* excellent divers.
Many are supportive of the administration's stance.
Several of the teachers *were* angry.

The following pronoun subjects use either a singular or plural verb depending on the meaning of the sentence: any, all, most, none, some:

Some of the merchandise *was* stolen.

Some of the dresses *were* stolen.
All of the fruit *is* ripe.
All of the bananas *are* ripe.
None of the construction *is* completed.
None of the buildings *are* completed.

Whether the subject precedes or follows the verb, the verb must agree with its subject in number:

Has anyone seen Jim?
The *assignment was* scribbled on the chalkboard.
On the chalkboard *was* scribbled the *assignment*.
Here *comes* the *sun*.
Here *come* the football *players*.

Singular subjects joined by *or* or *nor* use a singular verb; when a singular and a plural subject are joined by *or* or *nor*, use the verb that agrees with the nearer subject:

Either the *lawyer* or the *witness is* lying.
Either the *lawyer* or the *witnesses are* lying.
Neither the *students* nor the *teacher knows* how to balance the
    equation.

A collective noun used as a subject takes a singular verb when the subject refers to a unit. If the subject refers to the individuals of a group rather than to a unit, use a plural verb:

The *audience is* thrilled with the performance.
The *audience are* clapping their hands wildly.
The *number* of car accidents *increases* each year.
A *number* of teachers *are* retiring in June.

When the subject of a subordinate clause is a relative pronoun (which, that, who), the number of the verb agrees with the antecedent.

He spread a <u>rumor</u> *that was* unforgivable.
He spread <u>rumors</u> *that were* unforgivable.
Sue is a <u>person</u> *who loves* music.
Sue is one of those <u>people</u> *who love* music.

Plural subjects which indicate amount, distance, or other singular units of measure require singular verbs:

A hundred *dollars is* a lot of money.
1,000 *miles seems* like a long drive.
Three *inches* off the bottom *makes* the skirt a lot shorter.

VERB TENSE

Do not mix present, past, and future time within a passage.

> Mr. Browning had been my friend for years. When I was a little girl he even took me horseback riding a few times. After I was saddled onto the horse, he <u>looks</u> at me and <u>says,</u> "I wish I had a little girl like you for a daughter."

The underscored verbs are present tense. Past tense should have been maintained by using the following verbs . . . he *looked* at me and *said,*"

When statements either occur in the present or are "timeless" (meaning true in both the present and the past), use the present tense even though the rest of the sentence or paragraph uses the past.

> Dr. Williams believed that Albert Einstein, who uncovered the principles of relativity and expanded on other laws of physics, <u>is</u> the first and foremost scientific genius of all time.

Use the present participle to indicate an action or state of being that occurs at the same time as the main verb:

> *Glancing* carefully from side to side, Eleanor *led* Jeramie across the street.
>
> *Being* the eldest, Sue *felt* responsible for her younger sister.

Use either the past participle or the perfect participle to indicate an action or state of being that occurs before the time of the main verb:

> *Left* alone by her wealthy husband's sudden death, my client naturally distrusted her flock of sudden admirers.   (past participle)
>
> *Having completed* the exam early, Jim went outside for some fresh air.   (perfect participle)
>
> *Concerned* by her son's sudden unwillingness to communicate, Mrs. Frank sought the help of a psychologist.   (past participle)

ACTIVE AND PASSIVE VOICE

An *active* voice verb expresses an action performed by the subject. A *passive* voice verb expresses an action performed upon the subject.

Active Voice

Passive Voice

action

His bat struck the ball.

action

The ball was struck by his bat.

Use the active voice, which is more immediate and lively, whenever possible in narrative and descriptive writing.

When the doer of the action is unknown or when the direct object (the receiver of the action) is of more interest than the doer of that action, use the passive voice.

On the way to the airport, I stopped at my bank's special services window and *was given* travelers' checks for cash.

THE IMPERATIVE

When giving directions, avoid shifting between the imperative and other verb forms.

Correct:

Before you go to bed, *turn* off the sprinkler, *cover* the plants, and *turn* off the lights.

Incorrect:

Before you go to bed, *turn* off the sprinkler, *cover* the plants, and *you need to turn* off the lights.

PLACEMENT OF MODIFIERS

Avoid "dangling" introductory phrases and clauses that do not sensibly and clearly modify a word in the main clause.

Strong:

Overcooked and tough, the meat was inedible.

Dangling Modifier:

Overcooked and tough, I could not eat the meat.   (*Overcooked and tough* mistakenly appears to modify *I*.)

Strong:

Straining under a load of books, he caught his toe on the edge of the step.

Dangling Modifier:

Straining under a load of books, his toe caught on the edge of the step.   (*Straining under a load of books* seems to modify *toe*.)

Strong:

After I graduated from high school, my mother bought me a new car.

Dangling Modifier:

After graduating from high school, my mother bought me a new car. (*After graduating from high school* seems to modify *mother*.)

RUN-ONS AND FRAGMENTS

Be careful not to fuse two or more sentences together without using either a conjunction or the proper punctuation. Here are sentence-combining exercises which show how two simple sentences can be joined in different ways.

1. Joining with *and, but,* or *or*
    The apples were green_x   (, but)
    ꭗhe oranges were red.
        The apples were green, but the oranges were red.

2. Joining with a *semicolon*
    The apples were green_x   (;)
    ꭗhe oranges were red.
        The apples were green; the oranges were red.

3. Joining with *a semicolon followed by a conjunctive adverb*
    The apples were green_x   (; however,)
    ꭗhe oranges were red.
        The apples were green; however, the oranges were red.

A fragment is an incomplete sentence or a group of words that is not complete. Usually it lacks either a complete verb or a subject. Be sure not to let a fragment stand alone, as if it were a sentence. Here are a few examples of sentence fragments:

> The reason being that I was too tired to stick around.
> Although I could have done the job better than the person she hired.

There are two easily identifiable types of sentence fragments: the phrase fragment and the subordinate clause.
    Do not separate either a phrase or a subordinate clause from the sentence.

The Phrase Fragment

Complete sentence

> My parents' new townhouse is on the east side of a small Wisconsin lake in a wooded area full of ravines.

Fragment

> My parents' new townhouse is on the east side of a small Wisconsin lake. *In a wooded area full of ravines.* (Prepositional fragment)

Complete sentence

> As I drove by her house, I saw Jean struggling to push a clunky old lawnmower across a lawn overtaken by weeds.

Fragment

> As I drove by her house, I saw Jean. *Struggling to push a clunky old lawnmower across a lawn overtaken by weeds.* (Participial fragment)

The Subordinate Clause Fragment

Complete sentence

> Although I won't be able to attend next Monday's meeting, I will attend Thursday's session.

Subordinate clause fragment

> *Although I won't be able to attend next Monday's meeting.* I will attend Thursday's session.

Complete sentence

> When the rains come and the breeze is warm, it feels like spring.

Subordinate clause fragment

> *When the rains come and the breeze is warm.* It feels like spring.

Punctuation and Capitalization

COMMA

The comma (,) is the most frequently used punctuation mark within the sentence. When used effectively, it can make lengthy sentences easy to understand. When used carelessly, it can cause your reader to miss the point of your writing. The following examples show you how commas are used by many writers. Emphasis is placed on the kind of materials that you will be writing in school.

Commas Between Items in a Series

Three or more words, phrases, or clauses used together in a sentence make up a series (*words*, *phrases*, or *clauses* in this very sentence make a series of words). The commas help you use a shorthand form of repeating part of a sentence several times. Look at the following example:
The Great Hall was decorated with paper flowers.

The Great Hall was decorated with streamers.   (,)

The Great Hall was decorated with two giant gazeboes.   (, and)

> The Great Hall was decorated with paper flowers, streamers, and two giant gazeboes.

The commas allow you to say three things about the decorations in the Great Hall without repeating "The Great Hall was decorated with" three times.
   In this next sentence, the phrases in the series are expanded and moved to another position.
   Paper flowers decorated the Great Hall.
   Streamers of twisted crepe paper decorated the Great Hall.   (,)
and ,   Two giant gazeboes surrounded by green plants decorated the Great Hall.   (, and)

> Paper flowers, streamers of twisted crepe paper, and two giant gazeboes surrounded by green plants decorated the Great Hall.

A series ordered with commas can be made of single words:

<u>Nouns</u>

Jim placed in the semi-finals competition.

,   <u>Jose</u> placed in the semi-finals competition.   (,)

, and   <u>Michelle</u> placed in the semi-finals competition.   (, and)

Jim, Jose, and Michelle placed in the semi-finals competition.

Erica likes <u>pickles</u> on her sandwich.

, Erica likes <u>mustard</u> on her sandwich.   (,)

, and   Erica likes <u>sprouts</u> on her sandwich.   (, and)

Erica likes pickles, mustard, and sprouts on her sandwich.

<u>Adjectives</u>

The streamers made the gym look like a Fourth-of-July celebration.

The streamers were <u>red</u>.

, The streamers were <u>white</u>.   (,)

, and The streamers were <u>blue</u>.   (, and)

The red, white, and blue streamers made the gym look like a Fourth-of-July celebration.

If you add words that modify <u>red</u>, <u>white</u>, <u>blue</u>, and <u>streamers</u>, use the same two commas.

The red, white, and blue streamers made the gym look like a Fourth-of-July celebration.

The red was <u>brilliant</u>.

The white was <u>chalky</u>.

The blue was <u>royal</u>.

The streamers were <u>crepe</u>.

The brilliant red, chalky white, and royal blue crepe streamers made the gym look like a Fourth-of-July celebration.

A series ordered with commas can be made of simple sentences:

The clouds appeared.

, The wind came up.   (,)

, and The rains fell for hours.   (, and)

The clouds appeared, the wind came up, and the rains fell for hours.

A series ordered with words such as and, or, or nor does **not** need commas.

Neither Wind kept New Year's Eve motorists off the roads.   (Neither)

nor Snow kept New Year's Eve motorists off the roads.   (nor)

nor Ice kept New Year's Eve motorists off the roads.   (nor)

Neither wind nor snow nor ice kept New Year's Eve motorists off the roads.

Commas Between Pairs or Items

Two clauses are usually combined with commas even if the items are already joined with a conjunction such as and, but, yet, or, nor, or for.

Long independent clauses need commas:

This arrangement would be more convenient for me.

, but You must consider the others in the group.   (, but)

This arrangement would be more convenient for me, but you must consider the others in the group.

Short independent clauses do **not** need commas:

You go ahead.

and I'll come later.   (and)

You go ahead and I'll come later.

Dependent clauses in pairs do **not** need commas:

When   The trees begin to bud.   (When)

and   The ice melts.   (and)

It will feel like spring.   (, then)

When the trees begin to bud and the ice melts, then it will feel like spring.

Paired phrases of any length are not separated from each other by commas:

Adjective — Adverb Phrases:

mopping

While   Burt ~~mops~~ up the mess in the kitchen.   (While ___-ing)

answering

and   Burt ~~answers~~ the phone with his free hand.   (and ___-ing)

,   Burt had his first misgivings about having his own apartment.   (,)

While mopping up the mess in the kitchen and answering the phone with his free hand, Burt had his first misgivings about having his own apartment.

Verb Phrases:

We looked around everywhere.

but   ~~We~~ couldn't find him.   (but)

We looked around everywhere but couldn't find him.

Adjective Phrases:

The ball was quite large.

and

~~The ball was~~ somewhat deflated.   (and)

The ball was quite large and somewhat deflated.

Noun Phrases

The Sulphur Street gang met at noon.

their

and   ~~The Sulphur Street gang's~~ uptown rivals met at noon   (and)

The Sulphur Street gang and their uptown rivals met at noon.

Commas After Introductory Items in a Sentence

It is sometimes effective to set the stage for your readers with an introductory item before you give them the content of your sentence. When you do so, use a comma to set off the introduction from the main part of the sentence. If you don't, you might confuse your readers.

Introductory Words

> Above, the thick clouds began to disperse and let the sun peek through.
> Somewhere, somehow, we've got to get to the bottom of this.

Introductory Phrases

> By the way, Jim was looking for you.
> As a matter of fact, I am pretty tired of listening to you complain about school.

Introductory Clauses

> When you finish playing, the piano needs to be dusted.

Commas Before and After Items That Interrupt Sentences

Appositives

Words, phrases, or clauses in apposition are nouns that follow another noun in the sentence; appositives further explain or identify or restate the noun that they follow. Notice how the appositives interrupt the flow of the sentences they are in and add needed information.

Words

> Lena Wilson played the piano in the concert.
>
> ~~Lena Wilson is~~ a student.   (, —— ,)
>
> Lena Wilson, a student, played the piano in the concert.

Phrases

> Pierre is returning to Paris next week.
>
> ~~Pierre is~~ our foreign exchange student.   (, —— ,)
>
> Pierre, our foreign exchange student, is returning to Paris next week.

Miss Johnston loved to talk about Hamlet's insanity.

~~Miss Johnston was~~ our English teacher.   (, —,)

Miss Johnston, our English teacher, loved to talk about Hamlet's insanity.

She removed the egg carefully from the nest to examine it more closely.

~~The egg was~~ a small, fragile one.   (, —,)

She removed the egg, a small, fragile one, carefully from the nest to examine it more closely.

Clauses

Erica won the singles tennis competition without much effort

, She's my sister.   (, —,)

Erica, she's my sister, won the singles tennis competition without much effort.

Non-restrictive Clauses, Phrases, and Words

A non-restrictive clause is a dependent clause that modifies the noun it follows; it is an adjective. It does not change (restrict) the meaning of the sentence it joins. It simply interrupts it to add information the reader may not know. Non-restrictive phrases and words interrupt in the same manner. All non-restrictive items are set off by commas.

Clause

Arlene Turner is my best friend.

, who   ~~Arlene Turner~~ lives right down the street   (, who —,)

Arlene Turner, who lives right down the street, is my best friend.

Phrase

Jacquie reached the bottom of the slope in 35 seconds!

skiing
, ~~Jacquie skis~~ furiously through the storm.   (, -ing —,)

Jacquie, skiing furiously through the storm, reached the bottom of the slope in 35 seconds!

Words

Fido chased Fluffy away.

Fido is unfriendly.   (, —,)

Fluffy is friendly.   (, —,)

Fido, unfriendly, chased Fluffy, friendly, away.

Nouns of Direct Address

Sometimes you may interrupt your sentence to address your readers directly. You may simply want to get their attention or you may want to convince them of your seriousness. Set off their names with commas.

We are proud to present, ladies and gentlemen, "The Greatest Show on Earth!"

You can be assured, Carol, of the money by the end of the month.

Parenthetical Expressions

Parenthetical expressions are words or phrases used to explain, emphasize, or qualify a statement. Some common parenthetical expressions are: as a matter of fact, consequently, however, for example, for instance, I believe (think, hope), indeed, moreover, on the other hand, therefore.

He is, I believe, the only person who can do the job well.

Jim did say, however, that he would think it over before making his final decision.

The house next door, as a matter of fact, is for sale right now.

I can't wait around this town for two more weeks; consequently, we'll have to make the decision this week.

Embedded Questions

Short questions within a sentence are set off with commas as well.

Team A is the stronger of the two.

Don't you agree?   (, —,)

Team A is, don't you agree, the stronger of the two?

Phrases Used for Emphasis

A sleek limousine pulled into the driveway.

A limousine was hardly the car I expected   (, —,)

A sleek limousine, hardly the car I expected, pulled into the driveway.

Speaker Tags in Direct Quotations

"I am not the only student who thinks so!"

" She argued.   (," —,")

"I am not," she argued, "the only student who thinks so!"

"Those will have to do until I can afford new radial tires."

" Jim mumbled,   (," —,")

"Those will have to do," Jim mumbled, "until I can afford new radial tires."

Commas in Certain Conventional Situations

Items in dates and addresses:

On Monday, February 5, 1981, the building was destroyed.

He has lived at 1500 Park Avenue, New York, New York, since August, 1956.

The salutation of a friendly letter and the closing of any letter:

Dear Nancy,   Dear Father,   Love,   Sincerely,

Degrees and titles that follow names:

Joseph Lytle, Ph.D., authored the Preface to the book.

James Johnson, Jr., will talk on endangered species of birds in Newfoundland this Sunday.

SEMICOLON

There are three primary uses for semicolons in more formal papers:

Independent Clauses without Conjunctions

    Walter started walking toward the car.

;   Nothing would make him turn back.   (;)

        Walter started walking toward the car; nothing would make him turn back.

Independent Clauses with Certain Conjunctions   (for example, for instance, however)

    The bell rings at 11:30.

however   It has been late before today.   (; however,)

        The bell rings at 11:30; however, it has been late before today.

Between Word Groups Containing Commas

    The paper was full of humor.

,   ~~The paper was full of~~ life.   (,)

, and   ~~The paper was full of~~ happiness.   (, and)

; but   Its punctuation ~~was horrible.~~   (; but)

,   Its spelling ~~was horrible.~~   (,)

        were

, and   Its capitalization was horrible.   (, and)

        The paper was full of humor, life, and happiness; but its punctuation, spelling, and capitalization were horrible.

COLON

There are four uses for the colon in writing:

At the Introduction of a list of items

Our guidebook recommended the following items.

:   ~~It recommended~~ a knife.   (:)

,   ~~It recommended~~ a compass.   (,)

~~It recommended~~ a small backpack.   (,)

~~It recommended~~ some edibles.   (,)

~~It recommended~~ a canteen.   (,)

~~It recommended~~ matches.   (,)

~~It recommended~~ a sweater.   (,)

, and   ~~It recommended~~ a camera.   (, and)

Our guidebook recommended the following items: a knife, a compass, a small backpack, some edibles, a canteen, matches, a sweater, and a camera.

At the Introduction of a Formal Statement or Address

The world will never forget Theodore Roosevelt.

or   ~~The world will never forget~~ his famous words.   (or)

"Walk softly and carry a big stick."   (;)

The world will never forget Theodore Roosevelt or his famous words: "Walk softly and carry a big stick."

After an Independent Clause that is explained by a second clause

Clothing isn't made the way it used to be.

Seams tear easily.   (:)

Zippers break.   (,)

, and   Fabric isn't very durable.   (, and)

Clothing isn't made the way it used to be: seams tear easily, zippers break, and the fabric isn't very durable.

Certain Conventional Situations

Salutation of a formal letter:
    Dear Sirs: Gentlemen: Ladies: To Whom It May Concern:
In noting time:
    1:15 a.m.   12:30 p.m.
Biblical references and other bibliographical references:
    John 19:57   James 9:1   Hebrews 2:7   Proverbs 34:50
    Boston: Allyn and Bacon, Inc.

APOSTROPHE

You may use the apostrophe (') for three different purposes in writing: it can signal possession (Erin's book), plurals (I made two A's.), or an omission of letters (aren't for are not, we've for we have).

Possession

To show possession for one person or thing (any singular noun), place the apostrophe and then an s after the noun or indefinite pronoun ('s).

The opinion was written on the board.

The opinion belonged to the teacher　　('s)

The teacher's opinion was written on the board.

The taxi came to a screeching halt.

The taxi belonged to Gus　　('s)

Gus's taxi came to a screeching halt.

> Other Examples:　brother's gloves, Caroline's hat, the elephant's trunk, Rawl's grocery, Mr. Comb's glasses, bus's brakes, everybody's loss, anybody's guess, someone else's problem

To show possession for several people or things (any plural noun), place only an apostrophe after the noun　　(') . . .

The swimming pool is now empty.

The swimming pool belongs to the girls.　　(')

The girls' swimming pool is now empty.

If the plural form does **not** end in s. Plurals such as deer, children and women are made possessive by adding 's.

deer's,　children's,　women's

When two or more nouns possess something individually, indicate the possession (according to the rules above) for each noun.

The departments are on different floors of the store.

's
~~One department is for~~ men.   ('s)

and   's
~~Another department is for~~ women.   (and ___'s)

The men's and women's departments are on different floors of the store.

When words indicate joint possession, indicate possession (according to the preceding rules) for only the last noun.

~~The~~ records were the hit of the party.

's
The records belonged to Jose and Marguerita.   ('s)

Jose and Marguerita's records were the hit of the party.

Other examples: the cat and dog's dinner time,
mom and dad's vacation

When using a personal pronoun to replace any possessive noun, do **not** add an apostrophe.

The dress was two sizes too large for me.

her
The dress belonged to ~~Evelyn.~~   (her)

Her dress was two sizes too large for me.

Other examples: his gloves, its profit, their mistake   (Don't confuse the possessive pronoun, its with
the contraction of it is—it's. They are easy to mix up.)

Plural

To indicate the plural of numbers, symbols, letters of the alphabet, and words referred to as words, use 's.

How many is three 3's and four 4's?
Count the +'s and the −'s in this equation.
Occasion is spelled with two c's.
Try to cut down on the number of and's and but's in your paragraph.

Omission of Letters

We have only just begun.	('ve)	We've only just begun.
There is no doubt about it.	('s)	There's no doubt about it.
You have not told everything.	(n't)	You haven't told everything.

DASH

The dash is used somewhat as the comma is. It is more appropriate to use a dash than a comma . . .

when the shift in thought is *sudden*
> I hope that next time he has the sense to—but perhaps, we should first hear what he has to say for himself.

or when the interruption in the sentence is especially abrupt
> He could have—and indeed should have—been a bit more considerate.
> Other examples: His goal—if you can even call it a goal—should have been to get himself out of debt.

or when the series ordered by commas is long and possibly confusing
> You should use sections—the table of contents, chapters with headings, tables and graphs, appendixes, and references—to make your research paper easy to read.

HYPHEN

Use a hyphen between syllables to divide a word at the end of a line.
> regis-/ter
> oppor-/tunity
> indica-/tive

Be sure to leave more than one letter of a divided word at the end of or at the start of a line.
> e-/lope (faulty)   (Put the entire word on the next line.)
> speed-/y (faulty)   (Put the entire word on the line.)

When there is a prefix or a suffix, divide the word just after the prefix or just before the suffix.

inter-/dependent   (not in-/terdependent)
merri-/ment   (not mer-/riment)
sub-/ordinate   (not subor-/dinate)
elusive-/ly   (not elu-/sively)

Often, a good place to divide a word is between double consonants.

run-/ning
Missis-/sippi

Use hyphens when two or more words combine to form a modifier.

a would-be movie star
a well-kept beard
a don't-care-if-you-do attitude

If the first word of the modifier unit is an adverb ending in *ly*, do not use a hyphen.

a neatly dressed woman
a poorly worded sentence

Hyphenate compound numbers from twenty-one through ninety-nine, and fractions.

Thirty-three years old hardly makes you old!
A one-fourth portion goes to charity; the other three-fourths is needed to pay back expenses incurred.

Use a hyphen to avoid confusion or between awkward letter combinations.

re-collect   (collect again; prevents confusion with recollect meaning *to remember*)
semi-interesting   (avoids awkwardness of *semiinteresting*)

PARENTHESES

Parentheses indicate another kind of interruption in a sentence. When the interruption includes material most people already know, but some may not, use parentheses.

Mayor Daley (Chicago) had more political control than any other mayor in the country.

The make-up of carbon dioxide molecules (see Diagram B) consists of two atoms of oxygen and one of carbon.
The film *Gone with the Wind* (1939) was aired on television recently.
Sen. Percy (R., Ill.) was re-elected by a narrow margin.

All other punctuation near the parentheses must come after and not before them. When a parenthetical item is added to a clause that ends with a comma, extend the comma beyond the parenthetical information.
The ghost of Hamlet's father commanded Hamlet's friends to "swear by the sword" (the sword itself was, ironically, symbolic of the cross), forbidding them to tell anybody about his appearance.

BRACKETS

Use brackets to enclose explanations within quoted material when the explanation is not part of the quotation.
Mr. McDonough calmly addressed the audience with these words: "I am honored by it [the nomination for presidency], and if elected I will do my utmost to carry out the awesome responsibilities of this honored position."

Use brackets to enclose explanations within parentheses when the explanation is not part of the material in parentheses.
The molecular structure of more complex molecules is harder to understand. (See page 219 [Chart A] for detailed breakdowns of five complex molecules.)

THE PERIOD

Use a period to follow a statement or a command.
The trees shivered in the cold.
Please keep the noise down.

Use a period after abbreviations.
Dr.   Mr.   Mrs.   Ms.   Nov.   B.C.   Ave.

Abbreviations of various governmental agencies and social, professional, or business organizations are **not** followed by periods.
NATO   UNICEF   CIA   HEW
IBM   dbs (decibals)   mph (miles per hour)

Avoid abbreviating common words in ordinary writing.

> Unclear:
>> Two new mfg. cos. were just built on Co. Blvd. last Oct., just next door to my two bros., Chas. and Jim.

> Clear:
>> Two new manufacturing companies were just built on Colorado Boulevard last October, just next door to my brothers, Charles and Jim.

Indirect questions are followed by a period.
> She asked whether I wanted to come.
> We wondered how much longer we should wait.

Polite requests in formal business letters are followed by a period.
> Will you please send me ten extra copies and bill me for them.

THE QUESTION MARK

Use a question mark to follow a question.
> Do you want to come?
> How much longer should we wait?

A question mark should be placed inside quotation marks **only** if the quotation itself is a question.
> "Do you think you'll come?" he asked me.
> *BUT*
> Who said, "All the world's a stage . . ."?

THE EXCLAMATION POINT

Use an exclamation point after statements expressing strong, excited feeling.
> Wow! What a dress!
> "Cut it out!" he yelled at me sharply. (Note the period after *sharply* and the exclamation mark within the quotation marks.)

ELLIPSES

Use three periods to show where words have been omitted within a quotation; use four periods where words have been omitted at the end of a sentence or where two or more sentences have been omitted.

>I pledge allegiance to the flag . . . and to the republic . . . with liberty and justice for all.

>Speak properly and in as few words as you can, but always plainly, for the end of speech is not to make a show but to be understood. . . .

>Be reserved but not sour . . . cheerful, not light. . . .

QUOTATION MARKS

Use quotation marks before and after a person's exact words. If you aren't quoting a person exactly, you needn't use quotation marks at all.

>She told us to think about our attitude.

If the person's words ask a question, state a command, or simply make a statement, use the appropriate end punctuation inside the second quotation mark.

>I asked, "Why don't you go along?"

When a person's words are interrupted with a quotation stem (said mother, replied George), place a comma and quotation mark before and after the stem.

>"How would you feel," asked Mother, "if Aunt Ruth didn't even mention your birthday?"
>"Leave me alone," I shouted, "before I lose my temper!"

If you use a semi-colon which is not a part of the quotation, place it outside the quotation marks.

>Father said, "I don't want to discuss it at all"; unfortunately, Mr. Rogers thought it was an important matter and refused to drop it.
>He grumbled, "They just don't make clothes the way they used to"; from the looks of what he was wearing, I knew what he meant!

If the sentence is a question, but the quotation is not, place the question mark outside the quotation marks.

Didn't you tell Mark, "Forget it"?
You said to me, "Forget it!" didn't you?

Use quotation marks before and after words referred to as words.

Don't use "but" or "and" at the start of a sentence.
I tried to explain to the psychiatrist my hostility against the world and against the "dopes" that controlled it.

Use quotation marks before and after titles of songs, short stories, short poems, essays, articles, and subdivisions of books (chapters, sub-headings, etc.).

"Georgia On My Mind" is Ray Charles' most popular tune.
E.E. Cummings "In Just Spring" is my favorite poem.
I read a fascinating article entitled "Computer Art" in yesterday's newspaper.

BUT

No quotation marks are used for the title of a poem of book length.

Walt Whitman's *Leaves of Grass* is an American classic.

Begin a new paragraph each time a speaker changes.

"I can't wait until Christmas," Jamie babbled, "and school's out for awhile."

"I know what you mean," Sarah sighed wishfully. "I think I'm going skiing for the week between Christmas and New Years."

"Too bad it's not summer vacation coming up," Ralph intervened. "I have a good job this summer!"

When you quote the same person for more than two paragraphs, use quotation marks at the start of each paragraph and at the end of the final paragraph.

"I'll never forget that vacation, because everything seemed to go right.

"First, the weather was perfect. The sun was out every day, the snow was fresh, light, and powdery, just the way I like it. The slopes weren't even crowded. I remembered how sunburned my nose was at the end of the first day.

"Then Sue and Deborah came up. On Sunday morning we all went cross-country skiing, out away from the crowds into some of the back country. All of us worked up a sweat and laughed a lot. At one point, we even ran into a herd of elk and took some great photographs."

"Photographs?" Jim interrupted. "Do you have them here?"

Extensive quotations are indented five extra spaces from both the left and right margins (ten spaces if beginning a new paragraph) and single-spaced, even if the rest of the paper is double- or triple-spaced. Leave an extra line above and below the indented quoted material to separate it clearly from the rest of the copy. No quotation marks are necessary.

"However that may be," Taylor related, "neither the President nor Secretary of Defense Robert McNamara gave objective review to Westmoreland's operations." Townsend Hoopes further states:

> The Pentagon simply lost sight of the truth that protection for the people against Viet Cong terrors had to be achieved by means that did not themselves alienate the people by causing heavy casualties and wanton physical destruction.

Use single quotation marks to enclose a quotation within a quotation.

"What do you mean by saying, 'Put the news peg in the upper lefthand corner of the first page'?" I asked Mrs. Weber.

CAPITALIZATION

Capitalize the first word in any sentence or in any quoted sentence or fragment.

Everyone agreed that the rooms needed painting. "Do you think that we'll have time to do them next week?" asked Charles.

BUT

"Do you think," asked Charles, "that we'll have time to do them next week?" [Note: "that" is *not* capitalized since it is a continuation of the direct quotation beginning with "Do you think . . ."]

Traditionally, the first word in each line of poetry is capitalized. In modern poetry, while this observance is still common, it is **not** a hard and fast rule.

I think that I shall never see
A poem lovely as a tree . . .

Capitalize proper nouns.

Capitalize the names of persons.

Miles Davis   Picasso   Hamlet   Charles Dickens   Mr. McDonald   Mrs. MacDuff   John O'Brien

Capitalize geographical names, including:

Cities, counties, states, countries, continents

Atlantic City, New Jersey, Boulder County, Canada, Europe

Bodies of water

Atlantic Ocean, Black Sea, Lake Michigan, Mississippi River, Beaver Pond, Chipmunk Creek

Islands, peninsulas, straits, canals, beaches, mountains

Hawaii, Florida Peninsula, Strait of Gibraltar, Panama Canal, Daytona Beach, Grand Tetons, Longs Peak

Streets, specific buildings

Broadway, Main Street, Birch Boulevard, Fifty-ninth Street, Highway 119, Sears Tower, White House, Conrad Hilton Hotel

Parks, forests, dams, canyons, valleys

Yellowstone National Park, Pike National Forest, Hoover Dam, Poudre Canyon, Beaver Valley

Recognized parts of the country or world

the North, the Middle East

Note: The words *north, south, east,* and *west* are *not* capitalized when they refer to directions, but *are* capitalized when they refer to sections of the country.

Drive *east* from Colorado for 1,000 miles and you will be in the *Middle West.*

Capitalize the names of ships, boats, planes, trains, awards, and monuments:

S.S. Titanic, the Lucille (name of boat), the Blue Angels, Olympic Gold Medal, the Statue of Liberty

Capitalize the brand names of consumer products—do **not** capitalize any common nouns which may follow the brand name:

Seven-Up, Crest, IBM typewriter, Volkswagon Rabbit, Jay's potato chips, Butternut bread, Sunkist oranges

Capitalize the names of specific rooms and other nouns followed by a numeral or letter;

Room 607   School District 12   Chapter 8   Diagram B

Capitalize the names of school classes—however, the words *freshman, sophomore, junior, senior* are not capitalized when they refer to either a student or a year:

Jim Stone is valedictorian of the *Senior Class.*

They were a fine group of *Seniors.*

Sue is a *junior* this year.

Al's grade point average rose dramatically his *sophomore* year.

Capitalize the names of specific business firms, and governmental, scholastic, professional, and social organizations or departments

Business firms

United Airlines, Xerox Corporation, Sperry Rand, Inc., Flatirons Theatre, Fred's Cafe

Governmental, scholastic, and social organizations

Congress; Department of Health, Education and Welfare; United Nations; French Club; American Honor Society; Phi Beta Kappa; Lions Club, Shriners, Pep Club; Photographic Society of America

Institutions

Harvard University, Lawrence College, Glenbard East High School, Ford Foundation, Institute for Peace Studies, Language Arts Department

Capitalize the names of nationalities, races, and religions

American, French, Oriental, Caucasian, Protestant, Moslem, Catholic, Jewish

Capitalize the names of specific deities or prophets and possessive pronouns or nouns referring to those deities

God, Christ, Buddha, Mohammed, John the Baptist, Zeus, Apollo, Simon Peter

God gave the world *His* only *Son.*

Capitalize proper adjectives, but not the common nouns that follow them.

America, American *people*   Canada, Canadian *winters*

Elizabethan *drama,* Gothic *architecture,* Renaissance *literature*

Capitalize the names of events

Capitalize historical events and periods of time

World War I, Civil War, Battle of Bunker Hill, Dark Ages, Iron Age, the Renaissance

Capitalize special events

the Super Bowl, the Olympics, the World Series

Capitalize political or religious holidays

Fourth of July, Memorial Day, Christmas, Easter

Capitalize calendar items including the days of the week and the months of the year

Book Week, National Secretaries' Week, Sunday, April

Do **not** capitalize the names of seasons unless personified.

I can't wait for spring.

BUT

There was Spring, tripping in all dressed in green with flowers in her hair.

Capitalize specific titles of persons

Capitalize the title of a person when used preceding a name

Superintendent John Knolls   Reverend Philips
Dean Williams   General Eisenhower

Capitalize a title either used alone or after a name only if referring to a high government official or in order to show special respect.

Hello, Reverend   What next, Coach?   President Roosevelt
Jim Withers, president of the Senior Class
John Daley, ex-Mayor of Chicago (**Note:** the prefix *ex-* is not capitalized.)
the Senator

BUT

a committee of six senators
the Chief of Police
Vice-President Johnson (Two capitals are required only when referring to the Vice-President of a nation.)

Capitalize the first word and all important words in titles of books, short stories, poems, plays, periodicals, articles, documents, songs, films, and works of art. Articles (*a, an, the*) and conjunctions and prepositions of fewer than five letters are not capitalized unless they are the first word in the title.

Have you ever read the *Chicago Tribune?*
"Snows of Kilimanjaro" is, perhaps, illustrative of Hemingway at his best.
I Never Promised You a Rose Garden is the story of the rehabilitation of a precocious, teen-age schizophrenic named Deborah.
The award-winning film, "One Flew over the Cuckoo's Nest," was aired for the first time on television in 1979.

Capitalize the titles of academic subjects only if they refer to languages or specific course titles.

French, Spanish, English, History II, Algebra I, American Poetry, Advanced Placement English

BUT

home economics, history, algebra, chemistry

Capitalize words showing a family relationship when used with a person's name or in place of that person's name, but **not** when preceded by a possessive.

> my *u*ncle, his *a*unt, Uncle Remus, Aunt Sally,
> my *c*ousin Ralph, my *s*ister Ruth
> I told my *m*other all about it.
> *BUT*
> I told Mother all about it.

Always capitalize the pronoun "I."

> *I* know what *I* know when *I* know it.

UNDERLINING (ITALICS)

Underline (or use italics) for titles of books, periodicals, names of ships, and works of art. Do not underline or italicize *a*, *an*, or *the* preceding a title unless it is part of the title.

> *The Scarlet Letter* by Hawthorne
> Have you read the *Wall Street Journal?*
> My favorite painting is *Portrait of an Artist's Son* by Renoir.
> The *Titanic* is a well-known ship.

Underline (or use italics) for words, numbers, letters, and figures referred to as such.

> The number 6 looks like the number 9 upside down.
> The word *and* is the most common conjunction.

Underline (or use italics) for foreign words or phrases.

> She always used the words *c'est la vie* when something problematic but unavoidable happened.

Commonly Confused Words

The following words are commonly confused. Sometimes the problem is with spelling; sometimes it is with meaning.

accept/except	I accept your settlement offer except for the part on the first page.
advice/advise	I advise you to take my advice and be careful.
affect/effect	The smell affects me so much I feel sick. What effect does it have on you? Could you effect a change in the ventilation?
already/all ready	John has already gone. My friends, are you all ready to go?
alter/altar	We can't alter the past. The altar was covered with flowers.
altogether/ all together	I don't altogether dislike the taste. The flavors are blended all together in the drink.
angel/angle	A triangle has three angles. Much early art portrays angels as babies.
assent/ascent/ ascend	Will your parents assent to your making the ascent? Don't ascend without their permission.
bath/bathe	I decided to bathe in the warm bath water.
bear/bare	The only kind of bear I have seen is a bare bear.
berth/birth	She gave birth to a baby in the berth of a Pullman car.
bore/boar	Bore holes in the tree and attach the fence. That will keep the boar away. However, without any excitement, the country may bore you.
born/borne	Where were you born? They have borne their troubles well.
brake/break	Step on the brake lightly. These glasses I'm holding break easily.
capital/capitol	Springfield is the capital city where they voted on capital punishment. It takes lots of capital to start a business. The Capitol building is in Washington.
cite/site/sight	He cited Shakespeare in his paper. The site of our new home has not been picked yet. A beautiful sight greeted us when we saw the lovely valley.

cloths/clothes	There are six new wash cloths under the pile of clean clothes in the linen closet.
coarse/course	The wool shirt felt coarse against my skin. The plane followed a straight course. Chicken Kiev was the main course. I signed up for the course in Latin.
consul/council/ counsel	I called the British consul in Rome to get help. Jeremy was elected to the school council. I tried to get counsel from the best lawyer in town. She agreed to be my counsel.
desert/dessert	The Sahara Desert is huge. Grandpa would never desert the family. We had chocolate mousse for dessert.
diary/dairy	I once wrote in my diary about my experiences milking cows at my uncle's dairy.
dissent/descent/ descend	Did your parents dissent when you asked them if you could make the descent? You didn't descend in spite of their dissent, did you?
formerly/formally	She was formerly Miss America. She formally addressed the group.
forth/fourth	Go forth to battle in the fourth company of infantry.
its/it's	The cat licked its paws. It's too late now.
later/latter	I'll see you later. I'll choose the latter of the two.
lose/loose	Don't lose your temper. I have to tie up some loose ends.
moral/morale	You have to have strong moral character to keep your morale high these days.
miner/minor	My father was a coal miner. A sixteen-year-old is considered a minor in some states. I have one minor objection.
muscle/mussel	There are many mussels at our beach. The athlete has very strong muscles.
pair/pare	Please pare a pair of apples.
past/passed	Grandma lives in the past. We drove right past your house. I passed up a great opportunity.
peace/piece	I feel at peace in the mountains when I have a big piece of pie.
personal/ personnel	I don't want a personal involvement. I took the job because I liked the personnel working there.
plane/plain	They hired four planes to spray herbicides. She had a plain dress on. The settlers traveled across the plain.
precede/proceed	I will precede you as you proceed down the aisle.

presence/presents	She had a mysterious, self-contained presence. We opened our presents on Jim's birthday.
principal/ principle	Greed was his principal motivation. Who is principal of the school? He has strong principles.
prophecy/ prophesy	Does the prophet prophesy? Or is his prophecy just a lot of words?
quiet/quite	Be quiet. I'm quite sure we'll go.
rain/reign/rein	The king began his reign in a heavy rain; it was pouring so hard his horse would barely respond to the rein.
sheathe/sheath	Sheathe your sword in its sheath.
stationary/ stationery	The seats were stationary and couldn't be moved. I received a letter on perfumed stationery.
straight/strait	We went straight through the Strait of Gibraltar on our ship.
than/then	I am taller than he. If he puts on elevator shoes, then he'll be taller.
their/they're there	It's all their fault. They're waiting at the club. Put the flowers over there. There are three of us.
to/too/two	Give it to me. He is too young for me. I'm coming, too. Here are two of my best recipes.
waist/waste	She has a 24-inch waist. Do you know what we should do with nuclear waste?
weather/whether	We're going whether the weather cooperates or not.
wholly/holy	The group was wholly in agreement. The saint was holy.
whose/who's	Whose hat is this? Who's responsible here?
your/you're	This is your copy. You're too young to drive.

Lie and Lay

Lie means "to recline" or "to be in a horizontal position." The verb *lie* is intransitive; it never takes an object. *Lay* means "to put or place something down in a resting position." The verb *lay* is transitive; it requires an object.

I think I'll *lie* down.   (intransitive)

Lay the book on the table.   (transitive; *book* is the direct object)

Below are the principal forms of these verbs:

Present	Present Participle	Past	Past Participle
lie	lying	lay	lain
lay	laying	laid	laid

Lie down. I *am lying* down. Five minutes ago, I *lay* down for a nap. Perhaps they have *lain* down for a while.

Lay the book on the table. He *is laying* the book on the table. He *laid* the book on the table. I *have laid* the book on the table.

Sit and Set

Sit means "to assume an upright position." *Sit* is almost always an intransitive verb; it rarely takes an object. *Set* means "to put or place something down." *Set* is a transitive verb; it usually requires an object.

Sit down on the sofa.   (intransitive)

Set the packages down on the table.   (transitive)

Below are the principal forms of these verbs:

Present	Present Participle	Past	Past Participle
sit	sitting	sat	sat
set	setting	set	set

Sit down over there.

He *is sitting* on the floor. He *sat* on the floor.

We *have sat* here waiting for you for hours.

Set the packages on the table. Jane *is setting* the groceries on the front steps.

They *set* the boxes on the floor. We *have set* the larger boxes on the floor.

Rise and Raise

Rise means "to go up" or "to get up." It is intransitive; it never takes an object.

Raise means "to force something to move upward." *Raise* is transitive; it takes an object.

What time does the sun *rise*?

Can you *raise* the flag?

Below are the principal parts of these verbs:

Present	Present Participle	Past	Past Participle
rise	rising	rose	risen
raise	raising	raised	raised

Rise to your feet. He *is rising* to his feet. The crowd *rose* during the Pledge of Allegiance. The moon *has risen* at sunset for the last five days. *Raise* the flag. The janitor *is raising* the flag. Two students *raised* their hands. I *have raised* my hand three times in the last five minutes.

A List of Frequently Misspelled Words

The following list includes many of the words in English which are thought to be difficult to spell. You can solve many spelling problems by checking this list or a dictionary.

A

abbreviate
absence
abundant
accelerator
accidentally
acclimated
accommodate
accompanied
accompaniment
accomplishment
accumulate
accuracy
achievement
acknowledgment
acquaintance
acquire
adequately
adolescent
advantageous
aerial
aggravate
allegiance
allusion
amateur
among
analysis
analyze
angel
angle
annihilate
anonymous
answer
anxiety
anxious
apologetically
apparatus
apparent
appearance
appreciate
appropriate
arctic
argument
arrangement
ascend
ascent
assent
association
atheistic
athletic
attendance
audience
auxiliary
awkward

B

bachelor
ballet
bankruptcy
barbarian
bath
bathe
bear
beggar
beginning
behavior
beneficial
benefit
benefited
berth
bibliography
birth
biscuit
blasphemy
boar
bore
boulevard
boundaries
breath
breathe
brilliant
buffet
buoy
bureau
business
busy

C

calendar
campaign
candidate
captain
carburetor
caricature
catalogue
catastrophe
category
cellar
cemetery
certain
changeable
characteristic
choose
chose
circumstantial
colossal
column
committee
communist
comparative
compelled
competent
competitor
completely
complexion
compulsory
conference
confidentially
connoisseur
conscience
conscientious
consciousness
consistent
controversial
criticism
criticize
curiosity
curious
curriculum

D

dairy
decadent
deceitful
decision
definite

descend
descendant
descent
describe
description
desirable
despair
desperate
devise
diary
different
dilapidated
dilemma
diligence
disappear
disappoint
disapprove
disastrous
disciple
discipline
discrimination
dissatisfied
dissent
dissipate
divide
divine
doesn't
dormitory

E

ecstasy
efficiency
eligible
eliminate
embarrass
emperor
emphasize
endeavor
enthusiastically
environment
equivalent
especially
espionage
exaggerate
exceed
excellent

exceptionally
exhaustion
exhibition
exhilaration
existence
extraordinary
extremely
exuberant

F

familiar
fascinate
fascism
February
feminine
foreign
forfeit
forth
forty
fourth
frantically
freight
fulfill
fundamental

G

gaiety
galaxy
gauge
generally
government
governor
grammar
grammatically
grievous
guarantee

H

handsome
harassment
height
hereditary
hindrance
holy
hospital

horizontal
humorous
hygiene
hypocrisy

I

illusion
imaginary
immediately
incidentally
incredible
independent
indispensable
inevitable
influential
ingenious
initiative
innocent
intellectual
intelligence
interesting
interpretation
interrupt
irrelevant
irresponsible

K

kerosene
knew
knowledge

L

laboratory
larynx
legitimate
leisure
liable
library
license
lightning
liquor
literature
livelihood
loneliness
luxurious

M

magnificence
maintenance
manageable
maneuver
marriage
martyr
mathematics
meant
mediocre
melancholy
melodious
merely
miniature
minute
mischievous
misspell
moral
morale
mortgage
mosquito
municipal
murmuring
muscle
mussel
mysterious

N

naive
necessity
neither
neurotic
nickel
ninety
ninth
noticeable
nuclear

O

obedience
occasion
occurred
omission
opinion
opportunity

optimistic
orchestra
original
outrageous

P

pageant
paid
pain
pamphlet
pane
parallel
paralysis
parliament
particularly
pastime
peasant
penicillin
permanent
permissible
perseverance
persistent
perspiration
persuade
phenomenon
physically
physician
picnicking
playwright
pneumonia
politician
possess
practically
precede
preference
preferred
prejudice
presence
prestige
presumption
prevalent
privilege
probably
procedure
proceed

prominent
pronunciation
propaganda
prophecy
prophesy
psychiatrist
psychoanalysis
pursue

Q

quantity
quietly
quite

R

rain
rebellion
receive
recognize
recommend
reference
rehearsal
reign
rein
religious
remembrance
reminiscent
remittance
repetition
representative
respectful
responsibility
restaurant
rhyme
rhythm

S

sandwich
satisfactorily
saxophone
schedule
secretary
seize
separate

sergeant
sheath
sheathe
siege
significant
similar
sophomore
souvenir
speak
specifically
specimen
speech
sponsor
straight
strait
strictly
stubbornness
succeed
success
superintendent
supersede
surprise
surroundings
susceptible
syllable
symbolic
symmetrical
symphonic
synonymous

T

tariff
temperament
temperature
tendency
thorough
together
tolerance
tomorrow
tortoise
tragedy
transcend
tries
truly
twelfth

typical
tyranny

U

unanimous
undoubtedly
universal
unmistakable
unnatural
unnecessarily
unscrupulous
until
usually

V

vaccine
vacuum
valuable
variation
various
vegetable
vehicle
vengeance
versatile
vigilant
village
villain
vinegar

W

weather
Wednesday
weird
whether
whisper
whistle
wholly
withhold

Y

yacht
yawn

Spelling Helps

VISUALIZING

One of the most successful techniques for remembering the spelling of a word is to see the word in your "mind's eye." If you have this ability, you will be able to retrieve a correct spelling easily, and you will be able to spot misspelled words, too. Most visualizers look at the word on a page, then look away and try to "see" the word in their memories.

MNEMONIC TECHNIQUES

Some people remember correct spellings by developing "hints" which are based on some characteristic of the words they are to spell. The following examples are presented so that you can see how the process works. Only a few of these "hints" are presented, since the best way to use this process is for you to develop your own. Use the examples here as suggestions; then, make up your own tricks to help you remember.

absence	I will "c" you at the end. ab*sen*ce
accompanied	An "a" is accompanied by two "c's" in this word. *acc*ompanied
captain	Don't let it r*ain* on the capt*ain*.
describe	There is a *scribe* in de*scribe*.
excellent	There is a prison *cell* in ex*cell*ent.
fundamental	*Fun* is *mental*.
independent	Put a *dent* in indepen*dent*.
knew	The "k" is new.
paid	How is it that *I* always get involved when something is to be *paid*?
parliament	Can there be a *liar* in a par*lia*ment?
pronunciation	A *nun* always has good pro*nun*ciation habits.
speak	Give him an "*a*" and let him spe*a*k.
succeed	It takes double letters to su*cc*eed.
vegetable	Your vege*table* is waiting at the *table*.
Wednesday	We hope to *wed* on We*d*nesday.

SELECTED SPELLING RULES

IE or EI

Use I before E except after C for the long "E" sound.

		after C
believe	priest	ceiling
fiend	relieve	conceit
grievance	retrieve	deceive
niece	shriek	receive
piece	thief	

Learn the exceptions to this rule by memorizing this nonsense sentence (Note the spelling of each word):

Neither financier seized either species of weird leisure.

Use E before I when the sound is not a long "E"

freight	neighbor
height	weight

Adding Prefixes

When you add a prefix to a word, the spelling of the word itself does not change.

un + natural = unnatural   over + run = overrun
mis + spell = misspell   im + mobile = immobile
un + excused = unexcused re + supply = resupply

Adding Suffixes

When adding the suffixes -NESS and -LY, the spelling of the word does not change.

dry + ness = dryness   mere + ly = merely
kind + ness = kindness   shy + ly = shyly

Exceptions: For words that end in Y not representing the long "I" sound, change the Y to I before adding -NESS or -LY.

happy + ness = happiness   ready + ly = readily

Drop the final $\underline{E}$ before adding a suffix that begins with a vowel.

hope + ing = hoping   live + able = livable
use + able = usable

Retain the final $\underline{E}$ after $\underline{C}$ or $\underline{G}$ if the suffix begins with $\underline{A}$ or $\underline{O}$.

advantage + ous = advantageous   notice + able = noticeable
courage + ous = courageous   service + able = serviceable

Retain the final $\underline{E}$ before adding a suffix that begins with a consonant.

care + ful = careful   hope + ful = hopeful
Exceptions: argument, awful, ninth, wholly, wisdom

For words ending in $\underline{Y}$ preceded by a consonant, change the $\underline{Y}$ to $\underline{I}$ before adding a suffix. Retain the $\underline{Y}$ if it is preceded by a vowel.

funny + est = funniest   boy + ish = boyish
happy + ness = happiness   enjoy + ing = enjoying
merry + ment = merriment   stay + ing = staying
Exceptions: Retain the y in words such as *babyish, ladylike, studying.*

Double the final consonant before adding a suffix beginning with a vowel if both of the following two conditions exist: 1) the word has only one syllable *or* the accent is on the second syllable; and 2) if the word ends in a consonant preceded by a vowel.

control + ed = controlled   propel + er = propeller
occur + ence = occurrence   quit + ing = quitting
plan + ing = planning   refer + ed = referred

BUT
cancel + ed = cancelled (Accent not on last syllable, but final
    consonant is doubled)
prefer + able = preferable (Accent shifts to first syllable)

Add $\underline{K}$ before adding $\underline{ING}$, $\underline{ED}$ or $\underline{Y}$ to words ending in a hard $\underline{C}$.

picnic + ed = picnicked   mimic + ing = mimicking
panic + ed = panicked   traffic + ing = trafficking

Plurals

To form the plural of nouns, observe the following rules:

The most common way to form the plural of a noun is to add S.
   book, books   table, tables   desk, desks

The plural of nouns ending in S, SH, CH and X is formed by adding ES.
   box, boxes   church, churches   dress, dresses

To form the plural of nouns ending in Y *preceded by a consonant*, change the Y to I and add ES.
   army, armies   enemy, enemies   fly, flies

To form the plural of nouns ending in Y *preceded by a vowel*, add S.
   donkey, donkeys   key, keys   monkey, monkeys

To form the plural of most nouns ending in F or FE, add S. However, the plural of a few nouns ending in F or FE is formed by changing the F to V and adding either S or ES.

chief, chiefs	dwarf, dwarfs
BUT	
calf, calves	elf, elves
hoof, hooves	knife, knives
leaf, leaves	loaf, loaves

To form the plural of nouns ending in O *preceded by a vowel* add S. If the final O is preceded by a consonant, the plural is formed by adding S or ES.

(O preceded by a vowel)
rodeo, rodeos   radio, radios

(O preceded by a consonant)
domino, dominoes or dominos   tomato, tomatoes
hero, heroes

All words ending in O that pertain to music, form the plural by adding S.

   alto, altos   piano, pianos
   crescendo, crescendos   solo, solos

To form the plural of compound nouns written as one word, add <u>ES</u> if the word ends in <u>S</u>, <u>SH</u>, <u>CH</u> or <u>X</u> and <u>S</u> if it ends in anything else.

   spoonful, spoonfuls   strongbox, strongboxes

The plural of hyphenated compound nouns consisting of a noun plus modifiers is formed by making the noun plural.

   mother-in-law, mothers-in-law   passer-by, passers-by

Some nouns are the same in the singular and plural.

   deer, sheep, species, trout

Many words of foreign origin have two plurals. Others have a plural that is irregular by English standards. When in doubt, check your dictionary.

Singular	*Plural*
alumna (feminine)	alumnae (feminine)
alumnus (masculine or mixed)	alumni (masculine or mixed)
curriculum	curriculums, curricula
appendix	appendixes, appendices
beau	beaus, beaux
focus	focuses, foci
memorandum	memorandums, memoranda
fungus	funguses, fungi
index	indexes, indices
analysis	analyses
basis	bases
crisis	crises
criterion	criteria

The plural of numbers, letters and symbols is formed by adding an *apostrophe* and <u>S</u>.

   two 5's,   three x's,   How many +'s are there in that equation?

The Research Paper

A research paper is a formal composition that includes information from a number of sources. It is essentially a summary of the information the writer has discovered about a particular subject.

Many research papers simply present the information the writer has found. Others attempt to draw a conclusion which persuades the reader to adopt a particular point of view. A paper on the origins of American jazz would probably be informational; one on ways in which the federal tax system could be reformed could proceed from the facts to a conclusion and then to a recommendation for a future course of action.

Strictly personal opinions are usually out of place in a research paper. As a result, the word "I" is seldom used. It is important in a research paper to "let the facts speak for themselves." You should let the authorities you cite carry the weight. It is much more convincing for a research paper to say, *"Thomas Jefferson* thought the taxing system should . . ."* than to say, *"I* think the taxing system should . . ."

If you wish to draw a persuasive conclusion in a research paper, you should generally present a series of facts in an "If . . ., then . . ." statement such as:

> "If Jefferson's view that . . . can be applied today, and if the constitutional principle that . . . is still valid, then the tax system of the United States is not what the Founding Fathers intended."

This writer presents information from one of the Founding Fathers (the argument would probably be stronger if the writer had presented information from others as well); there are also appropriate facts from the U.S. Constitution. Then, in a conclusion, the writer brings those facts together into a summary statement. The careful reader would probably have picked up the differences between present practice and the intent of the Founding Fathers as they were presented throughout the paper. By stating the conclusion in the final paragraph, the author makes sure that no reader misses the point.

Parts of the Research Paper

1. Title Page

The title page includes at least the title of the paper and the author's name, both centered in the middle of the page. Often, the name of the course, the teacher's name, and the date are also included on three separate lines in the lower right-hand corner of the page (see Figure 1).

figure 1

USING EXISTING KNOWLEDGE AND TECHNOLOGY
TO DEAL WITH THE ENERGY DILEMMA

By

Susan Spangler

Introduction to Science
Mrs. Pomranka
April 6, 198—

2. The Abstract (optional)

An abstract is a brief summary of the content of the paper. It should state the central idea and main divisions of the paper as well as summarize any inferences made or comparisons drawn from the author's research. If the paper attempts to solve a problem or recommend a future course of action, the abstract should also state how the author arrived at the problem, how the research was done (reading, interviews, questionnaires, etc.), how the results were compiled, and how the conclusion was formulated.

3. Table of Contents

The Table of Contents lists the main divisions of the paper and their corresponding page numbers (see Figure 2).

4. List of Illustrations (if any)

(see Figure 3).

5. Introduction (optional)

The purpose of an introduction is to inform the reader of the intent or purpose of the paper and the extent of the research involved. If the paper covers a problem or a controversial issue, the problem should be clearly introduced, the necessary background given, a statement included about the method of research, and information given telling how the conclusions are derived.

Figure 2

TABLE OF CONTENTS

Figure 3

LIST OF ILLUSTRATIONS

6. Text

(This is the main body of the paper).

7. Appendixes (if any).

Supplementary or explanatory material not essential to the text but of importance should be included in the appendixes at the end of the paper.

8. Bibliography

The bibliography is a listing of all reference material used in preparing the paper. It includes published material such as books and magazines; it also includes such things as interviews, letters, and the like which may have been used but which are not commercially published. A later section provides specific information about the form to be used in the bibliography.

Choosing a Topic

Choosing a topic is the most important part of writing a research paper. If you choose an unsuitable topic or write on one which is too broad, your paper will not be successful.

Here are two suggestions which are very important to consider in choosing a topic. First, be sure to *select a topic which you find interesting*. If you write about something you have no interest in, you will probably not write well.

Then, be sure *the topic is in an area you would like to learn more about*. Having insurance against boredom is important for anyone writing any paper, but it is especially important in the case of a research paper, since you will spend a considerable amount of time with the topic.

Where do ideas for topics come from? For most writers, they come from one or more of at least three places:

1. Often topics come from *assignments given by teachers*. Usually a teacher will provide you with a broad area, however, and you will be expected to narrow the topic to something specific which you feel to be an important dimension of the area and something which is interesting to you.

2. Many times topics come from *your own experience*. For example, if you were concerned about the conservation of energy resources, you certainly could find a specific topic for research in that area. Sometimes, your interests and general topics assigned by a teacher coincide in strange ways. A student interested in engineering might respond to an assignment to write a research paper on Shakespeare's plays by writing about the stage machinery which performers of Shakespeare's time used.

3. Sometimes, especially as you read widely, you will find topics arising from *articles or books which you read*. If you keep your eyes open and search for topics when you are reading, you will find some excellent ideas. Most often, you will find the main thrust of the article provides an idea for a topic. But sometimes you will be struck by a single sentence or idea hidden in an article. If you are alert, always looking for ideas to write about, you will spot those hidden topics.

When you choose a topic, you should keep in mind the availability of materials that you will need for your research. Once you have an idea, go to your school, community, or home library and see if there is sufficient material to use as a basis for a paper. If you can't find at least ten sources which apply to your topic, you should probably look for another area. Use the card catalogue, the *Readers' Guide to Periodical Literature*, and other appropriate indexes to determine whether your library has enough material to provide you with a good base to work from.

Limiting the Topic

Once you find you have enough material, limit your topic. Imagine trying to write a paper on a topic such as "World History." You could literally write for a lifetime and never complete the work. You need to narrow that broad topic.

The key to limiting your topic is to select a subject for writing which you can cover *completely* in the time available to you. You must also consider the length of your paper. An illustration of the process of limiting a topic follows:

History
    U.S. History
        The Depression Years
            Roosevelt's Anti-Depression Activities
            Government Work Programs
                The Works Progress Administration (W.P.A)
                    Highways Built by the W.P.A.

An eventual title for a paper emerging from this process might be "The Impact of the W.P.A. on Transportation in the United States from 1935 to 1950." Included in the paper could be a description of W.P.A. sponsored activities, the costs of W.P.A. highway building programs, and the like. It would be possible in such a paper to develop a conclusion based on the benefits of the activity as it is related to its cost.

Taking Notes

Prepare a preliminary outline to guide you in note-taking.

In order to begin researching a topic in an organized way, you need to write some kind of outline that includes the topics on which you need information. Sometimes you will need to begin reading before such an outline can be written; at other times you will already know enough about your topic to anticipate the main sections of your paper.

    Suppose you were going to write a research paper on the origin of modern-day blues music. Your tentative outline might look something like this:

1. The music of black Africa
2. The importation of black Africans to America and the treatment of black slaves.
3. Early black work songs, religious and gospel spirituals, and "plantation blues"
4. The emergence of urban blues in cities with high black populations
5. The music of early blues greats such as Louis Armstrong, Bessie Smith, and Billie Holliday
6. The influence of New Orleans ragtime and big band sounds on the blues
7. Progressive problems of black people and how these problems changed their music

Prepare a "heading card" for each topic of your outline.

A heading card is a single card, usually 3″ by 5″, which you use at the front of all note cards containing information on that particular area. An example of a heading card is shown below.

Heading Card

1.   The Music of Black Africa

As you read, you may find that topics need to be added to your outline. As you add them, prepare heading cards for them as well.

Prepare a "bibliography card" for each source you use.

The moment you begin using a source (book, magazine, interview, letter) prepare a bibliography card for it. Use cards that are the same size as your heading cards.

The bibliography card serves two purposes: First, it provides a correct identification for each note you will take, and it saves you the effort of writing the complete source on each note card. Second, it provides a bibliography entry in correct form so that when the final draft of the paper is written, you need only arrange your "bib" cards in alphabetical order and copy them on the page.

If you were writing a research paper on energy conservation, you might use a book by Davis and Schubert entitled, *Alternate Natural Energy Sources in Building Design*. Your "bib" card would look like this:

Bibliography Card

Davis, Albert J. and Robert P. Schubert,
Alternate Natural Energy Sources in Building Design,
New York: Van Nostrand Reinhold Company, 1977.

Specific directions about how to prepare bibliographic entries are included in the "bibliography" section of this Handbook. Be sure to follow the directions very carefully. If your "bib" cards are carefully and accurately done, you will save yourself considerable time and trouble later on.

Prepare a note card for each potentially useful idea you encounter in your sources.

When you encounter something in your reading which you feel may be useful for your paper, either write it on a 3″ by 5″ notecard in your own words (paraphrase it) or copy it directly. If you copy it directly, enclose it in quotation marks. If you paraphrase the material, be sure you do not use the author's exact words.

Once you have written your note, write the author's last name, the publication date, and the page number(s) of the source at the top left of the card. At the top right, write the number of the topic (from your outline) to which the note refers. Here is an example of a notecard from Davis and Schubert's book, *Alternate Natural Energy Sources in Building Design:*

Note Card

Davis and Schubert, 1977, p. 42   #4
   "There are three basic types of light. First there is <u>direct</u> sunlight, which originates from the southeast to southwest (high angle), and east to west (low angle). <u>Ground</u> light, a secondary source, is reflected from the earth's surface and varies in intensity in relationship to ground surface, angle toward the sun, and the slope of the ground. <u>Diffused</u> light or skylight is direct light diffused by the particles of the atmosphere."

You know several things from the form of the notecard: first, you know the source from which the material came; second, you know the page from which it came; third, you know that it is quoted directly (note that the material is enclosed in quotation marks); finally, you know which outline topic the quoted material refers to (#4 refers to topic number 4 in the outline).

Notice that you do not write the entire bibliographical entry on each card, but only the author's name, date of publication, and page. You also do not write out the entire topic from the outline; rather, you simply identify the card according to the number of the topic from the outline.

When you have finished the notecard, place it immediately behind the header card for the appropriate outline topic. Most people like to place rubber bands around the cards to keep them together.

It is important that you use a fresh notecard for each idea you identify, so that you can have all cards for a single topic together and not have single cards which fit under several headings. Also, when you arrange your cards in the best order to help organize your paper, you will be able to shift ideas around as you shift cards. If you have many ideas on a single card, it becomes much more difficult to organize your paper. Most students get a pack of 100 3″ by 5″ notecards when they begin a research paper. Those following good procedures will frequently use all of the cards as they prepare a 10-12 page paper.

Writing the Paper

Review your outline.

As you have been taking notes, you have probably been modifying your outline. You have probably encountered new topics, and found that certain topics you originally felt important are no longer worth including. As you modified your outline during the notetaking stage, you probably modified the numbers on your notecards to conform to your changing outline. However, once you finish your notetaking, it is important to step back for a short time and look at the outline carefully. Ask yourself the following questions:

1. Do the main topics reflect the major ideas I want to present?
2. Are the topics reasonably independent of one another?
3. Are the topics arranged in the sequence that will be the most effective in presenting the information?
4. Do the topics lend themselves to an appropriate conclusion?

Based on your answers to the questions, modify your outline as necessary. You may find this to be a good time to add sub-categories to help you organize your materials even better. Some people like to develop very detailed outlines at this point; others go directly to the first draft of the paper.

The Thesis Statement.

Some writers like to write a single sentence which sums up where they intend to go with their research before the research effort gets underway. Most beginners like to let the major idea of the paper evolve as they become familiar with the sources they intend to use. Whatever your preference is, the first step in writing the first draft is to write a *single sentence* which sets the stage for what you will write in your paper. You may never use the precise sentence you write as your initial thesis sentence; in fact, you will probably revise it several times before you write your final draft. However, that single sentence is very important to you. It guides you as you organize your material and as you select which material to use.

A good thesis statement does at least two things: it tells the reader what your paper will be about, and it captures his or her interest. In the case of a research paper which intends to persuade, it also hints that the reader will be asked to accept the writer's conclusions. The following thesis statements may serve as examples:

1. The emphasis in the Constitution of the United States on the rights and responsibilities of the common person is due in large measure to Benjamin Franklin.
2. The world has a serious energy problem, but it can be solved through the intelligent use of existing knowledge and technology.
3. Jane Smith has the qualities Hamilton looked for in a governor.

Usually the thesis statement appears in the final draft of the paper at the end of the first paragraph; however, under some circumstances, it may not be explicitly stated until the end of the paper. A useful model for the research paper is the following:

First paragraph.

This sets the stage for the paper by catching the reader's attention; then it quickly moves to the thesis statement. The following is an example of an introductory paragraph:

The world's fossil fuels will be used up in less than one hundred years if consumption continues at present rates (Ernhardt, 1981, p. 18). Numerous high-technology solutions such as generation of electricity through panels in space with micro-waves transmitting the energy to earth have been proposed to solve the problem. Most solutions involve considerable governmental expenditure. What has been ignored by officials is the abundant supply of answers to the energy problem that we already have. The world has a serious energy problem, but it can be solved through the intelligent use of existing knowledge and technology.

The Text.

Once the first paragraph (with its thesis statement) has been written, organize your notecards according to the outline and begin to juggle them until they seem to fit an appropriate order within the topics. Then, using the notecards, begin writing, using the cards as guides. Often you will use only bits and pieces of the material on the cards; sometimes you will have to go back to the original source to get additional information (although if you have been careful in the notetaking process, this will rarely happen).

Sections of the paper should correspond to the topics of the outline, and you may wish to title those sections. Should you wish to do so, center the titles on the page and underline them. They should be included in the Table of Contents once you finish your final draft.

The Conclusion.

Usually research papers will have a conclusion. More often than not, the conclusion is a re-statement of the first paragraph and its thesis statement. The following is an example of a concluding paragraph:

> The intelligent use of the energy sources supplied by the wind, by the seas, and by the sun can eliminate the problem posed by rapidly diminishing fossil-fuel supplies. But rather than waiting for high technology to capture those energy sources, the common, ordinary citizen can make a common-sense application of techniques that go back to the cave dweller and thus delay the onset of a crisis in energy. Ultimate answers to the energy problem may involve complex technology, but immediate answers involve common sense and common people.

Conventions

Headings.

Most research papers use three levels of headings to sub-divide the content and to provide helpful cues to the reader.

A centered main heading

A flush-left side heading

An indented paragraph heading

Here are examples of the three headings:

> METHODS OF RESEARCH
> Library Research
> Procedure
> Written Results
> Questionnaires
> Writing the Questions
> Procedure
> Written Results

Proper Presentation of Numbers

When referring to numbers in a research paper, use *words* to express the following:

The numbers zero through nine
five others
We questioned *eight* doctors regarding their knowledge of the latest in cancer research.

Any number that begins a sentence

Sixty percent of those questioned answered, "yes".

One hundred forty students were given scholarships.

Use figures to express

Numbers 10 or greater

They tabulated a total of 48 responses.

Units of measurement or time

He was given 500-mg doses for 2 weeks.

Ages

Her daughter is 7 years old.

Times and Dates

8:25 A.M., January 29, 1988

Percentages

A total of 18% responded to the letter.

Ratios

The people voted 4:1 in favor of the bond issue.

Exact sums of money

Each person who completed the petition was paid $5.

Page numbers, figure or table numbers

Table 4 on page 26 shows the 1952 election results.

Numbers grouped for comparison within a single sentence

Of the 25 cases, 11 were settled out of court, 3 were settled in court, and 1 is still pending.

Commas in numbers

In figures of 1,000 or more, use commas between groups of three digits.

1,000 children 84,396 Libyans

Illustrative Material

Illustrative material such as tables, figures, charts, graphs, and photographs can increase understanding of the text in ways that words cannot. Just as "one picture is worth 1,000 words," one table or chart can show pages of written description at a glance, making it easy for the reader to assimilate and compare vital information.

- Figures, charts and graphs should be clear, properly labeled, and easy to read.
- Use heavy lines for vertical and horizontal axes clearly labelling the units in which they are measured.
- If possible, color-code each separate line placed on graphs.
- Number each figure, chart, or graph throughout the paper.
- If there are many figures within each chapter, number the figures by chapter (figure 3.8—the 8th figure in chapter 3).

Footnotes

There are three common kinds of footnotes, each serving a different purpose:

1. Content footnotes

Content footnotes explain or amplify the information in the paper. An example of a content footnote would be a reference to something in an appendix.[1]

[1]See appendix B for Solar Tables for North America.

> Most often, especially in short papers, you will place information such as this in parentheses at an appropriate point in the paper instead of putting it at the foot of the page. (See Appendix B for Solar Tables for North America.)

2. Reference footnotes

Reference footnotes are used to inform the reader about the source from which material was taken. Footnotes of this sort are used for all ideas taken from other sources, whether or not the sources are quoted directly. Avoid the mistake of footnoting only quoted material.

The most common way of indicating the source of referenced material is to use the following format: (Davis and Schubert, 1977, p. 42) immediately following the quoted material. The sequence of material is: a parenthesis, the name(s) of the author(s), the date of publication, the page(s) on which the material appeared, and a parenthesis. This reference appears in the text of the paper, not at the bottom of a page. Should the reader wish to find the specific article to which the reference refers, he or she should go to the bibliography, where a book entitled, *Alternate Natural Energy Sources in Building Design* appears under the authorship of Davis and Schubert.

3. An older system of footnoting

This system placed reference notes at the bottom of the page on which the quoted or referenced material appeared. This system was troublesome for a number of reasons: first, it required the reader to shift from the text to the bottom of the page, thus interrupting the flow of the reading; second, it was extremely difficult for a typist to allow a precise amount of space at the bottom of a page for anticipated footnotes; and finally, scholars who read research papers tend to be the ones who check footnotes, and they usually know the contributions of authors rather than the precise names of books or articles. Thus, they appreciate the appearance of the author's name in the text rather than at the bottom of the page.

The system advocated here is the one most widely accepted in scholarly writings today. It is also the most commonly accepted system in colleges and universities for research papers.

Bibliography

When writing a bibliography, observe the following details of form:

- Items should be arranged alphabetically according to the last names of authors.

    If the source has more than one author, alphabetize it under the first author's last name. The names of co-authors are written first name first.

- It is not necessary to number the sources in a bibliography.
- Anonymous items such as encyclopedia articles are alphabetized by the first word of their titles, unless the first word is *the*, *a*, or *an*, in which case it is alphabetized according to the second word in the title.
- If an item occupies more than one line, the second line should be indented so that the author's name stands out on the page.
- Type bibliographical entries using single spacing leaving a double space between entries.

Follow the following format when compiling a bibliography:

Books

Kotzwinkle, William, *Dr. Rat: A Wild Novel About the Ultimate Revolt of Mother Nature*, New York: Bantam Books, 1977.

Newspapers and Magazine Articles

"GOP Unveils Tax Relief Ideas," *The Boulder Daily Camera*, March 22, 1979. (no author given)

Attaway, Roy, "A Viking in the Keys," *Motor Boating and Sailing*, April 1979, pp. 67–70 ff. (*ff* means the article is continued later in the magazine.)

Encyclopedias

"United States of America: Racial Composition," *Encyclopaedia Britannica*, vo. 22, Chicago: Encyclopaedia Britannica, Inc., 1966, pp. 18–19.

Interviews

Davis, James S., Interview, Oct. 14, 1981.

A Glossary of Grammatical Terms

Sentence

A sentence is a string of words that makes good sense and is complete. The following strings of words are examples of sentences:

The elephant died.

Drop your packages off at the drugstore.

Every person at the celebration overate.

My dog chased the neighbor's cat into the street.

If a string of words that makes good sense is not complete, it is called a *sentence part*. The following are sentence parts:

On the chair next to the broken window

The carnival manager socked the

The man in the third row from the top of the balcony

Sometimes strings of words make no sense at all. In that case, they are called *non-sentences*. "Dribbled jumped the by and if the man" is a non-sentence.

Sentence Types

Most English sentences are statements or *declarative* sentences. The following are *declarative* sentences:

The book was large and difficult to carry.

Sammy is the nicest cat we've ever had.

The first baseman caught the fly to retire the side.

Another type of sentence is the question or *interrogative* sentence. The following sentences are *interrogative*:

Can you stop and pick me up?

Will John ever grow up?

A third type of English sentence is the command, often called the *imperative* sentence. The following are examples of *imperative* sentences:

Hit the deck.

Please go with me to the movies.

Enter the room quietly and take your places in your assigned seats.

Parts of the Sentence

A sentence consists of a *subject* and *predicate*. The subject is the part of the sentence something is said about; the predicate is the section which says something about the subject.

The Subject

The *subject* normally occurs at the beginning of the sentence. It contains the noun or pronoun which the predicate says something about. That noun or pronoun is called the *simple subject*. The subject is underlined in the following sentences, and the simple subject is enclosed in a box.

The boy ran fast.

The boy *who lives in the house next to mine* ran fast.

We noticed the boy who lives in the house next to mine running down the street.

Sometimes the subject is not at the beginning of the sentence.

Everywhere there was *laughter.*

The Predicate

The *predicate* usually occurs at the end of the sentence. It contains the main verb in the sentence and says something about the subject. In distinguishing between subjects and predicates, it is often useful to identify the verb first. Once that is done, finding the subject is usually quite simple.

In the following sentences the predicates have been underlined and the main verbs enclosed in boxes:

The boy *ran fast.*

The boy who lives in the house next to mine *ran fast.*

We noticed *the boy who lives in the house next to mine running down the street.*

Sometimes the predicate is not at the end of the sentence.

Everywhere there was laughter.

The Direct Object

The *direct object* is the noun or pronoun which receives the action of the verb. It is a part of the predicate. The direct objects in the following sentences are in italics:

The boy chased the *dog.* We saw *him.* He was chasing a *cat.*

The Indirect Object

The *indirect object* is a noun or pronoun which comes before the direct object in the sentence. It tells for whom or to whom the action of the verb is being done. Indirect objects in the following sentences are in italics:

Mary gave *Susan* a birthday card.

The donkey threw *Henry* a baseball.

Predicate Adjective

The *predicate adjective* is an adjective in the predicate which tells something about (modifies) the subject, and is joined to it by a linking verb such as the verb *to be*. The predicate adjectives in the following sentences are in italics:

The lake is *quiet* today.

The throat of the fire-eater became *sore* after yesterday's performance.

My mother's health seems *better* after her stay in the hospital.

Predicate Noun or Pronoun

A *predicate noun or pronoun* appears in the predicate. It is the same person or thing as the subject, and is joined to it by a linking verb such as the verb *to be*. The predicate nouns and pronouns in the following sentences are in italics:

My mother is the *Representative* from our congressional district.

Jim was the *candidate* who won the election.

It was the Jones *family* coming up our drive.

The culprit could be *she*.

Parts of Speech

Noun

A noun is the name of a person, place, thing, or idea. Here are some examples of nouns.

Henry gave his *brother* the *apples*.

> *Henry* is a proper noun as all names are. It is the SUBJECT of the sentence. Proper nouns are capitalized.

> *Apples* is a common noun and is the DIRECT OBJECT of the verb; it tells directly what was given.

> *Brother*, another common noun, is the INDIRECT OBJECT of the verb; it tells to whom the apples were given.

Beauty is everywhere.

> *Beauty* is an abstract noun and is the SUBJECT of the sentence.

Pronoun

A pronoun is a word that takes the place of a noun. In one of the preceding sentences, *he* can replace *Henry*, *him* can replace his *brother*, and *them* can replace *apples*.

Verb

A verb is a word which shows action or expresses a state of being.

When she *is* at home, they *visit* her.

Is expresses a state of being; it does not describe an action of any kind.

Visit is an action verb.

Adjective

An adjective is a word used to modify (more fully describe) a noun or pronoun.

The *full* moon peered over the *Chinese* junks.

Full is a common adjective modifying the noun *moon*.

Chinese is a proper adjective modifying the noun *junks*. Since it is proper, it is capitalized.

Adverb

An adverb is a word used to modify (more fully describe) a verb, an adjective, or another adverb.

The *very* small child ran *extremely quickly*.

Very is an adverb, modifying the adjective *small*.

Quickly is an adverb, modifying the verb *ran*.

Extremely is an adverb, modifying the adverb *quickly*.

Function Words

Most of the words you use fit in the above five classes of words (parts of speech). These are called *content* words; they carry the majority of the meaning in sentences. Since certain pronouns replace and carry the content of nouns, they are *content* words.

Of course, content words aren't the only classes of words you use in speaking and writing English. Other words are called *function* words. They connect the content words according to the patterns of the English language. They include:

Pronouns

Sometimes pronouns are used to connect two sentences together and form one.

The man lives in Korea.

We met the man today.   (whom)

The man *whom* we met today lives in Korea.

Preposition

Words that connect nouns or pronouns to the rest of the sentence are called *prepositions*. The noun or pronoun is called the *object of the preposition*.

A friend *of* mine lives *in* Canada.

Conjunction

A *conjunction* is a word that connects two parts of a sentence. If the conjunction connects two parts that are similar in structure, it is called a *coordinating* conjunction.

Mary *and* Jim like ice cream, *but* I don't.

And connects two words. *But* connects two sentences.

If the conjunction connects two parts that are different in structure, it is called a *subordinating* conjunction.

Jeremy continued to fight *until* the bell rang.

Until connects a sentence (independent clause) with an adverb clause (dependent clause).

Articles

The, a, and *an* are articles. They always precede a noun and modify it. Thus, they are a kind of adjective. *The* is used when the noun it precedes refers to a specific object or idea.

The man left *the* dream of his boyhood behind.

A or *an* is used when the noun it precedes does not refer to a specific, but rather to a general object or idea.

An elephant can drink *a* gallon of water in seconds.

A and *an* refer to any or all elephants and to any and all gallons of water.

Interjection

An *interjection* is an exclamation that has no grammatical connection with the rest of the sentence. Many times interjections are used to show strong feeling. The following are examples of interjections:

Oh! Oh! There's a mouse in the house.

Please! Don't you know this is a library?

Alas, poor Yorick; I knew him well. (Shakespeare, *Hamlet*)

Multiple Classes

Words that you use in speaking or writing can fall into any number of the previous classes. For example, the word *up* can be used in the following sentences:

Preposition: The men's room is down the hall, *up* the stairs, and to the right.

Verb: Our neighbors *upped* the price of their house $3,000 last week.

Noun: "*Up*" was written on every sign around the hall.

Adjective: The *up* escalator stopped while we were between floors.

Adverb: Anyone going *up*?

The Prepositional Phrase

The *prepositional phrase* is a string of words which begins with a preposition and ends with a noun or pronoun. The noun or pronoun which ends the phrase is called the object of the preposition. The prepositional phrases in the following sentences are in italics:

The girl *with the baseball glove* is my sister.

My sister is the one *with the baseball glove*.

In the afternoon, we went *to the beach*.

On the other hand, we knew the burglar in the house would take the television set *near the family room*, the silverware *from the buffet*, and the coin collection *on my dresser*.

Prepositional phrases may be either adjectival (modifying a noun or pronoun) or adverbial (modifying a verb, adjective, or adverb).

The Clause

The Independent Clause

An *independent clause* is a string of words which could stand alone as a sentence. It is complete and makes good sense by itself, but it is a sentence that is connected to another independent clause or to a dependent clause. The following are examples of independent clauses:

I met a classmate, and *we went to the cafe for a soda*.

The man whom I expected to meet *wasn't there*.

I met a classmate whom I haven't seen in five years.

Dependent Clause

A *dependent clause* is not a complete string of words. It cannot stand alone as a sentence. The dependent clauses in the sentences below are in italics:

I met a classmate *whom I haven't seen in five years.*
The man *whom I expected to meet* wasn't there.

Verb Tense

Present tense verbs indicate action which is taking place at the present time:

The group *is going* to the film.
The singer also *plays* piano.
Ann *does play* the violin well.

Past tense verbs indicate action which took place at a previous time:

The group *went* to the film last period.   (past)
The birds *have returned* from the South.   (present perfect)
The rock band *had finished performing* when the star *appeared.*   (past perfect and past)

Future tense verbs indicate action which will take place at some time in the future:

The group *will go* to the film.   (future)
They *will have left* by the time you arrive.   (future perfect)

Voice of Verbs

Active Voice

The *active voice* verb makes the subject the chief actor, as in the following examples:

The dog chased the cat.
Henry ate his food quickly.
Sarah carried the whole load of firewood.

Passive Voice

The *passive voice* verb places the actor in the predicate, as in the following examples:

The cat was chased by the dog.
The food was eaten quickly by Henry.
The whole load of firewood was carried by Sarah.

Sometimes the passive voice is used when the actor is unknown:

The silver *was stolen*.

An error *has been found* in the ballot count.

Number of Verbs

Verbs may be either *singular* or *plural*. Singular verbs go with singular subjects as in the following sentences:

John (singular) chases (singular) deer out of the family garden nearly every night.

The students (plural) visit (plural) a neighboring school each year.

The book (singular) lies (singular) open on the desk.

Grammatical Relationships

Coordination

Coordination means that two equal things are connected in some way. The following sentences show coordinate relationships between elements:

The *boy* and his *father* walked to school.   (coordinate subjects)

The cat *lapped* the milk and *dripped* it on the floor.   (coordinate verbs)

The teacher thanked *Sandy* and *Martin*.   (coordinate direct objects)

The lady gave *him* and *me* candy bars.   (coordinate indirect objects)

Grandma spoiled Jim, and *Grandpa told her not to*.   (coordinate independent clauses)

They went *over the river* and *through the woods*.   (coordinate prepositional phrases)

The shark was *huge* and *ugly*.   (coordinate predicate adjectives)

Subordination

Subordination means that two unequal things are connected in some way. These sentences show subordination of one element to another:

When I get tired, I find it hard to get to sleep.   (dependent clause followed by an independent clause)

My teacher, *who has been teaching for ten years*, is an expert on language.   (dependent clause connected to an independent clause)

Modification

Modification means that a word, phrase, or clause makes the meaning of another element of the sentence more specific. The following sentences illustrate modification:

The *big* cat walked *quietly*.   (*Big* tells something about cat; *quietly* tells something about how the cat walked)

The man with the heavy coat left the movie.   (*With the heavy coat* tells which man left.)

In the beginning of the film, the hero finds a horse.   (*In the beginning of the film* tells when the hero finds the horse; it gives a time element to the verb, *finds*.)

Pronoun Antecedent

An antecedent is the word which a pronoun replaces. The following paragraph illustrates the relationship of pronouns and their antecedents:

Father turned on the news to watch the weather forecast. He (father) said that it (the forecast) warned of a major storm on its (the storm's) way. "Too bad," he (father) mumbled. "Looks like my (father's) golf match will be cancelled."

Pronoun Reference

Sometimes it is not clear what the antecedent of a pronoun is. For example, in the following sentence a reader could misunderstand the meaning because of an *ambiguous reference*.

The soldiers fought with the invaders until they were nearly destroyed.

Who was nearly destroyed? The soldiers? The invaders? Because the reader cannot be sure of the antecedent of the pronoun *they*, this sentence should be rewritten so that the antecedent is absolutely clear. Placing the pronoun very close to its antecedent usually eliminates the possibility of confusion.

THE BUSINESS LETTER

A business letter should include the following elements. Their numbers may be identified on the sample letter which appears on the facing page.

1. The Heading includes the street address; the city, state, and ZIP code; and the date. Always abbreviate the name of the state, since the recipient of your letter may write back to you, and he or she will want to use your return address on the envelope. The U.S. Post Office asks that names of states be abbreviated on envelopes to make sorting easier.

2. The Inside Address should be identical to the address on the envelope in which you send the letter. It should contain the name and address of the company or person to whom you are writing.

3. The Salutation will always include the name of the person included in the inside address. However, if you are writing to a company, not a specific individual, you have a small problem. Avoid the salutation, *Gentlemen.* That assumes an all-male company, something that almost never exists. If you address someone by title in the inside address (Executive Director, for example), you might write, *Dear Executive Director* or *Dear Director*. If you are writing to a firm and have no idea what area your letter should be directed to, simply wirte, *To Whom It May Concern* as your salutation. That is a bit formal, but if you are quite indefinite about the company, it may be best to be a bit formal in your whole letter. Whenever possible, include a specific name in your saluation.

4. The Body of the letter contains the message you wish to send. It should be clear and concise; it should reflect a business-like tone.

5. The Closing will normally be something like *Sincerely*; however, closings such as *Very truly yours, Respectfully*, and *Sincerely yours* are each appropriate. Capitalize only the first word of the closing.

6. The Signature should appear immediately below the closing, with the full name of the writer typed below it. Generally, one should leave four spaces between the closing and the typed name of the writer.

7. The Envelope should be addressed exactly as is the letter. The return address should be identical to the heading, except that the date is not included; the address should be identical to the letter's inside address.

The following is a list of U.S. Postal Service abbreviations for the fifty states, the District of Columbia, and the several trust territories of the United States. Use of these abbreviations speeds handling of the mail.

State		State	
Alabama	AL		
Alaska	AK	Nebraska	NB
Arizona	AZ	Nevada	NV
Arkansas	AR	New Hampshire	NH
California	CA	New Jersey	NJ
Colorado	CO	New Mexico	NM
Connecticut	CT	New York	NY
Delaware	DE	North Carolina	NC
District of Columbia	DC	North Dakota	ND
Florida	FL	Ohio	OH
Georgia	GA	Oklahoma	OK
Guam	GU	Oregon	OR
Hawaii	HI	Pennsylvania	PA
Idaho	ID	Puerto Rico	PR
Illinois	IL		
Indiana	IN	Rhode Island	RI
Iowa	IA	South Carolina	SC
Kansas	KS	South DAkota	SD
Kentucky	KY	Tennessee	TN
Louisiana	LA	Texas	TX
Maine	ME	Utah	UT
Maryland	MD	Vermont	VT
Massachusetts	MA	Virgin Islands	VI
Michigan	MI	Virginia	VA
Minnesota	MN	Washington	WA
Mississippi	MS	West Virginia	WV
Missouri	MO	Wisconsin	WI
Montana	MT	Wyoming	WY

287 Beacon Street
(1)———→Boston, MA 02215
January 3, 198–

(2)

Director of Public Relations
Denver Museum of Natural History
1295 Colfax Avenue
Denver, CO 80209

(4)

Dear Director:←———(3)

    Please send me a copy of your bulletin "Artifacts
of the Plains Indians of Colorado." I am enclosing a
money order for $3.50 which should cover the cost of
the publication. If there is a fee for handling and
mailing, please bill me.

    I would appreciate your prompt handling of this
request. I am writing a paper on the Plains Indians
and need the bulletin immediately.

(5)———→Sincerely,

(6)——→ *Aaron Smith*

      Aaron Smith

(7)

Aaron Smith
287 Beacon Street
Boston, MA 02215

        Director of Public Relations
        Denver Museum of Natural History
        1295 Colfax Avenue
        Denver, CO 80209

A BRIEF GRAMMAR

Sentences

Most English sentences have subjects and predicates, and English speakers naturally expect to hear subjects and predicates when they hear the language spoken. Should a subject be omitted, they automatically supply one. For example, in this sentence

> Get out of here!

The English speaker probably understands something like, "*You* get out of here."

The sentences below have been marked with a slash (/) to show the division between subject and predicate. The subject is in the first part of the sentence and the predicate in the last under normal circumstances.

Some dogs   /   have nasty habits.
No two dogs   /   behave in exactly the same way.
All dogs, including the so-called barkless hounds,   /   have voices.
(You)   /   Watch out!

Elements of the Sentence

There are three basic elements of the English sentence: the simple subject, the simple predicate or verb, and the complement.

Simple subject	Simple predicate or verb	Complement
Dogs	*like*	*humans.*
Newspapers	*spread*	the *news.*
The *pioneers*	*founded*	*Valley City.*
The *school*	*is*	*large.*
Henry	*seems*	*ill.*

A complement is not always necessary to complete the sentence's message; thus, some sentences do not have complements. The following sentences have no complements.

subject	verb
Most *dogs*	*bark.*
Susan	*is thinking.*

Word order. The order in which words appear in an English sentence is very important in determining meaning. Read the following sentences to see how important word order is.

The lion ate Henry.

Henry ate the lion.

Simple subject. The simple subject is the main *noun* or *pronoun* in the subject. Simple subjects are italicized in the following sentences.

The *man* with the heavy coat / is my father.

The vigorous young *colt* / is the son of the winner of the race.

He / ate the cookies.

Simple predicate. The simple predicate is the main *verb* in the complete predicate. Sometimes the simple predicate contains more than one word. Simple predicates are italicized in the following sentences.

The man with the heavy coat / *is* my father.

The vigorous young colt / *is* the son of the winner of the race

He / *ate* the cookies.

Transitive verb. Transitive verbs are simple predicates which take direct objects as their complements. Transitive verbs are italicized in the following sentences.

Henry *chased* the intruder.

The caterpillar *made* a cocoon.

Direct object. The direct object is the most common complement. It receives the action of the verb. Direct objects are italicized in the following sentences.

Henry chased the *intruder.*

The caterpillar made a *cocoon.*

Indirect object. The indirect object is a special complement which may appear only when a direct object is present. It indicates the person or thing for whom or to whom something is done. The indirect objects in the following sentences are italicized.

> Sally gave a book.   Carrie showed her stamp collection.
> Sally gave *Sandy* a book.   Carrie showed *Jim* her stamp collection.

Object complement.   The indirect object always precedes the direct object; the object complement follows it. In the following sentences, the object complement is italicized.

> The voters elected Maria *treasurer*.
> The results made Sam a former *politician*.
> The couple kept their marriage a *secret* for ten days.

Linking verbs.   Linking verbs connect the subject with certain kinds of complements. Linking verbs are words such as am, are, is, were, was, be, being, been, seem, appear, become, smell, and taste. Linking verbs are italicized in the following sentences.

> Marv *became* a dragon for the school play.
> Sherril *is* the main character.
> The play *is* really good.
> The leading character *must be* terribly ambitious.

Predicate noun.   Predicate nouns are complements which follow linking verbs. The predicate nouns in the following sentences are italicized.

> Marv became a *dragon* for the school play.
> Sherril is the main *character*.

Predicate adjective.   Predicate adjectives are complements which also follow linking verbs. The predicate adjectives in the following sentences are italicized.

> The play is really *good*.
> The leading character must be terribly *ambitious*.

Basic Sentence Patterns

There are six basic sentence patterns in English. These patterns are the common ones, those which every native speaker of English understands naturally. These patterns reflect the order in which the elements of the sentence appear; thus, they contribute much to meaning.

Subject, Verb, Direct Object Pattern.   This pattern is the most common of the sentence structures in English. In it, the subject acts through the transitive verb on the direct object. The following sentences illustrate this pattern.

subject	verb	direct object
Our *dog*	*ate*	the *cake*.
He	*chased*	the neighbor's *cat*.

Subject, Verb Pattern. This pattern has no complements. The verb is called an *intransitive complete verb* because it is complete, not requiring complements. The following sentences illustrate this pattern.

subject	verb
Dogs	*bark*.
Birds	*fly*.
Henry	*sits* in the garden every night.

Subject, Linking Verb, Predicate Noun Pattern. In this pattern, the noun after the linking verb means the same as the subject. The following sentences illustrate this pattern.

subject	linking verb	predicate noun
The Mississippi	*is*	a *river*.
Elephants	*can be*	good *workers*.

Subject, Linking Verb, Predicate Adjective Pattern. In this pattern is much like the Subject, Linking Verb, Predicate Noun pattern except that the word in the predicate is an adjective. It tells something about the subject, rather than being another word for it. The following sentences are examples of this pattern.

subject	linking verb	predicate adjective
Candice	*is*	*ill* today.
Little *brothers*	*can be*	*troublesome*.
Defensive *backs*	usually *are*	strong *runners*.

Subject, Verb, Indirect Object, Direct Object Pattern. This pattern introduces a receiver of the direct object. The following sentences illustrate this pattern.

subject	verb	indirect object	direct object
Consuela	*gave*	her *family*	the *money*.
Mary's *mother*	*showed*	*everyone*	her baby *pictures*.
The *pitcher*	*threw*	the second *baseman*	the *ball*.

Notice that each of these sentences can be rewritten to place the indirect object in a prepositional phrase following the direct object.

subject	*verb*	direct object	phrase
Consuela	*gave*	the *money*	to her family.
Mary's *mother*	*showed*	her baby *pictures*	to everyone.
The *pitcher*	*threw*	the *ball*	to the second base-man.

Subject, Verb, Direct Object, Object Complement Pattern.   This pattern is the least common of those listed. The object complement follows the direct object and is a noun which means the same as the direct object. The following sentences illustrate this pattern.

subject	verb	direct object	object complement
The *couple*	*named*	their *baby*	*Harrington Spencer III.*
The *class*	*elected*	*Dennis*	*treasurer.*

Notice that in each instance you can connect the direct object and the object complement with "is." (Their baby *is* Harrington Spencer, III. Dennis *is* treasurer.)

Variations on the Sentence Patterns

There are a number of variations on the basic sentence patterns. These variations usually involve a shifting of the elements of the sentence, the addition of words, or the omission of words.

Questions.   Basic patterns are formed into questions in several ways. Notice the basic patterns below and the ways in which they have been changed to make questions.

Subject, Verb, Direct Object Pattern
Our dog ate the cake.
Did our dog eat the cake?

Subject, Verb Pattern
Dogs bark.
Do dogs bark?

Subject, Linking Verb, Predicate Noun Pattern.
The Mississippi is a river.
Is the Mississippi a river?

Subject, Linking Verb, Predicate Adjective Pattern
Candice is ill today.
Is Candice ill today?

Subject, Verb, Indirect Object, Direct Object Pattern
Consuela gave her family the money.
Did Consuela give her family the money?

Subject, Verb, Direct Object, Object Complement Pattern
The couple named their baby Harrington Spencer III.
Did the douple name their baby Harrington Spencer III?

Negatives.   The following examples illustrate some of the many ways that negatives may be made in English.

Samantha has slept much this week.	(positive statement)
Samantha hasn't slept much this week.	(negative through *n't*)
Samantha has not slept much this week.	(negative through *not*)
Samantha needs sleep.	(positive statement)
Samantha needs no sleep.	(negative through *no*)
Samantha needs little sleep.	(negative by diminution)
Samantha needs hardly any sleep.	(negative by diminution)
Samantha needs scarely any sleep.	(negative by diminution)
Samantha is kind.	(positive statement)
Samantha is unkind.	(negative by prefix)
Samantha is not kind.	(negative through *not*)

There are many other ways to form the negative in English; they usually involve shifting meaning by using different words.

Commands or Requests.   Requests and commands normally do not have directly stated subjects. English speakers usually understand the subject, however, even when it is unstated. If there is any question about the identity of the person to whom the command or request is directed, the listener normally asks the speaker to name the subject. The following are examples of requests and commands.

Please polish the car this morning.
Close the door when you leave.
Hit the deck!

<u>Passive Voice.</u>   Only Subject, Verb, Direct Object patterns may be changed to passive voice. This operation permits the Direct Object to function as the Subject of the sentence. In the examples below, the first sentence is in active voice; the second is in passive voice.

Active:	The alligator ate the duck.
Passive:	The duck was eaten by the alligator.
Active:	The president opened the meeting with a bang of her gavel.
Passive:	The meeting was opened by the president with a bang of her gavel.

Sentence Expansion

English would be a rather unexciting language if its speakers could only use the six basic sentence patterns without embellishment. In actual practice, one might think of the basic sentence patterns as a kind of framework on which the sentences of the language are formed. As one adds to that framework, the language fills out just as a building might take shape around its wooden or metal framework.

<u>Modification.</u>   One of the most common ways to expand sentences is through modification. Look at the following ways in which modification may take place in sentences.

<u>Single-word Modifiers.</u>   Words that modify (more fully explain or describe) nouns are called *adjectives*. Look at the following sentence-combining problems to see how basic sentence patterns are expanded through the addition of adjectives.

Basic sentence:	The car blocked the street.
Add modifiers from:	The car was <u>dirty.</u>
	The car was <u>old.</u>
	The street was <u>busy.</u>

<u>Expanded sentence:</u>   The *dirty old* car blocked the *busy* street. *Dirty*, *old*, and *busy* are adjectives. *Dirty* and *old* modify *car* (they tell us more about *car*); *busy* modifies *street*.

Words that modify verbs, adjectives, or other adverbs are called *adverbs*. The adverbs in the following sentences appear in italics. Notice how they make the meaning of the verb more specific by explaying *how*, *when*, or *under what conditions*.

I won *easily*.	(explains how I won)
I won *yesterday*.	(tells when I won)
I won *handily*.	(tells under what conditions I won)

Notice how easily adverbs may be moved around the sentence.

Yesterday I won the golf tournament.

I won the golf tournament *yesterday*.

I *easily* won the golf tournament.

I won the golf tournament *easily*.

Immediately I felt better.

I *immediately* felt better.

I felt better *immediately*.

In all modification, the basic sentence pattern remains. Adjectives and adverbs are added to make the meaning of the sentence more precise.

<u>Phrase Modifiers.</u>   Phrases (groups of words usually beginning with prepositions such as *of, in, between, among,* or *with*) that modify nouns are called *adjective phrases*. The adjective phrases in the following sentences are printed in italics.

The girl *in the car* shouted.

They built a cabin *in the mountains*.

The dog bit the man *with torn pants*.

The house *between the oaks* is ours.

The blade *of the knife* is very sharp.

We love our little house *among the pines*.

Phrases that modify verbs, adjectives, or adverbs are called *adverb phrases*. As with single-word adverbs, they often tell *how, when,* or *under what conditions*. They also may be placed in many different parts of the sentence. Adverb phrases in the following sentences are italicized.

We eat breakfast *in the morning*.

We eat breakfast *in five minutes*.

We eat breakfast *in the kitchen*.

We eat breakfast *with our friends*.

We eat breakfast *with Grandma's old silver*.

Notice how easily adverb phrases can be shifted to different places in the sentence.

In the morning, we eat breakfast.

We eat breakfast *in the morning*.

There is little change in meaning when adverb phrases are shifted within sentences. Emphasis, however, changes a good deal. In the examples above, the first sentence (In the morning, we eat breakfast.) suggests that you will tell a listener what you do at other times of the day in later sentences. We might expect you to say, "Then, we have lunch at noon," or something like that in your second sentence.

The second example suggests something else could follow, although not necessarily so. One might follow "We eat breakfast in the morning" with "Some people sleep so long they have to wait until noon for their breakfast."

Participial phrases are phrases that begin with participles (verb forms) and modify nouns. The participial phrases in the following sentences have been printed in italics.

Going full speed, the biker collided with a telephone pole.

A little boy *carrying a large bag* slipped on the ice.

The man *sitting there* is my uncle.

Clause Modifiers.   Clauses are groups of words that have subjects and predicates. Those that can stand by themselves, without the addition or deletion of words or phrases, are the same as sentences. They are called *independent clauses*. Those that cannot stand by themselves but must be included in the context of a sentence are called *dependent clauses*. It is the dependent clause which can serve as a modifier.

Adjective clauses are dependent clauses that modify nouns. Look at the following sentence-combining problem which produces an adjective clause.

Base sentence:	Vandals destroyed the house
Add modifier:	Vandals lived in our neighborhood (who)
Expanded Sentence:	Vandals who lived in our neighborhood destroyed the house.

Notice how "who lived in our neighborhood," a dependent clause, modifies the noun *vandals*.

Adjective clauses usually follow the noun they modify, just as adjective phrases do.

Adverb clauses are dependent clauses that modify verbs, adjectives, or adverbs. The following example illustrates the formation of an adverb clause.

Add modifier:	A storm had raged throughout the night. (After)

Basic sentence: We woke up to a yard full of fallen trees.

Expanded sentence: <u>After a storm had raged throughout the night,</u> we woke up to a yard full of fallen trees.

Or   We woke up to a yard full of fallen trees <u>after a storm had raged throughout the night.</u>

Adverb clauses begin with *subordinating conjunctions*, words such as *after, when, until, because,* and *if.* Adjective clauses begin with relative pronouns—*who, which,* and *that.*

<u>Joining.</u>   Basic sentence patterns can be joined together quite simply. The simplest way is through the use of a *coordinating conjunction* (*and, but, or,* or *nor*).

I like apples.

My sister likes plums.   (, but)

Result: I like apples, but my sister likes plums.

Two sentences may also be joined by using a semi-colon (;), thus avoiding the use of the coordinating conjunction.

I like apples.

My sister likes plums.   (;)

Result: I like apples; my sister likes plums.

Sentences that have similar subjects may be joined by stating the subject only once and incorporating the remaining words into the new sentence.

The angry elephant jerked the rope off the stake.

,   The angry elephant turned toward the stands.   (,)

, and   The angry elephant charged at the surprised spectators.   (, and)

Result: The angry elephant jerked the rope off the stake, turned towards the stands, and charged the surprised spectators.

Sentences that have similar predicates may be joined by stating the different subjects and then stating the predicate only once.

Jim checked his watch.

,   Charlie checked his watch.   (,)

, and   Kevin checked his watch.   (, and)

Result: Jim, Charlie, and Kevin checked their watches.

Words

Nouns

Nouns are naming words; they normally name persons, places, or things.

Kinds of nouns

Concrete nouns name things that can be observed with one or more of the senses. Words such as table, city, apple, and girl are concrete nouns.

Abstract nouns name things that usually cannot be observed with the senses. Words such as hostility, love, anxiety, and concern are abstract nouns.

Proper nouns include all nouns that specifically name people, places, or things. Words such as Sandra, Mt. McKinley, Broadway Avenue, and *The Washington Post* are proper nouns.

Common nouns include all nouns not included in the category of proper nouns.

Collective nouns are common nouns that refer to groups or collections of persons, places, or things. Examples are crowd, gathering, and family.

Functions of nouns.

Subject of a sentence.   Nouns are commonly used as simple subjects of sentences. The nouns used in this way are printed in italics in the sentences which follow.
>The *man* is nearly seven feet tall.
>Whether we like it or not, that *team* is going to win.

Direct Object of a verb.   Examples of nouns used in this way follow:
>Thoreau wrote *essays* in the nineteenth century.
>The jury made a *decision*.

Predicate Noun.   Examples of nouns used in this way follow.
>Texas is the largest *state*.
>The overcharge was really a *tax*.

Indirect Object.   Nouns used in this way appear in the following sentences.
>The French offered *the United States* soldiers.
>Henry gave *Lucy* a locket.

<u>Objective Complement.</u>   Nouns used in this way appear in the following sentences.

The judge appointed him *bailiff.*
The people elected him *chairman.*

<u>Object of a Preposition.</u>   The examples that follow are prepositional phrases (a preposition followed by a noun or pronoun, together with any modifiers). Nouns acting as objects of prepositions are printed in italics.

in the *house*
near an open *field*
outside the *law*

<u>Possessive.</u>   Singular nouns show possession as in the following examples.

Henry's automobile
Carolina's apples
the *law's* variety
the *crowd's* anger

<u>Forming plurals of nouns.</u>

The following rules may be helpful in determining the plural forms of nouns.

Most nouns form their plurals by adding *s*. Some notable exceptions are listed in the following items.

1. Nouns which end in *s, z, x, ch,* and *sh* form their plurals by adding *es.*
    Examples   lens, lenses; fox, foxes; wrench, wrenches; wish, wishes.
2. Most nouns ending in *f* or *fe* change the *f* to *v* and add *s* or *es.*
    Examples: knife, knives; calf, calves.
3. Some nouns have similar singular and plural forms.
    Examples: deer, sheep.
4. Hyphenated compound nouns (nouns which contain more than one word) usually form their plurals by making the first part of the word plural.
    Examples: Secretaries-of-State, mothers-in-law.
5. Nouns ending in *y* preceded by a consonant change *y* to *i* and add *es* to form the plural.
    Examples: fairy, fairies; cherry, cherries; spy, spies.

6. Nouns ending in *y* preceded by a vowel form their plurals by adding *s*.
    Examples: monkey, monkeys; alley, alleys.
7. Some nouns form their plurals by changing the entire word.
    Examples: man, men; woman, women; mouse, mice.
8. Nouns ending in *o* preceded by a vowel form their plurals by adding *s*.
    Examples: radio, radios; studio, studios.
9. Nouns ending in *o* preceded by a consonant form their plurals by adding *es*.
    Examples: potato, potatoes; hero, heroes. There are several exceptions to this rule, however. Some are: piano, pianos; solo, solos; soprano, sopranos.
10. Nouns with Greek roots ending in *-sis* form their plurals by changing the i to *e*.
    Examples: analysis, analyses; hypothesis, hypotheses.
11. Some nouns keep their foreign forms.
    Examples: datum, data.

Pronouns

Pronouns are words used in place of nouns. They may be classified as personal, relative, demonstrative, reflexive, or indefinite.

Personal pronouns refer to persons. They are classified according to person, case, and number. The following chart illustrates this classification.

	First person		Second person		Third person	
	Singular	Plural	Singular	Plural	Singular	Plural
Nominative Case	I	we	you	you	he, she, it	they
Objective Case	me	us	you	you	him, her, it	them
Possessive Case	my, mine	our, ours	your, yours	your, yours	his, her, its, her	their, theirs

Nominative case is used for subjects and predicate pronouns. Possessive case is used whenever ownership is expressed. Objective case is used for direct objects, indirect objects, and objects of prepositions.

Relative pronouns take the places of nouns as well as joining dependent clauses to the remainder of sentences. The relative pronouns are *who*, *which*, *what*, *that*, and *whom*. Examples of the use of relative pronouns in sentences are as follows:

> The fellow *whom* I saw in the store is following us.
> Those *who* step forward will get $8,000.

Demonstrative pronouns point out some definite person, place, or thing.

> Examples: *This* scarf is mine, *that* one is yours.
>   *These* seats are taken; *those* are not.

Reflexive pronouns are formed by adding *self* or *selves* to the personal pronouns. They may be used in the following ways.

Direct object:	He likes *himself* too much.
Indirect object:	He bought *himself* a candy bar.
Predicate pronoun:	The ducks are not *themselves* this morning.
Object of a preposition:	Play by *yourself* for a while.

Indefinite pronouns are words like none, something, nothing, anything, and everything. They do not require antecedents, since they stand for things that are non-specific.

Verbs

The verb is the chief function word in the predicate. It establishes a connection between the subject and the complements that follow, or it serves to complete the sentence's action.

Transitive verbs are verbs that express action and that take direct objects. The following sentences contain transitive verbs (printed in italics).

> Karl *hit* the fence.
> While we all looked on, Daphne *tied* the score.

Each of the above sentences is in the *active voice*, that is, the direct object receives the action (expressed by the verb) of the subject.

The *passive voice*, on the other hand, involves shuffling the sentence around. The following are the same sentences expressed in passive voice.

> The fence *was hit* by Karl.
> While we all looked on, the score *was tied* by Daphne.

Intransitive verbs either show no action at all or limit their action to the subject. The following sentences illustrate the *intransitive complete verb*.

The dogs *are barking* tonight.

The pianist certainly *plays* well.

Contrast the last sentence with this same verb used as a transitive verb. Note the presence of the direct object in the changed sentence.

The pianist certainly plays *Bach* well.

Bach is the direct object in the sentence; thus the verb *plays* is now transitive.

Intransitive linking verbs connect the subject to either a predicate adjective or a predicate noun or pronoun. Linking verbs are usually forms of the verb *be* (*is, are, was, been,* etc.), although others such as *seems, became, appear, feel, smell, taste,* and *sound* may also be used. The following sentences illustrate the use of the intransitive linking verb.

Henry is certainly a good basketball *player*. (*Henry* and *player* are connected by the linking verb *is*.)

Henry seems better today. (*Henry* and the adjective *better* are connected by the linking verb *seems*.)

The previously tame *tiger became* a *monster* in thirty seconds. (The subject, *tiger*, and the predicate noun, *monster*, are connected by the linking verb, *became*.)

Forms of Verbs

Verbs take two forms, regular and irregular. One of the reasons children or persons just learning English make errors such as "I holded the puppy" is that they are attempting to make the verb *hold* a regular verb. If it were regular, one would say, "I am holding the puppy," "I holded the puppy," "I have holded the puppy," and "I will hold the puppy." As you can see, when the same thing is done with a truly regular verb ("I am carrying the puppy," "I carried the puppy," "I have carried the puppy," and "I will carry the puppy"), *hold* is *not* a regular verb.

Regular verbs have four forms. The first, called the *infinitive form*, is the basic word from which all forms are created. The second is the *singular* form; it is used with singular subjects. Its regular form is made by adding -*s* or -*es* to the infinitive form. The third is the *past* form, used to express action which has occured in the past. Its form is created by adding -*ed* to the infinitive. The final form is the *present participle* form, made by adding -*ing* to the infinitive.

The following table shows the four basic forms of regular verbs.

infinitive	singular	past	present participle
carry	carries	carried	carrying
stop	stops	stopped	stopping
walk	walks	walked	walking
move	moves	moved	moving
hiss	hisses	hissed	hissing

Note the irregularities in spelling. Rules governing the spelling of regular verb forms are stated above. However, exceptions include the following.

1. When the infinitive form ends in *y* preceded by a consonant, as in *carry*, the *y* is changed to *i* and *-ed* is added to form the past.   (carried)
2. When the infinitive form ends in *s, x, ch,* or *sh,* as in *hiss,* add *-es* rather than the normal *-s*.   (hisses)
3. When the infinitive form ends in *e* as in *move,* add only *-d* to form the past and drop the *e* when adding *-ing* to form the present participle.   (moved, moving)
4. When the infinitive is only one syllable and it ends with a consonant preceded by a single vowel, as in *stop,* double the final consonant when adding *-ed* and *-ing*.   (stopped, stopping)

Irregular verbs do not appear to make their forms according to any systematic formula as do regular verbs. The following list illustrates the considerable number of irregular verbs. It also shows how common they are in ordinary usage.

infinitive	singular	plural	past	past participle	present participle
be	is, am	are	was, were	been	being
begin	begins	begin	began	begun	beginning
bite	bites	bite	bit	bitten	biting
choose	chooses	choose	chose	chosen	choosing
do	does	do	did	done	doing
feel	feels	feel	felt	felt	feeling
forget	forgets	forget	forgot	forgotten	forgetting
freeze	freezes	freeze	forze	frozen	freezing
get	gets	get	got	gotten	getting
have	has	have	had	had	having

infinitive	singular	plural	past	past participle	present participle
hold	holds	hold	held	held	holding
know	knows	know	knew	known	knowing
lie (recline)	lie	lie	lay	lain	lying
write	writes	write	wrote	written	writing
swim	swims	swim	swam	swum	swimming
go	goes	go	went	gone	going
make	makes	make	made	made	making
run	runs	run	ran	run	running
say	says	say	said	said	saying
sit	sits	sit	sat	sat	sitting
hurt	hurts	hurt	hurt	hurt	hurting
teach	teaches	teach	taught	taught	teaching
wear	wears	wear	wore	worn	wearing
thrust	thrusts	thrust	thrust	thrust	thrusting
think	thinks	think	thought	thought	thinking

Functions of verb forms

The infinitive form is used in the present tense and with the pronouns *I* and *you*. It may also be used with helping verbs such as *can, may, should, could, shall,* and *will.*

>   I *will begin* at the beginning.
>   I *feel* as good as new.
>   The man *will choose* the fabric for the uniforms.

The singular form is used with singular nouns and certain pronouns, in the present tense.

>   The detective *knows* the truth.
>   She *swims* well enough to win the tournament.
>   Horace *runs* the forty in twenty-seconds.

The plural form is used with plural subjects to express present tense.

>   The members of the class always *forget* to close the door.
>   They *hold* their new puppies so carefully.

The past form indicates past tense with either singular or plural subjects.

>   He *chose* to go skiing.
>   They *chose* to go skiing.

The past participle form uses the helping verb *had*, as well as related forms such as *should have, must have, might have, could have, should have,* and *will have.*

> We *had begun* our trip by eight o'clock.
> We *should have felt* relieved to be getting out of there.
> We *had run* as far and as fast as we could.
> We *could have worn* warmer clothes.

The present participle form uses helping verbs such as *am, is, are, was,* and *were.* It expresses action which is continuing, is anticipated, or had been happening.

> The champion *is swimming* around the pool.
> The children *were freezing* to death.
> I *am getting* out of here.
> They *are holding* the puppy.

Adjectives

Adjectives modify nouns in one of two ways; 1. they describe the noun or 2. they limit it.

Descriptive adjectives are the more common type, and are reflected in the following sentences.

> The *tired old* man straightened his *aching* back and smiled.
> It was a *solid* victory, and the team was *happy.*

In the second sentence, the adjective *happy* is a predicate adjective. It modifies the subject, *team,* just as if the sentence had begun, "The happy team . . ."

Limiting adjectives are of three types.
1. Numeral adjectives show how many or in what order things are considered.

> There are *three* types of limiting adjectives.
> The *first* item concerns the condition of the classroom.

2. Demonstrative adjectives indicate "which one" or point out specifics.

> *This* book should have been returned to the library.
> *Both* criminals were guilty.

3. Indefinite adjectives express an indefiniteness about a noun. They serve a writer by permitting the expression of a non-specific quantity or quality.

> *Some* students want the lunchroom closed.
> However, *many* want it to remain open.

All descriptive adjectives and some limiting adjectives have the potential for expressing comparison. The table below illustrates this quality.

adjective base	comparative form	superlative form
old	older	oldest
young	younger	youngest
fat	fatter	fattest
kind	kinder	kindest

Adjectives of one syllable normally form their comparative and superlative forms by adding *-er* for the comparative and *-est* for the superlative. However, those with two or more syllables often form their comparatives by adding the words *more* or *less* the words *most* or *least* being used for the superlative form.

adjective base	comparative form	superlative form
dependable	more dependable	most dependable
careful	more careful	most careful
foolish	less foolish	least foolish
careless	less careless	least careless

Some adjectives form their comparatives and superlatives on irregular bases. Following are some examples.

adjective base	comparative form	superlative form
good	better	best
bad	worse	worst
many	more	most
little	less	least

The comparative form of an adjective is used when one is comparing two things.

My father is *older* than yours.
That runner is certainly *faster* today than the last time I saw her.
I am even *more tired* today than I was yesterday.

The superlative is used when comparing more than two things.

My father is the *oldest* person in the room.
That time must be the *fastest* she has attained.
I am the *most tired* today that I have ever been.

Adverbs

Adverbs, like adjectives, modify other words. Adverbs modify verbs, adjectives, and adverbs. They can help a writer express time, place, manner, degree, and cause.

<u>Time</u> is expressed by adverbs such as *now* and *today* for present; *soon* and *tomorrow* for future; *before* and *yesterday* for past. Duration of time is shown by the adverbs *always* and *never*; frequency is shown by adverbs such as *frequently* and *sometimes*.

<u>Place</u> is expressed by adverbs such as *above* for position; *forward* for motion toward; *away* for motion from.

<u>Manner</u> is expressed by adverbs such as *quickly*, *slowly*, *better*, and *worse*.

<u>Degree</u> is expressed by adverbs such as *little*, *more*, *very*, and *almost*.

<u>Cause</u> is expressed by adverbs such as *consequently*, *then*, and *why*.

The following examples illustrate adverbs used in these ways.

Today we're going to the country.   (present time)
Soon we'll go to the country.   (future time)
Yesterday we went to the country.   (past time)
We're *always* going to the country.   (duration)
Sometimes we go to the country.   (frequency)
The picture is *above* your favorite.   (position)
Move the picture *forward* just a bit.   (motion toward)
Get that cat *away* from me!   (motion from)
Let's get this over *quickly*.   (manner)
Move it just a *little* to the right.   (degree)
If we don't want to get fired, *then* we'll have to work harder.   (cause)

Many adverbs end in *-ly*, and are easy to identify. However, some adjectives also end in *-ly*, thus creating a problem. Also, there are many adverbs which do not end in that suffix.

It is probably best to think of adverbs as answering questions like "When?", "Where?", "How long?", "How often?" and "How much?" Look at the following sentences.

adjective   We all need *daily* bread.
adverb   We all need bread *daily*.

Note how *daily* in the first sentence modifies bread. It functions as *wheat* in *wheat bread*. In the second sentence, however, *daily* functions as an adverb in that it answers the question, "when?" Therefore, it modifies the verb *need*. It tells the reader when the bread is needed.

Some adverbs which are commonly used but which do not end in *-ly* are the following.

almost	here	never	straight
already	instead	now	then
back	late	often	there

Prepositions

Prepositions are used with a noun or pronoun to make a phrase called a prepositional phrase. Such a phrase acts as an adjective or adverb in a sentence.

The following is a list of commonly used prepositions.

about	at	but (except)	into	through
above	before	by	near	to
across	behind	down	of	toward
after	below	during	on	under
against	beneath	for	out	underneath
along	beside	from	outside	until
among	between	in	over	up
around	beyond	inside	past	with

The following sentences illustrate the use of prepositions.

The man *with the Western hat* is a singer.   (adjective phrase)
We always eat *on Grandma's best china.*   (adverb phrase)
The rope *around the tree* keeps insects *from the leaves.*   (adjective phrase; adverb phrase)

INDEX

Art Credits

Photo Credits